Praise for Mark Singer's
Mr. Personality

"**Mark Singer knows the most interesting people in America.** His gallery in *Mr. Personality* will hold the reader more rapt and enthralled than Scheherazade ever did for that Near Eastern politician."

—Richard Condon

"Singer deserves a wider audience. Apart from his own wry, oblique style, **his most conspicuous talent is for capturing the special language people speak when talking about themselves.** . . . Among Singer's considerable skills are a greedy eye for detail and a deft hand with physical description."

—John House, *Seven Days*

"Singer is not only a writer of great craft but also a reporter. **His stories brim with the color, rhythms and dialects of New York City.** He has an ear for conversation, an eye for detail and the ability to capture both on paper."

—Valerie Berg, *The Milwaukee Journal*

"**There's something, and somebody, here for everyone.**"

—*Publishers Weekly*

ALSO BY MARK SINGER

Funny Money

Mr.
Personality

Mr. Personality

PROFILES AND TALK PIECES

MARK SINGER

COLLIER BOOKS
MACMILLAN PUBLISHING COMPANY
NEW YORK

Collier Books
Macmillan Publishing Company
866 Third Avenue, New York, NY 10022
Collier Macmillan Canada, Inc.

Library of Congress Cataloging-in-Publication Data
Singer, Mark.
Mr. Personality : profiles and talk pieces / Mark Singer.—
1st Collier Books ed.
p. cm.
ISBN 0-02-029822-6
1. New York (N.Y.)—Social life and customs—Anecdotes.
I. Title.
F128.52.S54   1990
974.7′1′00992—dc20   89-25265   CIP

Macmillan books are available at special discounts for bulk
purchases for sales promotions, premiums, fund-raising,
or educational use. For details, contact:

Special Sales Director
Macmillan Publishing Company
866 Third Avenue
New York, NY 10022

First Collier Books Edition 1990

10 9 8 7 6 5 4 3 2 1

PRINTED IN THE UNITED STATES OF AMERICA

FOR WILLIAM SHAWN

Contents

PROFILES

Acknowledgments

I feel especially indebted to the following people—all present or former colleagues at *The New Yorker*—for their assistance: Dwight Allen, Martin Baron, Peter Canby, Charles Patrick Crow, Bruce Diones, Hal Espen, Ann Goldstein, Lex Kaplen, Charles McGrath, Eleanor Gould Packard, Richard Sacks, Thomas Teal, Rob Tiller, and William Whitworth.

Introduction

One summer while I was in college, I worked as a reporter for one of my hometown newspapers, the Tulsa *Tribune*. My only other job offer was as a steam-gunner in a car wash. I had never previously written for a newspaper or enrolled in a journalism course—to this day I haven't had the fundamentals explained to me by a certified professor of journalism. I took the job at the *Tribune* with the idea that this might be fun. The newspaper city room had air-conditioning.

My first assignment came on the heels of a tornado. I was asked to write a brief notice stating that the trash dump on the west side of town was filled with storm debris and was closed, and that everyone should therefore haul his or her fallen tree limbs to one of the other dumps. It took me most of a morning and six elaborate paragraphs to formulate that information. I submitted what I had written to the assistant city editor, and around one o'clock that afternoon, when I saw the early edition of that day's paper, I recognized the value of thoughtful editing. There, on the first page of the back section—the page that I have since learned is called the "second front"—was my scoop about the dump. It had been cut to one paragraph, about a column-inch, headline included, and it said the dump on the west side of town was filled and if you had storm debris you should take it elsewhere.

I was proud of what my editor and I had accomplished, and that evening, at home, I showed my father the second front page. Right in the middle, just above the crease, was my dump-closing communiqué. "Dad, this one's mine," I said, and he reacted with pleasant surprise. It wasn't that he had any surplus storm debris. Rather, he could connect—for the first time, it seemed, or else

he was being paternal—a piece of writing to the person who had
written it. His pride in me did not appear to diminish when I
explained that I had composed the *War and Peace* version of the
dump-closing and a literal-minded editor had boiled my work down
until it was pure extract of dump-closing. He appreciated that a
real person had written something he was reading in a publication.
I was impressed that my father was so impressed.

My senior year in college, I wrote a twenty-five-thousand-word
essay about the nonfiction of Ernest Hemingway and Norman Mailer.
Ten thousand of those words were shameless filler material—not
the literary criticism that was expected of me but a parody sung
in the narcissistic voice of Norman Mailer's journalism. ("The brave
student searched for a gambit. He was committed to a project and
his restless sense of honor, a sizable jump ahead of his flagging
stamina, demanded honorable results. The tolls of his many over-
indulgences began to burden him. And to make matters worse, a
one-night stand's worth of boozing and ego-glorying had shoved
him into a nasty little corner. He had met the man, locked stares
with him . . . 'Shall I send you the whole paper or edit it for you
first?' he asked Mailer. . . .") That spring all six of the law schools
I had applied to turned me down. One of the faculty members who
read my senior essay used a colorful phrase to describe both Norman Mailer and me: "elephantiasis of ego." I took that to mean I
had a vocational prospect after all. I was now a writer.

Two years later, in the spring of 1974, I found myself one
afternoon seated in the office of William Shawn, the editor of *The
New Yorker*. This came about because for several months I had
been corresponding with another editor at the magazine, a gentle
man named Robert Bingham—sending him ostensibly humorous
pieces of my writing—and one day Bingham had phoned to say
that William Shawn wanted to meet me. I had a vague sense of
who William Shawn was, most of it gleaned from a recent reading
of James Thurber's *The Years with Ross*. I knew that he was a shy,
polite genius who had been the editor of *The New Yorker* for about
as long as I had been alive and that the whole world called him
"Mr. Shawn." My wife and I were newlyweds, living in Connecticut.
When I told her I had an appointment to meet the editor of *The*

New Yorker, it seemed natural that she would join me for the ride to the city. She came with me to the building on West Forty-third Street where the magazine has its offices. Together, we went up to the nineteenth floor and sat in a small foyer until Robert Bingham came out to greet us. I assume Bingham asked himself why the hell this guy had brought along his wife to a job interview. If he had asked me, I would have explained that it hadn't occurred to me this might be a job interview; my wife and I were tourists, and the *New Yorker* headquarters were on her sightseeing itinerary. When Mr. Shawn was ready to see me, my wife stayed in Bingham's office, where she worked a crossword puzzle. Bingham, I imagine, spent the next twenty minutes wandering the hallways.

Certain elements of the scene in Mr. Shawn's office that day remain fixed in my mind—the broad dark-maple desk; the orderly clutter of manuscripts, proofs, and glass paperweights on the desktop; the jar of freshly sharpened pencils; the Windsor armchair; the manual typewriter on a table in one corner; the photograph, resting against a window behind the typewriter, of Harold Ross—because I had conversations with him in that room again and again, until he left *The New Yorker*, in 1987. My other memories of our first meeting have never been vivid, however, because most of what took place had an out-of-body quality. Mr. Shawn offered me a job as a "Talk of the Town" writer. I heard him say that, and I heard myself explaining that I wouldn't be able to start work for a few months. He said that would be all right. We shook hands. I returned to Bingham's office and reported to my wife what I thought had happened, Bingham told us goodbye, and we left the building. Our *faux pas de deux* turned out to be a lucky thing. "No, I was there," she reassured me, more than once, in the weeks that followed. "You were hired."

In the fall of that year, we moved to New York City, where I had never lived before, and I began looking for things to write about. I was twenty-four years old. Mr. Shawn started me out with a couple of assignments. He sent me to cover a rally organized by citizens opposed to a plan to build a superhighway along the lower West Side of Manhattan (a subject I have written about six or eight times since then; the highway still hasn't been built), and he sent me to a convention of Beatles memorabilia collectors and to the opening of a store on the upper East Side that sold not only pets but entire environments for the pets to live in. Then I started finding stories on my own. Ideas materialized. Every serendipitous subway ride to Brighton Beach, every trip to Hester Street to buy pickles, loomed as a potentially tax-deductible adventure. The five boroughs of New York City and the west bank of the Hudson were over-populated with entertaining people who had things to say I had never heard before. My object was to get down on the page not only what they said but how they said it. I tried to leave out the dull parts. Eager to capture dialogue as accurately as possible, I enrolled in a shorthand course. I spent nights on the town with middle-aged hockey players, bibulous wholesale grocery salesmen, and nonsense-spouting friends of my father-in-law from the Bronx whose main virtue was that they had great nicknames (Whitey, Stabber, Loony, Kotz, Skate-O, Lock, The Actor, Chick), and I spent days with pigeon fanciers, stonecutters, and the occasional stuffed-gorilla vendor. I was looking for individuals who were living their lives unencumbered by public-relations flacks, who were en-gaged in endeavors they enjoyed.

What I enjoyed was how it felt to walk down Seventh Avenue, in Chelsea, and discover a live rooster in the window of a locksmith shop. I had been walking past this particular locksmith shop several times a week for several months, and this was definitely the first time I had noticed a rooster. This was not a celebrity rooster who had already gotten the treatment from the *Times*, the *Enquirer*, "Live at Five," and *Rooster News*. I knew it was my responsibility to go inside and talk to the rooster's colleagues. Journalistic balance required that I go next door to the Café Borinqueneer and interview the rooster's former colleagues.

I would submit a story on a Wednesday afternoon and, if I hadn't dropped the ball, I could see it in print the following Tuesday. Mr. Shawn had the habit of extending overly generous praise. Sometimes my phone would ring:

"Hello, Mr. Singer."

"Hello, Mr. Shawn."

"That's an ingenious and wonderful piece you wrote."

"Thank you very much."

"Thank you for doing it."

No, actually, thank you. William Shawn believed that the most important thing an editor could give a writer was freedom. Which is not to say he granted this freedom with no strings attached. He once assigned me and a few other "Talk" writers to cover the Democratic National Convention, dispatching us with this admonition: "Remember, please—no politics." He also had a low tolerance for meanness or arrogance. I got paid to do my work, yet regarded myself, and continue to regard myself, as a professional amateur. The subjects of all my reporting pieces—"Talk" stories and much longer Profiles—have been people who, for reasons other than mercenary ones, interested me.

A friend from Oklahoma tells me that on a visit to Manhattan a while back he was standing at a crosswalk in Times Square when a man with a llama asked him for directions. No one else, my friend claims, was paying the llama or his handler any mind. I tend not to believe this story. New York City is too tough a media town for a llama in Times Square to slip by unchronicled. One morning several months ago, I had an appointment in the garment center with a German-refugee zipper specialist whom I wanted to watch in action, and I was running late. I decided to take a taxi instead of the subway. The taxi driver was a friendly Haitian country-and-western music lover. His first name was François, and he said he was teaching himself to play steel guitar and it was his dream to go to Nashville someday and record an album. Over and over—we got stuck in traffic—François's tape player serenaded us with a song called "All My Ex-es Live in Texas." The experience had a logic I have grown comfortably familiar with: the where I was going, the sensations along the way, the hair-tearing frustration, the uplift of dislocation. My session with the zipper specialist worked out all right, and the result is in this book. I ought to have followed up with François. But I didn't, so that story isn't in this book. For all I know, François has given up music and is well on his way toward building a llama ranch in Far Rockaway—in which case, perhaps we'll meet again. The A train goes there.

Mr.
Personality

Talk Pieces

Yabba-Yabba, Doodle-Doodle

As soon as Antoinette and Clem Blafford get around to building a prototype of their new invention, an automatic dog washer, they will be in a position to establish their reputations as the Bell and Watson of canine hygiene. At the moment, the Blaffords, who live in Bensonhurst along with their dog, Max, have just made the leap from the drawing board to the United States Patent and Trademark Office. Patent No. 4,056,078, which was issued a couple of weeks ago, recognizes the Blaffords as the developers of Doggie Washer, a device that the inventors frankly believe is inferior only to the self-cleaning dog. The basic Doggie Washer concept seems sound. Before the Blaffords set out to market thousands of the Doggie Washers, however, they might want to consider changing the name. A doggie, most puppy behaviorists agree, is a little animal that sits in the kitchen sink and maintains equanimity during a bath. A creature worthy of machine-cleaning runs closer to the dimensions of Max, a full-grown red Doberman pinscher, who in greeting a visitor to the Blaffords' home likes to rest his forepaws upon the visitor's shoulders and render a totally convincing portrayal of a difficult-to-wash dog. It was not actually Max who inspired the Doggie Washer. That honor belongs to the late Duke Blafford, a German shepherd who was in the family for eleven years before he died, last winter.

"Oh, washing Duke, don't even ask," Mrs. Blafford, a small, fair-haired woman in her forties, said the other day, as she sat at her kitchen table, along with her husband and their fourteen-month-old grandson, Michael. "Giving Duke a bath was a big ritual. He weighed a hundred pounds, and first you had to get him to go down to the basement and into an old-fashioned four-legged bathtub. Then came the soap-and-water part—maybe a half hour of scrubbing and rinsing, plus all the towels it took to dry him. Don't ask."

"Not to mention the floor getting completely wet," said Mr. Blafford, lighting a cigarette.

"Not to mention the floor," she agreed. "And not to mention that when he got out of the tub and shook himself he gave the person washing him a shower. Then, if it was summertime, he had to stand outside in the sun to dry. During the winter, we used a hair dryer. It took about two hours in all, which gave me time to think, and one day about three years ago I thought, Dogs are wonderful to hug and kiss, but they often discourage you by seeming to need a bath—right? So I thought of a dog-washing machine. Then I took my idea to an engineering firm. They did the drawings for the machine."

"It's really my wife's invention," Mr. Blafford said with a mixture of pride and sheepishness. "When I first heard the idea, I thought it was ridiculous. But I used to help her wash Duke, so when we applied for the patent she named me as co-inventor."

"He helps me to wash Max now," said Mrs. Blafford. "And Max is as much trouble as Duke was."

"It took us five months to replace Duke," said Mr. Blafford, exhaling smoke in Max's direction. "I finally went to see Mr. Lucky, the A No. 1 dog trainer in all of Brooklyn. His first name is Lester, but he goes by Mr. Lucky. You could say that Max is attack-trained."

"But he has a very good disposition," Mrs. Blafford quickly pointed out. "He's wonderful with the baby."

The baby, Michael, had finished eating a bowl of pasta and was now walking around the kitchen, subtly avoiding Max. Mrs. Blafford watched Michael for a moment and then picked up an envelope that had been lying on the table and removed a copy of her patent application, which included a technical description of the Doggie Washer and a schematic drawing done by the engineering firm. The machine resembles a squat, front-loading automatic clothes washer. However, it actually loads from the rear, and instead of a glass window in front there is a baffled opening for the dog to stick his head through while the rest of him is being bathed. "It's got pipes in the walls and overhead—see?" she said. "And the water comes out like a shower spray and gets him wet, then the detergent sprays hit him, then a rinse cycle, and then there are pipes that blow hot air to dry him."

"You forgot to mention the soap," said her husband.

"The detergent," she said. "The soap is the detergent."

"About the dryer," said Mr. Blafford. "Right now, we see it as being in the same compartment as the washer, but there might be a separate dryer for people who wish it. Either way, when you get him out, he's clean and dry." Mr. Blafford paused a second, then continued, "I can see these things all over Brooklyn—all over the world, even. I envision this as an international invention, because there are dog lovers everywhere. We need a few Arabs to buy these things. How about twenty coin-operated dog-washing machines in a row in a store? You get your change from a change machine, put your dog in the Doggie Washer, do your yabba-yabba, doodle-doodle—you know, whatever you do while you're waiting in a laundromat—and then go home with a clean dog."

By this time, the Blaffords had succeeded in thoroughly articulating their Doggie Washer master plan. The only remaining question concerned the Blaffords' listing in the Brooklyn telephone directory, in which their name is misspelled. "Oh, yes," said Mrs. Blafford. "We purposely had them spell it B-l-a-f-f-a-r-d, instead of B-l-a-f-f-o-r-d, to discourage unwanted calls. We could have had an unlisted number, but you know they charge for those. I didn't want to pay the extra fee. But this way my friends can look it up and they know they've got the right Blafford."

Clem Blafford was smiling now. "My wife is an extremely unusual person," he said. "She thinks of everything."

1 9 7 7

With Leo

If you operated a resort hotel in the Catskills and your oven stopped working the same day that the talent for tomorrow night's dinner show took sick, you could solve both problems with a call to Leo Hoffman. In the past fifteen years, Leo Hoffman has repaired some forty thousand kitchen ranges—products of the Welbilt Corporation, his employer. For eighteen years before that, he worked on the Welbilt assembly line, in Maspeth. His monologues contain equal parts candid criticism ("I cannot believe the dirt inside this stove. Even mice wouldn't want it; I don't understand why they aren't here picketing") and candid self-admiration ("I like my job. I'm not a doctor, I'm not a podiatrist or a dentist, but I tell you this: When people call me, there's a problem. When I leave, there might be a problem, but it has nothing to do with the stove"). He speaks about three hundred words a minute. One of Leo's mottos is "If it's broke, I fix it." Another is "The wrong people don't touch the stove, I don't get a headache. They touch the stove, I get a headache." Another: "You wait for Leo or you eat at Wendy's."

One recent morning, Leo responded to a service call at a residential hotel on West Eighty-sixth Street. Leo drives a 1985 Buick. In the last eight months, commuting from faulty range to faulty range throughout the five boroughs, he has put nineteen thousand miles on the odometer. Parking his car in a garage near the hotel, he told the attendant, "Fifteen, twenty minutes, no longer." Walking across Eighty-sixth, he said, "I always tell the garage fifteen or twenty minutes, because, with most jobs, it shouldn't take much more than that. What could the problem be? I'll fix it, that's all. Anyway, you can't tell the garage any longer. They'll bury the car."

Leo's wife, Millie, came up with the idea of installing clear-

8

plastic upholstery covers on the driver's seat and the left-front-door panel of the new car. On the job, Leo gets dirty. When he goes home at night—he has lived in Bensonhurst for thirty-five years—he removes his soiled work clothes before he walks through Millie's clean living room. Millie cooks on a range that Leo helped build twenty-seven years ago, in Maspeth. "I made the range, but Millie doesn't want it anymore," he said the other day. "She says she wants an up-to-date range. But that's ridiculous. *I made the range*. It's a beaut. Why does she want to change it? You tell me. But she's a good cook. And I love food, I really do. Some people enjoy food. I love food."

Evidently, Leo does not skip many meals. He has a solid fifty-nine-year-old physique, a full, round face, more than one chin, a broad jaw, a narrow mouth, white crewcut hair, and brown eyes. He wears one pair of thick black-framed eyeglasses for reading and close-up work and an identical-looking pair for distance. Most weeks, he works six days, and most days he repairs ten ranges. He carries his tools in a shoulder holster: vise grips, adjustable wrenches, socket wrenches, open-end wrenches, a hacksaw, four Phillips screwdrivers, wire cutters, needle-nosed pliers, regular pliers, adjustable pliers, and three hammers. In the pockets of his shirt and trousers and parka go electronic-ignition modules, safety valves, ignition wires, broiler wheels, stove-burner switches, thermostats, friction tape, wire nuts, and aerosol lubricant. In uniform—blue work clothes and a black-mesh baseball cap with a Welbilt emblem—he looks like someone who has come to fix the oven.

Entering the lobby of the building on West Eighty-sixth, he said, "The work ticket on this reads, 'Oven don't work.' I'm assuming it's the electronic ignition."

The front desk was a glass enclosure. The clerk, a bespectacled man in his fifties, sat inside. "Hey, I remember him," Leo said. "The guy with no hair. Sam." Through an opening in the glass he announced, "You've got a broken oven. Lead me to it."

"The tenant says the stove at the bottom," said Sam.

"I'll take care of it. Just let me look at it. That's the end of it."

Before Leo could take care of anything, however, Sam had to

rummage through a drawer filled with keys. Each bout of rummaging was followed by a trip upstairs. After ten minutes of waiting
in the lobby, Leo said, "Actually, today is nothing. I came here
once and there was *nobody* here. Nobody on the desk. Nobody
even to not be able to find the key." Five minutes later, he said,
"You like this system? You think I haven't got aggravation?" Finally, the key materialized, Sam led Leo to a freight elevator, and
they rode up together and entered a studio apartment that contained
some paintings by the tenant and autographed glossy photographs
of Johnny Carson, Barbra Streisand, George Burns, Joan Baez,
and Arnold Schwarzenegger. The kitchen had finite charm. Leo
started testing the stove burners.

"He says the oven," Sam said.

"Excuse me," Leo said. "But this stove is not working."

"Sorry."

Lifting the top of the range, Leo found the crispy remains of
what might have once been urban wildlife. "This is nothing," he
said. "I went to see an oven once. I don't scare easily, but I jumped
that time. A mouse who knew I was coming leaped out when I
opened the door. That was the appetizer. Inside I found the rest
of his family. Big family."

Ten minutes later, the range was fixed. Leo had replaced a switch
on one of the stove-burner controls, reattached a thermostat wire
inside the oven, and recalibrated the oven-control knob. When he
was ready to test the thermostat, he turned on the gas, watched
the oven burner ignite, and said, "Boom. Done."

On the way out, Sam pointed to a canvas on the wall—a female
nude of superhuman proportions—and said, "This guy, he's a very
well-known artist."

"Doesn't turn me on," Leo said. "You know what turns me on?
A nice warm pastrami sandwich."

Leo has few opinions; mainly, he has positions. His position on
where it is easiest in New York City to repair a range is that the
Bronx is easiest, because he grew up there and can find his way
around blindfolded, and because in the Bronx he rarely has trouble
finding a parking spot. He does not consider it the fault of the
Bronx per se that he once discovered eleven million roaches living

inside a cast-iron oven burner on St. Ann's Avenue, in Mott Haven. His position on the popular oven cleaners is negative. "Listen to me," he said. "I'm dead set against that stuff. People see it advertised on TV and they get careless with it. They put it on the hinges, the capillary tubes, the mercury valve, the manifold panel. Eventually, it eats through the broiler rollers and the burner caps. It destroys. You know what's the best cleaner? Water and ammonia and a soft, soapy sponge. If I ever go on TV, the oven-cleaner people are out of business."

Leo has the following position on explosives: it is a bad idea to store them inside an oven. "One time in Chinatown, on Bayard Street, I got a call to fix an oven," he said. "What made me look inside before I turned the knob I'll never know—but I looked inside. It was crammed full of fireworks. Imagine. I'm not talking little firecrackers, either. I'm talking Roman candles, fountains, aerial bombs. Why were they inside the oven? I have no idea. I don't speak Chinese."

It is Leo's position that many people do not understand the proper way to use a kitchen range. As a result, they often cause themselves inconvenience and unhappiness. "On the East Side—I forget the street—I go to repair an oven, and the Fire Department has arrived by the time I get there," he said. "I work my way through the crowd, go to the kitchen, find the customer. She's reported that something's wrong with the broiler. I open the oven and look inside. There's no bottom to the oven, just a hole. Through that hole I should be seeing the floor, but I don't see the floor. Then I realize I'm looking through a hole in the floor—into the apartment downstairs. This lady had put charcoal briquettes inside her oven, in the broiler pan. That's what she thought the oven was for. The charcoal burned a hole in her oven and then the floor, right through to the neighbor below. I think that's what she said. I didn't hear everything she said. I was yelling most of the time. What a hole that was!"

Leo's next stop was a renovated three-bedroom apartment in Washington Heights, where there was a six-month-old oven that had never been cooked in. While driving there, he referred to a clipboard and said, "This one says, 'Oven control is off. Clicking all the time.' That's easy. Easy. Less than ten minutes." Now, inside the kitchen, he moved the range away from the wall, inspected the red plastic ignition module in the lower rear, and unhooked a wire from it. "Heh-heh-heh," he chuckled as the module made a clicking noise. "You see the sparking at the back?" Blue sparks danced across the gap where the wire had been attached. "That means the module's good, the wire's no good."

When Leo's work goes well, he usually sings and repeats to himself that he is some kind of genius. As he replaced the wire, he hummed "Over the Rainbow." When the burner failed to ignite, however, he became quiet. "Wait, wait. I'm doing something. Just a sec." After a pause, he said, "I'm gonna bet on something which I haven't seen in a long time. I've got an ignition, but there's no gas coming through the thermostat. I bet there's a little piece of paper in there, blocking the gas, it can't get through. I bet it's there from the factory. Now, don't smoke, because I don't shut nothing off."

He removed the oven-control knob and thermostat, using an index finger to plug the gas that came rushing through. His diagnosis of an obstructionist piece of paper turned out to be incorrect, but this did not faze him. "You gotta check out the entire range," he said. "If you don't check out the entire thing, you're a bad mechanic." His next hypothesis—that the building superintendent had fiddled with the oven burner and broken it—was also mistaken. Nor were the two gas feeds inside the oven clogged. Leo had been working in near-silence for several minutes when he took apart the mini-pilot assembly and removed a tiny thimblelike part called an orifice. Inspecting it, he decided that it was clogged. He fitted a new orifice into the assembly, replaced it and the oven burner, and turned the control knob. There was a delay of a few seconds, followed by the clicking sound of the electronic ignition, and then the entire burner flamed.

"You gotta go step by step," Leo said, chuckling again. "It won't work otherwise. Process of elimination. Figure it out. There's not a thing you can't fix when you want to. It's when you *don't* want to . . . See, I know what I'm doing. I checked the thermostat. No problem there. I checked the burner. I broke the main gas feed and the feed from the pilot. There's gas coming through. So where's it not coming through? The assembly. So I just opened it up, checked the orifice, put in a new orifice, and—voilà. The kid's good, huh? You think so? I *know* so."

Replacing the range against the wall, he sang "Happy Days Are Here Again." One last time, he checked the stove burners and the oven control. "Always check the burners after it's put away," he said. "You might have knocked something loose moving it. Then you have to come back for free."

The tools were returned to his holster and he was ready to go; there was a smoking range waiting in Brooklyn Heights. As he headed for the door, he said, "Well, you notice that the oven works—and it didn't work before—so the guy who lives here can't squawk. If I can't fix that oven, I'm eating crow. I'm so good I can make it talk. People complain sometimes to the main office. They say Leo Hoffman has an attitude. Whaddya *mean*? The range is dirty, I tell you it's dirty. Did you break it? First I tell you you broke it. Then I fix it. That's not an attitude. That's me, Leo. I do what I do. What do I do? I *fix*."

1 9 8 6

Jerome's Bus

This is Jerome's bus. It belongs to Jerome Weinberger, whose calling card describes him as a teacher-sculptor. About Jerome: he's in his late forties, short, well built; trim beard; lives in Long Beach, out on the Island. About the bus: it's a '67 Chevy; Jerome bought it on Staten Island last year, painted it off-white, and then added blue racing stripes and white lettering on both sides. The lettering says "Discoveries in Sculpture." Jerome calls the bus the Mobile Sculpture Gallery. Admission is free, but you're welcome to make a contribution. According to a pamphlet (also free), Jerome and the bus have won praise from Ed Graff, principal of the Lido Elementary School, in Long Beach, and from Adria Braverman, supervisor of art at Thomas Jefferson High School, in Brooklyn, among others. Several original Weinbergers are on display inside the bus, including the llama and baby llama made out of brushes; the football placekicker made from a stapler; the samurai warriors made of vises and clamps and corkscrews; and the motorcycle-inner-tube/sardine-can/light-bulb tableau, which is an example of Jerome's more daring recent abstract work.

Jerome's great strength lies in the area of the found object. With found objects, he makes the stuff that he puts in the bus and brings to SoHo on Saturdays in the spring and autumn. His most coveted found object is this parking space on West Broadway, between Prince and Spring streets, right in front of the Castelli Gallery. Jerome always aims for this exact parking space. With Jerome today is his good friend and associate Phyllis Hart. Earlier, shortly after they arrived in SoHo and parked, Phyllis suggested that Jerome take a white banner with black letters—the banner says "An

Experience Through the Imagination"—and hang it upside down
on the left side of the bus, the side that faces the traffic. The banner
on the other side had already been hung right side up. Phyllis
mentioned the upside-down banner just as a throwaway idea, but
Jerome thought it was a marvelous suggestion, and when Phyllis
realized that he had actually *done* it she thought it was brilliant,
too—just the sort of thing that Jerome would do. This approach
—using the imagination to break down the preconceived notions
we have about our visual reality through the use of the most ordinary
objects in new and ingenious associations, as Jerome has described
it many times—goes on all the time with the Mobile Sculpture
Gallery.

Some other highlights from this Saturday afternoon aboard Jerome's bus:

*Jerome talks with Jim, an actor, about the nature of imagination,
and Phyllis inadvertently interrupts:*

Jerome: "Jim, your role as an actor is to bring awareness to
others. To let them know that what they're doing is not allowing
their imagination to become reality. Most people have a fear of
living what their own imagination tells them to do. It's because
they've got their own fears. And, hey, don't think I don't have my
own hangups."

Phyllis: "Jerome, you're blocking the doorway."

Phyllis discusses what it's like to assist Jerome in his endeavor:

"I straighten out the plastic runner that protects the carpet, I
do the lettering on some of the signs in the bus. Like the letters
on *that* sign faded—the one where Jerome describes his philosophy—so I just relettered that sign. Jerome doesn't worry about
those details. He's very busy with his work. I also play the music.
Here's a folk-and-ragtime tape. We try to leave Long Beach at
eight o'clock on the dot. The whole way driving in, Jerome's
apoplectic that he's not going to get this parking spot. I was late
in getting ready today and we forgot one of the pieces, an old
tricycle that Jerome calls 'The Acrobats.' Forgetting it was a hor-
rible experience. Don't ask. What we usually do while we're here
is at some point I'll like go for a walk. Maybe I'll go buy juice.
We bring some other food. Jerome's a vegetarian—not a strict

vegetarian but a vegetarian. It's an integral part of his life—the nonwaste attitude. I find it very stimulating, too."

Jerome and Phyllis discuss the reality of parking the Mobile Sculpture Gallery on West Broadway:

Jerome: "I've had a lot of people from Connecticut come in, for some reason. And I've inspired a lot of people to duplicate what I've done, although they'll probably go further. I had a fellow from Venezuela and a fellow from France. They both stopped by and said that this is just what they wanted to do."

Phyllis: "One Saturday last spring, we were wall-to-wall people all day long. We had a Venezuelan and a Colombian back to back today. We had an ambassador in here once. He grilled Jerome about what he was doing, and when he decided Jerome was O.K. he gave him his card. Very distinguished."

Jerome tells how he fixed up the burlap-covered panels on the interior walls:

"First, I laid the burlap out across a piece of plywood and attached it to the back of the plywood with staples. Then I pulled it in the other direction, so it was real tight, and I stapled it on that side. Then I stretched it across the top and stapled it there and then I stretched it around the bottom—you have to be very careful that you don't get any wrinkles there—and I stapled it there. Then I took a drill and I drilled these holes in the corners and I screwed the whole thing in place. See the screws? It's not as complicated as it sounds."

Jerome talks about his artistic past and future:

"For a long time, most of my life was interior; I never gave myself over to the artistic life and the role that the artist finds himself in. This bus is a reaching out—a desire to communicate and let my presence be felt. I've literally changed a thousand different objects from reality into sculpture. I put in fifty thousand miles on beaches, just walking, looking for found objects. I wore out quite a few pairs of shoes and feet. I'm trying to get people to break down their own reality structures in order to open them up to new channels of communication. Break down their way of conceiving reality. I see myself as an educator.

"I've met over thirty-five hundred people this way. Meeting all those people, I began to experience my own capacity to stimulate them—children, teenagers, young adults, middle-aged people, old people. I can't tell you all the amazing things I've done here with *people*. It seems they yearn to be nourished, they're starved for somebody to make them conscious of the potential of a human being. I don't know where all this is leading me. I still haven't clarified my motives to myself. I'm still amazed at the kind of situation the imagination can lead a person into. And yet inside me I feel I've accomplished nothing. In many ways, I'm nowhere near my potential."

1 9 8 1

Mr. Personality

When Paul Schimmel does his regular work—he's involved in the printing business—he's just plain Paul Schimmel. When he plays his clarinet during rush hour on the F train, he physically resembles just plain Paul Schimmel, but his inner self has actually metamorphosed into Mr. Personality. The money that Mr. Personality collects from passengers in the subway Paul Schimmel in turn uses to underwrite free concerts in hospitals and nursing homes. Paul Schimmel arranges the concert dates, and then he arranges for Mr. Personality to show up with his clarinet. In the end, the Goodnicks of America—Paul Schimmel happens to be the founder and at the moment the only member of this organization—gets credit for a good deed. Full circle comes the enterprise.

Seven days a week, Paul Schimmel ventures into the subway with his clarinet. In the IND station at Sixth Avenue and Forty-second Street one recent afternoon, he paid his fare with a free pass. Various good deeds and diplomatic gestures across the years have enabled Paul Schimmel to forge friendships with employees of the Transit Authority who evidently believe that he qualifies for a senior citizen's discount. In fact, he is only sixty-three. He was wearing black slacks, a blue blazer, a light-blue shirt, a blue necktie, a black topcoat, a brown leather cap with earflaps, and black shoes with a fresh shine. "For the shoes, today I decided to splurge," he said. He wears eyeglasses with thick lenses and thick black frames, and he has gray hair, a round, jowly face, and the torso of a born Santa Claus. On the downtown platform, he paused. After assembling his clarinet, he left its case open at his feet and spread a hand towel across it. Atop that he rested a straw basket, and then he displayed a plastic-sheathed copy of a letter from Mary

Duffy, an employee of the geriatric-psychiatric-services division of Coney Island Hospital. The letter verified that Mr. Personality is a habitual doer of good deeds.

Warming up, Paul Schimmel said, "I can imitate Benny Goodman. Wanna hear?" He played "Let's Dance." "I can imitate all the bandleaders. Let's say Artie Shaw—all right?" He played "Begin the Beguine."

A shuttle train went by on the local tracks, followed a couple of minutes later by an F train. Paul Schimmel has access to a computer inside his brain, which goes to work as soon as he enters a subway car, sizing up the audience. A soft, sweet song usually breaks the ice. Aboard the F, he braced himself against a pole and played "The Shadow of Your Smile" and then "Sorrento," each song punctuated by loudspeaker announcements explaining that there was congestion at Thirty-fourth Street and the train would begin moving shortly. Paul Schimmel's idea of a perfect audience is a bunch of jolly young professionals "that appreciate artistic endeavor." When he finished "Sorrento," he said, "I belong to the Goodnicks of America. Our motto is 'Happiness through music.' Ladies and gentlemen, any contributions you make will go to support concerts in nursing homes and hospitals." By the time the train reached Thirty-fourth Street, there was fifty cents in the straw basket, and Paul Schimmel's transformation into Mr. Personality was complete.

Mr. Personality is partial to less-than-full trains—he needs room to maneuver—and to Broadway musicals. When he plays songs from *South Pacific*, he interlards them with impersonations of Ezio Pinza, Mary Martin, and Juanita Hall. He does the voice of Carol Channing announcing that Mr. Personality will now play "Hello, Dolly!" Offering a synopsis of *West Side Story*, he says that Tony and Maria once planned an assignation aboard the F train.

He worked his way through Tommy Dorsey (a medley, beginning with "I'm Getting Sentimental Over You"), Count Basie ("Stomping at the Woodside"), and Duke Ellington ("Folks, never mind what train you think you got on. This is now the A train"). He has been known to segue from "Take the 'A' Train" to "Chattanooga Choo Choo." His Tommy Dorsey medley is preceded by a set speech:

"Ladies and gentlemen, in 1938 Tommy Dorsey came to the Paramount Theatre, a theatre that contained all the juvenile delinquents of that day, who are the grandmothers of today. They attended the shows illegally, because they were truants from New Utrecht High School or someplace. The truant officers would come in and say, 'All you kids, go back to school.' And they'd dance in the aisles and ignore the truant officer. If you don't believe me, ask your grandmother. Tell her Mr. Personality says, 'Ask your grandmother.' "

A sanitation worker in green work clothes and an orange cap boarded at Fourteenth Street, accompanied by a brown-haired young woman wearing black leather and carrying a stereo boom box. The sanitation worker said, "Hey, Benny Goodman."

The young woman said, "I played clarinet for two years. Then my lips got tired."

Mr. Personality's musicianship is such that he gets the melodies mostly right. He doesn't necessarily land on every note as precisely as Rodgers and Hammerstein, Billy Strayhorn, or Leonard Bernstein might have preferred. Once in a while, a passenger suggests that maybe Mr. Personality should consider playing his clarinet on another train or in a large empty space. When this happens, Mr. Personality does what he can to restrain himself.

"Ladies and gentlemen," he said as the train rolled out of the West Fourth Street station, "I'm now going to take you on an imaginary trip to Brazil. We're gonna leave on an imaginary airline. I'm the captain of the ship. We're about to land in Rio de Janeiro and we're looking over Copacabana Beach, and there are half-nude Cariocas dancing and swaying and you hear the music, and it's this." He played "Corcovado" and "The Girl from Ipanema," saying when he had finished, "Excuse me. Mariachi dancers and Margaritas are now being served in the bar car. It should only happen, right?"

Approaching East Broadway and Canal, he detoured to Paris by way of "La Vie en Rose." He told two young women to think of him as Charles Boyer or Maurice Chevalier, either one. Under the East River, he played "Gigi." On a good run—say, from midtown Manhattan to downtown Brooklyn—he brings in about ten dollars.

At York Street, the first stop in Brooklyn, he usually gets out, because it is possible to cross the platform there and catch a Manhattan-bound train without climbing a stairway. Paul Schimmel knows all the Brooklyn subway stations, because he has lived in Brooklyn most of his life. He learned to play the clarinet as a teenager but gave it up at the age of nineteen, when he went into the printing business. Now, as Mr. Personality, he feels that he is carrying out a preordained plan. "There's no question that when I do this I'm fulfilling my destiny," he said. "So I'm a late bloomer is all."

In the summer of 1983, Mr. Personality and his clarinet logged a lot of hours at the Brighton Beach Baths. For two years, he worked at Bonaparte's Restaurant, on Avenue M, in Midwood. "That's where I practiced my craft," he said. "That's where I learned how to banter."

On the F train back to Manhattan, he spotted a Chassidic passenger, and the computer inside his brain told him to play "Bei Mir Bist Du Schön." That somehow led into "Oklahoma!" and on to "Camelot." When the train reached Thirty-fourth Street, he decided to take a rest.

"The body tells me when to cool it down," he said while carrying his paraphernalia up a stairway and a ramp. "But Mr. Personality is coming through today, right? If I feel fatigued or a little stilted, it's no good. It doesn't give Mr. Personality a chance to take over. Mr. Personality has to generate his own fuel. *I* wouldn't know what to say for a whole hour onstage. But *Mr. Personality* does. The key is improvisational ability. I don't know what I'm going to do in the next thirty seconds, you understand. Here you got a guy—*I* don't know Mr. Personality any more than *you* do. He's a third dimension. Follow? It's improvisation and unpredictability that give you the edge. That's the beautiful part of Mr. Personality. You wanna get an ice-cream cone?"

At a refreshment stand near the top of the ramp, he said, "Gimme a custard. Vanilla."

Between bites, he discussed a concert he gave not long ago at a Bronx nursing home, where his mother, who is now ninety-five, resides. Evidently, fifty years ago she discouraged him from pursuing a career in music. The recent concert forced her to reconsider. "Now she says to me, 'O.K., Paul, you wanna play the clarinet, play the clarinet.' "

When the cone was gone, it was time to go back to work. Instinct told Mr. Personality to switch from the Sixth Avenue line to an uptown N train. "I'm a gambler in life," he said. "I'm a great believer in the laws of probability. Do you believe in ghosts? I sort of believe in ghosts. If I go into a subway car and spill all my stuff—unfortunately, it's happened—I have a feeling that some ghost did that to me. It's a very artistic feeling. I don't believe anything happens accidentally. Everything has a destiny, and you have variables. Now, we're gonna take the N train next. O.K., maybe the F train will blow up and I'll think, Gee, how lucky. But it was *meant* to be that way. Anyway, I want to get on the N train because it has a more artistic crowd. It stops at Fifty-ninth Street, near Bloomingdale's."

A possibly artistic woman passenger on the N train read an Edith Wharton novel and ignored Mr. Personality while he played "Sorrento," "Danny Boy," "Glocca Morra," "Cabaret," and some klezmer tunes. A possibly artistic girl in chinos and a denim jacket snapped her chewing gum and smiled at all his jokes. Mr. Personality played snatches of the theme from *The Godfather* and also "Over the Rainbow," "June Is Bustin' Out All Over," "It Might As Well Be Spring," "In the Mood," and "Marie." When he paused after "Marie," a middle-aged woman in a red wool coat looked up at him and said, "Tommy Dorsey! I feel like I'm in my living room."

1 9 8 7

Approachable

Out on the Coast, Hank Grant has been doing his job, turning out five fourteen-hundred-word "Rambling Reporter" columns a week for the *Hollywood Reporter*, taking an occasional four-day weekend (only rarely a longer vacation), basically giving the entertainment community his uninterrupted best efforts for twenty-five years, keeping track of the movieland subcurrents with as much diligence as Miss Rona and a lot less moralizing, and then, from nowhere, along comes some guy—someone nobody's ever heard of—who feels like giving Hank a hard time. It puts Hank in an unfair position. Hank Grant used to be a performer himself—in the late forties, in Chicago, he had a half-hour radio show called "Let's Have Fun," and then he did a couple of local Chicago TV shows called "What's Wrong with This Picture?" and "The Teens and Tunes Club"— and because Hank has worked the other side of the street he has always taken the position that a columnist for one of the trades should be easily approachable. By now, the smart people in the business have figured out that if they just drop Hank a note sometimes or a card from wherever they're locationing (and Hank Grant can name *quite a few people* who have done this from Rio or London) he'll see what he can do with it. When Hank goes with an item in the column, he wants to report tomorrow's news today, not yesterday's news tomorrow, so he's approachable. "In other words," Hank Grant says, "I don't live in an ivory tower."

Now, historically, Hank's relationship with Bobby Vinton, the singer, has been excellent. Bobby Vinton has kept in touch with Hank. A couple of times a month, Bobby calls Hank on the phone. In addition, Bobby's press agent, Jules Levine, sends in enough items so that Hank Grant can go with at least one a week in his column. Recently, Hank has been able to pass along such information as:

Bobby Vinton now has an honorary Doctor of Music degree from Duquesne University in Pittsburgh (but will he make house calls?).

The current jitters in Poland over possible Soviet intervention has postponed indefinitely the naming of a street in Warsaw after Bobby Vinton. But Bobby does have the consolation of a street awready named after him in his hometown of Canonsburg, Pa.

Bobby Vinton pulled a switch. Last year, he gifted his sec'y with a two-week vacash in Hawaii. Now he's paying the freight for a Hollywood vacation for Ruth Gillette, the prez of his fan club in Honolulu.

All worthwhile items. Of course, Hank Grant is hardly running a Bobby Vinton News Service; Hank's covering an entire town, an international industry. He's keeping his eyes and ears open when "WKRP in Cincinnati"'s Loni Anderson reaches a two-hundred-G alimony settlement with ex-hubby Ross Bickell or when Erik Estrada slips a goose-egg-size diamond ring on Beverly Sassoon's engagement finger or when Don Knotts and his wife, Loralee, are having dinner at Emilio's or when Ernie and Tove Borgnine go for a bite at Ah Fong's. In other words, Hank, who works without the services of a secretary or a legman, is busting his hump for the readership, so he understandably gets upset when a guy who signs himself Don Barde writes a letter to the editor of the *Hollywood Reporter* which begins, "I wonder how many other readers out here are also wearied yet curious about the daily inclusion in Mr. Grant's column of the witticisms and professional happenings of one Bobby Vinton." After the opening sentence, it gets even worse. This Don Barde goes on and on, in a generally insulting manner. Naturally, something like this provokes considerable response from the readership—more than three dozen letters—and the editor subsequently publishes four of the replies (including one from Jules

Levine). Hank Grant doesn't see all the mail, but he hears that it's unanimously pro-Bobby and pro-Hank.

You would think that that would settle the matter, and it would have settled it except that a few days later along comes *another* letter, this one from a guy who signs himself Samson De Brier, and this Samson De Brier writes the following: "It was interesting to read in the *Hollywood Reporter* all the letters written in behalf of Bobby Vinton. Very nice. By the way, who *is* he and what does he do?"

Hank Grant has every right to be suspicious of a question like "Who is Bobby Vinton?," inasmuch as it implies that Bobby Vinton has never published an autobiography titled *The Polish Prince*, in which he tells what it has been like to sell thirty million records, or that Bobby has never recorded such hit songs as "Roses are Red," "Blue Velvet," and "My Melody of Love," songs that have brought joy to people in shopping malls and elevators and enclosed spaces everywhere, songs that have kept Bobby riding high on the charts and have kept him busy on the Strip in Las Vegas, including a phenomenal three consecutive monthly bookings at the Riviera Hotel, bookings that have enabled Bobby and his wife, Dolly, and their five children to carry on a certain life-style, which includes a beautiful home in Pacific Palisades, for which Bobby paid something like six hundred thousand dollars and for which, at the latest word, he turned down an offer of three and a half million. They are asking "Who is Bobby Vinton?" when, of course, the question should be "Who is Don Barde to criticize Hank Grant for running those items about Bobby Vinton?" and, for that matter, "Who is Samson De Brier to write a letter to an editor asking 'Who is Bobby Vinton?' "

Well, here's the kicker, which Hank Grant has recently learned and doesn't mind passing along: Don Barde apparently *doesn't exist*. He's an impostor. Nobody can find that name in the Los Angeles telephone directory. And it leads up to a very important point that Hank Grant would like to make about his life and his work. "I have the word from Jules Levine, who tried to track this thing down, that there's no such person," says Hank Grant. "I don't know about the second guy, De Brier, but the first guy was evidently

somebody who had an axe to grind. Possibly Bobby Vinton slighted
him in some way over the years. Possibly it's a publicist who resents
his client not getting as much exposure as Bobby Vinton. But I
have to make a very important point here. Bobby Vinton does not
stand alone in this particular regard. As a columnist, I cannot
every day just keep calling people and begging them for items.
The ones I favor the most are the ones who send me personal letters
or give me long-distance calls and say, 'Hey, I'm doing this next
week. This is happening to me.' Bobby Vinton is one of those
people. Since I have been doing my column, I have found that the
bigger they are, the nicer they are. Bobby Vinton is very nice. He
still looks like a young boy. I have no idea how old he is. You
know how tough it is to get people's ages in this crazy business.
But he's always kept his nose clean. He and his wife and his family
are very tightly knit. There's never been a breath of scandal, like
he's messing around with a chorus girl. Nothing like that, and
certainly the opportunities are very large in Las Vegas for that
stuff. Now, I heard from Bobby Vinton about this Don Barde guy,
this impostor, and Bobby was very pleased when the letters of
support came in, because at first he thought this Barde guy or
whoever he is was going to hurt his reputation. But it turned out
very well. Now I'll tell you a story about Bobby that I didn't even
get from Bobby—I got it from an employee in Ah Fong's restaurant,
in Beverly Hills. Bobby was having dinner there one night and
some guy at the next table was making some pretty lousy Polish
jokes. And Bobby turned to him and said, 'You know, you're
spoiling my dinner. I happen to be Polish. Would you please stop
it?' And the guy said, 'Go fly a kite,' only he said it worse than
that, and Bobby stood up and said, 'Come on. Let's go.' And he
went outside and beat the heck out of the guy. And, well, I went
with that item in the column. I was able to use that item in a nice
sort of way, without using foul language or anything. And Bobby
didn't mind me using it, and I'll tell you why: because it was true."

1 9 8 1

The Rooster

Haim Gabai, the owner of S.O.S. Locksmith, on Seventh Avenue in Chelsea, firmly denies that the live rooster in the window of his shop is there to attract business. Rather, he explains, deciding to provide a home for the rooster was a selfless, humanitarian gesture. Three months ago, Mr. Gabai rescued the rooster from the Café Borinqueneer, a tavern next door where English is occasionally spoken. A sign above the entrance to the Café Borinqueneer indicates that the place is available for catered weddings and christening parties, but the business card of the proprietor, Miguel A. Del Rosario, places the emphasis upon two attractions described as Go-Go Girls and Shows Latinos. Early last fall, shortly after the rooster, not long out of the shell, arrived on these shores from his native Puerto Rico, he went to work at the Borinqueneer. At the time, his given name was Ye-Ye, and his main duty was to strut along the bar and divert customers during slack periods between Shows Latinos and performances by the Go-Go Girls. When he wasn't doing that, he was confined to a back room, where he made so much noise that Haim Gabai, in his locksmith shop, could hear him. Eventually, Mr. Gabai went next door and persuaded German Roman, a Borinqueneer employee and the erstwhile owner of the bird, that a bar was not a healthy place for a young rooster, and that a young rooster might not be a health asset to the bar. Mr. Roman, who had entertained thoughts of training Ye-Ye for the fight ring, agreed to sell him to Mr. Gabai instead, for fifteen dollars.

"I bought food for him, and he was really hungry," Mr. Gabai said the other day. "The people next door, I don't think they knew how to feed him correctly. He lives very well here."

Mr. Gabai spends many of his working hours on calls that take him outside the shop. While he is away, the rooster enjoys the company of two S.O.S. employees, Maida Dalama and Al Emmons, and they, for their part, enjoy studying the vagaries of rooster behavior.

"The only time he'll talk is when he's happy," Al Emmons said, not long after Mr. Gabai left the shop for a keys-locked-inside-the-car emergency. "He's happy when he's eating. He eats pickles, potato chips, cheese, ham, and eggs. Loves ham."

"He does not like eggs," Maida said, correcting Al. "He doesn't want to eat his own kind."

"He's never been in a fight," said Al.

"No," said Maida. "I think he was bred as a fighter, but I think Haim took him away from all of that."

"He sits in the front window because he likes to see people," said Al.

"Likes women," Maida added. "He definitely likes women. He definitely doesn't like Arty, who works in our new shop, in Queens."

"He loves aggravating Arty," said Al. "He has no special tricks. He just likes to parade around and, if possible, aggravate Arty."

Their observations have led Al and Maida to conclude that the rooster is undergoing a mild identity crisis. Studying his reflection in the window, he can see his gray-and-white mottled body, yellow neck feathers, deep-blue-green tail plume, and tomato-red comb and wattles; thus, he instinctively realizes that he is a rooster. Occasionally, however, he becomes imperious and behaves like a watchdog; he moves around suspiciously when a stranger enters the shop. Also, he isn't quite certain of his name. After making the move from the Café Borinqueneer, he had to unlearn Ye-Ye, because Haim and Maida had decided to rename him Scottie, in honor of a West Indian locksmith who works for Mr. Gabai.

"We call Scottie the locksmith Scottie No. 1," Maida explained. "Scottie the rooster is Scottie No. 2."

"My full name is Omar Scott," said Scottie No. 1 when he showed up a few minutes later. "Like Omar Khayyam. I'm also full of romantic poetry that I pour out to fine ladies like her." As he spoke, he smiled at Maida.

Lately, Scottie No. 1 has been trying to get Scottie No. 2 to answer to yet another name—Louie. The fact remains, however, that the rooster reacts more alertly to "Scottie" than to "Louie." He also reacts vigorously to dogs passing in front of the store. Their presence causes him to twitch and cluck. If the traffic on the sidewalk bores him, he wanders to the back of the store and nibbles birdseed and corn from a red feeding trough or has a drink of water from his plastic bowl. When he needs exercise, he flies from a roost behind the counter, above a sign advertising Medeco locks, to the front window, where he settles down amid a display of cylinder guards, chain door locks, key window locks, padlocks, and police locks. Upon landing, he likes to balance on one leg and preen a bit. He is a self-assured bird.

On a clear day, every fourth or fifth passerby notices Scottie. This makes his view of the world approximate an extended episode from "Candid Camera." It is in the late afternoons, when people are on their way home from work, that he draws the most attention. A few regulars drop in frequently to inquire about his welfare.

The other afternoon, a young couple stopped by to have a set of keys copied. The man was the urban-cowboy type, with a dark beard, boots, jeans, and a leather jacket. The woman was tall, with light-brown hair and bright-pink cheeks, and wore jeans, boots, a gray wool coat, and a straw hat.

"Is that a rooster, and is he here all the time?" the young man asked.

"Yes," said Maida. "He likes it here."

The young man nodded sagely, as if to signify that, in a cosmic sense, the arrangement struck him as all right.

Shortly after that, a middle-aged woman with an arm full of packages stopped outside the store, looked in at Scottie, and began to offer a cartoon-version imitation of a rooster. "Buh-*bok*-bok-bok-bok-bok-bok-bok," she said. "Come on, rooster. Buh-*bok*-bok-bok-bok-bok-bok-bok." Scottie stared at her for a while and then bobbed his head several times. On the other side of the glass, the woman's clucking grew more insistent. After a moment of contemplation, Scottie abandoned modesty and erupted into an aria—first a couple of preliminary crows, then a haughty string of five or six more.

Outside, standing in the falling snow, the woman now dropped her packages, spread her elbows, and began to crow herself—heartily, full-throated. Hunched over as she was, she blocked the window almost entirely, so that anyone passing by at that instant would have had a hard time seeing that there was a rooster inside the locksmith's shop.

1 9 7 8

Not Strictly All Business

As far as the Social Security Administration is concerned, Bill Schifrin is officially retired. Before he retired (it's been almost a year now), he sold wedding rings—for forty years, *only* wedding rings—from a booth in the National Jewelers Exchange, on West Forty-seventh Street. Mr. Schifrin is confident that he knows more about marriage than anyone else on the planet. Therefore, when he shows up at his former place of business—now owned and operated by his son-in law, Herman Rotenberg—he has a tendency to speak in the present tense.

"The fellow at City Hall doesn't talk to the couples. *I* talk to them," Mr. Schifrin was saying one day not long ago. "It takes a customer at least a half hour to pick out the wedding bands. So I talk. I'm interested. Why? Because maybe I'm just a busybody. What I know is I'm the only one that knows as much about couples as I do. I'm the only one who knows where girls should go to meet high-class fellows. You want to know? This time of year, you go to Central Park, Fifth Avenue and Ninetieth Street, any Saturday or Sunday morning from seven to ten o'clock. There's three hundred guys in running clothes to every girl. Is now a busy time of year in the wedding-ring business? Not particularly. Years ago, people got two weeks' vacation in the summer. So they got married in the summer. There was no such thing as a winter vacation. Maybe you don't know that, but I know that."

How to look dapper—Mr. Schifrin knows that, too. He has some gray hair, light-green eyes, a suntan, and a trim physique. He could pass for Jack Klugman's first cousin. The other day, he wore a blue blazer, gray slacks, black loafers, a white shirt, and a maroon necktie. He wore a gold pinkie ring with a round diamond on his right hand, a gold bracelet around his right wrist, and a plain gold wedding band on his left ring finger. Attached to his shirt collar was a gold monogram pin. "It's a new style," he explained. "Nobody wears a tie tack anymore."

Herman Rotenberg, who is tall, fortyish, graying, and usually easygoing, was having some frustration with the telephone. "How do you sue the phone company?" he said.

"A fellow that sells a bracelet is not necessarily interested in people," Mr. Schifrin went on. "I genuinely am. I hear what people have to say. I hear if they're complaining about the in-laws even before the wedding. I play mental games with myself. Say a fellow comes here and says, 'I'll bring my fiancée in at four o'clock.' As four o'clock approaches, I try to picture her. Usually, I guess right. It's a cliché that love is blind, but only I *know* it is."

The older of Mr. Schifrin's two daughters, Ivy, was in the booth, as was his wife, Doris. "This is my daugher who's married to a diamond dealer," he said. "My other daughter, Gayle, Herman's wife, is at home taking care of her kids." Mr. Schifrin says about his wife, to whom he has been married for forty-five years, "She doesn't work. She helps out. She drops in to see the daughter and son-in-law." Mrs. Schifrin says about her husband, "He's never dull."

"From right where we're standing, I watched the sexual revolution happen," said Mr. Schifrin. "How did I know when it started? Well, I had read about these things. But here's how I found out for sure. A girl came in to see me and she wanted two wedding rings. Where's her fiancé? He's working, he can't take off. So I give her my ring sizer and tell her to bring it back the next day. She comes back the next day, and I say, 'Did you get his size?' And she says, 'No. When I left this morning, he was still sleeping.' That hit me. I knew the world was changing."

A casually dressed couple—late twenties, both with light-brown hair—approached the booth, accompanied by a blond little girl about four years old. "Nothing surprises me anymore," said Mr.

Schifrin. "I'm confident this little girl isn't the one getting married. Otherwise, nothing surprises me. One girl came in pregnant and asked me to engrave a ring '3-2-81, Better Late Than Never.' Another girl came back after three months of marriage. Tears in her eyes. They broke up. She wanted to sell the ring back. I looked inside the ring. It said '6-21-79—Forever ever ever ever.' That's why I don't care much for engraving. By the way, I don't believe the statistics that say women past a certain age have no chance of getting married. People still get married. Only, they get married *later*. Sooner or later, they get married. *Everybody* gets married."

Seven or eight years ago, when Mr. Schifrin noticed that quite a few customers he was selling wedding rings to said their parents had bought wedding rings from him, he began to contemplate retirement, and eventually Mr. Rotenberg, who was then training to become a psychotherapist, decided to switch careers. Selling wedding rings, Herman Rotenberg believes, is "much more exciting" than psychotherapy. He gets along fine with his father-in-law. "Bill Schifrin is a gregarious man," Mr. Rotenberg said. "*I* would buy a wedding ring from him."

"Herman's a natural when it comes to relating to people," said Mr. Schifrin. "He's better than I am. The only difference is I joke around more. People come in, I ask them, 'Are you sure you know what you're doing?' Or I say, 'If you're already standing here, it's too late.' My son-in-law doesn't speak like that. If a couple seems nervous, I might say, 'You both made good choices.' Hey, I know what to say. I never considered this strictly all business. If people walked away without buying, I said, 'All right. But remember, my wedding rings are lucky.' The girls' eyes always lit up when I said that. If someone complained about price, I would tell them, 'A wedding ring is the least expensive part of getting married.' I know all the answers. I told them, 'The wedding ring costs less than the cake. The flowers die the next day. The ring lasts forever.' "

The business cards that Mr. Rotenberg and Mr. Schifrin hand out say "1,873 Unusual Wedding Bands."

"We're always moving rings. Maybe we have more, maybe we have less," Mr. Rotenberg said. "I have no idea how many we actually have in stock." The inventory includes 14k.-gold rings, 18k. rings; "classic" rings, multilayered rings, flexible rings; diamond rings, sapphire rings, diamond-and-sapphire rings, diamond-and-ruby rings; rings of yellow gold, white gold, rose gold, and green gold; antiques, reproductions of antiques; multicolored, multishaped; sharp-edged, asymmetrical, four-sided, five-sided, ten-sided, twelve-sided; handwoven, handwrought; nuggety, Byzantine-looking, baroque-looking, custom-designed by-the-customer, and animal-figurine rings. There are rings designed not to look like wedding rings, and rings for people who are missing ring fingers.

Anyone who needs to buy a ring on the run can be accommodated. "One guy came in with a tuxedo," said Mr. Rotenberg. "He needed one on the spot. Another time, a best man came in with a tuxedo and he needed *two* rings. He'd lost them both. A fellow came in once in a desperate mood. He'd come to town for a convention and had misplaced his ring. Not only did he want a replacement just like it—he wanted us to make it look twenty-five years old."

A sign on the back wall of the booth says "No REFUNDS. EX-CHANGE OR CREDIT WITHIN 7 DAYS." "That's an old sign," Mr. Schifrin explained. "It was there because I didn't want my wedding rings used for immoral purposes. Used to be a fellow'd come here Friday afternoon, buy a ring, and try to return it Monday morning. Why? Because the fellow was conning the girl. That doesn't happen anymore—because a girl doesn't need a wedding ring to go away for the weekend."

A couple of young professionals in business suits approached the booth. Mr. Schifrin whispered, "Take a look. Take a look. *Class?* A perfect match. They're gonna hit."

"Take your time," Mr. Rotenberg told the couple. "This is not something people do often."

The A. & O. Diamond Dairy restaurant does business on the mezzanine above the National Jewelers Exchange. Suddenly, Mr. Schifrin got in the mood for a vegetarian-chopped-liver sandwich on rye, so he walked upstairs to the A. & O. As he ate, his mood became reflective. "When I finished high school, my father arranged for me to go to work for a diamond setter," he said. "And

I did it, because in those days you did what your father told you."
After spending almost four years in the Army during the Second
World War, he returned to diamond setting. "The only piece of
jewelry I was really interested in was wedding rings. I made them.
I designed them. Soon I devoted all my time to them. Somebody
buys earrings, somebody buys a bracelet—so what? But a wedding
ring is interesting. I succeeded because I talked to people. A clerk
in a department store can't sell a wedding ring. It's an emotional
purchase. The one who understands it has to be the one who sells
it. In my career, I hit. You know why I had such a good time here?
I saw girls at their best. All day long, I saw happy people."

Mr. Schifrin spotted a couple at an adjacent table—he had a
dark beard and tinted wire-rimmed glasses, and wore a three-piece
gray suit; she wore a yellow sweater and black slacks. The man
leaned across the table to kiss the woman.

"Watch this," said Mr. Schifrin. He reached inside his jacket
pocket, removed a business card, passed it to the couple, and said,
"Here, when you get ready to make it official, come see me."

The young man looked at the card, waved his left hand in the
air, and said, "We're already married. And we got the rings from
you."

Mr. Schifrin didn't miss a beat. "O.K., then, if you know any
other fellows as foolish as you, send them to me."

1 9 8 7

Rafting-Up

Because Captain Jack Eichholz has the look of an avid indoorsman, someone meeting him for the first time would not immediately suspect that he is a totally committed boatman. But then he would open his mouth to speak, and something about struts, shafts, props, and rudders would come out. Captain Jack has a fair complexion and lank blond hair that is turning silver—the image of someone who spends his spare time in the basement tending mushrooms. He is tall and has sloping shoulders, and he walks head down, as if he were waiting for one of his shoes to come untied. Weekdays, Captain Jack sells Chevrolets in Yonkers. When the weekend arrives, he usually heads for open water. For the past twenty years —he's now forty-seven—Captain Jack has held a commercial boat-captain's license. This explains his title. Once, he tried a career as a yacht broker on City Island, in the Bronx, but after a while he went back to selling Chevies. For more than a year now, Captain Jack has been the commander of Bronx Power Squadron No. 101, which is a unit of United States Power Squadrons, a private boating fraternity that is something like an Odd Fellows at Sea. You don't have to own a boat to belong to the Power Squadron, and at the moment Captain Jack happens not to. He doesn't own a Chevrolet, either. Whether he's dealing in cars or boats, he likes to be called Captain.

When the Captain can find the time, he serves as a free-lance pilot of charter fishing boats out of City Island. Some of the nicer things that have happened to him have taken place on the water. For instance, he met his wife, Peggy, on a charter boat ten years ago. Just the same, he doesn't forget that things can go wrong every now and then; the unpredictable or the marginally avoidable can arise, and there you are, stuck on a sandbar. Even when Captain Jack is having a good time, he doesn't like to get carried away. When a volunteer asks, "Can I give you a hand, Captain?" he usually says, "No, no. Make yourself comfortable." He says this in a speaking voice that comes partly from the upper Bronx and partly from the upper reaches of his sinuses. It's easy to keep track of what's happening aboard ship when Captain Jack is in command, because he has a habit of announcing what he's doing as he does it. "O.K., we'll check out the engine and get things percolating," he says. "O.K., I've got the VHF and the scanner tuned in. O.K., now I'm going to get the charts ready."

As far as the members of the Bronx Power Squadron are concerned, Captain Jack's tenure at the top of the bridge—that's what the squadron calls its slate of officers: "the bridge"—has been a conspicuous success. The major annual events—the moonlight sail, the predicted-log contest (using compasses but not watches, contestants predict how long it will take to cover a prescribed nautical course), the cooperative charting project (squadron members survey a stretch of water while studying nautical charts, look for discrepancies like missing buoys or nonexistent landmarks, and report their findings to the Coast Guard and to the National Ocean Survey), the Change of Watch dinner dance (that's when a new bridge is installed)—have all turned out quite well. The Bronx Power Squadron held its annual rafting-up cruise one recent Sunday, and Captain Jack was in command of a thirty-foot Trojan sport-fishing cruiser that he had borrowed from a generous friend. Afterward, Captain Jack was forced to concede, in all modesty, that it, too, had been an excellent event.

In principle, a rafting-up works this way: the squadron commander and all those members who feel like coming along agree that at a certain time on a certain date they will rendezvous at a prescribed spot. Specifically, rafting-up Captain Jack–style means getting up early and driving to a marina on City Island; taking along a few friends; taking along enough food and drink to last several months, in case you should get shipwrecked and stranded in Great Neck; cruising around Long Island Sound for a couple of hours; talking back and forth to your Power Squadron mates on the two-way VHF radio; joining them at a prearranged spot in Manhasset Bay; dropping anchors; hanging rubber fenders over the gunwales; lashing all the boats (twelve) together in a row; watching yachts, sailboats, runabouts, and other cruisers (*Cohn-Tiki, Buoy Crazy, Boom Boom*) pass by; spending the afternoon eating, drinking, swimming, and climbing from boat to boat; watching in distress as some squadron members take turns tossing each other overboard; getting a mild headache from overexposure to the sun; taking a couple of Anacins and waiting an hour until the headache goes away; watching Bill Quinn, the executive officer of the Power Squadron, dive for clams in the black ooze at the bottom of the bay; watching John Ciano use a putty knife to scrape barnacles from the hull of his cruiser; watching Ciano's German shepherd, Tarky, swim while wearing a canine life vest; listening to shoptalk ("Last year, I came to the raft-up with no trim tabs. I used forty-five gallons of gas that day"); willfully ignoring the fact that Manhasset Bay on a sunny Sunday in late summer is the nautical equivalent of the Seventh Avenue I.R.T. at rush hour; and then cruising back to City Island. Cruising back is the amazing part. The full moon is rising and the sun is setting, and Manhattan's silhouette, to the southwest, resembles pieces of slate propped against pink marble. All sorts of illusions are possible. In fading light, from an odd angle, Co-op City looks like Miami Beach.

1 9 8 0

No Fooling Around

According to Eugene Tso's résumé, his expertise encompasses "Kolomeyka, Windmueller, Hopak, Bavarian Ländler, Dreisteyrer, Neapolitan Tarantella, Kreuz Koenig, Zillertaler Ländler, Dodi Li, Parado de Valdemosa, Krakowiak, etc."—which means that Mr. Tso's expertise is international folk dancing. License No. 672, issued by the New York City Department of Parks and Recreation, specifies that for a few hours a week, from mid-April through late October, a lovely spot in Battery Park belongs to Mr. Tso. If the weather obliges, shortly after noon every Saturday—and also on Memorial Day, the Fourth of July, and Labor Day—Mr. Tso, wearing a shoulder bag and pulling a shopping cart, leaves his apartment, on the upper West Side, and takes the Broadway local down to South Ferry, the end of the line. When he reaches his designated spot—a patch of grass and pavement just west of the war memorial, about twenty-five yards from the tip of Manhattan, and centered between two evenly spaced rows of euonymus trees—he unpacks. He spreads out two plastic ground cloths, sets up two aluminum snack tables, props open the shopping cart, and, by resting Masonite boards on top of it, creates a shelf for an electric amplifier. A tape player and a portable power source stand on the snack tables, along with a couple of cigar boxes filled with tapes. Atop the amplifier goes a black plastic sign with raised white letters: "EUGENE TSO." Attached to that is a smaller sign that says, "EVERYONE IS WELCOME TO JOIN IN THE DANCING."

On a recent Saturday, Mr. Tso wore a short-sleeved white shirt, tan slacks, and a wide orange leather belt. He is slender and slightly stooped, and has coffee-brown eyes and sparse gray hair. Almost fifty years ago, Mr. Tso immigrated to the United States from China. During the nineteen-forties, he belonged to a Y.M.C.A. in Brooklyn, where he swam, did calisthenics, and played basketball and bridge. One day, a bridge partner suggested, as a change of pace, folk dancing. "We go to Washington Irving High School for folk-dancing class," Mr. Tso recalled while he was setting up his equipment. "I watch it and say, 'I could do better.' Next, I go to music library near Lexington Avenue. I spend the whole day there, looking for material. I discover books about folk dancing, but I also discover that people don't write well, they make mistakes. So I study many books and I dance and I write books myself."

Mr. Tso is now the author and publisher of four dance manuals—*Folk Dance Instructions, Volumes I–IV*—and he pays attention to new trends. "Nowadays, there are so many new good dances coming from *Israel*," he said. "If the people want it, we follow the *people*. I never go to Israel, I never go to European countries, I never go to Russia. I only study *books*. I have my principles. First principle is: No fooling around with the steps. *Maximum* accuracy is *very* important. If you fool around with the steps, the people will *find out*. Some folk-dance leaders—they don't *teach*. They don't *lead*. The reason? I don't know. They just like to play the tape recorder, I think."

Even when Mr. Tso is merely pushing a button on a tape recorder—that is, even when his feet are stationary—other parts of him dance. Frequently during conversation, he leans his head back and looks skyward and his arms levitate as if he were in a pool of salt water, floating effortlessly. At other moments, his features intensify—"Eureka!"-like—and for emphasis he moves his hands as if coaxing birds to fly. Mr. Tso does not display a sign that says that everyone is welcome to contribute. He does, however, keep an empty cigar box handy. If anyone cares to make a donation, he does not complain. "No, not supposed to charge," Mr. Tso explained. "Only *donations* accepted. You donate by *free will*. Some people donate a quarter. Some people donate *two* quarters. Some people—the dancers—give a *dollar*."

There was a time when Mr. Tso taught in various public and private schools around the city, and he now conducts weekly folk-dancing sessions at a senior center in the East Village and at a Y.M.C.A. in Chelsea. Most of the regulars who show up on Saturdays in Battery Park are his contemporaries, more or less. Chances are they did some dancing in their youth and then allowed thirty or forty years to slip by with no dancing. They seem grateful for the opportunity to make up for lost time and to exercise their critical faculties:

Encomium—"He runs a better session, Eugene does. There's no comparison. Most of us like to dance what he plays, because he plays what we like."

Rhetorical monologue—"What is this? Who knows? If I don't know, I make up my own dance. Who cares? I forgot my knee brace. It's in my husband's car. So, fancy I'm not doing today. Right?"

Historical perspective—"He goes by the book. But the book was written eighty years ago."

Sweeping dismissal—"*That's* what they do here? I thought this was supposed to be folk dancing. This isn't folk dancing. You wanna see dancers? Go to Central Park."

Self-analysis—"I want you to know I walk with a cane and I have a bad heart condition. But the doctor wants me to do this. So if I'm tired sometimes I'll come in, like, on the third chorus."

Idle observation—"I had my hair done yesterday. I'm worried about rain and low-flying birds. Come on. Let's dance."

The dancing lasts from two to six, and the regulars, many of whom commute from Brooklyn, tend to arrive early. Fifteen or twenty show up each week: Ann, Max, Jean, Martha, Lily, Irving, Sid, Esther, Lenore, Isabel, a couple of Roses—about twice as many women as men. They bring plastic shopping bags packed with lunches and insect repellent and other paraphernalia, and when dancing time comes they place their belongings on one of Mr. Tso's ground cloths. The women wear pinks and limes and lavenders and floral prints, along with sensible shoes and, on bright days, baseball caps. Periodically, foundation garments are adjusted. Nobody dances every dance. Some people sit for a while, some take a walk for five minutes, some eat a peach.

There are times when the group dances, consecutively, a hustle, a Rumanian line dance, a rumba, and an Israeli military march. As the music plays, the dancers eye Mr. Tso or each other and talk to him or to each other or to themselves. "Face me . . . The other way . . . Right foot. Four out, four in. It's one-two, two-two . . ." And "It's back-forward, back-forward. Two to the right, two to the left, and then you do with the cockamamie feet." And "You've got to make it a little faster, Eugene."

Often, at the end of a dance Mr. Tso bows solemnly toward the harbor. A nonstop flotilla—sailboats, ferryboats, hydroplanes, tugboats, and the side-wheeler *Andrew Fletcher*—passed by the other day. A blimp floated overhead. Hundreds of smiling strollers paused to watch: a Pakistani tour group, a Japanese tour group (busy with cameras, grateful to have come to New York and found something so exotic). A police car crept past, followed by a trio of roller skaters wearing Walkmans and sunglasses. At one point, as the dancers were doing a complicated Israeli circle dance—lots of handclapping and slow pirouettes—accompanied by a klezmer tune called "Dumyah Dumyah," one of the women said aloud, to no one in particular, "He's in all his glory today—Eugene is." A not exactly petite married couple in matching red shirts and candy-striped slacks rose from a bench. For some time, they had been only watching, but now they suddenly abandoned inhibition: they stepped right in, maneuvering with the grace of barges in rough water. They wore serene smiles. They had joined the dancing.

1 9 8 5

Violations

In your life you've never seen so much gratitude. A glow of gratitude is what it amounts to. Pilgrims arrive at the Parking Violations Bureau, on Park Avenue South, radiating this glow. You go to the third floor. It's a take-a-number arrangement: you take a number from one of the women at the reception desk—the women who before they landed jobs with the city worked as Alpine guides, or maybe not—and then you wait a damn long time. The waiting room: literally breathtaking. Every molecule—beige linoleum floor, matching Formica countertops, dark-brown beams, black molded-plastic chairs, uniformed security personnel, posted warnings of penalties for offering or taking or soliciting a bribe—does something to your lungs. Without knowing that this was the Parking Violations Bureau, you might mistake it for one of the new double-threat restaurants—cold cuts and mass income-tax audits, say, or express Chinese takeout and home-improvement-loan rejections. The Parking Violations Bureau exists because there are mornings when law-abiding citizens wake up feeling just a little too good about things in general. When you are feeling just a little too good about things, what you are actually feeling is that at some unpredictable moment in the near future the euphoria will dissolve into bitter disappointment. That is why efficiency-minded people are grateful for the Parking Violations Bureau. It cuts out all the suspense.

All walks of life turn up—pacers, hair-tearers, face-rubbers, knapsackers, stray United Parcel deliverers, an occasional motorist in a corduroy motoring cap, and many young unemployed actors who wear mobile-phone pagers and who moonlight driving mini-vans that they are constantly double-parking while dropping off day campers. The hair-tearer in the kelly-green jogging outfit has received a summons for a hydrant violation on West Eighty-second Street. With accumulated penalties, he's up to ninety-five dollars, even though he never even saw a copy of the original summons, which—how could he have seen it?—he does not deserve, because at the time of the alleged offense he was practically in Westchester, at a mall, helping his brother-in-law Jack buy a new transmission cable for the lawnmower. He was *nowhere near* West Eighty-second Street, much less parked next to a hydrant on that block.

A hearing examiner will soon listen to this explanation and many others. Right now he is waiting inside a hearing room, wearing a red-white-blue-and-yellow checked sports jacket and maroon beltless slacks, grinding his eye sockets with both fists and looking as if at any minute the heat could interfere with his love of due process. He is going to have a good time with the man carrying the three back issues of *Golf Digest*—the one who lives on the Island and drives a Buick LeSabre that somebody double-parked one night near a construction site in midtown. Some traffic-enforcement agent has thrown the book at this situation—double-parking where it was No Parking Any Time; front license tag missing; inspection sticker expired—and when the hearing examiner has heard just about enough he will give thought to tacking on a couple of citations for civil contempt. The Buick LeSabre owner, however, does not see this coming. In the waiting room, he says to one of the pacers, "They've got a nerve giving tickets to guys like us."

Everyone testifies under oath. The lady wearing the Walkman earphones and the Hullaballoons T-shirt and carrying the large white vinyl handbag knows in her bones that she transgressed a bus stop on Memorial Day. She is smoking a long cigarette and thinking about claiming Sunday-regulations-in-effect, but she will probably end up saying, "Hey, this can't be my ticket. My car never left the garage, because my kid was throwing up all day long," even though that way she runs a serious risk that the examiner will ask, "Do you have a parking receipt or some sort of note from a doctor?"—in which case she would do just as well invoking the Adolfo Defense. The Adolfo Defense goes, "It isn't even my car! It belongs to my friend Adolfo. He lent it to another friend. I don't live near where the ticket happened. Adolfo had a medical emergency and told me to come here. Adolfo's friend lives not far from where the ticket happened, and . . ."

The man with the freshly barbered beard, the three-piece blue pinstripe suit, the silver ring with the blue sapphire, the purple-tinted aviators, and the unlit cigar the size of a salami—this man's problem is justice. He has a wife whose arm is in a sling. She fractured her shoulder, he was taking her to the hospital for a checkup, he makes one little stop on Thirty-fourth Street and leaves his rear flashers on, the battery runs down, then he's waiting for a jump, and instead of help he gets cited for Loading Zone No Standing. Forty-five dollars. This would never happen to the chief executive officer of a Fortune 500 company. It would never happen to anyone you see when the Academy Awards are on television and the camera pans the audience. The hearing examiner announces that after your case is heard you are supposed to hold on to the disposition slip for eight and a half years—also the receipts and the canceled checks. Where is justice?

The wide black raincoat and wide black wing tips belong to an out-of-towner, a young fellow from Syracuse. He stares hard at his parking ticket, which he still cannot believe. He has been towed, and that is even more incredible and expensive. All the way from Syracuse for this—plus a hearing examiner who will congratulate him for "the most unique interpretation of the arrows on street signs" that the hearing examiner has ever heard. Brand-new in town and already he's a celebrity. He has told the hearing examiner that the arrows on the "No Parking" signs seemed to be pointing to the *opposite* side of the street. Now he must listen respectfully as the hearing examiner says, "This is a rental car, correct?"

"Yes."

"How long have you been here?"

"Four days."

"If I were you, I wouldn't drive in Manhattan. No one should. It's a very dangerous place. I don't understand people like you. After you leave here, I want you to turn the car in. I want to ask you a question: Why do you think we have buses and subways?"

1 9 8 5

Destiny

Sometimes an idea feels a little lonely. What it could really use is another idea, to provide loyal companionship, to share long walks, to be there for a warm snuggle in the easy chair next to the fireplace at the end of a long day. Don Mensh is the person who came up with the Montrose Pet Hotel idea. The slogan "Introducing a hotel so exclusive it doesn't accept people"—Don Mensh invented that. He also deserves credit for "spacious, private suites, complete with comfortable sleeping areas and a continuous supply of sparkling-fresh drinking water"; rooms "cleaned and disinfected daily by a modern high-pressure washing system"; "extra human contact that we provide—that extra scratch behind the ears"; "specially designed disposable feeding bowls—a fresh table-setting at every meal"; "comfort for your pet—and peace of mind for you"; and "the ultimate in in-town boarding and grooming." The Montrose is on Ninety-fifth Street between First and Second Avenues, and it has rooms for a hundred and thirty-four dogs and eighty-four cats. Don Mensh's partner, Richard Messina, says, "We're primarily a Manhattan demographic." When Richard Messina, who is an attorney, shows a visitor the carpeted cat-exercise area in the front window of the Montrose, he says, "That's where they scratch and whatever. Whatever cats do."

The scene at the registration desk as Choo-Choo or Pookie or Coco or Missy or Duffy or Dudley or Sabrina or Cleo or Caviar or Woofer or Little Bear checks in for the weekend—the handing over of the familiar items with the smell of home (the beanbag chair, the old bath towel, the panty hose); the writing down of special diet instructions and emergency phone numbers; the last-minute purchase of rawhide bones or puppy chips or realistic-looking fur mice from the Montrose Pet Hotel gift shop; the moist goodbyes—Don and Richard hired Sam Arlen to manage all that. Sam sits opposite a sign that says "HOTEL RESERVES THE RIGHT TO DIP GUESTS CHECKING IN WITH FLEAS OR TICKS." When the phone rings, Sam answers, and if it's Mr. and Mrs. Mooney calling from Barbados to ask whether someone couldn't please bring their schnauzer Marlene to the phone, Sam gets on the intercom and says, "Billy, come to the front, please." Then, when Billy, a factotum, comes to the front, Sam says, "There's a long-distance call for Marlene Mooney, in Room No. 61. Get her and bring her to the phone, please."

Sam has heard every joke: the joke about the poodle and the Irish wolfhound who sign the guest register "Mr. and Mrs. Joe Jones"; the joke about the all-dog and all-cat cable TV; the joke about the in-heat suite; the joke about the Magic Paws mattress massage. If you are a dog, a room at the Montrose runs from sixteen to nineteen dollars a night, depending upon your weight. If you are a cat, the price is ten dollars. Long-stay discounts can be arranged. The lady who owns the nineteen cats—she has delivered them in installments—perhaps qualifies for a long-stay discount. Or perhaps, considering the several hours she spends visiting every day, she, too, should be charged rent. The Montrose can accommodate a limited number of cockatoos and cockatiels and other birds with strong personalities. Rabbits, guinea pigs, and ferrets are welcome. "I'm a little wary of reptiles," Sam Arlen says. "We had a chance to take a six-foot iguana, but we weren't quite set up for it, with heat lamps and everything."

Don Mensh means what he says when he says, "The idea is a hotel for pets. But, in reality, what are we talking about? We're talking about *quality care* for pets."

The Critter Car ("Have You Taken Your Pet for a Ride Today?") was Barbara Meyers's idea. There are actually two Critter Cars, but they're the same idea. Each is a Chevrolet Cavalier wagon with enough cargo space to handle three Great Danes or at least eight cat carriers or a six-foot iguana if it had anywhere to go, and each is operated by a skilled, pet-sensitive driver who wears a beeper and has a mobile phone to facilitate maximum communication as he proceeds with his job, which is to insure a safe, stress-free ride. Barbara Meyers dispatches the Critter Cars from her office, in Old Mill Basin, in Brooklyn. For ten years, she was a nurse, and for five years she drove a taxi, accompanied by a toy poodle named Skila. She now owns, besides the Critter Cars, a mini-fleet of taxis and a filling station. When you talk to Barbara Meyers on the phone, she says, "That sound you hear is a cat purring. If he got any closer, he'd be in the telephone." The Critter Car idea came to her during a time when her German shepherd Duke had to make regular trips to a vet in Manhattan. A photograph of Duke (now the late Duke) has been attached to the glove compartment of each Critter Car.

It was destiny, of course, for Barbara Meyers to discover the Montrose Pet Hotel, and vice versa. The Montrose used to operate a guest-pickup-and-delivery service, but about nine months ago it turned that job over to Critter Car. Jim Viviano and John Feyko are the skilled, pet-sensitive drivers. About one in ten Critter Car trips terminates at the Montrose. The other morning, Jim Viviano had a ten o'clock pickup on West Twenty-third Street—a golden retriever named Max Goldstein. He went inside the building lobby and announced himself to the doorman, the doorman made a call on the intercom, and two minutes later Max was shaking the doorman's hand. Jim Viviano led Max outside and into the Critter Car. He drove east on Twenty-sixth Street and then north on First Avenue, heading for the Montrose. Along the way, he said that he regarded Max as an ideal Critter Car passenger, because although Max was a celebrity dog—he once appeared on a television program called "Weekend Style"—he was not an arrogant or demanding celebrity dog. Before Jim drove a Critter Car, he drove a limousine. "That was a real demanding crowd," he said. "I didn't care for most of the clients. Then I happened to see an ad in the *Village Voice*. It mentioned an exciting new opportunity for people who liked animals. Getting in on the ground floor sounded good. I thought, Gee, I like animals and I like to drive, so . . ."

In addition to celebrity dogs, Jim Viviano has had a celebrity's dogs in the Critter Car—the Shih Tzus of a popular female singer whose career goes up and down but who is nevertheless a bona-fide celebrity. Jim likes a challenge. There were the two guard dogs he gave rides to—one from Alexander's and one from the Frick Collection—each without his handler. And the time a Siberian husky gave birth inside the car. Jim's most difficult client was a Doberman from downtown that he was taking to the Montrose. "He gave me a look that said, 'I'm gonna do what *I* want to do.' What he wanted was to ride shotgun, up front, in the passenger's seat. I finally let him up here. The Doberman just wanted to put his head in my lap. Then he fell asleep."

The Critter Car had now arrived at the Montrose, where Max Goldstein would calmly go inside and, on the way to his quarters, get the once-over from Sam Arlen, who would say, "Max, look at the tartar on your teeth. Don't you ever brush?"

"We're providing a service that people want," Jim Viviano said. "We take reservations. We take you to the vet, we take you to the Montrose. You and your Saint Bernard are going to Acapulco? You've got a plane at J.F.K. at eight-thirty in the morning? We'll get you there. How many people are gonna get a cab at that hour, much less one that'll take a dog? Who do you call? Who will do what we do?"

1 9 8 6

The Gorilla

Those weekend drivers along West Street badly covet the gorilla, and yet they deny themselves. George Ellis, the gorilla's steward, sincerely believes that he has done what he can to find the gorilla a decent home. Meanwhile, however, the gorilla languishes on West Street. Several years ago, George Ellis and some business partners had the distribution rights for a soft drink called Afro-Kola, a venture that ultimately yielded sixty thousand leaking cases of soda and some heartache. George Ellis then took a vow to reduce the level of stress in his life. A gorilla seemed to be part of the answer. Before noon most weekdays and every weekend, George Ellis drives a yellow school bus he owns to one of two spots on West Street—either downtown, near Pier 40, where West Street intersects Houston, or farther uptown, between Thirty-third and Thirty-fourth, near the construction site of the Jacob Javits Convention Center. He parks, unloads a huge stuffed toy gorilla, and spends the rest of the day entertaining hollow offers to buy.

"If it's not bought today, O.K., I'm not in a hurry," George Ellis said one recent Sunday as he watched the traffic move past his uptown site. "Most peddlers, if they had the chance, would save up money so they could open a store. They want to get off the streets. I have no desire to leave the streets. A retail store means overhead, tension. Out here, a good business day is a relaxed day. You don't need to sell a gorilla to have a good business day."

In addition to the gorilla, George Ellis sets out two rows of cardboard cartons on the sidewalk and lays plywood sheets across them to create shelves. Then he liberates the other animals from his bus. Larger-than-life Saint Bernards sit on the back row, against a chain-link fence, along with not quite life-size ponies and Bavarian bears. Smaller creatures—puppies, rabbits, teddy bears, lambs—sit atop the front row of cartons. Giant frogs and pandas lean against these cartons. Predators—panthers, tigers, lions, leopards, grizzlies—congregate in one spot, accompanied by elephants, camels, giraffes, and kangaroos. The gorilla brings the entire menagerie into focus. You can't miss the gorilla. If the gorilla stood up instead of tilting and balancing on its fists, it would be six feet tall—as tall as George Ellis. The gorilla has gray fur, a red nose, and pink-and-blue eyes. People in a rush to get to a traffic jam miles away, on the Cross Bronx Expressway, invariably rubberneck for the gorilla on West Street.

Approximately one in three hundred drivers pulls over. Half the time, the drivers who stop just roll down the window; the rest of the time, they park and get out. They all ask the same question: "How much for the gorilla?" When George Ellis tells them—it's not an unreasonable price; actually, it's a fraction of what a live gorilla would cost—they change the subject. They say, "Oh, well, how much for the camel with the gold necklace?" or "How much for the bear with the lederhosen?" A young man in a blue Buick may hear the gorilla's price and ask, "How much for a poor boy?" He may end up buying a panda or a frog or a rabbit or a lamb or, quite likely, nothing. The gorilla would look dramatic riding off in somebody's blue Buick, but this never happens. George Ellis believes that "most people tend more toward hamburger than toward steak."

Some time ago, George Ellis went to see a designer in Brooklyn and described how a custom-built gorilla should look. The resulting gorilla has George Ellis's mouth—it looks skeptical, amused, and relaxed. George Ellis, who is in his early forties, is black and hefty. In addition to distributing Afro-Kola, he has studied filmmaking at New York University, worked as a sanitation man in Phoenix (where he picked up Barry Goldwater's garbage twice a week), delivered cakes in Boston, and traded rice by the carload and cement by the megaton. He enjoys peddling on West Street, he says, "because people come by here and they never stop laughing. They might buy without saying anything at all. They just laugh. They have different reasons. A guy might buy a grizzly bear because he wants to get back in the house."

On Sunday, a not very brisk business day, a red Toyota with Jersey license plates stopped at George Ellis's place of business. The driver, a middle-aged man, stayed in the car while his wife got out and dickered. "How much for the gorilla?" she asked George Ellis, and he told her.

The woman, who was stocky and had short gray hair, wore a red plaid parka and carried a large red vinyl purse. Upon hearing the gorilla's price, she asked, "How about something for twenty dollars?"

"How about something for fifteen?" George Ellis said. He held up a two-foot-high beige pony. "Nice pony. You can't leave a pony like this out on the sidewalk."

With a lit cigarette in her hand, the woman waved the pony away. She had become interested in the pandas and was studying one that was red and white and one that was yellow and copper. "Which color holds up better?" she asked.

"I don't know—either one," George Ellis said. "You buying this for a boy or a girl?"

"It's for me."

"Oh. A girl."

The woman examined the red-and-white panda closely. "This panda's dirty," she complained.

"That's not dirt," George Ellis said. "That's just pure New York City dust. You can't get that in New Jersey."

After a bit more deliberating, the woman bought the red-and-white panda and four little teddy bears. Then she contemplated a gray lamb. "How much?" she asked.

"Three dollars."

"Give it to me for two."

"No."

"Two-fifty?"

"Is it your birthday?"

"Yeah, it's my birthday." She smoked her cigarette. "No, it's not my birthday. But my anniversary comes up next week."

"Give me two dollars and have a happy anniversary."

This victory made the woman feel bold. She reached into her purse to get two dollars from her wallet and, without looking up, said, "Now let's hear you come down some on the gorilla." .

"You've got expensive taste," George Ellis told her. "All you need is money."

He packed the lamb and the teddy bears into a large plastic bag, along with the panda, and put it in the back seat of the car. The woman got in the front seat and nodded a thank you, and then she and her husband rejoined the traffic, heading uptown on West Street, toward the Lincoln Tunnel and New Jersey, in their red Toyota, gorillaless.

1981

Melnikoff's

Melnikoff's is a general-type store at Eighty-fourth Street and York Avenue. This time of year, it caters to the summer-camp crowd. You don't really belong there on a spring afternoon unless your name is Jared, Jamie, Jennifer, Jeffrey, Jonathan, Lauren, Dana, Courtney, Brian, Benjamin, Eric, Stacy, or something like that— the sort of name that's likely to be sewn into two pair white gym shorts, two pair green gym shorts, twelve pair athletic socks, one poncho, one terry-cloth robe, three nylon swimsuits, one duffelbag, etc.—or unless you are one of those happy but sad adults who have decided to spend two thousand dollars to send Jared/Jamie/ Jennifer away for eight weeks so that he/she can receive individualized attention and sensitive, experienced personal instruction while learning everything it is possible to know about art, dance, drama, music (jazz, rock, folk, chamber, opera), archery, riflery, water-skiing, tennis, night tennis, soccer, horseback riding, golf, painting, sculpting, graphics, white-water rafting, canoeing, backpacking, fishing, conservation of natural resources, go-carts, minibikes, rocketry, campcraft, ham radio, video, batiking, silversmithing, weaving, photography, lacrosse, and kayaking, with stress on citizenship and high personal values. If you happen to be such a happy but sad adult, go to Melnikoff's and take along about a thousand bucks.

"What's your name?"

"Ethan."

"Where are you going to camp?"

"Wildwood."

"I heard your mother mention that you go to school at Ethical Culture. So you're a philosopher as well as a camper, huh?"

"Dumb."

"Is it true that at the camp you're going to they make you eat your vegetables?"

"Yucch."

"Is it true that they serve *only* vegetables?"

"Yucch."

"How do you feel about insects?"

"Yucch."

"Wildlife in general?"

"Yucch."

"Ethan, when this man asks you a question can't you give more than a one-word answer?"

"Yucch-yucch."

No one named Melnikoff really has anything to do with Melnikoff's. The owner now is a Felenstein—Marshall Felenstein. Marshall Felenstein also runs a chain of retail clothing stores in the Midwest, called Marwen Stores. His wife, Diane, runs her own P.R. firm. She has just returned from Cuba. The children in Cuba lead different lives. In summer, they have activities and they learn crafts, but they have no minibikes, no video, and no lighted tennis courts. In Cuba, there is no Camp Winadu, no Camp Winaukee, no Camp Lakota, no Camp Towanda, no Camp Tegawitha. The children in Cuba are not nearly as fortunate as the children who shop at Melnikoff's.

"This size feels big."

"He's ready for a men's medium. He's just used to everything being so tight. He's going to a weight-watchers' camp next summer. The list says eight pair of socks. You want tube socks, Andrew? You want these with the colored stripes?"

"Look at those socks. You wouldn't wear those socks, Mom. Damn, you're cheap. I'm not wearing those socks. Everybody at camp's gonna think I'm gay if I wear those socks."

"That's enough of that! Try these shorts on."

"Maybe I got nice legs, but I ain't gonna wear shorts."

"Yeah, you have nice legs. Too bad they have to go with that big stomach."

"Shut up, Jill."

"Try this on. I don't have all day."

"What is this—a dressing contest? Don't *rush* me."

"Andrew, come on out now. I want to see how those fit."

"You're embarrassing me."

"I'm not embarrassing you. *You're* embarrassing *me*. Now, open the door."

"O.K. How does this look?"

"You gonna wear those with the waist all the way up around your chest, Andrew?"

"Yeah."

"You look like a dingdong."

"Shut up, Jill."

"*Stop it!*"

"Why?"

If you place your order before a certain date, Melnikoff's will sew in the name tapes free of charge. The name-tapers are Boris and Alex. Boris owns a tailor shop down the block from the store. Alex is his son. No question about it, free name-taping attracts a lot of customers. Marshall Felenstein supports free name-taping. Marshall Felenstein says, "Free name-taping's the hook. *That* plus personal service."

"I ordered these two extra shirts for my son, and they came late. Could you please sew name tapes in them?"

"Mr. Marcus, we already shipped your order and we mailed you extra name tapes."

"If I bring you the name tapes, could you just sew them in these shirts?"

"Mr. Marcus, it's only two shirts. Can't your wife just sew those in?"

"If she could sew them in, I'd still be married to her."

When you've put down your deposit for everything at Melnikoff's, the people there pack it in a cardboard box and put it downstairs in the storage room. If there are special-order items yet to come in, they wait for those, and when everything is ready they send the entire box to Boris and Alex for name-taping. When that job is done, it all comes back to Melnikoff's for final folding, packing, and shipping. You should plan ahead, but even if you

don't, don't worry. They'll ship the stuff to you or ship it directly
to the camp. They'll ship anything on your list of Necessary Articles
and Optional Articles, but they will *not* ship the following items:
live animals, expensive jewelry, stereo equipment, knives and
axes, explosives. So don't even bother asking. They won't do it.

"I see you're here with your brother. Are you going to camp,
too?"

"No."

"In a couple of years?"

"No."

"Have you already been to camp?"

"No."

"You're going to spend the summer in the park?"

"No."

"You're going somewhere, right?"

"Yes."

"Well, where else is there?"

"Italy."

1 9 8 2

Screened

Al Verssen, the owner of the Brooklyn Dodgers, which is one
of ten franchises in the professional Eastern Basketball Association, takes pride in knowing his personnel. When Mr. Verssen
contemplates the players on his team, he likes to say that they
are "a very screened group of individuals." In a way, the same
could be said of the fans who come to watch the Dodgers play
their home games—at Roosevelt Hall, a gymnasium building on
the campus of Brooklyn College. In fact, Mr. Verssen, a rotund,
bespectacled man in his fifties—too short to play competitive
basketball but just the right size to own a team—himself screens
all the individuals who attend the games. He does this while
taking tickets at the door. Mr. Verssen recognizes that he is a
rara avis among professional-sports moguls. He is his own factotum. "I'm the guy whose job it is to worry about everything,"
he said one recent Sunday night as he guarded the gate prior
to a contest between the Dodgers and the Providence Shooting
Stars. Several people got in without paying. This happened not
because of inattention on Mr. Verssen's part but, rather, because
he is generous. If someone sidles up to the ticket table and hes-
itates in an odd way, Mr. Verssen asks in a low voice, "You
a friend of anyone?" In many instances, the fan mentions the
name of one of the Dodgers, and the owner admits the friend
free of charge. This makes the Brooklyn Dodgers one of the few
professional sports organizations around that are run with the coy
ambience of a speakeasy. Usually, a couple of hundred paying
spectators attend the games. Once, when the Dodgers played
the Washington Metros, the gym was loaded to capacity—with
seven hundred and fifty people. For that occasion, the Dodgers

had distributed free tickets in Flatbush and Canarsie. The lack of a critical mass deprives the Dodgers of basketball's proverbial home-court advantage. As it is, the team owner wouldn't really mind if the Dodgers played all their games on the road, since this would obviate renting the Brooklyn College gymnasium. When he can, Mr. Verssen follows the team on its out-of-town trips. Last month, however, when the Dodgers flew to Alaska to play the Anchorage Northern Knights—the Anchorage team picked up the tab—he had to stay behind in New York, because of various other obligations. By day, he teaches mathematics at Monsignor McClancy Memorial High School, in East Elmhurst. Also, he owns a printing business in Greenpoint. He regrets not making the Alaska journey, even though doing so would have forced him to witness two consecutive losses by the Dodgers. "They were fairly close games, but we still lost them both," he said apologetically. "I think we ran into some jet-lag problems."

The Dodgers' roster for the game against Providence listed twelve players, seven of whom actually appeared in uniform. A couple of nonroster players also suited up. Wondering which of his players will or won't attend a given game leads Al Verssen to conclude that owning a minor-league basketball team "can place a person in a stressful situation." In addition to the players, the Dodgers' roster regularly lists Harold Tonick as head coach and Mr. Verssen as defensive coach. The myriad demands of sole ownership, however, have restricted the time that Mr. Verssen can devote to coaching defense, and he now relies upon Mr. Tonick to handle both jobs. In any event, defense is not an integral part of the game in the Eastern Basketball Association. Not long ago, for example, the Dodgers vanquished the Quincy Chiefs by 169–167 (no overtime).

"This is second-chance heaven," Mr. Tonick said as he and Mr. Verssen made their way to the sidelines to watch the Dodgers and the Shooting Stars limber up for the game. "The best players here, the younger ones, have tried without success to make it in the big league, the National Basketball Association, and now they are waiting for a second chance. Some of the others might be a little

older. They realize they've taken a step down, but they like
to play and they need the chance to do it against non-amateur
competition."

The Dodgers have some talented and promising players. Jim
Bostic, a forward, leads the E.B.A. in rebounds and in scoring.
Jackie Dorsey, who while playing for Brooklyn is actually under
contract to the Denver Nuggets, of the N.B.A., leads the E.B.A.
in shooting percentage. Mr. Verssen, for his part, probably leads
the league in pained expressions. As the Dodgers took the floor
during the pregame warmup, it was hard not to notice that the team
members wore green jackets inscribed "Pros." These were left over
from last season, before the Dodgers were called the Dodgers. One
of the Dodgers' forwards, a former member of the New York Knicks
named Ronnie Nunn, wore white shorts, while all his teammates
had on green.

Harris Parker, the team's general manager, said to Mr. Verssen, "Any chance we can get all these guys in the same kind of
shorts?"

Mr. Verssen ignored the question.

Mr. Parker muttered, "We gotta get uniforms in the budget."

The game was scheduled to begin at seven-thirty, but no one
seemed to be in a hurry. For one thing, when seven-thirty rolled
around, Jackie Dorsey, the star, had not arrived.

"So where the hell is Dorsey?" Mr. Verssen asked.

"Don't look at me," said Mr. Parker.

"Last week, he flew in from Atlanta for the last six minutes of
our game against the Metros," Mr. Verssen recalled. "He almost
pulled it out for us, too. Scored six points."

A few minutes later, a head attached to a six-foot-eight-inch
body appeared in the doorway. This was Jackie Dorsey. He greeted
the owner, the coach, and the general manager and then went off
to the dressing room to change.

Meanwhile, the public-address announcer, a Brooklyn College
student named Ira Klein, had begun the proceedings. "Good
evening, and welcome to Roosevelt Hall, home of the Brooklyn
Dodgers," he intoned. "For those of you who are attending your
first Brooklyn Dodgers game, welcome. For those of you who have
been here before, you're here again."

The game began, and after a few missed shots by both teams Providence took the lead on a jump shot by a guard named Erie Ferange. Although Ferange was listed in the printed program as six feet two inches tall, he looked as if he could do a much more convincing imitation of someone five feet ten. Within seconds, Brooklyn evened the score, and once Jackie Dorsey had entered the game, about five minutes after it began, the Dodgers seized control and began to turn it into a runaway. "I knew it would happen like this," said Harris Parker, who had taken a seat next to us. "The Providence team may wear uniforms that match, but we play better. We'll blow these guys off the court."

At halftime, Brooklyn led, 67–45. During the intermission, Vinnie Ernst, the Providence coach, stood outside the gym eating a doughnut and drinking coffee.

"What's our strategy for the second half?" he said. "Two choices. We're gonna either send seven men onto the court or lock the Dodgers' dressing-room door. If the whistle blows to begin the second half and they aren't here to play, we win by forfeit."

In the second half, the Dodgers came onto the court on schedule but they had some shaky moments. Most of these, however, were offset by some shaky moments that the Shooting Stars experienced, and Brooklyn held on to win, 130–113. Jackie Dorsey finished the game with 37 points and 11 rebounds.

Afterward, Mr. Verssen seemed subdued. Victory was hardly an indignity, but he had other matters on his mind. For one thing, the players had to be paid. He declined to reveal what the paid attendance had been for the game. "You know, there are two and a half million people living in Brooklyn," he said. "I figure we should get at least a thousand of them here for each game—that's the break-even point—but so far we haven't done it. I might add that no matter whom I talk to—politicians, businessmen, people who live in the borough—I always get good vibes. Nobody is disdainful of the Brooklyn Dodgers. I want you to know that I'm doing this in the best interests of basketball and the best interests of Brooklyn."

1 9 7 8

Luxury

Larry Cohen wants to rent you a car. Larry Cohen rents wrecks. Drivable wrecks. You wanna rent a wreck? Go see Larry. Let's suppose—just a supposition—you wake up one morning with a pounding urge to go to Jersey to rent, or lease, a car. Suppose, further, that you don't get any particular lift out of being strapped into those sleek and efficient late-model numbers that the well-established nationwide agencies have to offer—Nipponese compacts with only thirty-five hundred miles on the odometer, dripping-wet-clean Ford LTDs still reeking of Eau de New Car. No, your tastes run to the earlier classics—say, a road-ready '73 Nova hatchback, gray with potential air-conditioning (pending a pressure test of the cooling system), or a once blue '72 four-door Pontiac Catalina, a ninety-seven-thousand-mile veteran that stands only a brake job away from behaving like a twenty-thousand-mile cream puff. The man you absolutely have to touch base with is Larry Cohen, the proprietor and franchiser of Larry's Rent-A-Wreck, Inc. ("We Rent Used Cars at Used Car Prices"), which he operates on license from Bob's Rent-A-Wreck, Inc., of Raleigh, North Carolina. Larry wants you to drive away in the rented used car of your and his shared dreams. Larry's just that kind of guy.

To pay him a worthwhile visit, you cross the Hudson, take the New Jersey Turnpike to the Garden State Parkway, and—heading south—follow that to Exit 109, where you aim for the ocean until you hit Highway 35, in Shrewsbury. Take a right on Highway 35 and you can't miss it. There, across the street from Buxton's Country Restaurant (the look, feel, and approximate taste of a Friendly's), and between Ace Auto Tops and M. Silberstein's Interior Designs, stands a yellow cinder-block building with signs in the front window that proclaim "We Speak Volkswagen" and "Go Topless to the Shore. Rent-A-Convertible."

Inside, you find Larry Cohen, a portly young man in his late twenties, with a mustache, thick, black-framed eyeglasses, blue jeans—nothing obviously hard-sell about him. He's busy with a customer, so you tour the waiting room—two desks, two secretaries, a huge map of Monmouth County, and a 1953 Citroën, which is not for rent—and while you are doing this a blown-dry young blond guy appears and introduces himself as Bob Munnerlyn—Bob himself, proprietor and franchiser of Bob's Rent-A-Wreck, Inc., of Raleigh, North Carolina. Bob just happens to be in town for the day.

With almost no prompting, Bob recites his success story: how two and a half years ago he was damn near bankrupt; how he no longer contemplates bankruptcy; how he has *no* connection with Dave Schwartz, the rent-a-wreck man in West Los Angeles, who rents cars to the stars; how he has no connection, either, with a North Carolina outfit called Lease-A-Lemon. It seems that Bob's Rent-A-Wreck and Lease-A-Lemon used to be connected, but now they are opponents in some interesting litigation. Bob used to sell used cars, but he gave that up in 1976. "Ever since then," he says proudly, "Rent-A-Wreck has been my full-time gig. I have no partners. Larry Cohen is an associate. He works the entire Northern region."

Surging enthusiasm is one of Bob Munnerlyn's outstanding traits. He offers to help you get started with your own Rent-A-Wreck franchise. "We'll outfit you with everything—I mean it," he promises. "All you do is put down your up-front money, select a location—say, Camden—and come to Raleigh for at least one week of training, and when you get back to Camden we've set you up with pens, pencils, rental forms, insurance, license plates, desks, mechanics, advance ads in the newspapers, advance publicity, and, of course, cars. You've got a total operation the minute you walk in the door. Think about it."

While you are envisioning prime sites in Camden, Larry Cohen appears, and says, "Come with me." You follow him through the repair area, where a totaled green Monte Carlo is being cannibalized so that a blue Monte Carlo may live. Larry says, "This guy rented the green Monte Carlo from us, drove away, and called me five minutes later to say that he'd run a red light and hit another vehicle. We picked up the car, he paid the two-hundred-and-fifty-dollar deductible on the insurance, we put him in another car, and he drove away again. We have a very good atmosphere here. We enjoy our work. We don't have an attitude."

"Hey, Larry, you got a dealer plate?" someone hollers.

"There's a dealer plate in the trunk of the Mustang hanging off the two-car carrier."

The two-car carrier is parked out back, next to a chain-link fence that surrounds a half-acre of rental merchandise—a '73 Hornet, a '73 Ventura, a '72 Chevy wagon, a '73 Ford Country Squire wagon, two '73 Le Manses—along with an ambulance that has four tires and a pair of well-worn wheels where the afflicted usually ride, and a custom-built Volkswagen with a spaghetti-like tuned exhaust system and a grafted-on sleeping compartment that will accommodate two uncomfortably. The VW and the ambulance are not for rent. Many of the other cars go for flat rates of sixty, seventy, eighty dollars per week—depending. "Most of my customers want equipment," says Larry. "They want AM/FM. They want air. Maybe a tape deck. We use only Goodyears, no recaps. That '71 Delta 88 there—it's a big boat. Nobody thinks they want a big boat these days. I love 'em. I can buy 'em for a song. I paid three-fifty for that one. I'll fix it up and rent it. No problem."

In come Dan and Karen Wagner, an imposing-looking couple. Karen works in day care in Red Bank; Dan runs a drive-in movie theater in Eatontown. They've driven themselves to Rent-A-Wreck in a mid-size yellow school bus—Karen's, to use on the job. Now it's parked across the street at Buxton's.

"Our car just died," says Karen. "Technically, it's a total loss. We're talking about a rental that's ready to go now."

Larry nods, then lets them explore the premises. Getting into a '71 Chevy Caprice, Dan starts it up, sees that the air-conditioner doesn't work, climbs out. They shop some more, and finally decide that they like the station wagon.

"We're interested in the Country Squire," Dan tells Larry.

"Sorry, I've got commitments on that one," Larry says. "This customer wanted a first-class dress wagon. You want me to get another one, I can do it in a week. Meanwhile, I can put you in a temporary."

There is a moment of silence.

"Let me quote you out ratewise," Larry says. "You want air and stereo? You want a flat rate with unlimited mileage? I don't know how long you want it, but on a six-month lease the mid- or full size will run you two hundred and twenty-five dollars a month, with full service and maintenance. As a bonus to you I take off twenty-five percent the last month."

"I don't know," says Dan.

"As you can see, we are not small people," says Karen. "And I have three children plus a mother-in-law living with me."

"You wanna talk luxury?" Larry asks.

"I don't know," says Dan.

"Let him talk luxury," says Karen. "It wouldn't hurt."

Larry talks luxury. He also talks insurance binders, talks security deposit, talks Cadillac De Ville and Lincoln Continental. Karen writes it all down. Then she and Dan retreat to Buxton's to study the figures over a couple of Buxburgers (hamburger topped with cheese, bacon, lettuce, and tomato) and iced tea. A few minutes later, they are back at Rent-A-Wreck, ready to rent. They order a Lincoln Continental, AM/FM, 8-track stereo, air, lots of room inside. Larry tells them their car will be ready in a week. Until then, of course, they can have a temporary, but they decide to wait for the Lincoln. Smiling, Dan signs a few forms and pays the security deposit in greenbacks. Smiling still, he and Karen now cross Highway 35 again and board the yellow bus, thinking luxury, shifting gears, driving away, rumbling toward Red Bank.

1 9 7 8

Zipper Man

Herbert Stiefel's problem is that no one else in New York cares as deeply as he cares about zippers or will do what he will do to make things right with a zipper.

"If you saw some of the garments customers bring to me, the way they're manufactured, you'd see it's a crime," Mr. Stiefel said the other day at his workplace, in the garment district. "The manufacturers put in zippers without stops. That shouldn't be. The slider will come right off. People come to me with new pants. One, two, three—they're broken. That shouldn't happen. They bring me handbags—the zippers have pulled away from the fabric. For the last ten years, maybe, the whole situation has been deteriorating. Because nobody seems to care. There's something wrong with this mentality. Why is there nobody to take care of things? This city could use a place where people can get *zippers*."

In fact, Herbert Stiefel is the proprietor of a place where people can get zippers. He isn't eager to give the impression, however, that he is actually in business. To get to Mr. Stiefel's workplace, you pass through the main floor at Harry Kantrowitz Company, Inc.—an Eighth Avenue trimmings outlet where zippers, among other items, are sold in hefty quantities but generally not in small quantities—and climb a flight of stairs. At the top of the stairs, on the left, is Herbert Stiefel's domain, a low-ceilinged room with exposed pipes and no natural light which is lined with shelves stacked with cardboard boxes full of zippers and zipper parts: zippers in aqua, blue, teal, tan, gray, green, dark green, ruby, peach, pink, gold, rust, lilac; long bolts of zippers; precut zippers (twenty-four-inch, thirty-six, thirty-one, eighteen, twenty-three); zipper pulls and zipper stops; zippers in sizes from No. 3 to No.

9—about three thousand boxes in all. Despite the presence of so many zippers and also the presence of three ancient manual zipper-cutting machines—not to mention the steady stream of zipper-needy people who find their way to him each day—Mr. Stiefel says, "My sign is in the window downstairs, but I'm not in business anymore. I went out of business three years ago."

Mr. Stiefel's personal zippers—the ones on his clothing—never break. "I handle them right," he says. When he wears a jacket with a two-way zipper, for instance, he always unzips the bottom a couple of inches, so that, when he sits, the zipper doesn't stretch and come unhemmed. The other day, as he rubbed a white candle against the nickel teeth of a bunch of custom-made eight-inch No. 6 royal-blue zippers, Mr. Stiefel said, "When I get home, I hold these against a hot pot to melt the wax. Then the sliders go on easier. I'm a perfectionist. I'll make one or two or three zippers for you. Nobody else would do this. But I do it this way."

Although Mr. Stiefel is a naturally modest man, there are moments when self-restraint eludes him, and this was one of them. "I don't even want to say that I'm in competition with the other places that say they sell zippers or repair zippers," he said. "So they have zippers—but do they have what the customer needs? And what happens when they charge five times what they should charge? I enjoy it when people come up and say, 'I found you. I'm happy. I would have gone out of business if I hadn't found you.' I had a customer the other day—a stripper, she needed a zipper. Who else could she turn to?"

A gray-haired black woman wearing a pink Ultrasuede shift and a gray-and-white knit tam-o'-shanter entered the room, and Mr. Stiefel said, "When did they let you out?"

"When?" she said. "As of now."

The woman was Naomi Carpenter. She is a part-time dressmaker and a full-time city employee, and she had come on her lunch break to Herbert Stiefel because she needed three thirty-six-inch zippers for some pillow slipcovers, and six other zippers, of varying lengths. After she had recited her shopping list and Mr. Stiefel had gone to work with zipper pliers (jaws an inch wide, with fine-edged pincers), she said, "And don't let me walk out and leave everything behind, like I did last time." Then she turned to us and said, "I came here to get zippers. He can construct zippers like no one else. No one else."

"And I don't feel good about it," Mr. Stiefel said.

"It's like the buttonhole gentleman across the street," said Miss Carpenter. "He's the only one of those."

"Because no one else can make a living doing these things. Thank God, I don't need to make a living anymore. I just don't want to walk around with the old guys and listen to their aches and pains. And I try to stay away from doctors."

"The young people today need to be trained under him."

"I wouldn't train anyone," said Mr. Stiefel. "One year they stay, and then they're gone. I don't want to build up. I want to build down."

After Miss Carpenter departed, a queue of customers began to form. Sy Kantrowitz, the son of Harry Kantrowitz, the founder of the Kantrowitz zipper empire, came into the room for a moment, said, "Herbie, you better move a little faster—they're backing up," and then headed back downstairs.

Sy Kantrowitz isn't Mr. Stiefel's boss. Fifty years ago, however, not long after he arrived in America from Germany, Mr. Stiefel did work briefly for Harry Kantrowitz. Then he went out on his own. He had a wholesale zipper business on Thirty-fourth Street, moved it in the early fifties to a loft on West Thirty-eighth Street, and stayed there until six years ago. "I was sixty-six years old, the landlord wanted to raise the rent, and I wanted to retire," Mr. Stiefel said. "All these jobbers heard I wanted to get out, they grabbed me—'Come with us! Come with us! Come with us!' I'm not money-hungry, but I don't want to stay home, I've got to be occupied. I've got all these things people can't get anywhere else. Kantrowitz asked me to come here, so I'm here. Five days a week I'm here. But I'm really not here."

Mr. Stiefel wears wire-rimmed eyeglasses and has white hair and a vaguely ascetic look. Three or four times a day, when he says something that pleases him or when he is flirting with a Fashion Institute student, he smiles faintly. Otherwise, he maintains a cultivated deadpan—the nonspecific skepticism of a man who when it comes to zippers has seen and heard everything and then some.

His happiest time of day is the midafternoon, when he tunes in "The Bob Grant Show" on the radio. "Sometimes Bob Grant is obnoxious," he said. "But mostly I agree with him. Because I'm not perfect myself."

A bearded young man wearing a black leather jacket equipped with a lot of zippers, not all of them utilitarian, needed eight zippers for a sample garment he was designing. He was followed by Joseph Mayo, an elegantly dressed man who carried a silver-handled walking stick and had a well-trained, upsweeping salt-and-pepper beard.

"Is there another place that would sell me these?" said Joseph Mayo, who had come to buy ten No. 5 twenty-four-inch black zippers. "I think there's one on Thirty-seventh Street."

"You think or you know?" said Mr. Stiefel.

"I know. I've been there. It's downstairs."

Mr. Stiefel held up one of the freshly custom-made zippers. "They have *these*?" he asked.

"Uh, no," said Joseph Mayo.

A dry cleaner from College Point came by for six zippers in six different shades and sizes, and he was followed by a young businessman with curly brown hair who wore aviator glasses and a beige trenchcoat.

"You the zipper doctor?" the curly-haired man asked.

"I'm not a doctor," Mr. Stiefel said. "If I'm a doctor, I charge you thirty-five dollars for the first three minutes."

The curly-haired man had a problem with the nylon zipper on his nylon running suit: the teeth wouldn't mesh at the bottom. Mr. Stiefel worked on the slider with needle-nose pliers and in less than a minute had it fixed.

"What do I owe you?"

"Thirty-five dollars."

When the customer reached for his wallet, Mr. Stiefel waved him away.

Theodore Parham had a problem with his black nylon parka.

"How long a zipper you need?" asked Mr. Stiefel.

"Nineteen inches. Aluminum."

"Nickel silver is what you want, not aluminum. Nickel silver is the best."

While Mr. Stiefel cut a nineteen-inch zipper, Mr. Parham, a

black man in his fifties, said, "I've been coming here five years. I'm a retired merchant seaman. I've been all over the United States by myself. That's how I find places like this. But, see, he knows his business. He knows what it's all about with zippers. Do I know his name? No, I don't know his name. Just he's the zipper man." Mr. Parham paused, as if his memory might summon the zipper man's name. He pointed to the faulty zipper on his jacket and said, "It's a small thing, man. But it's a problem. It gives you a headache. But now the problem's solved. How much I owe you?"

"Fifty cents," said Mr. Stiefel.

"That's beautiful," Theodore Parham said as he handed over the money. "Yeah, that's all right. You're glad to pay somebody like him. Yessir. One of the best."

1 9 8 7

Idea

The other day, Robert Sparks gave a demonstration of an invention he has recently patented—the portable upright-sleeping device. This took place in his apartment, on East Fourteenth Street, near Union Square, where Mr. Sparks has no trouble making himself comfortable. He sat in a straight-backed chair with the prototype of the upright-sleeping device in his lap. The prototype was a Styrofoam box with a contoured base that fitted over his thighs. The top of the box almost reached Mr. Sparks' chin. He leaned on the top of the box, making a pillow with his forearms, and rested his head on the pillow. He closed his eyes and became very still, and created the impression that he was napping. The upright-sleeping device appeared to work fine. After about a minute, Mr. Sparks stretched his arms and yawned.

"If you were on a long bus ride—I've taken some long bus rides—you might want to store your valuables or some fresh food inside while you slept," said Mr. Sparks, removing the top of the box and revealing that it was hollow. He replaced the lid. "If you fell asleep in the waiting room of a hospital and you had this, your head wouldn't be rolling all over the place. This will make people more sociable. You can invite a friend over to spend the night even if you don't have an extra bed. Your friend can stay in your bed and you can sleep in a chair with one of these."

Mr. Sparks stood up and brushed away some Styrofoam crumbs that clung to his suit. It was a maroon polyester suit with tiny yellow dots. Underneath, he wore a blue plaid flannel shirt and a blue necktie with white dots. Mr. Sparks is a man in his early fifties who is modest by nature, except when he talks at length about the potential of the upright-sleeping device. In moments of

high enthusiasm, he compares the upright-sleeping device to the
wheel and the incandescent light bulb. When his attitude becomes
more sober, he points out, accurately, that the upright-sleeping
device shows greater promise than the self-wringing mop he thought
up in 1948, in Chicago. The problem with the self-wringing mop,
Mr. Sparks now believes, was that not everyone needed a mop,
and most people who did already had one.

Some of Mr. Sparks' other creations are the draw-anything-you-
can-see drawing board; a contemporary chessboard with built-in
ashtrays and coasters (more a design achievement than an actual
invention); and a perpetual calendar based upon the Book of Revelation. A couple of years ago, Mr. Sparks left his job as a statistical
typist, and he now considers himself a more or less full-time in-
ventor. Although he agrees that inventing is hard work, he believes
that success depends a great deal upon inspiration. Music inspires
him. A grand piano stands in one room of the apartment, near a
bright-colored oil portrait of a clown. Much of Mr. Sparks' time
has been devoted to generating an atmosphere in his apartment
which might be conducive to inventing. He owns a pool table, some
café booths and tables, curtains of hanging glass beads, a bust of
George Washington, and dozens of artificial plants. Mr. Sparks
mentioned that he prefers artificial plants to real ones, "because
I'm sort of a plant murderer." A potted tree that died some time
ago stands near the front door. The leaves that have not fallen off
have been spray-painted a bright green. They match a small grove
of artificial Christmas trees which stands in one corner, near the
contemporary-chessboard prototype.

"Those Christmas trees are like a broken clock," said Mr. Sparks.
"Once a year, they're right."

An electric wall clock with a severed cord happens to be mounted
not far from the Christmas trees. The clock, which is accurate
whenever the time is five minutes past eleven, hangs on the outside
of a wall surrounding Mr. Sparks' swimming pool. The pool is
circular, about ten feet in diameter, lined with plastic, and bor-
dered by siding material that makes it remarkably inconspicuous.
It is deep enough to hold four feet of water, but Mr. Sparks said
that when he uses it he puts in much less. "I get by with eighteen

inches," he said. "Eighteen inches lets you float around and still have a nice time."

Mr. Sparks called the swimming pool his "think tank," but that is not really where he does his inventing. Most of his invention ideas come to him while he is asleep. He was sleeping in a bed but envisioning an uncomfortable bus ride when the details of the portable upright-sleeping device manifested themselves to him. The engineering drawings that accompany Mr. Sparks' patent for the upright-sleeping device show several possible modifications. An inflatable model, for which no prototype exists, would include a chin rest and pouches that the hands could fit inside, as in a fur muff. Mr. Sparks said that he looks forward to test-sleeping this. The final design will depend upon some marketing considerations that he has not yet worked out. "I'll get to them soon," he said. "Or else they'll come to me. In a dream, I imagine."

1981

Pigeon Mumblers

One afternoon not long ago, three young men from Canarsie stopped by the Meeker Pigeon Exchange, in Greenpoint, on their circuitous way to watch the ponies run at Aqueduct. As the three customers passed through the Exchange's front room, heading for the pigeon coops, which are in the back room, Patrick Sottile, the proprietor, muttered something that sounded like "pigeon mumblers."

"You know, *pigeon mumblers*," he said. "Remember in school, the ungraded class, the yo-yos? That's pigeon mumblers. Actually, a lot of guys who kept pigeons never made it to the yo-yo class, because they didn't even bother to go to school, so when they talked they mumbled. Nowadays, it's mainly a term to describe someone who fancies pigeons. A guy doesn't have to mumble to be a pigeon mumbler, but you should watch out when you're talking to a genuine mumbler. He'll mispronounce everything, call a tippler a tiplet, or a teager a teaguh. One thing you gotta remember: when you get a real pigeon mumbler around, no matter what he's talking about, agree with him."

In New York City, there are about fifteen establishments that cater to the needs of serious-minded pigeon mumblers. Every pigeon emporium enjoys its distinctions. But it seems a safe bet that only the Meeker Pigeon Exchange—on Meeker Avenue, right alongside the Manhattan-bound lanes of the Brooklyn-Queens Expressway—has a live bird in the front window named Killer King. It also seems likely that no pigeon trader in town has more tattoos per square inch of arm space than Mr. Sottile has (none of the tattoos have anything to do with pigeons), and that no pigeon-exchange entrepreneur has a more relaxed attitude toward his work. A year ago, Mr. Sottile retired from the presidency of the Allied International Union of Security Guards and Special Police, and decided, at forty-five, to collect his pension and settle down full time with his pigeons. Mr. Sottile is a man *at ease*—far more at ease, certainly, than Killer, a pedigreed show king, who reluctantly shares the premises with a motley horde of birds, two calico cats, and a collie who has recently learned to answer to the name "Prince."

The cats have been standard fixtures since Mr. Sottile opened for business, last June; the pigeon population ebbs and flows with the customer traffic; and Prince, who almost certainly had a different name at his previous address, wandered in about two months ago. Prince gives every indication of having attended obedience school somewhere along the line, which makes him far better behaved than Killer, who lives in a cage with a nameless, relatively tame Great American Runt. The Runt seems well matched with Killer, both being about the size of respectable chickens. Their bulk makes them too heavy to fly, and their grandeur makes them not for sale. Killer is his most haughty self when he is perched atop a cardboard nesting bowl waiting for one of the Runt's eggs to hatch. Some Greenpoint pigeon mumblers who are familiar with Killer's irascible moods say that if he really put his mind to it, he could probably hatch a baseball.

As it happened, the Canarsie mumblers—George, John, and Steve—hadn't come to bother with, or be bothered by, Killer. George carried a small wire cage containing a blue teager and four Budapest tipplers—or Budies, as they're known in the trade. This meant that the mumblers had come not to buy but to sell—something that Mr. Sottile naturally understood—but he let the boys hang out in the back room for a while before he started to conduct his business with them. The front room at the Exchange contains cages, feed bins, a few birds, bulletin boards with race results and contest information, and a glass display counter with medicines, leg bands, and other pigeon accessories, but the real action is in the back room. Six coops there accommodate almost a thousand birds, including show homers and flying homers, show flights and flying flights, show turbits and flying turbits, and a variety of fancy Viennas, nuns, helmets, tipplers, and monks—about forty breeds in all. The birds come, of course, in all the appropriate, and peculiarly named, pigeon colors. A blue show flight looks gray to a non-pigeon mumbler, anything dun looks brown, yellow is gold, Dutch silver is red, red is sort of muddy, white is white, and black is black. The terms "show" and "flying" suggest that some birds are bred for beauty and others for their aerodynamic skills. This explains why a show flight caught off guard in a sudden gust of wind usually looks pretty silly.

When Mr. Sottile, who sells more flying flights than anything else, finally wandered into the back, the transaction was brief.

"I'm keeping the teaguh," George said. "But you can have the others. How much?"

"Haven't I seen those birds before?" Mr. Sottile asked.

"Yeah," George said. "You saw the mommy and daddy but not the babies. I sold you the mommy and daddy early last spring and bought 'em back in July. Here they are again."

"I'll give you three bucks apiece."

"Good enough," said George, and he accepted a ten and two singles from Mr. Sottile and put them in the breast pocket of his T-shirt. The T-shirt was inscribed "Maloney's, E. 42nd and Ave. D. Bklyn." George then placed the four Budies in a small cage along the wall, opposite the large coops.

"We're gonna let the teaguh go out at Aqueduct," George explained. "He's my smoker—a hot one. I liberated him one time up in the Adirondacks, two hunnerd fifty miles from home, and he makes it back in five hours. No, I don't have names for my birds. He's just a blue teaguh and he's my smoker. I sold the mommy and daddy Budies in the spring and bought them back in the summer because I liked them, and then they had the babies, and I sold them again today because I'm a little tired of them but mainly because I'm a carpenter and I've been out of work for a while because I hurt my hand, and we're going to the track now and I need twelve bucks to bet a horse—Sip Sip Sip, running in the fourth."

Ignoring for the moment the unfortunate fact that the newspapers the next day showed Sip Sip Sip to have broken from the gate in last place and stayed there, George's reasons for selling his beloved Budies accorded with the implacable logic that is the standard for most commerce at the Meeker Pigeon Exchange. Not long after the Canarsie mumblers left, for instance, two of their brethren, a couple of teenagers from Coney Island, dropped by the store. One of these mumblers, who explained that he had a plan for breeding golden flights, bought twenty-two carefully chosen birds for seventy-two dollars. His companion, who seemed less discriminating, paid twelve dollars for six birds, which he said he planned to add to his flock of five hundred. Why was he buying six more? "To watch them fly," he said.

Every self-respecting pigeon mumbler, then, has his own reasons. Mr. Sottile, who has been raising pigeons since he was ten years old, understands this, and, as a consequence, asks few questions. He also makes few rules, with the notable exception of a caveat posted on a bulletin board in the front room. The sign says, "I DO NOT BUY STREET RATS." A street rat is the garden-variety pigeon found everywhere in the city except in pet shops. Among pigeon mumblers, who will disagree on just about every other subject, contempt for street rats is a common denominator.

Mr. Sottile invokes one other rule—an unwritten injunction that prohibits schoolchildren from hanging out in the store during school hours. This is part of his plan to reduce the population of genuine mumblers in the Brooklyn area. The plan isn't intended, however, to rob Brooklyn of its distinction as a mecca for pigeon mumblers. When Mr. Sottile opened the Meeker Pigeon Exchange, he put up a small sign on top of the building to advertise the store. The billboard can be seen from the B.-Q.E., and its presence probably accounts for the homing instincts of the upwardly mobile mumblers who long ago made the move from Brooklyn to Nassau County but have somehow discovered Mr. Sottile's store back in Greenpoint. No one at the store claims that the mumbler migration to the wilds of Nassau County means that there is anything like a burgeoning pigeon chic afoot in the suburbs, but it's worth noting that Mr. Sottile has gone to the trouble to tack up a newspaper clipping next to the cash register which shows Yul Brynner nuzzling a pigeon.

"Oh, you get a lot of interesting people who raise pigeons," one customer told us. "James Stewart, Gene Autry, Roy Rogers, Henry Fonda. Also, Jerry Rosenberg—you know, 'So, what's the story, Jerry?'—and Dutch Schultz. Actually, Dutch used to pay a guy a hundred dollars a week just to take care of his pigeons for him." The customer neglected to mention Marlon Brando, who, as Terry Malloy in *On the Waterfront*, knew a thing or two about flying homers. As it is, the regulars at the Meeker Pigeon Exchange tend not to have names like James, Marlon, Yul, and Henry but run more to Rocky, Gus, Carmine, Butch, Richie, Joey, Frankie, and Vinny. Lots of Vinnys.

Because Mr. Sottile's vocation is an extension of his avocation, and because his union pension gives him a satisfactory income, he doesn't feel compelled to keep long hours—he opens at noon, and doesn't open at all on Wednesday—or even to dicker very strenuously when he is buying and selling. One of his regular customers, a thirteen-year-old called Obbie Santiago, came in with a friend after school the other day and handed Mr. Sottile some change. "Here's the fifteen cents I owe you, from the food," he said.

Mr. Sottile took the money but looked puzzled. "Are you sure?" he asked. "What happened—'dja get a call from my lawyer?"

Obbie said sternly, "I'm sure." Then he went into the back room with his friend.

While the two boys were among the coops, Mr. Sottile noticed some birds flying outside and went to the front door of the store to watch them. He pointed toward a group of pigeons on the other side of the Expressway. The birds rose and glided, whirling in a funnel-shaped mass, above a row of low buildings. "That flock there belongs to a customer who lives a couple of blocks away," said Mr. Sottile. "And see that other flock, over there? Probably a few birds from each flock will get mixed up with the other." For a while, it seemed that the two flocks might merge completely, but they never did. Between them, there must have been about four hundred birds aloft at that moment—four hundred birds who were demonstrating more sustained pigeon flight than most non-pigeon-mumblers witness in a lifetime.

"How high will those birds fly?" Mr. Sottile was asked.

"Those birds? How high?" Mr. Sottile hesitated for a moment, and then nodded in the direction of the pigeons. "Now, those *particular* birds will fly *sky*-high."

1 9 7 6

Tomato Bob

The multitalented Tomato Bob is, among other things, a capable mimic, whose repertoire includes Artie, his father; Joe, one of his two main tomato suppliers; Joe's wife, Helen; Veryle, one of his delivery drivers; Danny, an excitable produce buyer at an East Side steak house; and Kelly Kendig, a patrolman in the Lambertville, New Jersey, Police Department. Before he became Tomato Bob—back when he was Robert Polenz, a friendly guy with roots in Ringoes, New Jersey—he accumulated many interesting life experiences. He graduated from Muskingum College, in Ohio, enrolled in a Methodist seminary in Illinois, taught high school, gave piano and organ lessons in a music store in a suburban mall, worked as a janitor, cleaned houses, waited table, played cocktail piano and sang in nightclubs and a bowling alley, and acted on and off Broadway. In 1983, he sold tomatoes from a garden he had cultivated in Ringoes to a few restaurants in lower Manhattan. That summer and the next, when he officially became Tomato Bob, he sold ten or so cases of tomatoes a week. Now he has about sixty accounts and sells about five hundred cases of produce a week. His invoices and stationery say "Field ripened New Jersey tomatoes, peaches and sweet corn."

The tomatoes grow in Ringoes—an hour southwest of the Holland Tunnel, not far from the Flemington Fur Company—and are sold to "21," Hulot's, the Café Carlyle, Maurice, Memphis, the Café des Artistes, Café Luxembourg, Miss Ruby's Café, the Gotham Bar & Grill, Odeon, Provence, the River Café, and other places where you can eat if you remember to bring a fully loaded wallet. Tomato Bob picks his tomatoes ripe and sells them ripe, and that explains why, during tomato season, Tomato Bob is such a popular person.

The "TOMATO" on Tomato Bob's business card is all uppercase and chlorophyll green, and the "O" in "BOB" is a round, plump, deep-red tomato. Tomato Bob himself has blond hair, a fair complexion, and a smooth-shaven, lean, fit look. He's forty but could pass for thirty. On the job, he wears khaki shorts, white socks, white New Balance tennis shoes, and a white polo shirt with the "BOB" logo over the left breast. When Tomato Bob, dressed that way, gets into one of his two sleek white Toyota vans, he gives the impression that he's off to play a couple of sets of tennis and *then* deliver some tomatoes.

In moments of adversity, Tomato Bob tries to stay calm. "I don't want to have to yell in this business," he says. A pet saying of Tomato Bob's translates politely as "Stuff happens." When Tomato Bob says "Stuff happens," he means, without rancor, that unpleasant stuff happens but, hey, it's bound to happen anyway, you just try to work your way around it. Maybe you have a long run of dry weather and your second crop doesn't come in fast enough, and then, just as it ripens, maybe you get about nine inches of rain and your tomatoes swell and burst. Maybe sap beetles attack. Maybe ground rot. Maybe Veryle dents a fender and gets upset and dysfunctional. Maybe Danny, the produce buyer at the East Side steak house, gets upset by something that isn't even your fault and calls you every name in the book but Tomato Bob, and the steak house becomes a former big Tomato Bob account. Maybe some other stuff happens.

This happened the other morning: At four-thirty—Tomato Bob doesn't usually rise and shine until five-thirty—the phone rang in his apartment, in SoHo. It was Lyn Stires (Tomato Bob has five siblings; Lyn lives with his youngest brother, Jeff) calling from Lambertville, which is seven miles from Ringoes, to say that Tomato Bob's sleek white Toyota van (*not* the one with the Veryle-dented fender; the other one), which had been parked outside her and Jeff's apartment with, in the cargo area, twenty cases of assorted tomatoes, five cases of peaches, four hundred ears of corn, and three pounds of squash blossoms, and which Lyn had been planning to drive to New York that morning, had been borrowed, without authorization, by the seventeen-year-old sort-of husband

of Tomato Bob's niece Lucy (daughter of his older sister Patt)—
Bob's nephew-in-law, sort of; call him Ricky.

That morning, Tomato Bob spent a lot of time on the phone,
apologizing for not being able to make certain deliveries, and that
afternoon he drove his fourteen-foot Mitsubishi truck to Ringoes.
His first stop was John and Helen Rynearson's place. Two and a
half acres of tomatoes are planted in the Rynearsons' front yard,
and they include all of Tomato Bob's special varieties: Lemon Boys
(pale yellow), Golden Jubilees (large and orange), Sweet 100s (red,
cherry-size), Romas (red plums), White Beauties (ivory-colored
and big), two varieties of tomatillos (with a sweet flavor that Tomato
Bob describes as "earthy and tart"), Teardrops (yellow, pear-shaped,
cherry-size), and Sundrops (medium-sized yellow plums—the
type that eventually finds a home atop a designer pizza on Third
Avenue).

Two minutes after Tomato Bob arrived, Lyn Stires drove up in
the once-sleek white Toyota van. The left front headlight was smashed
and the right passenger window was missing. "I bet your customers
are saying, 'Boy, that Bob can make up any kind of excuse for not
delivering,' " Lyn said.

John Rynearson, who had been picking tomatoes with his wife,
headed off to an appointment with a chiropractor, and Lyn joined
Helen Rynearson out in the field. Tomato Bob took off his shoes
and socks and went out there, too. None of the plants were staked,
so he had to tiptoe through a morass of fruit and vines. He reached
for a white tomato. "There's a good one," he said, but when he
looked at it closely he saw that it was cracked. "Ach," he said.
"All this weather." After taste-testing a few tomatillos and yellow
plums, he loaded onto his truck everything that should have been
delivered that morning, and also an extra dozen or so cases of
small tomatoes, red field tomatoes, plum tomatoes, and tomatillos,
waved goodbye to Lyn and Helen, and drove a half mile to Bob
Perehinys's farm. Bob Perehinys had four hundred just-picked ears
of corn waiting in gunnysacks. Tomato Bob also buys pumpkins
and corn smut from the Perehinys farm. Corn smut is a fungus that
most American farmers spray their crops to avoid, but in Mexico,
where it's a delicacy, farmers try to cultivate corn smut. "These

farmers in New Jersey selling me corn smut—'gosh' is every other word out of their mouths," said Tomato Bob, who sells the Perehinys corn smut to Rosa Mexicano, on First Avenue.

The first of Tomato Bob's tomatoes are harvested in late July, and he hopes to harvest the last ones around Halloween, by which time he should have earned enough money to support himself through the winter. Tomato Bob's last acting job, as understudy for Frederic in the Joe Papp production of *Pirates of Penzance*, ended in the fall of 1982. That winter, he had a snowmobile accident and lost part of his singing voice. He thinks it's coming back now, and he hopes that by January, right around the time the seed catalogues begin to arrive, he'll be able to perform in an off-off-Broadway production of some Offenbach operettas.

The final stop on Tomato Bob's swing through Ringoes was at Joe and Helen Cvetan's place—a Cape Cod farmhouse on a busy state road, Route 31. Tomato Bob has been buying tomatoes from Joe and Helen Cvetan since 1983, his first season in business. The Cvetans plant only Pik-Reds—big red field tomatoes—and Tomato Bob buys four tons a week. He began loading forty twenty-five-pound cardboard cases of tomatoes onto his truck. He lifted the lid on one of the cases, inspected a tomato, and threw it aside, into an empty basket.

"What's wrong with that tomato, Bob?" Joe Cvetan asked.

"It had a bite taken out of it," said Tomato Bob.

1 9 8 7

Effects

The way things have been going lately at the Piccadilly Hotel Coffee Shop, on West Forty-fifth Street, it is entirely possible that anyone who wanders into the back room of the restaurant during the lunch hour will discover a grown man trying to make a teaspoon dangle off the end of his nose. The New York Magicians Table, a gathering of amateur and professional prestidigitators, convenes at the Piccadilly every weekday afternoon. Not long ago, an up-and-comer from Connecticut dropped by and, between the soup and sandwich courses, casually hoisted his teaspoon, lightly tapped its concave surface against his nose, and left it hanging there, handle down. This stunt appeared to defy gravity and was well received by the five other magicians who witnessed it. Since then, the spoon bit has caught on with the Magicians Table hard core, even though it is more of a gag than an effect—"effect" being the term of art that a self-respecting magician uses to describe what a layman might call a trick. Because "trick" implies unseemly deception, it is more or less a dirty word at the Piccadilly.

Daily sessions at the Magicians Table are never burdened with official business, because, as an organized entity, the Table has no dues and no agenda. Nevertheless, several members attend the lunches with orthodox devotion, even though doing so forces some of them to tear themselves away from demanding occupations. Larry Arcuri, who was a charter member of the Table when it started out during the mid-forties at the Dixie Hotel, happens to know an effect that changes one-dollar bills into fives. The rest of the magicians work for a living. One of the most peripatetic is Byron Wels, who, when he isn't off in some place like Atlanta training novice magicians for the Burger King chain or else at home in New Jersey trying to get his guillotine blade to slide properly, shows up at the Piccadilly virtually every day. Recently, Wels identified himself to a Magicians Table newcomer as "an editor and the author of one hundred and twenty-eight books." By the time his lunch, a tongue sandwich, had arrived, this awesome figure had begun to sound like "one fifty-eight." When it came time to pay the check, he casually mentioned that his œuvre included one hundred and eighty separate works. "I'm always busy with three or four at a time," he explained. "Most of them are the how-to variety. I wrote *New and Better Methods for Dog Obedience Training*; *The Medicine Cabinet*; *Basic Auto Repair*—stuff like that. Right now, I'm working on *The Layman's Guide to Personal Computers*. Also, I contribute a regular column to a magazine called *Custom Vans*. My best-seller is a magic book called *The Great Illusions*, a two-volume set. One volume contains nothing but diagrams. It sells for forty-seven fifty at Lou Tannen's magic shop, on Broadway. I know that sounds like a lot for a book, but that one took me a long time to write. How long? Four months. If you're gonna write books for a living, there's so little money in it you've gotta crank 'em out like sausages."

Larry Arcuri, who writes "Magic Whirl," a gossip column in *The Spellbinder*, a newsletter published by the New York Assembly of the Society of American Magicians, occasionally arrives late at the Piccadilly, because he has been eating lunch elsewhere. Around the time the others are finishing their coffee, he is apt to enter the room and announce, "I just ate two *wonderful* hamburgers." Then he winks and passes around a menu that he has pirated from Nathan's or some other well-established Times Square beanery. Arcuri dines around town this way because, as a charter member, he is dedicated to perpetuating the Magicians Table. Recently, the Piccadilly ownership changed hands. Just in case the new management decides to displace the magicians, Arcuri wants the group to be prepared to relocate with a minimum of fuss.

Besides Arcuri, the only charter member who is still a mainstay at the Table is Joe Barnett, a jowly, paunchy, white-haired attorney, who wears sober-looking suits and bow ties. The waist pockets of his jackets always sag, and his hands continually move in and out

of them, as if controlled by nervous habit. The exact contents of
Barnett's pockets are an abiding mystery at the Magicians Table.
Murray Celwit, a Table veteran, insists that they contain bundles
of checks that Barnett hasn't yet got around to depositing in the
bank. Whenever a newcomer visits the Table, one of Barnett's
compeers says, "How about a miracle, Joe?" Whereupon Barnett
asks the visitor to state his birthday. If the answer is, say, June
1, he produces, from a coat pocket, a small white piece of paper
that has been inscribed with the numerals 6 and 1. Various people
at the Magicians Table perform effects involving playing cards,
handkerchiefs, fire, money, and mentalism—some more fantastic
than others—but it is commonly agreed that Joe Barnett's flawless
ability to guess a person's birthday after it has been told to him is
a genuine miracle. Each time Barnett performs this miracle, Byron
Wels, who has a laugh like an asthmatic vacuum cleaner, wheezes
and says, "Joe, that's beautiful. You're a really beautiful guy."

The other day, when the Table was more crowded than usual,
a young advertising man named Barry Levy came to lunch. Working
with playing cards, Levy performs effects so impressive that Joe
Barnett shakes his head and says, over and over, "Vegas. I'm
telling you, the boy's ready for Vegas." Among so-called amateurs,
this is a supreme encomium. To add punch to his presentations,
Levy has purposely cultivated an abrasive running commentary.
Consequently, his adroitness with a deck of cards seems inversely
proportional to his personal charm. As an entertainer, this places
him somewhere along a continuum that is bracketed by Don Rickles
and Ilie Nastase. Within the New York Assembly of the Society
of American Magicians, he proudly regards himself as a dissident
member. "I decided to run for president of the organization in
1973, because I felt that it was time for some reforms," Levy said.
"Another young guy and I conducted a blitz campaign. I mean, it
was like a national political convention. We had stickers, we had
horns. Signs everywhere—'Vote for Barry Levy.' The guy I was
running against, meanwhile—a very nice man—was on a trip to
Israel during the election. So he sent in a tape recording of his
speech to the meeting the night the election was held. I got slaugh-
tered. I'm the only person in the history of the organization to get
beaten by a tape recording."

On this particular day at the Magicians Table, Levy did an effect called Card Thought and another called Thought Detector—both of which, as near as anyone present could tell, required sheer magic. At the conclusion of Thought Detector, someone asked to examine the deck. Larry Arcuri intervened. "Whaddya mean examine the deck?" he snapped. "Does Heifetz pass around his violin?" Then Levy began to explain his Thought Detector technique, describing it as "Barry Levy's version of Bob Corson's trick, as originally presented by Sam Schwartz, who stole it from Harry Houdini, who first heard about it from Pharaoh Ramses III." Murray Celwit turned to Byron Wels and said, "This is where it gets either interesting or boring."

Byron Wels, who wasn't paying close attention, seemed bored already. However, he explained that he was merely preoccupied with an examination that he was supposed to undergo that evening to try to gain membership in the Society of American Magicians. "The effect I'll be doing is Silk to Glitter," Wels said. To demonstrate, he rose from the table, stood about fifteen feet away, waved an empty palm once, and then pulled a red silk handkerchief from it. He stuffed the handkerchief into his other fist, made it disappear, and then opened his fist to fill the air with red glitter. When he sat down again, he watched Levy for a moment and said, " 'Pick a card, any card, pick a card'—that's not magic. Now, take Joe Barnett. *There's* a man who performs miracles."

Idly now, Wels lifted a spoon and tapped it to his nose. It hung there for an instant and then fell into his lap. Barry Levy noticed this. Interrupting his own disquisition on the Thought Detector, he said, "Lookit that, will you. And you want to know why the membership exam in the Society of American Magicians seems so difficult. You want some advice on how you can do that trick very easily, Byron?"

"How?" Wels asked.

"Epoxy," said Levy. "Epoxy."

1 9 7 8

Avenue P

The Avenue P players all talk rough, and they all hate to lose. Boy, do they hate to lose. Weekend mornings, especially in the warm weather, they play serious one-wall handball at Fourth Street and Avenue P, in Bensonhurst. You lose at Avenue P, it'll cost you—and probably several of your friends, too—some money. Temporarily, it might even cost you your friends. They'll be seated around the cement court in aluminum folding chairs, wearing golf hats, Bermuda shorts, knit shirts with holes where the ashes landed, reading the sports pages in the *News*, giving the game about half of their attention. And when you lose they'll wake up and realize that they had ten dollars that said you couldn't lose—certainly not with a partner like Phil, playing against a pair of bums like Sonny and Murray. Somebody—one of your former friends—is bound to holler at you what a no-good, lousy player you are, your backhand stinks, why don't you go to Coney Island and play with the old guys there. But the problem is, if you left Avenue P and went to the Surf Avenue courts, in Coney Island, pretty soon you'd start talking rough and trying to hustle the old guys into a money game, and then you wouldn't be welcome anymore on Surf Avenue. They'd tell you to take your sticks and go back to Avenue P. On Surf Avenue, the old guys call the wooden paddles "sticks," and they regard them with disdain. If it's a doctor or a dentist you're talking about, he doesn't want to hurt his hands, because he needs them in his profession—O.K., that's one thing. But what's with these other characters with their wooden paddles? The answer is the handicapping.

"Bernie, listen to me. Larry's got thirty dollars on this game. You want ten?"

"What's the game?"

"Stevie and I against Larry's left hand and Sonny."

"Give me a minute to think about it. Hold on. Hey, Sol, who'd you say's pitching today for the Phillies?"

The Avenue P players excel at handball—bare pink palms against hard black rubber—but they allow wooden paddles into the game when they need them for the handicapping. For instance, there's Stevie over there, with the knee brace and the fancy yellow shirt and tennis shorts that could get him into Forest Hills. He's thirty-seven years old now, a grownup. At Avenue P, the guys still call him Stevie because they remember when he was young, when he was so good at one-wall nobody would play against both his hands. Either he wasn't allowed to use the right or he wasn't allowed to use the left. Now he maybe uses both hands against a paddle. That's Stevie's handicap—his opponent's paddle. It makes the game fairer, gets people interested. But even when they're not interested they'll bet. On Avenue P, they'll bet on anything. They'll bet on how soon your shoelaces come untied.

"Christ-oh-mighty: Fourteen–three it was. It's now sixteen–fourteen."

"I know. I'm watching."

"Have you ever?"

"Never."

"Wanna bet on the final score?"

Nobody at Avenue P has a last name. There's Stevie, Phil, Julie, Murray, Manny, Doc, Sonny, Larry, Gary, Lou, Moe—the whole bunch. Not a last name among them. No last names and no fancy shoes and no credit cards. This is a cash-only operation. That's Doc, in the red bathing suit, playing over there on the far court. Well, he isn't actually a doctor. Actually, he fits glasses. But they always called him Doc, and, of course, he's friendly with several ophthalmologists. Last winter, he's down in Miami on a vacation and an old guy a couple of courts away keels over. Somebody calls for a doctor. Doc goes over and starts looking at the guy's eyes.

"How come you never call me?"

"What about all the times I call and you're not home?"

"If I'm not home, then it isn't a call."

"How about the times I call and leave messages?"

"Who do you leave them with?"

"Your wife."

"Then that's not a call, either."

"What do you mean? Doesn't your wife give you messages?"

"She doesn't talk to me. Now, excuse me, but would you mind moving a couple of steps to your right? I'm working on my sunstroke."

Normally, neighborhood handball doesn't require a referee. At Avenue P, however, on a Saturday morning, with a big crowd around, they make an exception. If there's a doubles game going, the referee is the fifth man. It's his job to call the close ones and to take as much abuse as the players have to offer. The fundamental philosophy of Avenue P handball is this: Blame somebody. It is against the rules to let a point pass without berating your partner or accusing your opponent of cheating. It is considered especially bad form not to find fault with the referee. He knows what to do. His job is to sit there in his aluminum chair, palms up, head shaking, brow wrinkled. His job is to do absolutely nothing right.

"How's your ulcer?"

"What are you talking about?"

"I thought you had trouble with ulcers lately."

"Nah, I just got hit by a car. An auto-pedestrian collision. Near the doughnut place. A guy was backing out of a space and didn't look at what he was doing. He had a lady with him. Got me in the left knee. I'm suing. I was with Harvey when it happened. The car sideswiped Harvey, too. He's still got great reflexes. When we got hit, Harvey let go with his hands and accidentally gave me a rap in the face. You know, Harvey the ex-lightweight. I'm standing there bleeding from the nose. Harvey says, 'I told you—always keep your hands up.' "

1979

Museum

Joe Baranyi, who has been living in the Trenton area all his life and is a valuable natural resource, worthy of billboards and high-concept four-color brochures, runs the finest museum in New Jersey devoted to the history of the state's penal institutions. Hesitating to specify his likes and dislikes doesn't fit Joe Baranyi's curatorial style. He comes right out and tells you that his favorite artifact in the collection is the twenty-penny nail that a prisoner once flattened and fashioned into a lock-pick device; that his second-favorite artifact is the phonograph needle and ballpoint pen that another prisoner converted into a tattooing machine; and that his third-favorite is the partial human finger. As a rule, a visitor to the museum—which doesn't have an official name, and consists of a room about twenty by twenty, with brown carpeting and blue walls, at the end of a corridor in the Correction Officers Training Academy, on the grounds of the New Jersey Department of Corrections, in a residential section of west Trenton—has to have been on the premises at least five minutes before Mr. Baranyi will bring around the partial finger.

"I'll show you something of special interest," Mr. Baranyi said the other day. He had just finished describing the contents of a double-kitchen-sink-size Plexiglas-covered display case, saying, "You're looking at about eleven buckets' worth of homemade weaponry of the knife variety. Back in 1975, over at the Wall—that's Trenton State Prison—there was a misunderstanding between the New World and the Old World Muslims. One inmate got killed or murdered or offed, or whatever you want to say, and a bunch of them got messed up pretty bad, and then there was a weapons shakedown. Most of these weapons turned up then, and I decided

they would make a good display. What do you think?" Then, from
a locked glass cabinet on one wall, he removed a rubber-stoppered
bottle. "This turned up when we were moving those eleven buckets'
worth of weaponry," he said. "I suppose you want to know how it
got into that jar. Well, somebody must have got paroled with a
fingertip missing. When I found it, I asked a pharmacist friend of
mine how you would pickle or preserve something like that, and
he said formaldehyde. But he couldn't give me any formaldehyde,
because it's—you know—primarily for licensed funeral directors.
But he said denatured alcohol will do as well—it's just that it
evaporates. So I have to keep putting alcohol in there. I'd say about
once a year I top it off. I made an investigation to try to find out
the who, what, when, and where of the whole thing, but I got a
dead end everywhere I looked. It just turned up in that pile of
weaponry. I recognized it when I first saw it, because it was in
pretty good shape. You could see the fingernail at the bottom of
the finger, or the top of the finger—I'll let you word that any way
you want."

Mr. Baranyi, who is in his mid-fifties and has green eyes, a pink
face, a dimpled chin, and dark, oiled hair, worked twenty-three
years as a correction officer at the Bordentown Youth Correctional
Institution, which he invariably refers to as "Bordentown, my alma
mater." For five of those years, he was president of the correction
officers' union, and this meant that back in 1976, when he started
the museum, he already had pretty good contacts throughout the
New Jersey prison system. The Dictaphone that sits against a wall
beneath the "Wanted" poster for one of John Dillinger's female
friends ("I think she's the one that ratted on Dillinger when he
came out of that movie theater and the G-men got him"), for instance, came from the Annandale Youth Correctional Institution.
"I wasn't that enthusiastic when I first heard about this Dictaphone," said Mr. Baranyi. "I thought it was going to be just like
a table-model tape recorder. But here it is, a Dictaphone on wheels,
patented by Thomas Edison, and it was used around 1915. After
we got this one, a custody supervisor at Rahway told me there was
an old one over there, in a tunnel, so that's how we ended up with
two of these things." He pointed to a second Dictaphone, across
the room.

A soup-to-nuts perusal of the collection can take about half an hour, unless you step back and encourage Mr. Baranyi to say whatever comes to mind, in which case it can take about half a day. He dwells and dilates upon every highlight and lowlight, among them:

A 1902 mug shot of William Ruppel, an average-looking and, according to the vital statistics accompanying the mug shot, average-sized fellow: "One of my favorite guys. Look at all these measurements. Guess what this meanie did. He stole a horse. So they measured his head. It was lopsided."

A metal immersion coil: "What's that weapon? It's not a weapon, it's a coffee cooker. But it *could* be a weapon."

A heavy metal chain outfitted with seven pairs of handcuffs: "Now, that is a seven-man hookup, and if one guy had to go they all had to go. That's got a one-link spread between the hands. When I hear remarks about how inhumane things are today, I say, 'Oh, yeah? How'd you like a one-link spread in your handcuffs?' "

A maroon thermos with a top that had been hollowed out to create a hiding place for a bullet: "The ingenuity of some of our inmates—if they ever put their brains to work, they'd be lawyers or millionaires in a minute."

The electric chair in which Bruno Hauptmann and a hundred and fifty-nine other people were executed is part of Mr. Baranyi's collection, and, of course, he has a lot to say about that: last-supper rituals ("They left it to the condemned man to decide the menu, and anybody on death row that wanted it got that special menu that night. Oh, they all partied good"), helmet sizes ("Now, the last guy was, I think, a size medium"), a condemned man he knew named Joe Ernst ("He was on my farm gang in Bordentown, my alma mater, and then he got out, and then he got back in for the crime of murdering his girlfriend. He was a little guy. About five five, smiling, good-natured. The love affair drove him to murder").

Several years ago, some representatives of Madame Tussaud's Wax Exhibition, in London, approached Mr. Baranyi with a special request. "They wanted to make a mockup of our electric chair," he said. "So they took measurements and made a replica, and the replica is over there right now, in Madame Tussaud's—the exact chair that was used at the Wall for our hundred and sixty death-row inmates—with a wax model of Bruno Hauptmann seated in it. And as part of that display they happen to have a correction officer in full uniform. And he stands there at the entrance to the death chamber, or the chamber of horrors, or whatever you call it, right next to the chair, and my impression is he is supposed to resemble me, Correction Officer Joe Baranyi."

Mr. Baranyi described in detail the chamber of horrors that he would, if his budget permitted, assemble in Trenton ("What I want to do is fix this *whole* place up"), and then he decided to go across the hall to an employees' lounge for a coffee break. He sat down on a couch and rested his feet next to a table made from a cell door that had once been installed at Trenton State Prison. "This door was made in 1836," he said. "I took it to a place out on Highway 130—it's no longer there—and they removed twelve coats of paint. They wanted seventy-eight dollars for the job, but when I told 'em what it was for, they said, 'Joe, it's on the house.' "

1 9 8 7

Positions Available

All over town, Pudgy Roberts has posted hundreds of notices that say "Wanted Reliable & Attractive Young Men & Women to Pass Out Flyers in Clown Make-Up. A Easy and Fun Way to Earn $$. Experience Welcome, but Not Necessary. Opportunity to Earn Unlimited Income. Excellent Benefits. Guaranteed Positions Available Downtown & Midtown. Call Pudgy Roberts—(212) 244-4270."

Sandra Seewald, who, along with her husband, owns Golden Path Jewelry, Ltd., at the corner of Sixth Avenue and Forty-third Street, looked out the window of their store one recent afternoon and said, "I'm sure my husband wouldn't have minded a Linda Evans type, but this is what Pudgy sent."

A woman who was dressed as a bride but was not in fact a bride stood, with her *faux* groom, on the sidewalk in front of Golden Path Jewelry and distributed advertising flyers that announced a spectacular sale ("Up to 75% below retail . . . Sign Up for Our DIAMOND Give-A-Way"). This was right after a lunch break, which the bride and groom had spent on the plaza next to the W. R. Grace Building, eating hot dogs. The bride, who looked much younger than Linda Evans—also less blond and less slender— was Denise. The groom was Marcos. Pudgy Roberts had sent them.

"The way I see what I'm doing is I'm trying to break a record here," said Denise as she informed passersby that Golden Path Jewelry was offering diamond-stud earrings for sixty dollars a pair. "When have you seen a bride spend this much time in a gown?" Denise, who has also earned unlimited income and excellent benefits dressed as a clown, was nearing the end of her second full week dressed as a bride. She wore a white gown and veil, a rhinestone tiara, purple sunglasses, white sneakers, and a Sony Walkman. Marcos had been a professional groom only three days. "Last week, I had three different husbands," Denise said. "But I think this guy will be with me for a while. The other ones—I don't know, they quit. This guy, I think he'll stay."

Before Marcos worked for Pudgy Roberts, he spent some time not working. Before that, he worked in a casino in Reno. Marcos had a goatee and a steady smile, and he wore a black tuxedo, black canvas sneakers, a white shirt, and a black velvet clip-on bow tie.

"Pudgy says this work is good therapy for yourself," Denise said. "You get in a happy mood, and you get other people in happy moods."

An elderly man in a gray pinstripe suit and a gray homburg accepted a flyer and said, "You just got married? How's it working out so far?" He was followed by two young women who looked at Denise and said, "Don't do it!"

"This wedding dress definitely attracts attention," Denise said. "Guys come by and say, 'Hey, I do.' And I say, 'Hey, too bad, because I don't.' But I like this job. You're not really obligated. You can, you know, take time off—I'm planning to go to Florida for a couple of weeks—and come back. You meet interesting people. It's not like being married."

Denise and Marcos have no plans to get married in real life. "I'm too young to get married," Denise said. "I have my whole life ahead of me." Not to mention that Marcos is already married and has three children.

"I know his wife," Denise said. "She's another clown."

The next morning, shortly after eight o'clock, Pudgy Roberts sat in his office at the international headquarters of the Pudgy Roberts flyer-distribution empire. On Liberty Street, south of the World Trade Center, there is a Roy Rogers Family Restaurant. The rear booth near the stairway on the second floor—that's Pudgy's office. "This is a central meeting point," Pudgy said. "I'm here every weekday. If I don't show up, that means there's no work." Usually, there is work. Seated in the adjacent booths were Marcos and his

wife, Sandy, and also Jerry, Angel, Carla, Ed, and Angelo. A
clown named Bob had already gone off to the Concourse Coffee
Shop, on lower Broadway, to wear a sandwich board. Sandy, Jerry,
and Angel were destined for various Crazy Eddie sites, as clowns,
and Carla, also a clown, had a date at Uptown Girl, on East Twenty-
third Street. The proprietors of 47th Street Photo, one of Pudgy's
steady accounts, prefer civilians, so Ed and Angelo would handle
that job disguised as themselves.

Although Pudgy Roberts is fifty years old, he believes that he
looks fifteen years younger. He has curly dark hair, brown eyes,
a significant nose, a small mouth, a cleft chin, and a broad, fleshy
face. The other morning, he wore a black-and-white shirt with
beige lions printed on it, and black shorts. By turns, Sandy, Carla,
and Angel sat across the table from Pudgy, and he applied their
makeup—white faces with red circles on the cheeks, red lips, and
a vertical black line below each eye. After being made up, each
clown received a costume: red satin pants, red-and-white striped
sweater, red-and-white neck ruffle, red fright wig. Jerry did not
require Pudgy's assistance; he had done his own makeup and put
on his costume at home. Each workday, he paints one eye orange
and the other eye yellow and puts on an orange wig and an orange
satin jumpsuit and then rides the subway to the World Trade
Center.

Before Pudgy got into the flyer-distribution business, he had a
few other careers. He decorated windows, drew portraits on the
boardwalk in Atlantic City, and wrote a gossip column. "I have a
book that's coming out later this year," he said. "I shouldn't tell
you the title, because it's too controversial. It will sell millions of
copies. It's called *Proof: There Is Absolutely No God*. I'm a great
compiler of reference material. I go to the library, do research,
study, and learn. The quest, to learn about life—that is everything.
And I know where to go to get the cheapest things."

Pudgy endeavors to run a low-overhead operation. The main
items in his expense budget are greasepaint, clown costumes,
photocopying, billboard paste, and subway tokens. On a good day,
a clown should be able to pass out two hundred and fifty flyers per
hour. "It's down to an absolute science," Pudgy said. "The main

obstacles to getting this job done right are weather and people's attention span. If it's raining or if the atmospheric pressure is low, most people don't take flyers. The people who harass you the most on the street are messengers. I'm not doing this because I'm just interested in making money. I'm interested in helping businesses grow. This is a good, helpful thing for the economy."

One of Pudgy's many talents is extolling his many talents. "I'm a writer and an artist, and I do everything very well, because I'm sincere," he said. "Here. Here's a flyer I drew. I often design my own flyers. It's excellent, isn't it? That's because I work my buns off. I'm dynamic and outgoing. I'm very good at art. I'm a mentor; I try to teach. My ideals are based on Louis Buscaglia. Or is it Leo? One of those names. I believe in love, honesty, and decency. My favorite singer is Jane Olivor. I've done everything in show business—magic, pantomime, impressions, costume design, anything in the creative field. I've been on all the talk shows. And I write poetry."

When Pudgy sends a clown or a bride or a groom on his or her way, he says, "See you later. Tell them there's more where you came from." This particular workday was already a couple of hours old. Pudgy still needed one more reliable and attractive young man or woman to check in with him at the Roy Rogers Family Restaurant and then be dispatched in a clown costume to Crazy Eddie's. Marcos had not yet been sent anywhere, because Denise had called to say that she wasn't feeling well; Pudgy had told her to try to come to work anyway. Perhaps Marcos would wind up at Crazy Eddie's in a clown costume, or perhaps Denise would materialize and they would return as newlyweds to Golden Path Jewelry. "She'll get here," Pudgy said. "She has to. I need a bride *and* a groom. I can't send out half the top of a cake."

In a clutch, Pudgy could have worn Denise's wedding gown himself—his published works include *The Female Impersonator's Handbook*—but he planned to devote the remainder of the morning to his executive duties. Also, he wanted some time to think. "I must meditate," he said. "I'm very resourceful and creative, but honest. I believe in basics. I'm a simple person. I don't smoke or drink. This honesty of mine is a jewel among the common stones.

I admit it. And there must be time in my day for the many types of volunteer work that I do—suicide hot line, save the whales, save the turtles, save all the animals. All this is a natural ability. It arises from my urge to make everything nice. It's because I am a perfectionist."

1 9 8 6

Sharp

Growing up, Lenny Binelli thought he might like to become an architect. His father, however, told him that unless he set his sights on becoming a doctor or a lawyer he would be better off sharpening knives for a living. The way things have turned out, Lenny Binelli, who is now in his mid-forties, knows how to say "knife" in Italian, Spanish, French, Portuguese, Greek, Yiddish, Arabic, German, Chinese, and English. "But that's about as far as I go with languages," Mr. Binelli said recently. "I got all I can do to speak English." Actually, Mr. Binelli has mastered the art of meet-and-greet palaver. On a busy day, he utters as many how-ya-doins and hey-amigos and hot-enoughs and have-a-nice-days and see-ya-next-weeks and take-it-easys as any affable doorman or elevator starter. He drives a white Chevy van with, on the driver's door, a drawing of a pair of crossed knives, a New Jersey phone number, and the name of his company—Edge Grinding Shop—and he fights Manhattan traffic, climbs in and out of his van about a hundred and fifty times, and maintains a cordial attitude all along the way.

When Mr. Binelli became a professional knife sharpener, he helped to prolong a family tradition. His father, who is no longer alive, sharpened knives, and so did both his grandfathers. Mr. Binelli has a cousin in Virginia, two uncles in Rhode Island, ten cousins in New York, and three cousins in Chicago who are in the same business. The cousin in Virginia also owns a chicken farm and sells chickens to Frank Perdue. "At least, that's what I heard lately," Mr. Binelli said. "The cousins in Chicago are like, I think, fourth cousins. They have a machine that they told me about: you throw the whole cow into a grinder and it comes out like chopped meat but without bones or gristle. These cousins are real big with McDonald's and Burger King. They've been to Spain. They're very big now. They bought up a bunch of small sharpening companies. Everything's on computer. The milk companies do that, and I've been watching the bread guys, too. It's all in the modern age, you know."

Mr. Binelli doesn't have a computer, but he does have a system—which if you're serving two hundred accounts and, some days, trying to complete seventy-five deliveries it makes sense to have. His son, Leonard, has recently joined him in the business. Between them, they have established a workable routine. Monday they spend together in their shop, in Fairview, New Jersey, putting clean edges on items that have to be sharpened by hand—cleavers, the occasional garden shears, the rare pair of barber scissors. "Barber scissors are the hardest, because barbers are the fussiest people," Mr. Binelli said. "If a barber calls me, O.K. But I don't go looking for those jobs." Tuesday through Thursday, Leonard Binelli works in the shop sharpening knives, and his father goes on the road, mainly to Manhattan. Friday, usually, after clearing up a little paperwork in the morning Mr. Binelli knocks off early, and he and his wife head for their cabin in the Poconos.

Mr. Binelli deals in cleavers, boning knives, French knives (for chopping), lox knives ("Technically, it's a ham knife, but people who slice lox don't want to hear it called that"), paring knives, steak knives, roast-beef slicers, vegetable peelers, slicing-machine blades, scissors, and shears, and his total inventory comes to about twenty-five hundred utensils. Edge Grinding's customers—restaurants, coffee shops, grocery stores, bodegas, delis—don't actually own most of their work knives; Edge Grinding owns the knives, and every time Mr. Binelli visits an account he replaces the dull-edged knives with freshly sharpened ones. When he needs new supplies, he usually buys them from Davpol Enterprises, on Lafayette Street. "I buy French knives by the gross," he said. "Every week, I'm in there. Hey, I buy a *lot* of knives." Davpol Enterprises sells more than just knives. If a customer of Mr. Binelli's has a need for twelve-inch fish splitters, meat tenderizers, veal-cutlet pounders, pizza cutters, dough scrapers, butcher saws, or electric

cheese graters, Mr. Binelli will procure any of those things at
Davpol. "I have access to these convenience items," he says. "You
know, you make a hit once in a while. It saves the other guy trouble
and I pick up a few bucks. Everybody's happy. You know what I
mean?"

In a cast of thousands you would come across Mr. Binelli's face
a few dozen times. He has light-brown hair, wide pink cheeks, a
short chin, and wispy gray sideburns. He wears wire-rimmed eyeglasses and dark-blue work shirts with "Lenny" stitched in yellow
over the right shirt pocket. One time, several years ago, as he was
leaving The Players, on Gramercy Park, a stranger asked him to
drop a letter into the mailbox on the corner. Mr. Binelli tried to
oblige, but, as it happened, the mailbox was welded shut and a
film crew from "Candid Camera" was recording his frustration. Mr.
Binelli was a good sport about this, and says that when the episode
appeared on television "a lot of guys in the knife-sharpening business recognized me because of the cardboard knife boxes I was
carrying."

Each customer's knives are kept inside separate cardboard boxes,
which are stored, upright, in milk crates that fill the back of Mr.
Binelli's van. When he makes a delivery, he gives the customer a
handwritten invoice and collects cash on the spot. Throughout the
day, he takes occasional breaks to sort and fold the receipts. "I
don't worry about carrying money," he says. "I'm also carrying
knives."

Mr. Binelli began one recent workday in lower Manhattan with
a six-thirty a.m. cup of coffee and a buttered roll at Moisha's
Luncheonette, a two-knife account (bread knife and French knife),
at the corner of Grand and Bowery. From there he went to two
Greek luncheonettes on Grand Street, then to two luncheonettes
in the Jewelry Exchange, at Bowery and Canal. "One of these
places is owned by a Chinese guy," Mr. Binelli explained of the
latter two. "He bought it from a Greek, who bought it from a Jewish
guy. The other place is owned by a Greek, but it used to be Jewish."

The reason Mr. Binelli can recite these provenances is that he
has been coming to the neighborhood for thirty-five years—since
the days when he accompanied his father on knife-sharpening

rounds. His next stops took him to a bodega, a Spanish restaurant, and another bodega, all on Allen Street; a Dominican restaurant on Delancey Street; a Chinese butcher shop and two bodegas on Eldridge Street; a Hispanic butcher shop on Madison Street; a Greek coffee shop on Market Street; a bodega in a housing project and an Italian restaurant–coffee shop, both near the East River; and back to Madison Street, to a grocery store that makes sandwiches, and then up the block to a fried-chicken place, a bar, a small grocery, and, at the corner of Pearl Street, a Sloan's supermarket.

In Sloan's, he went to three different departments—butcher, deli, and produce. In the produce department, a clerk tried to give him a meat slicer. "That's from the deli department—keep it," Mr. Binelli said. "Just give me the watermelon knife. Now, there's two small ones missing." As he left the supermarket, he said, "I prefer one-stop stores."

On East Broadway, he parked between Catherine and Market and circled the block on foot (Market, Henry, Catherine), hitting three consecutive Oriental seafood stores (scissors only, no knives); then he went to the Tin-Duc Food Market, where he parked behind a delivery truck from which two suckling pigs were being removed; then to a Vietnamese butcher shop down the block. At Delancey and Essex, he went into the Olympic Restaurant, on one corner, and a Greek doughnut shop across the street. "The Olympic used to be one half of a chain," he said. "The other half is down Delancey, near Clinton. I think it was owned by Greeks, and one of them had a Dominican wife, who ran that place." In the Essex Street Retail Market, he made a delivery to two butchers from the Dominican Republic who were selling something called "koshar franks" alongside sage sausage, spiced ham, cows' feet, tripe, and salchichón Dominicano.

A few stops later, at Ratner's, the kosher dairy restaurant on Delancey Street ("one of my most famous customers"), he exchanged friendly insults with Morris Breitbart, the manager, and then went to the kitchen. He gave the short-order cook, who was Chinese, a sandwich knife (eight inches long), a chef's knife (ten inches and heavy), and a bread knife. To the Puerto Rican in appetizers he gave two French knives and a lox knife. There was no one in the fish-and-vegetables department, but Mr. Binelli rounded up and replaced one French knife and two fish knives.

Down the block, in the Delancey Live Chicken Market, which used to be owned by Jews but is now owned by Chinese, there was plenty of wildlife—chickens, ducks, squabs, guinea fowl, rabbits—including some that had quite recently ceased being alive. At a supermarket a block away, Mr. Binelli exchanged five steak knives and four boning knives. There were quick stops at two bodegas on the block, then a drive to a kosher butcher at Grand and Abraham Kazan streets. Before entering a supermarket on Grand near Willett Street, Mr. Binelli said, "Here's a good one. This used to be owned by Italians. They sold it to Israelis, who sold it to some Spanish-speaking people. *They* sold it to some Chinese or Vietnamese, and it started to get shaky, so the Orientals sold it to some Puerto Ricans. They seem to be making a go of it." Inside, in the butcher's department, he did an inventory and announced that he was missing one boning knife. After searching under a pile of short ribs, he found what he was looking for. Then he was back on East Broadway: a kosher fish store, a bodega, and a Jewish nursing home, the Bialystoker Home for the Aged. In the bodega, the A & T Deli, a sign on the wall said, "We Will Not Serve Anything We Wouldn't Eat Ourselves."

On Stanton Street between Clinton and Attorney, there was a succession of five bodegas. One conversation went:

"*Amigo, cómo está?*"

"*Bueno.*"

"Everything *bueno?*"

"*Todo.*"

"*Hay caliente hoy.*"

"*Sí.*"

"Definitely *caliente.*"

"*Aquí.*" The bodega owner handed Mr. Binelli some dirty knives. "*Hay sucios,* O.K.?"

"O.K."

Parking at Rivington and Essex, Mr. Binelli said, "Here we've got a Dominican restaurant, across the street a Russian with appetizers, and then an Indian with one knife." After a detour to Chinatown, he drove to Greenwich Village. He found a spot on Minetta Lane near Sixth Avenue and made calls at Saba's (hot dogs and ice cream), Waverly Deli, Village Donuts & Coffee Shop, and Dallas Jones Bar-B-Q. It was early afternoon, and Mr. Binelli still had about thirty accounts left to serve, including twenty Italian restaurants, a French restaurant, two souvlaki places, a Russian appetizer store, a couple of Indian restaurants, and an Israeli restaurant on Macdougal Street (fifteen knives, biggest customer of the day). A light rain had begun to fall, and it felt like time to depart—there was still enough daylight left for a visit to the United Nations to catch a little of the gab in the General Assembly.

Mr. Binelli said, "O.K., no problem. Gooda see ya. Have a good one. Thanks for coming along. Hey—take it easy now."

1 9 8 6

King of All Kings

John Benjamin Alfred Redman, who is the sole owner and chief executive of V.I.P. Sewer Cleaning, a plumbing enterprise with headquarters in Brooklyn, prefers to be called Johnny Redd. When you come equipped with Johnny Redd's range of talents, you're entitled. Not many plumbers double as private investigators, but Johnny Redd does. Along with a partner, he owns and manages Verify Investigation & Protection Services. V.I.P. Sewer Cleaning has a slogan: "Try Us . . . You'll Like Us!" Verify Investigation & Protection Services' slogan is "Investigations Throughout the World." Although Johnny Redd possesses licenses and legal permits to operate a car and a motorcycle, to own a pistol, a shotgun, and a mobile phone, and to do private investigating and general contracting, when he beholds his plastic-sheathed plumbing license he says, "I prize this license over any other license I got. You could become a doctor or a lawyer much easier than a plumber." About three-quarters of Johnny Redd's working time is devoted to plumbing, the remainder to private investigating. Verify Investigation & Protection Services offers clients criminal-industrial undercover work, polygraph expertise, executive protection, armed bonded couriers, electronic security equipment, chauffeur service, armed escorts, missing-person searches, and a few other conveniences. When Johnny Redd is asked how he manages two such disparate businesses, he says, "Easy. Rockefeller did it. Paul Getty did it. You just got to have key people in key positions. The trick is to get the right people—remember that—in any business."

Johnny Redd is tall, black, muscular, and physically forthright. He has a round face, straight reddish-brown hair that would reach his shoulders if he didn't keep it tied on top of his head, an ample supply of vanity, and a fondness for bright-colored metal-studded leather clothing. He doesn't like to discuss his age, but he looks about forty. He is a graduate of Automotive High School, an ex-marine, a veteran of the New York Police Department, and an enthusiastic Republican. "I used to be in law enforcement, and then I realized that wasn't for me," he says. "I'm very law-abiding, but I got the hell out. That was just a stepping-stone. I'm a Republican because I'm strictly for people earning their living. It's terrible what's going on in this country. I'm against these people wantin' something for nothin'. You know, in Japan they don't even have holidays. That's how they got the jump on us."

On Waverly Avenue, in the Clinton Hill section of Brooklyn, Johnny Redd lives in the house he grew up in—a three-story row house that has pink metal awnings and a façade of pink and white stones, which give it a vaguely Mediterranean and vaguely Miami Beach appearance, and has a "BEWARE OF DOG" sign in the front window, which indirectly refers to a lot of nice stuff inside, including, Johnny Redd says, a basement "as elegant as a nightclub, with a water fountain in the ceiling." Like any busy chief executive, Johnny Redd moves around a lot. Sometimes you might call him at home early in the morning to make an appointment and he might say, "Come on by in an hour, and make sure you come." But then by the time you got to his place of business—it's a garage fifty feet from the house, directly opposite P.S. 11, the Purvis J. Behan School—something else might have come up. Someone who owes Johnny Redd a bunch of money might have unexpectedly got in the mood to pay up, or he might have suddenly had to run out to a big sprinkler job in Queens, so when you arrived he was unavailable for consultation. When this happens, it's comforting if someone else in the Johnny Redd organization is available for consultation.

The other morning, Darryl Walton, whose nickname is Mr. T., and whom Johnny Redd has referred to as "one of my lieutenants, a very loyal, dedicated employee in a key position," was situated in a key position on the floor of the garage on Waverly Avenue. Specifically, he was lying on an oil-stained Oriental rug ministering to Johnny Redd's motorcycle. The motorcycle is another manifestation of Johnny Redd's talent. Although Johnny Redd owns a silver 1965 Rolls-Royce (Silver Cloud), a red 1972 Cadillac Eldorado convertible with a vanity license plate that says "VIP REDD," a white 1976 Continental Mark IV, and a fleet of blue Chevrolet trucks, none of these comes as close to the core of Johnny Redd's being as his motorcycle. No other vehicle on earth resembles Johnny Redd's motorcycle. In one hand Darryl Walton held a tube of glue and in the other a strand of red rhinestones. Three times a week, Darryl Walton replaces any rhinestones that have fallen off the motorcycle. Rhinestones, chrome, and gold are essential elements of the Johnny Redd aesthetic. They have made it possible for Johnny Redd's motorcycle, which started life as a simple Harley-Davidson Electra Glide, to look now as if it were wearing a chrome Oscar de la Renta ball gown.

An overlay of scrolled chrome filigree has been applied to most of the metallic surfaces. The eagle atop the front fender is gold-plated. So are the dollar-sign-shaped rhinestone-studded hubcap covers and the crown that is fastened to the backrest. The front fender looks as if it came from Rolls-Royce, and so does the chrome radiator grille. Johnny Redd refers to the chrome Rolls-Royce emblem atop the grille as "the naked lady in front." He says, "That's my sweetheart." There is a plane of black leather between the grille and the windshield. Half of a chrome-plated .357 Magnum revolver has been welded to the right side of the gas tank, and an AM/FM quadraphonic radio and a tape deck have been built into the dashboard. An aquatic diorama has been countersunk into the red leather cargo compartment. There is an on-board computer. Red rhinestones on the dashboard spell "JOHNNY." The oil-pressure and voltage gauges look as if they were wearing red Dynel wigs. The running board is illuminated with red lights. "JOHNNY REDD" is spelled out in rhinestones on the backrest, and the gold-plated crown that is built into the backrest is studded with diamond chips that spell "KING OF ALL KINGS."

A sticker on the windshield shows a frontal view of a revolver and says, "NEVER MIND THE DOG. BEWARE OF THE OWNER." Three other stickers on the windshield say "WARNING! IF YOU VALUE YOUR LIFE AS MUCH AS I VALUE THIS BIKE, DON'T MESS

WITH IT." Some delicate floral patterns have been etched into the windshield and the standards that hold the rearview mirrors. Each mirror has an imprint of Johnny Redd's name in red script. The mirror mounts have rhinestone-studded gold-plated dollar signs. There is also a big chrome-and-rhinestone dollar sign on the cargo compartment. A five-inch portable color television set used to ride inside the cargo compartment, but Johnny Redd removed it a while back to give himself more storage room. Black leather fringe hangs from the cargo compartment and the driver's seat. The fringe goes nicely with the metal-studded black leather gloves that Johnny Redd wears when he rides. He also wears a medieval-looking helmet with a snakeskin bill, feathers, chrome filigree, and a crest made from broom bristles. If Johnny Redd doesn't feel like wearing that helmet, he wears one with a chrome crest and a black ponytail of human hair. He acquired these from a member of the New Breed Motorcycle Club when that organization folded a few years ago. The previous owner of the helmets didn't want to sell them, but Johnny Redd shrewdly approached him in a weak moment, when he needed the money.

Johnny Redd doesn't belong to any formal motorcycle club himself, but he has a certificate from the Pythons Motorcycle Club confirming that he has ridden in its Annual Bike Blessing Service and Parade. The certificate has been signed by all the officers of the Pythons, including Mr. Big Stuff, president; Crasher, vice-president; Sweet Andy, treasurer; Baby Huey, business manager; Run Joe, road captain; Beddie, road captain No. 2; Killer Joe, sergeant at arms; and Mr. T. (a different Mr. T.), second sergeant at arms.

One recent morning, Johnny Redd happened not to be occupied with other business and was therefore available for consultation. He cordially consented to extol the motorcycle's mechanical prowess. "I've owned three different show bikes, but this one surpasses them all," he said. "It took ten people five years to get this bike to look this good. It took me five years to pay for it. And what you're looking at in beauty, I had just as much put into the engine and operation of the bike. With all that jazz on it, I thought I needed that extra power. It's too powerful, really. Yeah, very, *very* powerful. It pulls a hill like it's nothin'. Very powerful. Plus I had special gearing put in it. See, nobody ever went this far out on a motorcycle, so I figured I might have trouble with it. So I had all that performance work done."

An attractive woman passed by the entrance of Johnny Redd's garage as he was explaining this. He greeted her by saying, "Are you looking for me?" It turned out she wasn't. Even the most beautiful woman in the world would not be allowed to take the motorcycle around the block for a solo spin. No matter how much you admire Johnny Redd's bike, he won't let you drive it. He'll let you sit on it, but that's all. He let a blond actress ride *with* him when they appeared together in a movie called *Satan Studs*, but he did the driving. Johnny Redd gets a little sheepish when he talks about that experience. "It wasn't what you'd call a Class One picture," he said. "It wasn't a *Rambo* or nothing." Once, two women were photographed sitting on the motorcycle "buck naked," but Johnny Redd doesn't recall all the details. Graciously, he has allowed two couples to get married on the motorcycle—not simultaneously—but, of course, they weren't able to borrow it for their honeymoons. Muhammad Ali sat on it once and asked to drive it, but Johnny Redd told him no way. On a number of occasions, Johnny worked for Ali as a bodyguard. He has done the same thing for Larry Holmes, Rocky Graziano, Mick Jagger, and Telly Savalas, and he has autographed photographs to prove it. He also has a letter from Jimmy Carter. "I spent a weekend in the White House with Jimmy Carter," he said. "Henry Jackson, the senator from Washington—Squirt Jackson—arranged it. He saw me on the street in New York with my motorcycle and said the President would like to see it. So I went down there for the weekend, and then Jimmy Carter sent me a letter to thank me for coming. Malcolm Forbes was interested in me, too. He wanted me to go on a cruise and then a motorcycle trip through China with him. But I couldn't leave my business." Johnny Redd admires all his luminary acquaintances, but he still won't let them drive the motorcycle. Rules are rules.

A red-and-white painted sign inside the garage enumerates some of the other rules that Johnny Redd lives by. If you lose a tool and it turns up later, that costs you five dollars. Losing it permanently costs you a bundle. Forgetting to put the keys to one of Johnny's five trucks back on the proper nail also sets you back five dollars, and so does failing to call headquarters when you're supposed to. Forgetting to leave a V.I.P. Sewer Cleaning fluorescent sticker at a job site when you finish a job—a fiver. No employee is permitted to throw out garbage without Johnny Redd's approval. Rule No. 15 says, "DO NOT WORK FOR ANY ATTORNEY UNLESS INSTRUCTED TO DO SO." Another "BEWARE OF DOG" sign is conspicuously displayed. This apparently refers to King, a Doberman pinscher who spends some of his time gnawing a rawhide bone the size of a rhinoceros femur and the rest of his time eyeball-to-eyeball with anyone who steps within the radius of his leash.

Whenever Johnny Redd rides the motorcycle, he takes with him several photographs of it. These he gives to doormen and security guards, so they will know to report a serious theft if they should happen to see anyone other than Johnny Redd cruising by on it. Johnny Redd hates to dwell upon the misfortunes that might befall his motorcycle. If you ask whether he has ever had a flat tire or a mechanical breakdown, he says, "Don't even mention it. Let's face it, I can't afford for that bike to break down nowhere. If I go to make a phone call, when I come back things ain't gonna be the same. I keep the bike in tip-top shape. I park it wherever I wanna park it, but I don't stay away from it too long."

Usually, wherever Johnny Redd parks the motorcycle it draws a crowd. Sometimes he hangs out in Manhattan at the Caliente Cab Company, on Seventh Avenue South, sometimes at the Spring Street Bar, in SoHo. He has also spent a lot of time at the CAT Club, in the East Village. At the CAT Club not long ago, Johnny Redd became friendly with some people in a rock band called Kill Me. Someone named Randy is in charge of the band, and he is arranging for a movie star named Dirty Hanky and a girl who is a movie star, too, to pose with the motorcycle for a rock video. Randy has already arranged to have some T-shirts imprinted with a photograph of the motorcycle.

"They put the bike on a T-shirt, and the bike looks beautiful," Johnny Redd said. "But they also put the name of the band on the shirt. So when I wear the shirt I'm going around with a shirt that says 'Kill Me.' Everybody be laughing when they see me in that shirt. I'm trying to spray-paint off the 'Kill Me' part. Why do I want to wear something that says 'Kill Me'? I got too much to live for. Me and the bike, we're supposed to be on 'Miami Vice.' We already did some shooting at the heliport and at the Water Club. You know who else I used to ride on my bike? Miss Rheingold. I met her at the Spring Street Bar. Everybody who sees that bike falls in love with it. Hey, I've done a lot of things with that motorcycle. I'm an interesting guy, right?"

1 9 8 6

Profiles

Court Buff

In all sorts of circumstances, certain people in Brooklyn will commit murder. This fact fascinates Benjamin Shine more than it appalls him. Shine is a peaceable gentleman from Borough Park who would hate to be asked which he prefers—a sunny afternoon stroll alongside the Belt Parkway with his wife, Tillie, or a dukes-up double-murder trial. He is a self-taught student of the behavior of criminals, innocents, witnesses, lawyers, judges, and jurors. He is a court buff. As a sideline, he happens to be a student of the behavior of his fellow court buffs. Most weekdays, a dozen or more buffs show up at the State Supreme Court Building on Cadman Plaza, in downtown Brooklyn. Shine attends as regularly as any back-seat jurisconsult in the borough.

Although Shine has lived in Brooklyn for most of his seventy-three years, he is no provincial. He acknowledges that the other boroughs of New York City have bred their own miscreants. Having spent the past dozen years watching criminal trials—mainly murder trials—in Brooklyn, however, he has found it sensible and convenient to become a specialist. Consequently, he takes more interest in a corpse that has been deposited in an airshaft in Flatbush than in one that has turned up in the trunk of an automobile at LaGuardia Airport or in a vacant lot near Hunts Point. Shine realizes that in addition to murderers there are antisocial types out there who have the capacity for rape, theft, burglary, kidnapping, arson, or aimless mayhem—at times, of course, overlapping occurs—but he devotes most of his attention to homicides. He is not ghoulish, merely curious. "Where there's murder," he often says, quite accurately, "you know something's doing."

Anyone who regularly conducts business in the criminal courts of New York City grows accustomed to seeing buffs seated in the back of the room. Many shortsighted lawyers think of court buffs as part of the furniture, and ignore them. But enlightened and resourceful lawyers regard knowledgeable buffs as jurors' jurors. On occasion, during trial recesses, they seek the buffs' counsel. Attention of this sort pleases a buff. Just because one buff tells another that an inept lawyer is stinking up a courtroom with his performance, it doesn't mean that he wants the lawyer in question to know he thinks so. A lawyer who solicits a buff's opinion usually hears words of reassurance. It is in a buff's interest to massage a lawyer's ego. Lawyers call witnesses to testify, and courtroom testimony is often amazing. The way a buff sees it, lawyers deserve encouragement; they book a lot of free entertainment. "I'd pay a dollar to see a good trial, I really would," Shine has said—grateful, just the same, that he doesn't have to. "Some of these buffs, though, I think if you charged only fifty cents you'd lose quite a few."

The State Supreme Court in Brooklyn—"Supreme Kings," in the parlance of the legal community—is an eleven-story building that covers two square blocks. It has a talc-gray concrete exterior punctuated by rows of rectangular windows, and it sits on Cadman Plaza like a Second World War battleship in permanent drydock. Inside, it is made of durable materials—pink marble, oak, brushed aluminum. All felony proceedings that originate with indictments are heard in the State Supreme Court; there were four hundred and thirty-six murder indictments in Brooklyn last year. Between trials, the buffs of Kings County shuffle through the corridors of the Supreme Court Building with the luxurious confidence of warehouse owners at a bankruptcy auction. A man named Harry Takifman, a colleague of Shine's, once explained this attitude to me in pragmatic terms. "In this joint, you got your rape cases, you got your murders, your muggings, your narcotics," he said. "So if you don't like what you see in one courtroom you can always go shopping somewhere else."

Like his friend Harry Takifman, Shine is not prone to lofty pronouncements about the nature of mankind. He subscribes to all Ten Commandments but never moralizes. He enjoys exercising his critical faculties, and avails himself of the chance to do so on a daily basis. From time to time, I join him at Supreme Kings and take in a murder trial or two myself. I met Shine one winter morning while we were both devoting our attention to *People* v. *DiChiara*, a homicide trial that contained ample measures of novelty and poignancy. After years of listening to hundreds of variations on a limited number of themes—toll collector discovers wife and up-stairs neighbor in flagrante, gun goes off six times; bongo player, father of four, dies of stab wounds outside East New York social club on a Saturday night—Shine has come to resemble an uncommon sort of naturalist, the bird-watcher who studies flocks of starlings in the hope that a green wood hoopoe will fly by. Eventually, one does. As I saw more and more trials in Shine's company, I came to realize that *People* v. *DiChiara*, while not quite a green wood hoopoe, was still a bird that had wandered away from its natural habitat. Shine is happiest when a trial appeals to what he calls "the composite powers of my mind." Shine has made up the verb "to composite"—or rather, has composited it. To composite, in his version, means to embellish; to embroider reality; to transport the facts to the exurbs of plausibility. A friend of Shine's, a buff named Leo Friedman, persuaded Shine to visit the Picasso exhibition at the Museum of Modern Art a while back. Shine came away saying that while he wasn't crazy about a lot of the artist's paintings he thought that "Picasso could composite—oh, and how."

People v. *DiChiara* had Shine compositing heavily. Frank DiChiara was a Brooklyn clothing-factory owner who had been accused of stealing fourteen thousand dollars—the entire savings of one of his employees, an Italian immigrant, and her husband—and, while burglarizing their home, of shooting the couple's only child, a thirteen-year-old girl, who, before dying, told the police, "My mother's boss, Frank DiChiara, shot me." The first day I sat in on the trial, I took a spot in the spectator gallery next to Shine. He nodded and smiled at me. A couple of minutes later, at the mention of Frank DiChiara's name, he nudged me with an elbow and tilted his head in the direction of the defense table.

"That's DiGennaro," he said softly, compositing with the pronunciation of the defendant's name. Frank DiChiara wore a well-cut suit and had dark hair, the physique of a stevedore, and a blank expression.

"*That* guy?" I asked, aiming an index finger.

"Don't point," Shine warned. "Don't point in the courtroom, and don't talk in the elevator if the other passengers have jurorly appearances. Yeah. That one. And that's his family to your right."

After a discreet pause, I turned slowly and looked at two men and a woman who shared the bench with us. She was pretty and had black-dyed hair and wore a white wool coat with a white-dyed fur collar. The men wore dark pinstripe suits and white shirts with French cuffs and gold links. Each had a copy of *Il Progresso* folded in his lap. In profile, both men distinctly resembled Frank Di-Chiara. Someone in the group smelled of Juicy Fruit. My own mind began to composite.

The evidence in this case, as marshaled by Harold Rosenbaum, a veteran assistant district attorney who is as familiar as Raymond Burr to Brooklyn homicide buffs, seemed conclusive. Rosenbaum saw fit to introduce into evidence, apropos of nothing that I could figure out, a pair of heavy green cotton bloomers that the victim, Germania Zurlo, had customarily worn underneath her parochial-school uniform. Elena Zurlo, the victim's mother, a gray-haired woman in her early fifties, was on the witness stand at the time. Seeing the bloomers reduced Mrs. Zurlo to misery, and no doubt impressed the jurors. When the time came, they pronounced DiChiara guilty. Shine accepted the verdict as inevitable, but a seed of doubt lingered and germinated. "I was reluctant to go along with that jury in DiGennaro," he said weeks later. "You saw the guy in court. You saw how he looked. I didn't figure him to be the sort who steals fourteen thousand on a breaking-and-entering. He didn't look the part. Here he was with a factory in Williamsburg, a nice suit of clothes. I think he's more the type with a weekend house in the Poconos, maybe a limousine with a horn that honks out the theme from *The Godfather*. A Poconos guy wouldn't be likely to try something like this." Shine paused and reshuffled the facts. "Don't get me wrong. I'm not saying fourteen thousand's not a good amount. Matter of fact, if you had a house in the Poconos already you could make some nice improvements with that much money." He paused again. "I don't think it would have happened if he hadn't panicked—this girl comes home from school and finds him there and he panics. And if the girl hadn't lived to say, 'My mother's boss shot me.' Now, there you have a classic example of a 'dying declaration.' The victim knows she's gonna die, and she names her assailant. That's really something. Rosenbaum called this detective to the stand, and the detective said this girl said that DiGennaro shot her. Normally, hearsay they don't allow. But if it's a dying declaration they allow the hearsay. It's an exception to the hearsay rule. She knows the end is near. So they allow it. On the other hand, you wonder about a guy who takes weekends in the Poconos. Of course, I'm only compositing."

When Shine wove this theory for me, it occurred to me that he might be an avid reader of mysteries and, perhaps, an underpaid literary critic. We had just eaten lunch and were taking a stroll. I asked him who his favorite compositors were.

"If I read too much anymore, my nerves fall asleep—which is what I want sometimes," he said. "I can listen to that guy Larry King on the radio and that puts me to sleep. I sleep the whole night through with the radio on. Reading—I used to like Maupassant and, yeah, Edgar Allan Poe and, whatis, yeah, Arthur Conan Doyle. Poe I like a little less, because he gets too colorful before he gets to the point he's trying to make. Also, it's not compositing. It's fantasy. It's not close enough to the real thing. The only thing that's better than the real thing is maybe Arthur Conan Doyle. I classify Doyle's work as classic. After all, he's dead quite some time now."

It was a warm day, and we were walking across Cadman Plaza, moving between shade and light beneath a row of tall London plane trees, in no special hurry to find out what José Rotger and Miriam Acevedo had done with the shotgunned body of José Martinez after rolling it up in a rug on St. Marks Avenue.

"And not too much poetry," Shine added. "One poem I remember very well, though. You know this one?" He recited the first stanza of Shelley's "Love's Philosophy," applying a Brooklynese flourish to the lines:

> The fountains mingle with the river
> And the rivers with the Ocean,
> The winds of Heaven mix for ever

With a sweet emotion;
Nothing in the world is single;
All things by a law divine
In one another's being mingle.
Why not I with thine?

"There's more than that, but I won't go on," he said.
"That was nice," I said. "When did you learn that?"
"Fifty years ago. That's what I recited to my wife when I first knew her. It gave me a lot of trouble. Since then, no more poetry."

Shine knows all about the uses of hyperbole. He also knows that Tillie Shine is a gracious lady. It doesn't bother her that her husband has taken an avocation and turned it into a full-time occupation. She lets him go his way each day without any complaint and without any urge to tag along. "I'm not bloodthirsty," Mrs. Shine once told me. "Not that Ben really is, either. He likes a mystery. He always liked to read them. I remember from when we were first married, he always went to bed with a mystery."

One morning not long ago, I rode out to Brooklyn and met Shine on the steps of Supreme Kings. We walked through the lobby and took the elevator to the seventh floor. A guard there waved Shine past a metal detector, and then they both watched as I emptied my pockets and submitted to being electronically frisked. Most of the courthouse personnel are familiar with Shine. They know his face, though they may not know his name. Someone new to the job could take a brief look at him and feel intuitively that he is not a man who would carry concealed weapons. He is myopic and, whether standing or sitting, seems always to lean slightly forward, as if in a perpetual state of aroused anticipation. The lenses of his eyeglasses are round, and the frames are thick and black. The eyeglasses suit his face, which is round and fleshy. He has peachy jowls, silky and plump, and they seem to have annexed the rest of him. From head to toe—a distance of five and a half feet—he looks like jowls with arms and legs. The top of his head is bald, but he has a fluffy fringe of white hair. Impressive salt-and-pepper tufts grow from his ears. Year round, he wears a hat. That day, it was a gray plaid snap-brim. It matched his gray plaid topcoat and gray vest, and managed not to clash with his blue plaid jacket, navy slacks, white shirt with blue stripes, and red-white-and-blue print bow tie. Before Shine became a court buff, he spent a quarter of a century as a traveling bow-tie salesman. During his career in bow ties, he traveled north as far as Buffalo, south to Richmond, east to Boston, and west to Chicago. Along the way, he always wore a nice piece of merchandise under his collar. Before he sold bow ties on the road, he owned a haberdashery. Each day now, he dresses with care. The act of selecting his daily wardrobe has a tonic effect. Shine believes that if he is going to spend a day in court he should make a businesslike appearance.

We walked down a corridor to Justice Edward Lentol's courtroom, where at that moment no business was being transacted. There were no jurors in the box, no lawyers or defendants in sight, no Justice Lentol seated on the bench beneath the engraved oak paneling ("The Welfare of the People Is the Supreme Law—Coke"). Two uniformed court officers sat in armchairs along one wall, making each other laugh. The bailiff stood nearby, reading the *Racing Form*. The clock on the wall above the spectators' section showed that it was almost ten-fifteen. At ten o'clock, proceedings were supposed to have resumed in *People* v. *Aviles and Aviles*—a case in which the charges included murder and attempted murder. When possible, Shine tries to watch a trial from the ceremonial first pitch and stay with it, for however long, until the jury departs to deliberate. The previous day, he had been in court for the opening innings of *People* v. *Aviles and Aviles*. It had looked promising.

These were the facts: The brothers Aviles—Carlos and José—were accused of the murder of Anthony Tinakos Goulias, who died at the corner of Fifty-eighth Street and Third Avenue in Bay Ridge, and the attempted murder of Nelson Ramos, who received a .22-caliber-bullet wound in the neck but subsequently recovered. At the time of the shootings, Carlos Aviles was the more or less constant companion of Cookie Adorno, Ramos' sister. Two of the first witnesses called by the assistant district attorney on the case were Carmen Ramos, the mother of Nelson and Cookie, and Nelson himself. Nelson, a lean, prematurely aging nineteen-year-old, told the court that he and his late friend Anthony Tinakos Goulias had paid a visit to Carlos Aviles one day after Cookie had complained that Carlos was being especially unchivalrous. As Cookie and Goulias looked on, Carlos and Nelson got annoyed with each other, Nelson struck Carlos, Carlos hit him back, Nelson struck Carlos again and headed for the door, making threatening remarks on the way out—something like that. A few hours later, on the street, someone shot Goulias and Ramos. One died; the other lived to tell the judge about it. This all happened on a Friday afternoon in July.

Near the start, the prosecution's case suffered because of these assertions by the defense: that Goulias had a widely known propensity for carrying a gun in his pocket even while he was running casual errands, and that Nelson, although he was still an adolescent, had accumulated a criminal record. Carlos Aviles' lawyer, a tall, gray-haired, crewcut man named Frederick D. Kranz, brought these facts to light during his cross-examination of Nelson Ramos. The state's case didn't improve at all when Carmen Ramos took the witness stand. The courtroom proceedings did not arouse Mrs. Ramos' enthusiasm—that, at least, was the impression she conveyed. She had orange hair, dark glasses, and a convincing scowl. Apparently, she was still annoyed that someone had shot Nelson, whom she naturally loved like a son, and whom, she acknowledged under oath, she "would lie to protect." During cross-examination, Kranz confronted her with an apparent discrepancy between her testimony at the trial and her testimony during the grand-jury hearing that preceded it. A delay ensued while Mrs. Ramos' private attorney, who happened to be in the courtroom, approached the witness stand for a consultation with his client. After he retreated and Kranz's question was repeated, the court's Spanish interpreter announced that Mrs. Ramos wished to invoke her right against self-incrimination, as granted by the Fifth Amendment. Upon hearing this, the assistant district attorney rested his forehead against his palms.

Now, in court for the next installment, Shine reviewed the proceedings with far greater relish than Mrs. Ramos had brought to her task as a sworn witness. "She made a bad move up there," he said cheerily. "When Kranz asked whether she lied to the grand jury, she should've said, 'I don't lie. I was mistaken.' After all, everybody makes mistakes, right?" The question of Nelson's credibility suggested a different approach. "With him, I'm undecided. He's a Nelson and he sings, but he's no Nelson Eddy. Does he have a credibility problem? For this, I say, let's be Solomonic. I say let's cut him in half and see what's doing there."

Such a confection—the epigrammatic point of law layered between trenchant appraisals of human nature—is a specialty of Shine's. Although he does not aspire to become a walking version of *Black's Law Dictionary*, he does keep a generous supply of buzz-phrases at his disposal. He summons them regularly, alternating them with thoughts about, say, what jurors No. 4 and No. 9 might have eaten while watching television the previous evening. I have heard his explications of the rules regarding photographic evidence, the protection against incriminating testimony by a spouse, the evidentiary relevance of a witness's prior criminal record, and the admissibility of confessions. Upon request, he will do what he can to explain the distinctions between circumstantial evidence, direct evidence, technical evidence, and evidence-in-chief. He has memorized most of the exceptions to the hearsay rule. Shine, who is an adherent of the ours-is-not-a-perfect-system-but-it's-the-best-one-around school of thought, says that Roy Cohn was the most effective trial attorney he ever saw. "He formulated sentences like a fresh-running brook," Shine says. "Very quick. It was a long time since I saw him. Two cases I saw, both in federal court. The one I remember, a guy hired out trucks. And one fellow didn't pay for the trucks, so he hired someone to break the fellow's legs. Roy Cohn lost, but he was very quick." In offering this compliment, Shine wasn't comparing Cohn merely with the best in Brooklyn. Last winter, Shine happened to be in Miami for a couple of weeks at a time when F. Lee Bailey was defending a murder case there. "It was a nice case," Shine recalled. "A guy accused of killing his mistress. A hung jury. Bailey was good, but he was only one of three lawyers on the defense team. I still say Roy Cohn had the sharpest mind."

To sit next to Shine in court and listen to his whispered running commentary often seems like watching a videotape with an out-of-sync play-by-play. He is adept at what amounts to simultaneous translation. As a lawyer rises from his chair to say "Objection, Your Honor," Shine mutters "Sustained" or "Overruled" before the judge ventures his opinion. Even more often, Shine raises a sotto-voce "Objection!" before the lawyer gets around to it. The lawyer, upon speaking, sounds like an amplified echo of Shine, who by then has ruled on his own objection. Instead of diminishing the suspense of the live action, this guessing game enhances the drama. Every now and then, Shine guesses wrong.

Many of Shine's jurisprudential ideas cannot be traced to any legal textbook. He enjoys speculating about how much certain lawyers earn, and he has opinions about how much their labor is actually worth. He gauges the degree to which a jury will be influenced by the similarity between a defense attorney's diction and a violin being played pizzicato. He knows intuitively when the wave in an accused man's pompadour amounts to a one-way ticket to prison. The crucial question in any criminal trial—superseding, ultimately, the absolute truth about guilt or innocence—is how the jury votes. Shine has heard a lot of perjury and feels confident that he can see a lie coming before the people in the jury box recognize it. Whenever he is asked to predict a verdict, he says, "I always say, 'With a jury, you never can tell.' " Then he proceeds to tell anyway. Shine tries to be soothing when he has to break bad news. "You're doing just great, just great," he is apt to tell a lawyer. "You're doing just great, but you aren't gonna win."

In certain circumstances, Shine will step forward to offer a lawyer an unsolicited opinion. A lawyer named John C. Corbett has been approached quite a few times with what Shine regards as a sound bit of strategic advice. Corbett, who is a former president of the Brooklyn Bar Association, is an imposing-looking man who usually wears a three-piece suit and a pocket watch and does his best to create the impression that neither he nor his client belongs in a criminal courtroom. During the past thirty-four years, he has defended two hundred and fifty accused murderers. Despite Corbett's efforts in their behalf, the vast majority of these people have gone on to become convicted murderers. It seems that one morning several years ago, Corbett and his pet dogs, dachshunds named Siegfried and Brünnhilde, were enjoying a walk along Avenue U, in Gravesend, when a city bus pulled over. The driver, who had once sat on a Corbett jury, emerged and began to tell the lawyer how skillfully he had defended the client. Recalling the case, Corbett pointed out that he must not have been skillful enough, because the accused man was sent away for twenty years. The bus driver was reassuring. "Oh, *him*," he said. "No, I just didn't like the looks of that guy. The minute I laid eyes on him, I told myself he was guilty." This episode impressed Corbett so deeply that he decided to make it the centerpiece of his closing arguments in the future. Nowadays, he ritually recites the parable of the misguided bus driver and implores jurors to judge his clients strictly on the evidence that has been presented during the trial. He includes graphic details of his stroll with Siegfried and Brünnhilde. After twelve years in the courthouse, Shine has heard this anecdote more times than he cares to, and he now makes it a habit, whenever he sees Corbett, to say, "The Humane Society wants to know when you're going to stop abusing those dogs." Or, "Hey, Mr. Corbett, isn't it about time those dachshunds were put to sleep?" Corbett, of course, pays no heed. Shine, however, regards such helpful admonitions as being part of a serious buff's unwritten contract.

Some court buffs believe that a criminal trial should be, in effect, a morality play—as if reality could be scaled down to the level of a tabloid-headline-writer's imagination. Shine does not share this notion. Which is not to say that he underestimates the importance of theatricality in the courtroom. A courtroom bereft of shameless posturing and caterwauling holds no more charm than an insurance office. The expectant tingle that permeates the air just before the opening of a trial can be matched only in a Broadway playhouse five minutes before curtain time. There is this important difference, however, between Supreme Kings and the Shubert Theatre: court proceedings are frequently interrupted by unanticipated intermissions of unpredictable duration. The fact was that nothing was destined to happen on this particular morning in the matter of *People* v. *Aviles and Aviles*, even though certain evidence indicated otherwise. Kranz, the defense attorney, entered the room carrying a brown leather briefcase, which he put down on the defense table. When Kranz's co-counsel, Harvey Greenberg, arrived a few moments later, Shine said, "Good. We're in business." As the two lawyers conferred, Kranz fiddled, first idly and then intently, with the lock of the briefcase. Either he had forgotten the combination or the latches were stuck; nothing worked.

"Case closed," Shine observed.

"He should take it to Rikers Island," another buff said.

"These Aviles boys must be innocent," Shine concluded. "If Kranz had a decent clientele, one of them would know how to open that." Finally, Kranz gave up. It didn't matter. The presence of Kranz and Greenberg suggested that the defendants might be brought into the courtroom at any moment, that their handcuffs would be removed, that Justice Lentol's arrival would be heralded, that all would rise in his honor, that the assistant district attorney would set up shop, that the court stenographer would enter and poise himself expectantly at the keyboard of his instrument, that the judge would at last tell a court officer to summon the jurors, that the court officer would disappear, that he would return in the company of twelve voting, taxpaying citizens of Brooklyn, and that Shine and his colleagues would indeed be in business. None of this happened. The briefcase latches didn't spring open. No Justice Lentol. No action. The occupants of the spectator gallery sat. They waited.

As a rule, Shine takes a seat in the second of the four rows of the gallery. The first row is reserved for policemen, for attorneys who drop in to kill time or to study someone else's trial work, and for members of the press. When there are significant facts that Shine wishes to remember—the street address where the corpse was discovered, the distance away that the head was found from the torso—he takes notes. He reaches into his coat pocket and removes a blunt soft-lead pencil, a giveaway from Brooklyn Better Bleach, Inc. With this, he scribbles on whatever is handy—the margin of a newspaper, say, or the paper bag containing his lunch. At the end of the day, before he boards the R train at the Borough Hall station and rides home to Borough Park, he tosses away the newspaper or the paper bag. If a trial attracts a lot of publicity,

Shine may clip a few relevant news stories and carry them in a
jacket pocket. After a couple of weeks, he throws them away as
well. Shine cannot recall the names or the details of most of the
trials he has observed or the nodding acquaintances he has made
along the way, nor does he care to. Much of the testimony he has
heard, he says, "the average man shouldn't want to know from."
Still, he takes pride in his attention to details and strives for
accuracy. If members of the press are available, Shine regularly
confers with them to verify his notes. When none are around, he
depends upon his fellow-buff Leo Friedman, who has perfect gram-
mar and lovely penmanship. Friedman is a retired social-studies
teacher from Sheepshead Bay. Once, when I had not been at the
courthouse for a few weeks, I received a note from him that said:

> Ben and I have been wondering about your absence from the
> court scene. You've missed some interesting cases. The last
> one—before the Honorable Justice Sybil Kooper—a lesbian
> convicted for killing a guy whom she found sleeping with her
> girlfriend.
> The best to you and your family.
>
> LEO

Not long before Kranz arrived with his recalcitrant briefcase,
Friedman had entered the courtroom in the company of several
other buffs. Friedman is Shine's closest friend among the Brooklyn
regulars. He has a trim build, gray hair, and a thin face creased
by a perpetual half-smile. Most of the year, his face is nicely
suntanned. During the winter, it is nicely windburned. Friedman
loves to fish, and he frequently takes day trips aboard Sheepshead
Bay party boats. An inverse ratio exists between the flounder population in the bay and Friedman's passion for justice. In the event
of sustained poor fishing, he rededicates himself to the pursuit of
the truth, the whole truth, and nothing but. He always returns from
a marine sabbatical in a refreshed frame of mind. Whenever Friedman makes a court appearance, he and Shine eat lunch together.
From time to time, they are joined by Louis Entman, Sol Kenare,
Moe Spector, Harry Takifman, Max Silverman, Charlie Rader,

Charlie's sister Jean, and, on rarer occasions, Ann Lieberman, Sam Rosalsky, John Fulton, Anita Warrington, Murray Lauer, or R. C. Frank. These people make up the core of the Supreme Kings buffs.

Entman, Kenare, and Spector are a virtually inseparable triumvirate, who call each other by their nicknames—the Landlord, the Grocery Man, and Kissinger, respectively. The Landlord anointed the two others, and they, in turn, christened him. Louis Entman, the Landlord, is a slack-jawed man who once owned most of Flatbush—or, at the very least, four or five buildings. He still has some property there. The first days of each month, he tends to arrive in court late. Quite a few of his tenants need prodding. When he does manage to collect a nice lump of rent, he celebrates by taking a shave and changing into a relatively clean shirt. He owns a gray sharkskin suit, which has acquired a fine antique sheen, and a couple of neckties, which came into his possession around the time that Chief Justice Rehnquist entered law school. The Landlord has baggy eyes and looks somewhat like a bulldog who has just bitten into something unpleasant that was crawling in the garden. He blinks a lot. He is an enemy of dullness and a master of the one-sided conversation: "Can a wife testify against a husband? I don't know. Wait. I'll ask Kissinger. He'll know. He doesn't even know his own address. See him sitting over there smiling? He smiles because his underwear's too tight. I notice you don't work for a living. You must have a rich wife. I've got a rich wife, too. No fooling. I saw her bankbook. A hundred and fourteen dollars. Her mother left it to her. Yeah. She had a mother. My mother-in-law. Right. She finally learned how to write. I think she went to night school for a week. She took a vacation to Florida and sent me a postcard. It started out, 'Dear Lousy.' She knew me very well. What? This defendant needs a character witness? I'll be a character witness for him. Sure. Tell him I'll do it for twenty-five bucks. You want to know why the judge called a recess? I'll tell you. He has a date to play basketball. Look at that judge. I think he gets his clothes at the Fairchild funeral home. Hey, nice shirt you got on. You oughta buy it." When Entman is not talking, he pantomimes. His head bobs and his hands flutter. Every now and then, a bailiff who happens to be in a foul mood will throw the Landlord out of his courtroom. The Landlord can usually keep up his pantomime for as long as he has an audience. All buffs manage to catch up on their sleep at some point during a working day. Even Shine would not deny that at times he has rested his eyes in the courtroom. So have more than a few judges and jurors. Piping Muzak into the courthouse—up-tempo in the late morning and in midafternoon, or however the Muzak people do it—probably wouldn't help a bit. Whenever a puzzling technical question arises during a trial, the less attentive buffs consult first with Shine and then with the Landlord—unless these experts have briefly nodded off. The other buffs admire the Landlord's business acumen. He is one of the few members of the fraternity who are still engaged in a remunerative enterprise.

Kissinger is a retired tobacconist who faintly suggests an eighty-year-old version of the former Secretary of State. Like Henry Kissinger's parents, he has an intelligent son whose name appears in *Who's Who*. The Grocery Man, a widower in his eighties, used to run a mom-and-pop market in Coney Island. He now follows trends in the business by clipping discount coupons from the Wednesday newspapers. Most buffs are avid clippers of all sorts of coupons. More than once, Shine, reaching for his Brooklyn Better Bleach pencil, has instead come up with a handful of promises of cheaper mouthwash, say, or free French fries at Burger King. Once—this happened during the trial of two young men who were accused of robbing a laundromat owner named Oscar Biggs at gunpoint and then threatening to run him through a ten-minute cycle in an electric dryer—all the buffs came to court with green cash-register receipts. It seemed that a supermarket chain was redeeming small bales of these scraps for gift items, and Kissinger badly wanted a tote bag.

Perhaps more than any other buff, Kissinger has the ability to draw remarkable conclusions from apparently insignificant events and details. He does this despite a hearing problem that is advanced enough to disqualify him for jury duty. I was seated next to him one morning when a lawyer named Mario Marino appeared in the courtroom to argue a motion. Kissinger whispered to me, "That

Marino used to shop in Sol's grocery store. During a summation, I saw him pull out a photograph of a herring and say, 'This is what the district attorney is trying to fool you with—a red herring.' I think he might have bought the herring from Sol." Later, when I asked Sol, the Grocery Man, to confirm or deny—I had learned early on that within the halls of justice, where life and death and the law are paramount, little things can count for a lot—he said he remembered that Marino had been a customer and he remembered selling herring, but he could not recall ever selling herring to an Italian.

Kissinger, a restless man, has adopted the role of scout. On an average day, he leaves the courtroom and returns in an excited state half a dozen times. After each constitutional, he reports his findings to the Grocery Man and the Landlord, and they pass the news along to the other buffs. The calendar clerk, whose office is on the seventh floor of the courthouse, maintains an up-to-date list of trials. Any buff who was inclined to consult with the clerk could avoid a lot of legwork. For their own reasons, however, buffs operate a private, word-of-mouth intelligence-gathering system. Kissinger, suddenly impatient, now said, "So what are we doing sitting here? We could go see the Mets. Anybody want to go to Aqueduct? I think there's a rape case down the hall. What are we waiting for?"

"We're waiting for the angel of death," Shine said as Kissinger headed for the door.

There was a brief silence after Kissinger left, and then Leo Friedman said, "This waiting in these state courts is a shame. You'd never find this in federal court."

"You know better than to compare federal and state courts," Shine replied. "In federal, it's all different."

"My point precisely," Friedman said. "And when a federal judge announces a lunch recess and says that court will resume at two o'clock you can be sure that court will be in session at two o'clock. Here, you sit around till two-twenty, two-thirty. Nothing happens. Nobody complains."

"But you can't compare federal and state," Shine insisted. "For one thing, they don't know from murders over there. Plus, in federal the caliber of the crime is on a much higher scale. You get a much higher-caliber judge, you get a higher-caliber lawyer, and you get a higher-caliber criminal. And a higher-caliber buff. Don't go comparing."

This observation disarmed Friedman, who seemed to turn his thoughts to less irritating topics, like whiting and fluke. Before long, Kissinger returned and announced, "There's a rape next door and a kidnapping down the hall."

The Grocery Man and the Landlord rose and departed with Kissinger, as did Harry Takifman and a couple of other buffs. Only Friedman and Shine remained, along with their fellow-buff Max Silverman.

"I saw that kidnapping," said Silverman. "A complete bust. If that was on television, I'd change the channel. All the time, the district attorney's saying, 'I object, I object.' So what? *I* object to the district attorney. The defense lawyer was a woman. Real heavy-set. Strictly from hunger. If someone kidnapped her, after an hour they'd send her back."

"So what do you want to do?" Friedman asked Shine.

"You wanna go up to Davis?" Shine said. His tone sounded tentative.

Silverman smacked his lips—something he does often. He has a flat, rubbery face. A few years ago, Silverman had a job making deliveries for a dentist. Part of his compensation was in kind—a poorly fitted set of false teeth. On certain rare occasions, he wears the teeth. Otherwise, he leaves them at home and spends the day in court smacking his lips for effect. The name "Davis" provoked him. For a long stretch of time, a Brooklyn buff could say "You wanna go up to Davis?" and he might as well have said "You wanna go to the Statue of Liberty?" It was certainly worth seeing, but if you missed it today you could always catch it tomorrow. *People* v. *Davis* stood out as one of those expensive monuments to the Fifth and Fourteenth Amendments, with their guarantees of due process, and to the political clout of the Patrolmen's Benevolent Association of the City of New York. A former convict named Cleveland McKinley (Jomo) Davis, who had been a leader of the Attica prison rebellion in 1971, went through three long-running trials for the murder, in 1978, of Norman Cerullo and Christie Masone, two New York City police officers. Davis's first trial, in the spring of 1979, lasted eleven weeks and ended with a hung jury. The second one, which began later that year, lasted twelve weeks and ended the same way. A third trial began in April of 1980 and ended, after nine weeks, in acquittal. Justice John R. Starkey presided at the first trial, Justice Lentol at the second, and Justice Robert Kreindler at the third. Their respective courtrooms were on the ninth, seventh, and ninth floors, so it was usually a matter of "going up" to Davis. Going up to Davis did not appeal greatly to Shine, who likes a mystery to have a beginning, a middle, and a firm conclusion; still, *People* v. *Davis* was a murder, which Shine considers preferable to rape or kidnapping.

In the elevator on the way to the ninth floor, Friedman asked, "Ann the Blonde's there, right?"

Shine nodded and said, "She's taking it by the week. No meals."

Ann Lieberman is a skeptical woman who is drifting into her golden years with a head of pale-yellow-tinted hair. A buff could stay away from the Davis trial for days—despite its notoriety, it was a rather boring case—and all he had to do was track down Mrs. Lieberman and she would fill in the gaps. She had made *People* v. *Davis* her specialty. Because the defendant was an observant practitioner of Islam, the trial recessed on Fridays, the Muslim day of rest. She was "up to Davis" the four remaining weekdays, in a lathered state most of the time. Nothing she did could have concealed her contempt for the defendant, so she didn't bother trying. Not that Jomo Davis, if he noticed, should have taken this personally. It seems that Mrs. Lieberman has never seen a defendant who wasn't guilty—if not guilty of the crime in question, then of some other offense. This is a common buff point of view, although it is not one that Shine inclines to. Being literal-minded, he takes the Constitution at its word. Also, he loves suspense. Therefore, he sincerely presumes innocence.

"When I start a trial, I have an open mind," he says. "I divest myself of all prejudice. I put the district attorney on trial and let him put the defendant on trial. The defendant is presumed innocent all the way through. When the jury comes out and says he's guilty, then he's guilty."

Friedman used to share this sentiment, but then he was mugged one weekend afternoon while he was walking along Eastern Parkway. Four youthful offenders, none of whom, if they had been apprehended, would have been old enough to get their names printed in the newspaper, made off with Friedman's wristwatch, wallet, subway pass, library card, and goodwill.

"Oh, gee, Leo, I'm sorry," Shine had said when he heard the news.

"What do you mean, 'sorry'?" said Friedman. "Where were *you!*"

"What time was it?"

"Two o'clock."

"Two o'clock, I was by the Oceana Theatre," Shine recalled. "It was a double feature—*Hurricane* and *Foul Play*. Two disasters for three dollars. I have a two-dollar pass, but you have to use that on a weekday."

"Anyway, they just lost an objective juror," Friedman concluded.

"Oh, don't take that attitude," Shine said, sounding genuinely dismayed. "Take their money. They're paying twelve dollars a day now, plus carfare. Don't tell them anything. If they ask were you ever mugged, say, 'I don't remember.' "

"And I'm a City College boy," Friedman said reflectively. "I didn't always feel this way."

"I'm a confirmed capitalist," Shine said. "I always have been."

A young woman with frizzy light-brown hair sat on the witness stand in the Davis courtroom. Her name was Laurie Weinman, and she was a witness for the defense. The buffs and I took seats in the row in which Mrs. Lieberman sat. An open spiral notebook rested in her lap. She saves all her voluminous jottings, and she doesn't mind homework. The courthouse doors are locked each evening at six o'clock. A jury that deliberates past that hour sometimes consigns Mrs. Lieberman to a phoneside vigil. Justice Sybil Hart Kooper, whose demeanor on the bench is more denmotherly than Portia-like, is a favorite with the Supreme Kings buffs. Justice Kooper remains in her chambers at the courthouse until a jury retires for the night, and during such waits she has received quite a few after-hours phone calls from Mrs. Lieberman.

As a rule, Mrs. Lieberman speaks with the judge's law clerk, Mark Smith, and asks what's taking that jury so long to convict. At the end of the conversation, she says, "O.K., Mark. Tell Sybil I called." Mrs. Lieberman would have a hard time winning a smile contest even in her most buoyant moments. Now she looked as if she had just sucked on a lemon under duress. Laurie Weinman was describing her meetings with a man named Flaco, who had dropped out of sight after the gun battle in which Cerullo and Masone were killed—and in which Davis was wounded. Davis's attorneys contended that Flaco, and not the defendant, had fired the murder weapon.

"The defense is calling its witnesses," Mrs. Lieberman said to me, in more of a stage whisper than I felt comfortable with. "A bunch of phonies. The prosecution had excellent witnesses. Beautiful witnesses."

Robert Bloom, one of Davis's attorneys, showed Prosecution Exhibit No. 7 to Miss Weinman and asked her to describe it. She identified it as a 9-mm automatic pistol.

"Nice girl," Mrs. Lieberman said. "She didn't mind that this Flake-oh had guns. He went to her house. Nice kid. She went to college. A nice girl. Her parents sent her to college so she could learn about guns."

Mrs. Lieberman has the ability to contort her face in striking ways. Occasionally, she gets so emotionally wrapped up in a case that a judge or a defense attorney suggests that maybe everybody would feel better if she were to indulge this gift in a different courtroom. Now she was scribbling in her notebook, looking up to glance at the jury, and twitching around the eyes and mouth. When she saw me noticing this, she said, "I get involved. I talk to everybody. I talk to the assistant D.A.s. The judges. I've even talked to defense attorneys."

I looked at the inscription engraved in the wall above the judge's bench. It said, "Justice Is Truth in Action—Joubert." Then I looked at the back of the bench in front of us, where someone—actually, several someones—had applied sharp objects that had eluded the metal detectors outside the courtroom. "ROSA + AL-FONSO" were in love, as were "SPEEDY + ALTHEA," "ANTHONY +

PEACHES," "LIVINGSTON + AUDREY," "ANGEL + SARITA," and a few other lucky people. As Laurie Weinman testified about her meetings with Flaco and her belief in Jomo Davis's innocence, Mrs. Lieberman clucked her tongue.

"I've got four children and eight grandchildren," she told me. "Two of my sons are C.P.A.s. My other son's in business with my husband. Two of my daughters-in-law are teachers. My son-in-law and daughter are teachers. They didn't live together before they got married. They didn't leave home. No guns. Knock on wood." She rapped "ANTHONY + PEACHES" with her knuckles. "It's a new age? Some age. Too good it isn't."

A few minutes later, Miss Weinman completed her testimony. On her way out of the courtroom, she smiled warmly at Davis and his lawyers. Mrs. Lieberman made a muffled gagging noise. When I turned to Shine and Friedman to see if they had any reaction, I realized that they weren't focussing intently on the proceedings.

"Ben, one of the jurors is eying you over," Friedman was saying.

"A man or a woman?" Shine asked.

"A woman."

"Oh, yeah? The one with the long dark hair?"

"No. The one who looks like Rocky Marciano."

From Shine's vantage point, the problem was that the Davis trial had political overtones. When Governor Hugh Carey announced his intention, in 1976, to finally "close the book" on the Attica rebellion, a report by the special prosecutor had recommended pardons for all but three of the inmates who had been charged with crimes stemming from the uprising; one of the three was Jomo Davis. Less than two years after Davis was paroled, he was arrested for the murders of the two policemen. During Davis's three trials, a cadre of sympathizers appeared each day in the courtroom. The spectators and the flavor of the trials seemed like ghostly anachronisms, throwbacks to recent history—Davis had become a sort of exhumed, junior-varsity Huey Newton—and Shine had no real appetite for that sort of history. Crime—Shine's kind of crime, anyway—has its roots in something less murky than politics. He feels at home with unadulterated motivations: passion, money, sin. *People* v. *Davis* featured complicated technical and forensic testimony—details that might have interested Shine if Davis's principal attorney, Robert Bloom, had been less plodding in his methods. Bloom's approach—halting diction, long pauses between questions, frequent short walks from the witness stand to the defense table to consult notes ("Excuse me, Your Honor, this will take just a moment"), then another pause—was more than a little soporific. Many years ago, Shine was spoiled by a Brooklyn district attorney named Benjamin Schmier.

"This Bloom's a real schlepper," Shine said. "Slow. I've never seen anything this slow. Maybe he figures if he goes slow it's that much longer before his client has to go to the penitentiary. Meanwhile, he's showing absolutely no respect for the buffs. I know that every lawyer has his own style, but I don't understand why somebody would want to have a *boring* style. He should have taken lessons from Ben Schmier. What a following he had. He's passed away. He loved to turn to a defendant during a closing argument and point his finger at him and shout, '*You are a murderer!*' It had a very good effect. Not so much with the defendant, but very good with the jury. Now, your best D.A. in Brooklyn today is Harold Rosenbaum, who did the DiGennaro case. He did a very good summation with that one."

"It was a masterpiece," Friedman agreed.

"Rosenbaum's coming here?" Max Silverman asked.

"No, not here," Shine said. "He was at Lentol."

"I thought so," Silverman said. "So who's this lawyer here? Rosenzweig?" He pointed at an assistant district attorney.

"No, that's someone else," Shine said. "No relation to Rosenbaum or Rosenzweig. Rosenbaum's I think on the fourth floor. He's an assistant district attorney. There's another assistant D.A. named Rosenzweig. There's a lawyer named Rosenblum. And a court clerk named Rosenberg. You gotta keep your Rosens straight, Max."

"What floor are we on?" Silverman asked.

"Nine."

"We move around so much sometimes I forget where I am."

"Stick with me, Max."

• • •

Because state governments, rather than the federal government, write the homicide laws, Shine spends only a modest amount of time on the upper floors of the United States District Courthouse, Eastern District of New York, which is two blocks north of Supreme Kings, on Cadman Plaza. For the sake of variety, he has watched enough federal cases to have established diplomatic relations with many of the higher-caliber buffs of Brooklyn. Nevertheless, his appearances in the federal courtrooms are sporadic, and when he does show up in one he is often obliged to endure a mild form of hazing. The colloquy usually runs like this:

First federal buff: "What's the matter? You run out of murder cases down the street?"

Second federal buff: "No. There was so much blood they ran out of bandages."

Third federal buff: "How do you like the way these guys think they can just show up here whenever they feel like it? They try to sit in the front row. They don't pay dues. They never apply for membership."

Shine: "Hoo, boy."

As the situation stands now, Shine takes a walk to the Emanuel Celler Federal Building almost every day, but he spends most of his time in the basement. The cafeteria there does a brisk lunch business between noon and one-thirty. Shine enjoys passing an hour or so in the dim fluorescent light, resting his elbows on a Formica tabletop, munching a tuna on rye, and engaging in a measured and thoughtful discussion of why someone would confess to having raped an eighty-seven-year-old woman if he hadn't in fact done it. Most of the other Supreme Kings buffs also make the daily pilgrimage to the cafeteria, where they commingle with the buffs who keep office hours upstairs. If the state courthouse had its own cafeteria, this trip wouldn't be necessary. Some of the Supreme Kings buffs seem ill at ease in the federal building. It strikes them as uncomfortably clean, too austere. Confusing abstract art hangs in the lobby. The restrooms have soap but no graffiti. When destiny guides certain buffs to the

upper floors of the federal building, they tend to sniff the air
suspiciously.

Shine's patience with the spectacle of the Jomo Davis trial began
to diminish as his midday hunger pangs grew. He mentioned this
to Silverman, who, being toothless for the day, declined a luncheon
invitation. Shine and Friedman and I left Supreme Kings together
and walked across Cadman Plaza East. When we reached the corner
of Tillary Street, we encountered a friend of Shine's—a federal-
court buff called Bill Abramson.

"What's new?" Shine asked.

"Oh, a very good trial with Judge Nickerson," Abramson said.
"Drugs."

"Not again," Shine said.

"No, this is a nice one," Abramson said. "This morning, they
had a witness—she's a concert pianist, she looks like a charwoman,
but she's an anthropologist or something, she ran a travel agency,
and I don't know what else. It's cocaine. There's money all over
the place. It's conspiracy the government's trying to prove. Oh,
they had about a hundred defendants, but a lot of them copped
pleas already. Come up and watch."

Abramson walked off in a different direction, and we entered
the federal building. As we went down a flight of stairs to the
cafeteria, Shine said, "We should go see that one, Leo. I think
they'll convict this woman."

"Why?"

"Normally, conspiracy's a tough charge to prove," Shine said.
"But if she's a pianist, it's easy—'acting in concert.' "

Friedman said, "Ben. Please."

"Hey, I write 'em, kid. You want more? I got more."

"No. One a day is enough."

While Friedman and I waited in line to buy sandwiches, Shine
found an empty table. When we had paid for our food, we saw him
at the opposite end of the room, waving with both hands, like a
signal corpsman coaxing in a distressed cargo plane. Bringing lunch
in a brown paper bag means that Shine gains a makeshift note pad
and a saving for the day of about three dollars. Though he has
nothing against a bargain, this predilection is more of a habit than

a necessity. He carries a typewritten list of his stocks and bonds in a clear-plastic envelope, which he keeps in his coat pocket, filed away with his grocery-discount coupons and the newspaper clippings from recent memorable trials. From time to time, he removes the list and reviews his portfolio, just to reassure himself. There is a brokerage house on Montague Street, not far from the courthouse, and he sometimes drops in to check the latest stock-market quotations. Shine has prudently diversified his holdings. Therefore, he didn't turn glum or get agitated when the accident occurred at the Three Mile Island nuclear power plant in 1979, even though he then held quite a few shares of General Public Utilities, the company that owns the plant. After almost four hundred murder trials, it would probably take a fully realized apocalypse —something on the order of the death of his automobile—to reduce Shine to grief. He drives a 1962 Mercury Meteor with eighty-five thousand miles on the odometer. Often, on Sundays, Shine and his wife take a pleasure trip along the Brooklyn shore. They park the Mercury in a convenient spot, walk a bit, rest a while, and then drive home. Shine is a skillful and dependable driver. Just that morning, he had awakened at four-thirty to drive to Kennedy Airport to pick up a niece who was flying in from Israel to visit her parents, in Flatbush.

"My wife's one of ten children, and I'm one of nine; I have twenty-seven nieces and nephews," Shine said, referring to his predawn excursion. "One's a physicist, another's a psychiatrist, there's a rabbi, lawyers on both sides, one nephew works for IBM, another's an engineer who does calculations for rockets to the moon. I have one son, Lester, who lives on Long Island, in Ronkonkoma. He works for an electronics firm. My granddaughter Rhonda just graduated college and my granddaughter Caryn's in Hollywood, being an actress. Do my relatives know that I watch these trials every day? They know. I don't hide anything from them."

I asked Shine whether he had ever considered a career as a lawyer.

"It seems like an awful lot of work to me," he said. "I never gave it much thought. It wasn't practical, because you had to pay to work as a law clerk. Not like these young lawyers today. I know they make pretty nice salaries. I was born on Rutgers Street, on the lower East Side, and we moved to Brooklyn when I was still an infant. I was the seventh of the nine children. My father had a clothing company, wholesale and retail, at East Broadway and Market Street, near Chinatown. The name of it was Strong Built. I worked there with him for quite a few years, until he moved to Israel. He moved there during the Depression, before the war, when it was still Palestine. During the Second World War, the government made me a uniform inspector for the Department of the Navy. I wanted to see combat, but I was too valuable as a uniform inspector. Yeah. They rated my work 'E' for excellent. When my father left for Israel, he gave the business to his sons. But, being there were five of us, I decided to go out on my own. I wanted to struggle all by myself. Yeah. When I still worked for my father, I'd go by the courthouse on Madison Street now and then to watch trials, but I didn't have that much time to do it. After the war, I opened my own place, Bentley Men's Shop, on West Twenty-third, near the Flatiron Building. How did I get the name Bentley? It was very simple. I took 'Ben' and 'Tillie' and put them together. Yeah. One day an immigrant came to me and said, 'You want to buy a lot of bow ties at a very low price?' I thought the price was good, so I bought. I bought so low I resold them both wholesale and retail. I had a haberdashery at street level and the wholesale business upstairs. Eventually, I went on the road with the bow ties—made it strictly wholesale. I went everywhere. I even went down in a coal mine—one hot summer day in Dickson City, Pennsylvania. I thought *my* business was bad, but you should try a coal mine sometime. When the bow-tie business tapered off, I went to long neckties. Then that tapered off, and I decided to retire. This was about twelve years ago, when a lot of these guys started with the open collars and no ties. Yeah. So I retired. I needed something else to do, so I started coming here every day to watch the trials. It's different from bow ties."

Shine's autobiographical discourse was interrupted by Charlie and Jean Rader, who stopped by to say hello. They are the only brother-sister buff team in Brooklyn. Jean, the elder, wears harlequin-framed tinted eyeglasses and warm clothing in every season and has the air of a woman of leisure on a cool day in Miami Beach. For Charlie, being a buff is like being on a permanent busman's holiday. In 1963, he retired from the New York Police Department, where he had risen to the rank of detective, second grade, during a career that lasted thirty-one years. All that time spent in the company of lawbreakers had a peculiar effect on Charlie's interest in crime. As a courtroom bystander, he prefers not to get involved with anything really heinous. Instead, he and his sister spend most of their time on the third floor at Supreme Kings. This is where the big-money civil cases—often involving complaints of medical malpractice—go to trial.

"We've just been on three," Charlie told Shine and Friedman. "Malpractice. Paralyzed from the neck down. Two point seven million the jury awarded this young fellow. I'm telling you, they brought him into the courtroom on a stretcher and it was *very effective*. Twenty-nine years old. His wife divorced him after what happened to him. Two point seven million. There's more where that came from. You should come watch."

"Maybe we will," Shine said, and the Raders soon departed. When Friedman had finished his cigar, we rose and carried our plastic trays toward the cafeteria exit. There was a small window near the door, where we stacked the trays and silverware on an idle conveyor belt.

"Someday I'll take you to a place where judges eat lunch," Shine said, rubbing his palms together. "I have a cousin—my cousin Paul Widlitz—who's an administrative judge in Mineola, Long Island. I went to see my cousin Paul one day. I didn't tell him I was coming. I just walked into the courtroom while he was holding a divorce hearing. It was two deaf people—no, wait a minute, I'm mixing up. That was another time, in Judge DiGiovanna's courtroom, in Brooklyn. That was a case with two deaf people who wanted a divorce and they spent the whole time arguing in sign language. Afterward, I told Judge DiGiovanna, I said, 'You know why those two people are getting a divorce, Your Honor? They can't communicate with each other.' "

Friedman's face took on a pained expression. "Ben, I told you: one a day is enough."

We rode an elevator from the basement to street level—a silent ride—and when we hit the sidewalk Shine resumed talking. "Yeah, no, but by my cousin Paul, the judge, that was just a straight divorce. He saw me come in and he stopped the proceedings immediately and gave me a tour of the premises. Oh, that was a nice setup. A beautiful library, a place to eat, with the stoves and the Frigidaires. I told my cousin, 'Hey, Paul, you've got a real racket here.' It's nice to see how the other half lives."

"I don't hold with these buffs and judges being on a first-name basis," Friedman said. "For instance, I know that Judge Mishler, the federal judge, hardly ever goes downstairs to eat in the cafeteria."

"You're right," Shine said. "And Judge Barshay, at State Supreme—he's died, but he used to have a Frigidaire in his chambers, and he took lunch there."

Friedman lowered his voice and said, "I heard he kept it *very* well stocked with cream cheese and gefilte fish."

There is a row of wood-and-iron benches in the shade beneath the tall plane trees that line Cadman Plaza. Louis Entman, the Landlord, sat alone now on one of the benches. It was almost two o'clock—the hour when most trials are scheduled to resume after the lunch recess. A few yards ahead, Kissinger, the Grocery Man, and Charlie and Jean Rader were walking slowly toward Supreme Kings. When the Landlord noticed Shine and Friedman approaching, he called out, "You see Charlie Rader?"

"Yeah," Shine said. "Two point seven million dollars. That's hard work."

"Two point seven million," the Landlord repeated. "If I had that much money, I would have ordered the soup today."

"Where are you going now?" Shine asked.

"I sent the Grocery Man and Kissinger up to Davis," the Landlord said. "We're thinking of splitting up the business. I might end up there or I might go to Judge Lombardo. I hear he's supposed to have a new homicide. Where are you going?"

Shine looked up at the sky. It was cloudless, faintly breezy, an unspoilable afternoon. "There's a lot of possibilities," he said. "There's drugs at federal court. Charlie's got the malpractice. We saw some of Davis this morning. You say there's a murder at Lombardo. And that kidnapping down the hall from Lentol. That's it—Lentol. I'm going to Lentol. With those brothers. Aviles. Maybe that lawyer Kranz got his briefcase opened by now. I think I'll head back to Lentol. I want to see what's doing."

1 9 8 0

Professional
Doppelgänger

Some people who live and work in Los Angeles have the impression
that New York City is a franchise owned and operated by a hyperactive and highly intelligent man named Sam Cohn. These people run the movie studios. They spend their days deciding which
motion pictures will be made—and more often, of course, which
ones won't be made. Reflecting upon Sam Cohn, one studio president said not long ago, "I think he's the Mayor of New York."
Most days, the telephones in Cohn's offices, on West Fifty-seventh
Street, ring about two hundred times. The people who live and
work in Los Angeles frequently call to say that they will be in town
next Monday or Wednesday. They definitely want to get together
with Cohn for lunch or dinner. Cohn maintains steady habits. Lunch
means the Russian Tea Room—for him, a brief stroll west on Fifty-
seventh Street. Dinner usually means Wally's, a steak house eight
blocks south and one avenue west of the Tea Room. Cohn does
not arrive for these appointments with a police escort, nor does he
make occasional trips to Rego Park or Sheepshead Bay to take the
pulse of the voters. In truth, he is not the Mayor of New York. He
confines most of his activities to a fraction of midtown Manhattan.
According to a certain view of reality, however—say, the trans-
continental view from the Warner Brothers lot in Burbank—his
seigniory is vast. Cohn seems ubiquitous. He inspires hyperbole,
deep faith, and extravagant investments of other people's money.
   Cohn is a motion-picture and theatrical talent agent. Many people who regularly do business with him, as well as many people
who wish that they regularly did business with him, contend that

he is the most effective agent in circulation. During the past few years, former agents have presided over virtually all the large motion-picture companies. These executives lead dynamic lives; they come and go. Cohn has stayed put. Several times, he has received lucrative offers to try to run a studio. He has declined these tempting opportunities. He prefers to try to manipulate Warner Brothers, Paramount, Universal, Columbia Pictures, Metro-Goldwyn-Mayer, Twentieth Century-Fox, and all their brethren from three thousand miles away. Besides, if his office were on Sunset Boulevard rather than on Fifty-seventh Street it would make for a long commute to Broadway, which also falls within Cohn's sphere of influence. At International Creative Management, the agency where he works, his title is "head of the New York motion-picture department." An agent from the William Morris office, ICM's chief competitor, was feeling expansive recently and said, "Sam Cohn is the single most important force in the motion-picture business in New York. What he is doing now has as much to do with how movies are made—is as significant—as the role the studio pioneers played in the early days." The woman who made this remark was born after *Gunga Din* and *The Wizard of Oz* were released and has therefore never had dealings with the likes of Louis B. Mayer and Darryl Zanuck and Irving Thalberg. Nevertheless, she has had dealings with Cohn, and she speaks with conviction. Another woman, a movie producer, has said, "You simply aren't in the movie business in New York if you don't have a working relationship with Sam Cohn." A friendly rival agent said not long ago, "When in doubt, assume that Sam Cohn's involved somehow." Encomiums such as these are always delivered in grave tones.

By nature, Cohn is diffident and modest—not necessarily useful traits in his chosen profession. To compensate, he has developed an orally aggressive manner—a confident staccato, as unstoppable as a bunch of marbles rolling down a hill—that could easily be mistaken for unrestrained egotism. His conversational style is as crisp and breezy as a morning d.j.'s. He laughs a lot—a popping laugh that sounds like a can of beer being opened, followed by a wheeze. Transacting business, Cohn proceeds forcefully. He charms.

He needles. He behaves in a preemptory and seemingly rude fashion. His charm can be exasperating. His rudeness can beguile. Robert Montgomery, the head of the entertainment department of the law firm Paul, Weiss, Rifkind, Wharton & Garrison, said recently about Cohn, "Where he's a great agent is in his ability to know the client's needs. He senses what the creative people in the business want, and he serves them brilliantly. I think he's adorable, and I also think that he's a monster to do business with—especially when he's on your side. When you're on opposite sides, it's not so bad, because he's not the sort of agent who sets out to exact onerous terms in a deal. It's just the way he acts. He views the lawyer simply as a functionary. He's unbelievably cavalier. He tries to hector you into submission. I'm very fond of him. And I'm just delighted, whenever a Sam Cohn deal turns up in this office, if I can somehow avoid getting involved."

Cohn can be trusted to try to dominate any set of circumstances, business or nonbusiness, regardless of how many other parties are involved. Several years ago, when a smoky fire broke out in the offices of ICM, Cohn took charge and herded forty of his co-workers into a glass-walled office, where they spent two panic-stricken hours before being rescued. Later, the survivors—everyone survived—presented him with a fireman's helmet. In the summers, on eastern Long Island, Cohn plays in a regular Sunday softball game. The other participants implicitly acknowledge that they are members of "Sam's team." They indulge him in his insistence upon pitching every game as well as his tendency to castigate anyone who is thoughtless enough to commit a fielding error. Apparently, Cohn owns the softball. His etiquette on the tennis court—he plays doubles every weekend, year round—approximates his demeanor on the softball diamond. Frequently, when Cohn attends a business meeting in someone else's office, it will at some point occur to everyone he is conferring with that he has appropriated the host's chair and has his feet propped on the desk. It is said that Bernard Jacobs, the president of the Shubert Organization, remains seated when he sees Cohn enter the room.

The reality of Cohn clashes with the stereotype of the mythical show-business agent—particularly the Hollywood variety. It is no coincidence that Cohn does not consider Los Angeles a fun place. Whenever duty forces him to spend time there, he burns a fair number of calories complaining about the programming on the local classical-music radio station or making caustic remarks about "the parking-lot attendants to the stars" or visiting friends in their carefully decorated offices at the studios and saying things like "Hmm, pretty tacky" and "I get such an *up* feeling here." According to the stereotype, most agents are named Morty or Marty and go around wearing shirts that show off their chest hair and saying things like "We'll max it at three hundred thou." A friend of Cohn's, intending to be flattering, said not long ago, "Sam's success reminds me of what Karl Marx said about John Stuart Mill—that 'his eminence is due in large part to the flatness of the terrain.' " Praising Cohn's intellect, Jeff Berg, the president of ICM, has called him "the Adlai Stevenson of the agency business."

Cohn lacks the well-tailored, lean-and-hungry style that many agents, for whatever reason, seem to cultivate. If he has cultivated anything, it is bagginess. He is five feet eight but seems shorter, because of a tendency to wear old cuffed trousers that barely reach his ankles. Cohn also likes to wear white wool socks with what were authentic Gucci loafers until he took a razor blade and removed the buckles. The rest of his wardrobe is often a bit frayed. The net effect could be called preppie dishabille. He frequently wears sweaters—Shetland and cashmere crew necks and V necks, usually thinning at the elbows—along with vintage button-down cotton Brooks Brothers shirts or polo shirts. In cold weather, he often puts on a tan corduroy jacket. Striding into the bitter winds, with his hands dug deep in the pockets of this jacket, he strongly resembles a baseball manager on his way out to settle the pitcher down. Physically, he is an odd combination. One often hears Cohn described as "a fat fellow," but the characterization is inaccurate. Rather, he is an almost spindly man who for the time being, out of a healthy affection for rich food and drink, elects to wear a larger person's midriff. His face has a squarish cast, and it also has dimples. There is a considerable gap between his front teeth. He has lank auburn hair that has now mostly gone gray. Despite this, he does not look his age, which is fifty-two. He has a thin,

crinkled mouth, a pink complexion, and blue eyes that can't see
very far. Behind his eyeglasses—thick lenses in translucent flesh-
toned frames—he squints. The squint gives him a look that is a
mixture of curiosity and amusement. If Cohn were less nearsighted,
he could see the same expression on the faces of many people who
know him well and are anticipating his next move.

Cohn's world is remarkably snug. Its dynamics are reminiscent
of animated film strips for beginning chemistry students—the ones
that show bright-colored gas molecules bouncing off the narrow
walls of a stoppered flask, frequently colliding and frequently bond-
ing. This is because Cohn seems to view the making of a movie
or the staging of a play as a potentially cooperative venture that
stands to benefit the maximum number of his clients. He represents
dozens of directors, writers, and actors who, in various permuta-
tions, often work on the same productions—and thereby constantly
exposes himself to the inference that he represents potentially
conflicting interests. He is often referred to as a "creative agent."
It is hard to know whether this is a euphemism or means something
usefully specific. It is hard to know, in other words, how to describe
just what a Sam Cohn does. Sue Mengers, a well-known agent who
spent much of her career at ICM in Los Angeles, has addressed
herself to the enigma of Cohn by describing him as an "agent
auteur." She means this as a compliment.

Moviemaking, whether high art or low commerce, is supposed
to be a collaborative enterprise. Across the years, the creative role
of the studio in this collaboration has steadily dwindled. Instead
of keeping the same actors, writers, directors, and producers on
the payroll for long periods of time—instead of operating a huge
repertory company—the studios have largely ceased to function
as motion-picture manufacturers. They have become, for the most
part, oligopolistic jobbers with polished marketing skills and long
lines of credit. They buy services and goods from independent
contractors and resell the finished goods to the ticket buyers. Meanwhile, vacuums have been created, hierarchies of authority have
been reordered. Different dates and events are cited as marking
the so-called demise of the studio system and the dawn of the age
of the independent motion-picture producer. For the sake of ar-

gument, let us say that it happened within the past thirty years. Subsequently, the sources of financing for films have become quite disparate, and independent producers have had to look to lawyers and agents to negotiate their deals for them. The processes of financing films and making films have diverged. This development has led to a considerable growth in the influence of certain agents and entertainment lawyers. Cohn, who happens to be a lawyer by training as well as an agent, has a reputation for becoming inordinately involved in the creative decision-making process. Along the way, he has been called a packager—a term that he resents. Although he is acknowledged to have high standards and good taste, he does not enjoy being called a packager, because, like the word "agent," the word "packager" carries some negative connotations.

"Sam Cohn's a very shrewd packager," a man named Mark Rosenberg has said. One morning not long ago, Rosenberg, trying to illustrate what he meant, began rearranging some objects that were cluttering the desk in his office, at Warner Brothers, in Burbank, California. It was a large antique pine desk. Rosenberg is a production vice-president. "Sam's not a hard-sell artist," he said. "He will find a buyer for what he wants to sell, and he'll find a market for it. But he's not a traveling salesman. I mean, he's not a hype artist. Now, I am aware of motion pictures in which Sam has had clients, and there might be people involved whom Sam does not love, and he might drop very interesting hints that if So-and-So would go home he could find someone else to fill that slot. But he never says that sort of thing outright. Agenting is not necessarily what it appears to be."

As Rosenberg spoke, he began to move several objects on his desk—a couple of matchboxes, a copy of *Publishers Weekly*, a pack of Marlboro cigarettes, a paperweight, a large pair of scissors. His intention was for each object to represent a different element in a hypothetical movie package—a package of Cohn's clients—that his imagination was at that moment assembling. "Now, let's say I'm your agent and I call you up and I say, 'O.K., there are two offers this morning. The first one doesn't have a title yet, but it's being directed by Bob Fosse, and Steve Tesich is writing the screenplay, and Meryl Streep and Woody Allen are going to star in it. Your pay is twenty thousand. And the second offer is produced by Sandy Howard and it's called *Meteor*. You're going to be the star and your pay will be a hundred thousand.' I suppose that's not a fair example, because you obviously take the twenty thousand. But it's one example that comes up often in an agent's life. The agent has a fiduciary responsibility to the client. It can become very muddy water. Sam is best at steering through that muddy water. Or he'll call up the studio and say that *he* has an element of a package—a package that's already largely intact. It's a Bob Fosse film with a screenplay by Tesich, and Sam wants it to star Leonard Sternfeld, whom he's just seen do something by Molière off-Broadway. The studio will say, 'You're out of your mind. We're paying a million to Fosse and half a million to Tesich, and we think Leonard Sternfeld's a lox.' "

At this point, Rosenberg rose from his chair in a manner that, for a moment, seemed personally threatening. However, he simply wanted to offer a creditable imitation of Cohn. "So," he continued, "the studio says Leonard Sternfeld's a lox. And Sam comes back, 'Well, *Fosse* thinks Leonard Sternfeld's *brilliant!*' And that's supposed to settle the matter." Rosenberg had the objects on his desk gathered in an appealing geometry, and now he lifted a sharp brass letter opener with his right hand. "So there's the package, and almost every other agent in the business would concede defeat and walk away. But here comes Sam, champion of Leonard Sternfeld"—he brought the letter opener down forcefully in the midst of the tableau, damaging the desk—"and Sam Cohn does not walk away!"

Eye-watering loyalty is a Cohn specialty. His attitude toward his clients has been described as being, variously, maternal, paternal, fraternal, godfatherly, avuncular, and mother-in-law-like —all of which characterizations assume, incorrectly, a margin of detachment and distance between Cohn and the client. More than merely representing a client as agent, he has a propensity—in public, at least—to merge with the client. He is a perfect specimen of the professional doppelgänger. One of my earliest encounters with Cohn took place just after I attended a preview of a film called

Eyewitness. The screening was held at Magno, a small, comfortably furnished private theater in the M-G-M Building, at Fifty-fifth Street and Sixth Avenue. Magno was rented for the evening, because *Eyewitness* was not an M-G-M picture. It was a Twentieth Century-Fox release, which, when it finally opened, a few months later, started off looking commercially promising but turned out to be a modest money loser. Not that that, Cohn would hasten to point out, reflects upon the film's intrinsic merits. At any rate, *Eyewitness* was an in-between movie. It had some thrills, some fine acting, and some funny lines at expected and unexpected moments. It also had an excess of plot. I came out of the screening room thinking that I had just sat through several movies (a murder mystery, an espionage story, a couple of family dramas, a romantic tale, a black comedy), a pilot for a weekly detective series, and a soap opera. There in the lobby, wearing his corduroy jacket, stood Cohn. "What'd you think?" he asked. His tone was hushed, as if he were a member of the immediate family asking the surgeon whether the patient would ever regain motor control.

Eyewitness was directed by Peter Yates and written by Steve Tesich. It starred Sigourney Weaver and William Hurt, and co-starred Christopher Plummer and Irene Worth. Of that group, only Hurt was not represented by Cohn. The film was edited by Cynthia Scheider, a client who is married to the actor Roy Scheider, another client. Being aware of this shrewd packaging, I felt distinctly put on the spot. I mumbled something about how I thought *Eyewitness* was pretty good, I nodded, and I did my best to put this man at ease while remaining noncommittal. Then I mentioned some minor things that hadn't seemed to work—bits of dialogue that didn't ring true, a twist of plot that lacked clarity. Suddenly, I got the feeling that my opinion no longer mattered, and I was correct. Cohn didn't respond to anything I had said. His face went blank, and in an instant he was off talking to someone else. I felt that I had just disappeared.

More often than his competitors, Cohn manages to become involved with films and plays that actually get produced. During 1981, ten

feature films and nine Broadway or off-Broadway plays opened that
were written, directed, or produced by one of his clients or in
which a Cohn client had a major acting role. The films were *Prince
of the City* (directed by Sidney Lumet, an ICM client, who co-wrote
the screenplay with Cohn's client Jay Presson Allen, who was also
the executive producer); *True Confessions* (directed by Ulu Grosbard); *The French Lieutenant's Woman* (starring Meryl Streep);
Atlantic City (directed by Louis Malle, who is now a client, and
written by John Guare); *Arthur* (starring Liza Minnelli, a client of
Cohn's, and Dudley Moore, an ICM client, with Charles Joffe as
executive producer); *Four Friends* (written by Steven Tesich, directed and co-produced by Arthur Penn, with Julia Miles and
Michael Tolan as executive producers, and featuring Reed Birney,
who has since become a client); *Ragtime* (novel and first version
of screenplay by E. L. Doctorow); *Superman II* (written by, among
others, Leslie and David Newman); *Paternity* (featuring Paul Dooley);
Student Bodies (produced by Allen Smithee, the pseudonym of a
client); and *Eyewitness* (practically everyone but the teamsters who
drove the equipment trucks). Not all these movies did great box
office. Some—*Arthur, Superman II*—made big money; *The French
Lieutenant's Woman* performed well but not spectacularly; *Prince
of the City, True Confessions*, and *Ragtime* did so-so; *Eyewitness*
drifted off the Top Fifty Grossers chart and into oblivion. More
than a dozen other films involving Cohn clients—among them
*Annie; Deathtrap; The World According to Garp; Sophie's Choice;
Still of the Night; Silkwood; Barbarosa; Personal Best*; two untitled
Woody Allen movies; *The Sting: Part II*; and *Superman III*—were
in preparation or in production. The extent of Cohn's involvement
in any given project is hard to quantify. It varies from case to case,
depending on the client. He is more wrapped up in the careers of
certain clients—Doctorow, Tesich, Mike Nichols, Meryl Streep,
Robert Benton, Sigourney Weaver—than others. The others accommodate themselves to this fact.

The Cohn-connected plays that opened within the last year or
so were *The Floating Lightbulb* (written by Woody Allen, directed
by Ulu Grosbard); *Alice in Concert* (written by Elizabeth Swados,
starring Meryl Streep); *Woman of the Year* (with music and lyrics

by John Kander and Fred Ebb); *The Amazin' Casey Stengel* (starring Paul Dooley); *Beyond Therapy* (starring Sigourney Weaver); *It Had to Be You* (written by and starring Joe Bologna and Renée Taylor); *Lunch Hour* (directed by Mike Nichols); *Grown Ups* (co-produced by Nichols, starring Bob Dishy); and *Foxfire* (co-written by Hume Cronyn, and just staged at the Guthrie Theatre, in Minneapolis). *One Night Stand*, a new musical by Herb Gardner, was previewed for a week at the Nederlander Theater, but it never officially opened. Three earlier plays were having long runs on Broadway: *Annie* (produced by, among others, Mike Nichols and Lewis Allen, directed by Martin Charnin); *Dancin'* (a Bob Fosse enterprise, produced by Jules Fisher); and *Amadeus* (directed by Peter Hall). In addition to representing all these clients as individuals, Cohn made an interesting arrangement with a new theatrical division of Paramount Pictures. Cohn thus advises Paramount on its theatrical investments and productions, and ICM takes an agent's commission on any profits. Paramount thereby becomes a client to whom Cohn could conceivably sell the goods and services of another client. Never mind appearances. Much of the time, Cohn seems to work in a hall of mirrors; his range is wide and cozy, vast and narrowly circumscribed.

Many agents can book an actor into a preëxisting entity or sell a screenplay. What Cohn does is secure commitments to have a film made or a play staged, and he does so more expeditiously than the average agent. "Can Sam Cohn sell air?" I once heard a motion-picture executive ask rhetorically, as if to express his pride that Cohn had never sold him any. If the germ of a movie—an idea, a rough plot, a not-yet-published novel—appeals to Cohn, he will line up financing for the writing of a screenplay; as the screenplay evolves through several drafts, he will arrange for a director, usually a client, to be hired to supervise its development; he will (perhaps scribbling on a napkin during lunch) project a budget for the finished movie; he will urge the studio to decide quickly whether to go ahead and make the movie; and he will play an integral part in influencing that decision. If the studio ultimately turns him down, he will seek a financial commitment from another studio or production company (this is the most difficult part, a step

that can take months or years or, in some cases, an afternoon);
once this occurs, he and the studio will agree on a date to start
filming. In general, he will risk more of his personal credit than
an agent should have to. Along the way, if the movie happens to
be made in New York City—and an unusually large number of
the movies that Cohn has a hand in are made in New York—he
will watch some of the shooting. As things proceed, he will call
up the director to remind him that there is a budget and that the
studio wants him to respect it. When he finishes that telephone
conversation, he will call the head of the studio to urge forbearance,
explaining why the budget is less important than the aesthetic effect
that the director is seeking. (There will be several such conversations, some of them heated.) He will monitor the weather reports,
hire the publicity people, tell everyone he bumps into at the Russian Tea Room that the picture is going to be either fabulous or
terrific. When the preliminary editing has been completed, he will
watch a rough cut of the film, recommend changes, watch the next
cut, attend previews, detain and interrogate members of the preview
audience as they are leaving the screening room, remind the studio
that the director hasn't received the latest installment of his pay,
and interject himself into the studio's planning discussions for
distribution of the film. If it's a project to which he feels especially
committed, and if, as in the case of *All That Jazz*, it's a movie to
which he must devote two or three years before he finds a studio
that is willing to make it, he may see a dozen more versions of the
film before it is ready to be released. Depending on the circumstances, he may lose his composure and involve himself unnec-
essarily in efforts to influence the movie's Motion Picture Association
of America rating. When the movie opens, he will read every review
and check the box-office figures, theater by theater, in the big
cities. If he happens to be in California at the right time, he may
make an appearance in the marketing department of the studio to
say a word or a thousand about the graphics of the newspaper-
advertising campaign. If the project in question is a stage play
rather than a motion picture, he will proceed through the theatrical
parallel of each of these steps. In many instances, he will invest
some of his personal funds in the play's production. Then, either

before or after the play opens, he will negotiate the sale of the movie rights.

To try to understand the making of any of Cohn's deals requires grappling at some point with the ineffable. Apart from the question of how much the services of a given actor or director or playwright are worth, most agreements conform to certain long-standing formulas. Cohn insists that the majority of the business discussions he participates in are mundane and unstimulating. Even if that is true, there are worthy exceptions. Rare among agents, Cohn can decipher a profit-and-loss statement. He understands gross receipts and net profits and escalator clauses the way most people understand sales tax. Above all, he senses when the standard terms and conditions don't apply.

"I find Sam Cohn to be refreshingly vague," the president of a large motion-picture company has said, describing what it is like to negotiate with Cohn. "What do I mean by 'vague'? It's all *mushy*. A deal with Sam seems mushy." Because the formality of committing an agreement to paper takes time, Cohn does not usually address himself to the finer points of contract law. Obviously, where expediency counts, he regards mushiness and vagueness as virtues. Quite often, the final employment contracts for a motion picture are not drafted and signed until after filming has been completed. Not long ago, a theater director went to Cohn's office to discuss a venture—a musical comedy—with which Cohn was having a brief romance. An ICM client who was trying to produce the musical wanted Cohn and the director to meet.

"I believe in this project," Cohn said.

"I believe in it, too," the director said.

"The musical theater needs to take a new direction," Cohn said.

"I definitely agree," the director said.

"I love this play," Cohn said.

"May I ask a dumb question?" the director said.

"I don't know," Cohn answered.

"What's your role in all this?" the director asked.

"I'll manage," Cohn said, and then he paused. ". . . I'll manage to find an economically rewarding role for myself in this somewhere."

In his theatrical pursuits, Cohn frequently does business with Bernard Jacobs and Gerald Schoenfeld, the president and the chairman of the Shubert Organization. At the moment, there are three projects on Broadway and off-Broadway in which Cohn and the Shuberts—as Jacobs and Schoenfeld are commonly called—have shared interests: *Dancin'*, *Amadeus*, and *Grown Ups*. Jacobs, who has said that he would consider Cohn his peer as a negotiator "except that I like to think that I have no peers," feels reluctant to cite Cohn's specific gains at the Shubert Organization's expense.

"The problem is, if I start giving you examples where I've been had, I make myself out to be a fool," Jacobs said. "The danger with Sam is that he can put a package together in such an expensive way that it becomes impossible for anyone but his clients to make money. If you give Sam an opening, it doesn't lie there very long. Sam likes to try to make the whole greater than the sum of the parts. Take *Dancin'*. Thanks to Sam's machinations, his client, Fosse, turns out to be one of the show's producers as well as the director, author, and choreographer. The show has run now for almost four years, and, as a result of Sam's imaginative arranging of the deal, it's recouped, it's begun to make a profit, and the road company has recouped and now makes a profit, but, most significantly, it's made a ton of money for Fosse. Sam happened to be an investor in that show, but mainly there's an example of his doing much better for his client than for himself."

Jacobs's partner, Schoenfeld, restated this proposition in a poetic way: "Sam gets away with more than anybody else I know can get away with. He does more what he wants to do when he wants to do it and in the way he wants to do it than anybody I know, and gets away with it."

A few years ago, Cohn got away with arranging a meeting between the Shuberts and James Nederlander, for the purpose of deciding whether the Chicago road production of *Annie* would play in a Shubert theater or a Nederlander theater. Between them, the Shubert Organization and the Nederlander Organization control twenty-six—or approximately two-thirds—of the legitimate theaters in the

Broadway district. Around the country, the Shuberts own five more theaters, the Nederlanders eighteen. There have been times when getting James Nederlander and the Shuberts in the same room has amounted to the Broadway equivalent of peace talks at Camp David. Schoenfeld and Jacobs have never been fond of Nederlander or his partners, and the feeling is returned. Considerable intrigue went into planning the meeting. Cohn had to cajole Schoenfeld and Jacobs into gathering at Nederlander's office. This meant yielding what they regarded as a territorial prerogative. They were gratified, however, when, after about five minutes, the proceedings having become ad hominem, Nederlander stalked out. When he took his bearings and realized that he could not go home, because he was already there, he decided to reenter his office. At this point, Cohn intervened and delivered a brief sermon, at the end of which the warring parties shook hands and resolved their immediate dispute. Not that that particular peace lasted, however.

"I admire Sam for his total involvement," Schoenfeld said recently. "But I would not abdicate to substituting his judgment for ours. We do not agree that he knows our business better than we do."

"Sam likes to be a producer ex officio," Jacobs said. "And he would like to be a capitalist entrepreneur."

"Without any capital contribution of any magnitude," Schoenfeld added.

Though Jacobs and Schoenfeld consider Cohn to be a trustworthy friend, they are often a bit wary of him. In 1978, shortly after *The Gin Game* opened, to strongly positive reviews, Cohn and his client Mike Nichols, who had directed the play, invested quite a lot of their valuable energy in calling the box office at the Golden Theatre, a Shubert house, to find out how many times the phone would ring before someone answered it. This sort of behavior gets on the Shuberts' nerves. Cohn would say that he was just carrying out his fiduciary responsibility to a client.

"Sam Cohn has great taste and great passion," Michael Eisner, at the time the president of Paramount Pictures, said a while ago.

"He wasn't born joined at the hip to people like Woody Allen, Robert Benton, Mike Nichols, and the rest of his clients. I think he has elicited their confidence not because of the deals he makes but because of his understanding of and enthusiasm for what it is they're trying to express. I find him to be like a high school junior who falls in and out of love constantly—always with total passion."

Because Cohn develops so many passions, he seems able to focus on one only briefly before moving on to the next. All that concentrated passion, though, makes him extraordinarily persuasive. What also makes him persuasive is the urgent tone in his voice whenever he begins a sentence "You really should . . ." On various occasions, Cohn has convinced me that I really should read a certain screenplay by a certain client, I really should see a certain movie—not necessarily a good movie—starring a certain client, I really should take a certain shortcut while driving in Nassau County, I really should try the red-wine jello at the Russian Tea Room. An adventurer of average pliability inevitably succumbs to Cohn's earnest goading. "It is never easy to pass on Sam Cohn," a vice-president of United Artists has said—"to pass on" being Hollywoodese for "to say no to." (It is part of the lexicon that also includes "to take a meeting," "to go into turnaround," "to have a step deal," and "to give good conference call.") Occasionally, when Cohn does get passed on by a studio, he feels obliged to mention that this blunder will probably ruin the studio permanently. A week later, if he has not yet found a buyer, and if he is feeling generous—and if the studio has not yet collapsed—he will call back and offer the passer a second chance.

Robert Montgomery, the entertainment lawyer from Paul, Weiss who believes that it is easier to appear opposite Cohn in a negotiation than to be on the same side, has said, "Sam has an odd manner of speaking. He'll go on and on about an idea, a deal. He becomes very combative. He tells you why he likes something, and he'll follow you across the room making points. He says what he thinks you're going to say and then he tells you why you're mistaken. You say, 'But *I* didn't say that, Sam. *You* did.' Sometimes an evening with Sam is more than anybody can take."

Montgomery has never fully recuperated from the experience,

in 1977, of ushering the Broadway musical *Annie* to the stage. In effect, Cohn and Montgomery jointly represented Mike Nichols and Lewis Allen, who were two of the play's six coproducers. The legal agreements between the authors, the producers, the major investors, and the minor-interest owners in *Annie* were extremely intricate. For complicated reasons, it became necessary late in the proceedings to raise several hundred thousand dollars within a few days—an undertaking in which Montgomery played a crucial role. Attorneys were tripping over one another. In the center of the tumult was Cohn, a lapsed lawyer who generally regards lawyers as obstructionists. "I represent artists who get paid only when they get work—they're like migrant workers," Cohn once said, overstating the case colorfully. "And the lawyers and the business people, who draw weekly salary checks, always want to stand in the way of their getting paid. They say, 'We're worried about the force-majeure clause, and unless you can work out the typhoon contingency there's no way we can sign these contracts.' " At any rate, the money was raised, the theatrical version of *Annie* proved vastly successful, and the authors, producers, agents, and investors all became rich. Upon the subsequent sale of the motion-picture rights, they became even richer. Cohn, managing the transaction singlehanded, persuaded Columbia Pictures to pay nine and a half million dollars for the rights—a record sum. (ICM's share of this was in excess of seven hundred thousand dollars.) "We found someone with a tremendous desire to own it," Cohn said when he was asked how he manipulated the sale. Frank Price, who became the president of Columbia Pictures after the *Annie* deal was consummated, tried at one point to renegotiate the sale agreement. He was unsuccessful. "It is one of the enduring mysteries at Columbia Pictures," Price has since said. "Who made the deal to buy *Annie* for nine and a half million dollars? The answer doesn't seem to be clear."

One morning in midsummer, Cohn walked a few blocks from his apartment, on Central Park West, to an appointment at the Gulf & Western Building, on Columbus Circle. It was only ten o'clock, but the day had become uncomfortably warm. Cohn wore a light-weight yellow hopsack jacket, a yellow button-down cotton shirt, gray slacks, brown loafers, and white socks. The slacks had blue ink smudges on both calves, and the shirt was faintly coffee-stained. Cohn took an elevator to the fifth floor, to the office of Dino De Laurentiis, the movie producer. He pushed open a heavy glass door and strode through a reception area as if he were heading toward his own office. As he turned a corner, a dark-haired young woman named Mindy Alberman greeted him in a familiar way and then led him down a long corridor toward De Laurentiis's suite.

"Why aren't you out in the Hamptons?" Mindy asked Cohn.

"I have to work," he said as they passed a pair of red leather tub chairs in the corridor. "Terrible. Terrible."

"Yes," said Mindy. "It's so *hot*."

"I'm not talking about the weather," Cohn said. "I'm talking about those chairs."

When De Laurentiis saw Cohn enter the room, he rose from his chair and walked around his huge mahogany desk. All the furnishings in the suite were dark except a large conference table of light-gray marble, near the entrance. Vertical blinds made of a deep-red fabric were turned to screen the bright light from outside. As Cohn came forward, De Laurentiis met and embraced him.

"How are you, Sam?" De Laurentiis asked. His tone sounded as genuine as the Italian inflection of his voice.

"I am well, Dino," Cohn said.

The two men hugging made an interesting picture. Although they are the same height, De Laurentiis is trimmer and is in every respect Cohn's sartorial opposite. That day, he was wearing navy-blue silk pinstripe pants, a monogrammed light-blue shirt with gold cuff links, a knitted black necktie, and black shoes of soft leather. His eyeglasses had thick black frames and egg-shaped lenses.

"I have just been talking to Peter," De Laurentiis said, referring to Peter Maas, a client of Cohn's, three of whose books De Laurentiis has made into movies—*The Valachi Papers*, *Serpico*, and *King of the Gypsies*. Since the film version of *The Valachi Papers* was produced, in 1972, De Laurentiis has financed, in whole or in part, several other movies in which Cohn was an interested participant, among them *Buffalo Bill and the Indians*, *Ragtime*, and *Loon Lake*, which has not yet been produced.

That day, Cohn had a Peter Maas project that he wanted to discuss with De Laurentiis, but it was not the first item on his agenda. He took a seat in a black leather chair opposite De Laurentiis's desk and propped his right foot on the edge of the desk.

"Coffee, Sam," De Laurentiis said as Mindy Alberman appeared in the doorway. "You will have American or Italian?"

Cohn chose American coffee, and then asked, "Is Fred here? I'm going to need him to translate something."

As if on cue, Fred Sidewater, a dark-haired man as dapper as De Laurentiis, came in and sat down in a chair next to Cohn. Sidewater is executive vice-president of De Laurentiis's company. Cohn was now ready to proceed.

"Dino," Cohn said. "You remember Abscam—the scandal with the government, the representatives, the senator? The F.B.I. was involved. And they were dressing up like Arabs? And there was a fat guy named Weinberg? Mel Weinberg?"

"I remember. I know."

"And this guy Weinberg was a con man, and he was actually working for the government?" Cohn's tone was quizzical, but De Laurentiis was nodding. "Louis Malle and John Guare have been talking to John Belushi and Dan Aykroyd about it. They want to do a comedy based on this story."

"Byoo-tee-ful," said De Laurentiis. Cohn had barely had time to utter the name of his client—John Guare—and De Laurentiis seemed to be reaching for his checkbook. "Byoo-tee-ful. For me, it is enough Louis Malle and John Guare and you, Sam."

"You want to commission a script or you want to make the picture?" Cohn asked.

"For me, if is Louis Malle, it is a picture. You know, Sam, Louis Malle loves you, but he is very upset with you. He calls you. You never answer the phone calls."

"That's been worked out," Cohn said.

"If is Louis Malle, I make it," De Laurentiis repeated. "I am ready to give a commitment to Louis Malle."

"That was tough," Cohn said. Although his coffee had not yet arrived, he had, it seemed, accomplished what might have taken six months of work. He called out to De Laurentiis's secretary, "Where's the coffee, Mindy? Are you harvesting in the mountains of Colombia?"

A few moments later, as she arrived with a small tray holding two cups and saucers, Cohn launched into the next discussion. "Now, Dino. You called me about the script I sent to you—*The Pope of Greenwich Village.*"

"Who is the director?" De Laurentiis asked.

Cohn said, "Ulu Grosbard." What he meant was that he was trying to help the producers of a proposed film, based upon Vincent Patrick's novel *The Pope of Greenwich Village*, find financing, because his client Ulu Grosbard wanted to direct it. The studio that had initially developed the movie—had financed the writing of a screenplay—had lost interest, but Grosbard had not.

"We can change the director?" De Laurentiis said—a statement in the form of a question.

"You don't want to. He's a wonderful director."

"What has he done?"

Cohn recited Grosbard's accomplishments, the most recent being the film based upon the John Gregory Dunne novel *True Confessions*, which was not then in the theaters.

"It is not a good movie," De Laurentiis declared.

"It's a *wonderful* movie," Cohn countered.

"I hear it is so-so," De Laurentiis said, and he made a waving motion with the palm of his right hand. "You saw? You say it is good?"

"De Niro and Duvall," Cohn said. As he mentioned the two leading actors in *True Confessions*, traces of De Laurentiis's inflection crept into his voice.

There were a few seconds of silence, which De Laurentiis broke by saying, "I would like to know why this *Pope of Greenwich Village* will cost twelve million dollars."

"Dino, this man is the best. He won't go one cent over budget."

"What will he guarantee?"

"He'll guarantee fifty thousand dollars."

De Laurentiis laughed as if he had just heard an old joke. "Fifty thousand dollars is one minute of shooting."

As if by telepathy, the two men digressed for a while into a discussion of *Ragtime*, a De Laurentiis film that was nearing completion. The film was directed by Miloš Forman, since the original director, Robert Altman—now a former client—had been fired by De Laurentiis. But Cohn was still quite concerned about *Ragtime*, because E. L. Doctorow, a client, had written the first draft of the screenplay, adapting his own novel.

Eventually, Cohn brought the conversation back to *The Pope of Greenwich Village*, saying, "Now, what do you think about *The Pope*? Do you want to talk with the director about the budget? He's in town."

"O.K. When does he want to begin shooting?" De Laurentiis asked.

"November," Cohn said.

"Why November? With the bad weather in New York. Why no October first with the weather?"

"He could be ready by October first," Cohn said. "You know what it's about? Two guys in Little Italy—in Little Italy today. They're cousins. One is half Italian and half Irish, and the other is all Italian. They work together. One's a waiter and the other's a headwaiter."

A puzzled look crossed De Laurentiis's face. He deferred to Fred Sidewater.

"*Cameriere e capocameriere*," Sidewater explained.

"So they decide to do a robbery. They get a guy who's a safecracker in the Bronx, but he's not able to handle a big job—"

"Is a comedy, no?"

"Oh, yes," said Cohn.

After a bit more plot recitation, followed by a discussion of the pros and cons of casting certain actors in certain roles, Cohn said, "You want to meet the director? He's in town."

De Laurentiis said, "Who is the name again?"

"*Ulu Grosbard*. Ulu. U-l-u."

"O.K. I see him tomorrow." De Laurentiis consulted a calendar on his desk. Before he looked up, his eye was caught by a copy of a novel. He fingered a corner of the book and said to Cohn, "I have something to send to Sidney Lumet."

Cohn removed his foot from its perch on the edge of the desk and leaned forward and recognized the book. "You know who's very good to do that? John Avildsen."

"I am sending it to Sidney Lumet."

"John Avildsen is very good. He's not even my client."

"He is on my list," De Laurentiis said. "But he is busy making a movie in New York."

"Not anymore," Cohn said. "Sidney will read it, but I tell you, John Avildsen is good for that movie."

De Laurentiis nodded.

"Now, do you want to talk about Peter's novel?" Cohn asked.

When De Laurentiis nodded again, Cohn outlined a proposal to give De Laurentiis an option on the film rights of a novel in progress by Peter Maas. "Instead of a price, you pay him one hundred thousand for one year."

"We'll just put him on the payroll," Sidewater said. "Give him medical benefits."

"You pay him for one year against the deal," Cohn continued. "You read the book when it's finished, and you have thirty days to negotiate. We make a deal or we don't make a deal. We don't make a deal, we have ninety days to try elsewhere. We don't make a deal elsewhere, we renegotiate. We make a deal elsewhere, we come to you and for five percent over our best offer you can acquire the book back. We make a deal elsewhere, they pay you fifty thousand dollars back."

"No!" said De Laurentiis. "I get one hundred thousand back."

Cohn shook his head.

De Laurentiis said, "If you are ready to make a deal now, I buy the whole thing."

This offer Cohn ignored. He brought up the final item on his agenda, asking, "Now, Dino. Do you want to make a deal about the detective?" He was referring to a screenplay titled *Double Standard*, which was based upon the life of a former philosophy professor whose new career as a detective was originally described in a nonfiction article by Calvin Trillin. Soon after the article was published, however, Trillin heard that Cohn had flown to California, where he made a deal directly with the detective, Josiah Thompson, to develop a screenplay—an act that sent Trillin off to have a talk with his lawyer. At the moment, however, the issue was moot. *Double Standard* had reached the same status as *The Pope of Greenwich Village*—had been developed to a certain extent by a major studio and then dropped, or, as they say, "put into turnaround." It had a screenplay by Judith Ross, a client of Cohn's, and he was proposing another client, Fred Schepisi, to direct it. De Laurentiis seemed mildly interested, and asked to read the script.

Cohn recapitulated the discussion: "All right. I've got to get Ulu to come over on *Pope of Greenwich Village*. We're O.K. on Louis Malle. And we've got a deal for Peter Maas. I'm gonna go home. I will have Ulu call you. You will love him, Dino."

Now De Laurentiis looked away from Cohn, as if he had already left the room, and he said, "Sam is a good man. But he's *sprecato*—how you say?"

"Wasted," said Sidewater.

"He is *wasted* as an agent. He should be a producer. A dee-vell-oh-ping producer."

When Cohn left the Gulf & Western Building, a digital clock on a roof above Columbus Circle showed that the time was ten-forty.

Cohn sees at least a hundred movies and seventy-five plays a year. Some he sees several times. He subscribes to the New York Philharmonic, the Philadelphia Orchestra, the Mostly Mozart Festival, and the Metropolitan Opera. Nights at the opera and the concert hall have no direct connection with his professional interests. Otherwise, his business life is indistinguishable from his social life. All but about five nights a year, he eats dinner in a restaurant— if not Wally's, then Parma or Joe Allen or, perhaps, Peter Luger, in Brooklyn. Although the chefs at Wally's make a sirloin steak with peppers and onions that Cohn admires, the food is not really what attracts him to the place several nights a week. Mainly, he feels comfortable there. No waiter has ever made a wisecrack about his shiny trousers or the vintage of his sweaters. If, for whatever reason, Cohn has to stray from Wally's for a few nights, the man-

agement greets his homecoming like liberated Parisians welcoming
the Allied infantry. The show-business gentry send several dele-
gates to Wally's every night. No regular is more highly esteemed
than Cohn. A large photograph of him in black tie hangs above
the coatroom doorway. It was taken during the Tony Awards cere-
monies a few years ago. Alexander Cohen, the Tony Awards im-
presario, had asked Cohn to rise from his seat at the Shubert Theatre
and prove that he owned a suit. The photograph of Cohn—bowing
slightly, waving faintly with one hand—is in distinguished company. On the wall next to it is a large candid portrait of Pope John
Paul II and Sonny Werblin, the president of Madison Square Garden (with Terence Cardinal Cooke looking on in the background),
on the occasion of the Holy Father's S.R.O. performance in the
Garden's main arena.

As a rule, Cohn arrives home after Johnny Carson has said good
night. He reads for a couple of hours before sleeping. Recently,
Cohn has suffered a recurring nightmare. In this dream, he seems
to be the last living reader on earth. Everyone else is a writer or
a writer manqué. The genuine writers and the would-be writers are
planning novels and movie scripts, but they are hesitant. "I'd like
to write it," they say, "but will Cohn read it?" Sometimes Cohn
experiences a version of this nightmare while he is awake. A while
back, the maître d' at Wally's slipped him a screenplay.

Around nine o'clock each morning, one of Cohn's two secretaries
phones and reminds him of his schedule for the coming day. Cohn
is fanatically attentive to certain details (last night's box-office
numbers, the audience response after a sneak preview in Phoenix)
and lax about others ("Who am I having lunch with today?" "What
was the title of that script I read yesterday, the one I liked so
much?"). "I think Sam's whole approach to life is 'O.K., on to the
next thing, whatever it is,'" Mike Nichols has said. Herb Gardner,
the playwright, has described Cohn as a man "condemned to live
in the present." It is not that Cohn has a contempt for the past per
se; he simply has no use for it and doesn't want it to crowd the
moment. This is a pragmatic attitude in a business ruled by only
a very few principles, one of which is that if someone tried to take
unfair advantage of you last week, that was, after all, *last week.*

The same manipulator, calling up today, should not necessarily be condemned or ignored. He might have a worthwhile proposition. The only thing that the caller has to do is catch Cohn during an unoccupied moment. He has a reputation for being extremely dilatory about returning phone calls. As a working method, this is defter than the "Don't call us. We'll call you" approach. Cohn's motto seems more like "Go ahead. Call me. I dare you." Filed somewhere in his memory is an invisible, protean "A" list—certain clients, certain people in the theatre, certain people at certain motion-picture studios at certain times—made up of those who, if they were to call and not get through to Cohn immediately, could expect him to call back within, say, twenty-four hours. Otherwise, he has made the unrequited phone call an art. His technique is intrepid and visionary: two or three successive calls to which he fails to respond can make for personal annoyance, while six or eight can blossom into temporary insanity; however, thousands of cases of neglect, spread through the populace, make for a mystique. Cohn, ensconced in unreachability, becomes desirable. Any emotionally healthy person who genuinely wishes to speak with Cohn must be diligent and must be careful not to interpret a failure to break through as a form of personal rejection. Taking it personally is a crucial mistake. Supplicants who feel personally rejected often respond by stepping up their efforts. They call eight or ten times a day for two or three weeks. More than a few of these callers are, of course, acute masochists who, if they could ever manage to engage Cohn in conversation, should thank him for making them feel alive. Several years ago, while Mike Nichols, a member of the "A" list, was on vacation in Paris, he received an urgent call from a movie producer in California who wanted him to intercede and persuade Cohn to respond to his phone messages. One client, a woman with a sense of humor, occasionally has a quarter and a note that says "Please call me" delivered to Cohn's table at the Russian Tea Room. Some clients have found it necessary to enlist the help of Marvin Josephson, who is the chairman of Josephson International, the company that owns ICM (which makes him Cohn's employer). They complain that they can't get Cohn to return calls. Whereupon Josephson explains that he often can't get Cohn to return *his* calls. Broadminded ironists dine out on tales of how they can't get through to Cohn. A fitting inscription on his tombstone, they say, would be "Here lies Sam Cohn. He'll get back to you." One reason that Cohn doesn't return calls, naturally, is that he is so busy talking on the phone. Two secretaries screen the calls. Each secretary has a telephone console with enough buttons to handle any emergency. There is an intercom—which Cohn often doesn't use, because it's easier to shout to his secretaries—and six outside lines. An additional feature called a Telepatcher makes possible five-way conference calls. Conference calls appeal to Cohn. They satisfy his penchant for bringing together people who might not otherwise converge. "O.K., plug in Roy!" he will holler to one of the secretaries. "*Roy*? Hi, pal. Listen, you're on the phone with Bob. *Bob*? Roy has some things he wants both of us to hear. Then we'll all gossip a bit." Silence descends for a few minutes while Roy says his piece. Then Cohn responds and Bob adds his part. The ensuing gossip lasts several minutes, and when it is over, Cohn hollers, "Take down Roy!" Then he reverts to mere two-party conversation with Bob. Dozens of lucky people are plugged in and taken down for Cohn's benefit each day.

Lester Gottlieb, a veteran television producer, had an office next door to Cohn's during the late sixties, when they worked at Creative Management Associates, an agency that later merged with another to form ICM. Gottlieb believes that Cohn began to master his telephone skills while he was still an up-and-comer. "People have priorities about answering the phone," Gottlieb has said. "You're going to incur a lot of discouraged people if you don't return their calls. Sam was trying to be a virtuoso. My office was next door to his, right? I hear him. He yells, 'Lester! Lester, get in here!' I amble in slowly. He doesn't like that, the slow response. He's got his hand over the mouthpiece. He says, 'Lester, pick up Line Three.' He wants me to pick up one of the other phones there in his office. 'Who's on there?' I ask. He's waving his arms—that means it doesn't matter. I pick it up and say, 'Yeah?' A voice says, 'Where's Sammy? Who is this?' My job is to say, 'Sam had to step away for a minute.' I then realize it's Lew Grade he's talking to at the moment. This was

before he became Lord Grade. Sam has to take another call, but
he doesn't want Lew Grade to hang up. He wants to talk to them
all at once. He was working out his priorities."

Years later, Cohn honed this approach, augmenting it with a
sort of Bermuda Triangle twist. He is now capable of vanishing
without a trace in mid-conversation. This usually occurs during
a three-way call, when one of the parties concludes a lengthy
monologue by saying something like "Well, what do you think
of that, Sam?"—only to realize that Sam thinks he would rather
take an incoming call on another line and has, in fact, already
done so.

Torture by telephone is not Cohn's only unsettling habit. There
is also, for instance, his quiet campaign to deforest North America.
On the average, he reads two or three plays or screenplays a week,
and he manages to eat a bit of each one. Sometimes he does this
to a newspaper or magazine review, favorable or unfavorable, of a
client's work. He doesn't swallow much, but he chews it all thoroughly. Robert Bookman, a former ICM agent who is now an executive with ABC Motion Pictures, recalls that at their first meeting,
several years ago, Cohn ate the sports section of the *Daily News*.
Some of Cohn's friends have fanciful memories of what they have
seen him ingest. It is possible that he didn't eat an entire sports
section, or even a page—maybe just a few box scores. People have
a way of exaggerating that sort of thing. Cohn likes his paper
products refined. He often has a large wad of tissue sticking out
of his mouth, as if he had just applied first aid to a lip injury.
Tissue crumbs cling to his sweaters. A movie producer named Paul
Lazarus III recalls first meeting Cohn in the early sixties, when he
was still nominally engaged in the practice of law. "I was just out
of law school myself, and looking for a job in New York," Lazarus
has said. "I went for an interview at this firm, and Sam was a
partner there. I was introduced to him—by accident, I think. He
was obviously so different from everyone else there. First of all,
he didn't want to talk about the current status of antitrust law, he
wanted to talk about the status of the Broadway theatre. He wore
a suit but I don't think a necktie. His collar looked as if it had
been chewed. And he was eating a book of matches."

A few years ago, Cohn and Herb Gardner flew to Los Angeles to attend a wedding. It was a quick trip; they made arrangements to return to New York immediately after the reception. Cohn also arranged to rent a car in Los Angeles. When the plane landed, they proceeded to a rent-a-car counter in the terminal, where Cohn showed them his credit card, signed a rental agreement, and was given a rectangular cardboard ticket, about three inches by five, which was attached to a loop of elastic string. The layout of Los Angeles International Airport makes it necessary to ride in a tram from the terminal to the rental-car parking lot. The cardboard ticket was Cohn's claim check; it contained the license number of the car that he had rented. When he and Gardner reached the lot, they found rows of unattended automobiles. Unfortunately, Cohn could not find the claim check. All he had was a piece of elastic string with a circular shred of cardboard dangling from it. "Sam said, 'I seem to have eaten it,' " Gardner recalls. "So we did what any two sensible people would do in that situation. We both fell down on the ground laughing."

It isn't always so funny. More than once, Cohn has conducted a complex negotiation during lunch, scribbled notes and numbers on a napkin, and returned to his office and found himself at a disadvantage because, while walking along Fifty-seventh Street, he had inadvertently masticated the terms of the deal.

Agents become agents, according to convention, by submitting to corporate Darwinism. They start out in the mail room, then elbow their way out and up. Cohn skipped that part. It is not that he necessarily planned to skip it. Becoming Sam Cohn, agent sui generis, is not the sort of thing that an ambitious young man—not even Cohn—could have carefully plotted in advance. Cohn was born in 1929, in Altoona, Pennsylvania, where his paternal grandfather, Benjamin Cohn, his father, Charles, and an uncle named Sam operated a family business called the Independent Oil Company of Pennsylvania. This enterprise marketed wholesale refined-petroleum products. In the late thirties, Standard Oil of New York bought out the Cohns, in exchange for Standard Oil stock. Sam,

being a perceptive child, realized early that he was in a position
to do what he wanted to do in life without worrying a lot about
money. He also realized that he did not intend to stick around
Altoona indefinitely.

When he was fourteen, he became a boarder at the Culver
Military Academy, in Indiana. The school's credo was "Culver
educates the whole boy." The military aspects of life at Culver did
not appeal to Cohn, and he was still a private first class when he
graduated. From there, he went to Princeton, where he majored
in English and German literature.

In the fall of 1951, Cohn entered Yale Law School. He had
spent three months there, during which he never quite got around
to opening any books, when he was summoned by the Army. Certain
aptitudes began to surface. Because Cohn had been enrolled in
the Reserve Officers Training Corps at college, he was commissioned a lieutenant. He was sent to southern Japan, to an Army
base near the city of Kokura, on the island of Kyūshū. The base
was the American Graves Registration Depot for Korean War casualties. The Army's job was to support a team of civilian anthro-
pologists whose job was to identify the not easily identifiable casualties
that regularly arrived from the front. Three months of law school
somehow qualified Cohn as the legal officer. Since there wasn't
much legal work to be done, he branched out and ran the Officers'
Club. The Army had many rules concerning what should and should
not take place in an Officers' Club. There was, for instance, a rule
that American officers would eat no beef that was not American-
grown. There were prohibitions against certain forms of fun. Cohn's
failure to rise through the ranks at Culver suggested his feelings
about military regulations and the education of the whole boy. His
reading of the situation in which he found himself on the island
of Kyūshū was that there was a war on. Furthermore, the dispiriting
nature of the work in the Graves Registration Depot meant that the
patrons of the Officers' Club needed an especially nice place to
unwind. Cohn gave them slot machines and Kōbe beef. The steaks
cost a dollar, à la carte.

After two years of service to country, Cohn returned to Yale Law
School. When he graduated, in 1956, he was twenty-seven years

old and was married—the marriage did not last—and the father
of an infant son; it was time to go to work. He knew that he had
no interest in a career with a Wall Street law firm. Instead, he
took a job in the legal department of CBS. During his first year at
CBS, his job was to read the personal files of William S. Paley,
the chairman of CBS, and Frank Stanton, then its president—a
task related to a study of the networks that was being conducted
by the Federal Communications Commission. Cohn noticed that in
the Paley executive suite there were white-coated butlers, elegantly
catered meals, and few abrasions. His time there was followed by
a year in the legal department proper, where there were no butlers
and no catered meals. In the legal department, there were merely
reams of contracts to be read and drafted. Cohn did not enjoy the
work. When a chance arose for him to shift to the business-affairs
department, he took it. In effect, the move signified the end of his
legal career and the beginning of his tutelage in the art of negotiation. At that time, CBS, which had financed the Broadway version of *My Fair Lady*, had decided to buy all the subsidiary rights
to the play from Lerner and Loewe, the authors. One of the lawyers
who represented Lerner and Loewe was a man named Burton Mayer,
who took a liking to Cohn. He invited him to lunch.

"He taught me a lesson for which I've always remained grateful,"
Cohn is fond of saying. "We were having lunch, and he said to
me, 'Listen, you're doing a terrific job, but you're making a great
mistake in your life. You're overcommitted. You're working too
hard for CBS.' I'd never thought of that. He said, 'You know, I
practice law for fun. I don't have to do this. And I'll tell you how
that came about. Ever since I was a young lawyer, each day I
would come back from lunch and I would close my office door, I
would sit in my chair, and for one hour I would quietly ruminate
on one question. And the question was this: Burt, what's in it for
you?' "

Cohn left CBS in 1959 to become a television producer. For
various and complicated reasons, this venture did not turn out
well. Its low point was an encounter with Lew Wasserman, the
chairman of the Music Corporation of America—which is now
an entertainment conglomerate but was then primarily a talent

agency and television producer—in the course of which, Cohn says, Wasserman advised, "If I were you, I would find work in another industry." During Cohn's fruitless campaigns to bring to life television specials like *The Great Zoos of the World*, he had a lot of dealings with Goodson-Todman, the television-production company. In 1961, when Goodson-Todman's counsel, a member of a large law firm, died, Cohn was hired to replace him. The firm, Marshall, Bratter, Greene, Allison & Tucker, took Cohn on as an associate and quickly made him the third partner in its entertainment-law department. He spent four amorphous years there, during much of which he concentrated upon the affairs of Goodson-Todman. He was part lawyer, part TV executive. The firm also represented Herbert Siegel, who is now the chairman of Chris-Craft Industries and was then the chairman of Baldwin-Montrose, a chemical company, which was the country's largest manufacturer of the pesticide DDT. When Siegel decided to diversify and bought a small, failing talent agency called General Artists Corporation, Cohn became one of his attorneys. GAC was a so-called variety agency, which means that it was involved mainly in booking nightclub performers. It also had a small television department. During the next two years, this imbalance was reversed. At first, Cohn's responsibilities to GAC meant spending several nights a week at places like the Copacabana studying the talents of Paul Anka and Nancy Sinatra and Allan Sherman. As the agency became increasingly involved in television packaging, he diverted his energies to such creations as *Hullabaloo* and *The Hollywood Palace* and *Voyage to the Bottom of the Sea*. In 1965, Siegel sold his interest in the agency, and the company passed into the control of a group of investors that Cohn had assembled. In addition to being an investor, Cohn, along with two other people, became the management of the agency. Three years later, Cohn decided to look for new partners. GAC had very few motion-picture clients, and that circumstance led him to a merger with an agency called Creative Management Associates.

"Creative management" was certainly a phrase that could describe the two movie agents who ran CMA—David Begelman and Freddie Fields. Their clients at the time included Barbra

Streisand, Steve McQueen, Paul Newman, and Robert Redford.
Fields is now the president of the motion-picture division of Metro-
Goldwyn-Mayer—a position that Begelman recently vacated to
become the chairman and chief executive officer of United Artists, which is owned by M-G-M. Their partnership with Cohn,
of course, began years before Begelman distinguished himself as
a successful motion-picture executive and then became something of a household name. Cohn was aware that most people
in the agency business rarely mistook Begelman and Fields for
apostles. This did not dampen his interest in the merger. At the
outset, Cohn told Begelman, "Don't lie to me. You can lie to
anybody you want, but not to me, and everything will be very
pleasant." During their careers as agents, Fields and Begelman
earned reputations as "signers"—they knew how to attract the
most worthwhile clients and how to find them the most remunerative employment. A few years later, while Begelman was
president of Columbia Pictures, he suffered an atavistic lapse
and signed other people's names on the backs of three checks
totaling forty thousand dollars—a deed that temporarily dis-
graced him in certain Hollywood precincts.

The merger of GAC with CMA was completed in 1968. Within
a few months, several coinvestors in GAC, who looked upon Fields
and Begelman with alarm, had been bought out by the surviving
company. And Cohn was in the movie business to stay. Cohn
has a basically fond recollection of his partnership with Fields
and Begelman. The agency packaged several television series
(including "All in the Family" and "The Kraft Music Hall") and
several movies (including The Sting and The Towering Inferno).
Six years elapsed before Cohn engineered yet another merger.
In 1974, by which time Begelman had left the company, CMA
was bought by Marvin Josephson Associates, which owned a
company called the International Famous Agency. Out of this,
yet another entity and another well-known set of initials—International Creative Management and ICM—were born. Along
with Fields, Cohn negotiated the merger, thus creating the institution that became and remains his employer.

"I look at this chain of events now and I think, This is what I wanted to do, without really knowing it," Cohn has said. "I wasn't ready to make the merger with Marvin Josephson until it became clear to me that it was essential. Stylistically, I had a wonderful time with Begelman and Fields—particularly Freddie. As far as Freddie was concerned, if you were looking to package, say, *Hamlet* and you happened to represent Vanessa Redgrave and Jerry Lewis and a director who was available, he would try to put them all together. That's not an example of one that actually happened, but it wouldn't have been inconceivable. It was very zippy. Freddie was mercurial and wild. The corporate management of that company . . . Let's just say that the Harvard Business School would not have been impressed. The management was us—Freddie, David, and myself. We looked at the books in a quixotic fashion. One day, David would say, 'This business is doing incredibly well,' everybody would get a bonus, and we'd have great big plans. We were all in on the decisions, but David had this sort of overwhelmingly compulsive and hysterical personality, and he could wear you down. Sixty days later, there would be another meeting, he would say, 'All the signs have turned bad,' and we'd have to cut back ten percent across the board. It was like doing business by witch doctor."

Since then, Cohn has retired from trying to run an agency. When circumstances make it convenient, he will tell a caller with a complaint, "As you well know, I have no part in management. I don't even have a title. I'm just sitting here doing the best I can." Actually, Cohn sits on the board of directors of ICM's parent company, but he owns no stock. For a while, he did own thirty thousand shares. When he sold them, several years ago, he used the proceeds to buy a twenty-room Victorian house in East Hampton. He is able to provide for the upkeep of the house and still have some walking-around money left over, because ICM pays him an annual salary of three hundred and fifty thousand dollars, together with a guaranteed bonus of at least fifty thousand dollars, and also pays for his lunches, dinners, movie and theatre tickets, and taxi and limousine rides. Cohn has invested his leftover funds widely and, it seems, wisely. He is the organizer of a group that, in 1980, started a restaurant in East Hampton called The Laundry. For better or worse, The Laundry has earned a reputation as the Elaine's of the white-duck-trouser set. Its success has inspired Cohn to consider branching out. What he has in mind is a restaurant on West Fifty-seventh Street. More specifically, he has in mind a place within walking distance of his desk that would come equipped not only with a well-managed kitchen but also with two motion-picture screening rooms. The main obstacle has been the unavailability of several thousand affordable square feet. "It just so happens that there's a vitally needed service in this town waiting for someone to provide it," Cohn says. "There's no place in New York where you can go to a screening and entertain people afterward." With the exception of this privation, Cohn manages to continue to live in the manner to which he has been accustomed since childhood. Part of what motivates him is the conviction that his clients, too, are entitled to this state of grace.

One morning late last spring—a few weeks before his meeting with Dino De Laurentiis—Cohn made another trip to the screening room in the M-G-M Building, to see *Four Friends*, a motion picture that was almost seven months away from being shown to paying audiences. Afterward, he walked two and a half blocks to the Russian Tea Room, where he had lunch with the head of a large film-production company. From there, he walked to his office. About fifty telephone messages were waiting for him. Cohn had some unsolicited calls that he wanted to make. He phoned one of the executive producers of *Four Friends*, who had been unable to attend the screening, to report that he liked what he had seen. "I love it. I think it's fabulous," he said. Since this was the third rendering of *Four Friends* that Cohn had viewed, his comments were brief and specific. He cited two lines of dialogue that should come out, a camera angle that seemed wrong in one scene, two scenes whose order should be transposed, an entire scene that deserved to be cut, and a couple of moments that now made more narrative sense to him than they had at a screening two weeks earlier. "And I think Liz's contribution is enormous," he told the producer. Elizabeth Swados had composed the background music for *Four*

Friends, and Cohn had just heard her score for the first time. At that point, it went without saying that Cohn was pleased with the way Arthur Penn had directed *Four Friends*, which was based upon a screenplay by Steve Tesich. Four years had elapsed since the idea behind *Four Friends* was hatched. Cohn had been close to the project all along the way. Now that he could see *Four Friends* coming together—successfully, he believed—he felt multiply uplifted. Arthur Penn and Elizabeth Swados are clients. Not only is Tesich a client but he is also one of Cohn's closest friends. The executive producer whom Cohn had phoned was Julia Miles. She is the associate director of the American Place Theatre, where several of Tesich's plays have been produced. She is also Cohn's wife and the mother of his daughter, Marya, and two daughters from her previous marriage. This was her first effort as a motion-picture producer. Her fee and contract for the film had been negotiated by Cohn, and that made her, in a manner of speaking, a client.

When Cohn finished that call, he made half a dozen others. He spoke to Jay Presson Allen, a client, who had recently written the screenplay for the film version of the Broadway play *Deathtrap*, which was in production under the direction of Sidney Lumet. Before that, she and Lumet had collaborated on the film *Prince of the City*. Cohn took a call from Ulu Grosbard, who had recently directed a Lincoln Center production of *The Floating Lightbulb*, by Cohn's client Woody Allen. He had a phone conversation about *The World According to Garp*, the film version of which was then in production. Two of Cohn's clients were involved—Tesich, who had written the screenplay, and Robin Williams, who had the title role. He sent materials regarding a potential lawsuit to Bob Fosse. At length, he spoke with Paul Mazursky, another client, who was concerned about how a possible strike by the Directors' Guild of America would affect his plans to begin shooting *The Tempest*, a new film that was loosely based on a romantic comedy by the English playwright William Shakespeare, who was not a client. Because Cohn was running late, he let a few dozen calls go unreturned.

Downstairs, a chauffeur and a limousine had been waiting for forty-five minutes. By the time Cohn was finally ready to make his getaway, early signs of rush-hour mortis had set in on Fifty-seventh Street. The stalled traffic was not giving the driver, a young blond Scotsman, a chance to demonstrate his skills. For a few moments, Cohn had a strained look on his face, as if he were resisting an urge to take over the wheel. Trying to relax, he propped his feet on an empty jump seat. Cohn regarded his plans for the rest of the day as an attenuated form of playing hooky. When the traffic at last began to yield, the limousine headed east, and Cohn was on his way to visit the set of *Still of the Night*, a murder mystery that was being filmed at a Long Island location. Shooting on the film had been under way for nine weeks and was expected to last four more. Cohn was making an appearance on the film set because he was on friendly terms with more than a few of the principals. The producer of *Still of the Night* was Arlene Donovan, a motion-picture agent at ICM and a close friend of Cohn's. To work on *Still of the Night*, she had taken a leave of absence from the agency—an unusual arrangement that Cohn had helped to bring about. Her services as the producer of *Still of the Night* had to be paid for by United Artists, the studio that was financing the picture. Cohn had negotiated her contract. Robert Benton was the screenwriter and director of *Still of the Night*, and the two leading roles belonged to Roy Scheider and Meryl Streep—all clients. Benton's preceding effort as a screenwriter-director was *Kramer vs. Kramer*, which in 1980 was nominated for eight Academy Awards. It won five, including Best Picture. Two of the Oscars went to Benton, for direction and for adapting a screenplay from another medium—in that case, a novel by Avery Corman, a client of Arlene Donovan's. Meryl Streep won an Oscar as Best Supporting Actress. Dustin Hoffman, who is not a client, had won as Best Actor. Justin Henry, who is a client, and who had played the role of Streep and Hoffman's six-year-old son, was nominated but did not win in the Best Supporting Actor category. Losing put him in company that year with several of Cohn's other clients—Woody Allen, Peter Yates, Bob Fosse, and Roy Scheider. Woody Allen was nominated for the original screenplay of *Manhattan*, which he wrote with Marshall Brickman, who at the time was not a client but has subsequently become one. Scheider was nominated as Best Actor for his portrayal of a Bob Fosse-like character in Fosse's cinematic autobiography, *All That Jazz*. That film won four Oscars—for editing, costume design, art direction, and musical adaptation—but Fosse lost the screenwriting and direction awards to Tesich and Benton. Yates was nominated for directing *Breaking Away*, but, like Fosse, he lost out to Benton. Tesich did win for writing the original screenplay of *Breaking Away*. His acceptance speech was a coast-to-coast tribute to the wisdom and magic of Sam Cohn. So were both of Benton's speeches.

The *Still of the Night* location was a summer home near Glen Cove, on the North Shore of Long Island—a slice of suburbia that has been zoned for residential fiefs. According to the script, the house belonged to the mother of the character being played by Meryl Streep. It was a farmhouse with an exterior of red brick and weathered shingles. After a forty-five-minute ride, the limousine arrived at the house. Cohn got out and walked to the end of a paved road and onto a dirt path, moving from sunlight into shade. As the path widened, a swimming pool and a spacious lawn occupied by several pieces of sculpture became visible. It narrowed again as it passed through a cluster of rhododendrons and magnolias. A patio behind the house had been roped off to discourage the movie folk from trespassing. Arlene Donovan, a slightly built, friendly woman with curly blond hair, was standing near the patio. She greeted Cohn and led him along a flagstone path, past a guesthouse, and into a garage. A telephone had been installed in the garage. Meryl Streep was talking on the phone. She smiled and waved at Cohn. Her long blond hair was pinned atop her head, and she wore a terry-cloth dressing gown. Cohn and Arlene Donovan went on through the garage and into the house. Before the moviemakers had descended, a good deal of furniture and art had been removed from the premises. Still, quite a bit remained, including a Matisse ink drawing of the lady of the house. An oil portrait of her—a handsome dark-haired woman—hung in a small sitting room. The crew was setting up a shot there. The room had rough pine walls and low beams. Even without the crowd that was gathering

there—camera operators, makeup and wardrobe people, a script
supervisor, lighting technicians, grips and gofers and assorted
others—the room would have made most people claustrophobic.
Because the day was hot and humid, it seemed especially uncomfortable. On the wall opposite the painting of the dark-haired
woman was a contemporary-looking portrait of a sharp-featured
bald man with a dark mustache. This turned out to be a small
conceit in the spirit of the enterprise. It was a painting executed
by Robert Benton's wife, Sally, of Nestor Almendros, the film's
cinematographer.

Two scenes still had to be filmed that day—a brief interior
scene with dialogue, between Scheider and Streep, and an exterior shot of Scheider driving a car (Benton's maroon Volvo se-
dan) down a long driveway. In all, an hour and a half of work
remained. One reason I made this excursion with Cohn was a
vague sense that subtleties and intangibles in his ways of doing
business would be revealed. This turned out to be a naïve ex-
pectation. What was going on that spring day on Long Island
was filmmaking—a distant remove from Cohn's specialty, which
is seeing to it that movies somehow get made, plays somehow
get produced, tickets get bought, people get entertained. One
suggestion did pop into Cohn's mind, and he mentioned it several times. He had thought of the appropriate score for *Still
of the Night*. ("Berlioz. Do you know Berlioz? 'Harold in Italy.'
You know the viola theme? Fabulous. Very romantic.") Otherwise, *Still of the Night* was running ahead of schedule and under
budget and no one was chronically misbehaving. When Cohn
had been on the set for half an hour, it became clear that there
was really nothing for him to do. In the sitting room, the first
take of the interior scene was being shot. Outside, Cohn stood
alone on a driveway, near the maroon Volvo. He wore a white
V-neck sweater and a blue button-down oxford-cloth shirt, black
loafers with white socks, and a pair of black slacks that had
a four-finger rip along the right outer seam, at thigh level. He
dug his hands deep into the pockets of his slacks. He chewed
on a Kleenex, then put it in his pocket. The expression on
his face was not one of curiosity and amusement but, rather,

that of an impatient child waiting to be excused from the dinner table on a late-summer evening while there was still daylight and time to spend in the tree house. For the moment, Cohn seemed helplessly understimulated. And, for the moment, he looked unmistakably sad.

1 9 8 2

Words Fool Me

Sharing Goodman Ace's company as he ambles through his seventy-ninth year of life, I often get the feeling that I'm watching a lucky and gifted veteran lion tamer work before a largely empty house. Risks ensue and minor mishaps sometimes threaten, but instinct prevails above all. Ace's primary instinct is to be funny, and he almost always is. He says funny things when he talks with his friends, when he rides in a taxi, when he orders lunch at the Friars Club, when he plays pinochle, when he buys cigars, when he goes to the doctor, and even, if his word is to be trusted, when he is all alone. Occasionally, he talks to inanimate objects—his mirror, his television set, his typewriter, his foot when it falls asleep—and because inanimate objects and most people never listen carefully enough, they miss a lot of humor. The accumulation of these missed opportunities creates the empty-house effect. The general public would benefit if at given moments Ace would slap his knee or laugh loudly or announce, "Joke there, folks," but such posturing would violate his principles. He remains, as his late wife, Jane, often said, a ragged individualist.

At other moments, when he isn't busy resembling a veteran lion tamer, Ace seems like a small sailboat listing nervously in the wind. He is six feet tall—or, as he claims, five feet twelve—and if he is feeling just normal he walks with a slight forward stoop, usually with his hands slouched in his pockets. A close friend of his, Jean Bach, is fond of saying that Ace has a tendency to back into airplane propellers, suggesting that he frequently courts small-scale disaster. Not long ago, Ace had a dinner date with Mrs. Bach. When he arrived to pick her up, she wasn't ready to leave, so he sat down in her living room to wait. She owns a cat. At some point, the cat must have wandered into the living room, because the next day Mrs. Bach found a scrap of paper on her coffee table which gave evidence of some arcane duel that had taken place the previous evening. It said:

ACE   CAT

Mrs. Bach had the piece of paper framed.

This *objet trouvé* doesn't firmly prove or disprove that Ace backs into airplane propellers. Rather, it suggests that he appreciates the intrinsic value of a private victory. In this sense, the lesser similes—lion tamer, the small sailboat—fall away, and a more precise image of the man emerges: the human domino. This is a sterling Aceism that was coined sometime during the thirties or forties, when he wrote, directed, produced, and starred in, along with Jane, "Easy Aces," a seminal radio situation comedy. Many incidents in his life, as Ace recounts them, resemble sitcom. The careful listener realizes that he is hardly in the presence of a garden-variety jokesmith. Goodman Ace's jokes always have proper contexts. He enjoys telling the best stories again and again, and they tend to improve with age. A fair example is his French-restaurant routine, which I have seen him execute several times, although never with any great success. At a certain moment in a French restaurant, Ace motions to a waiter and calls, "Uh, *gendarme, gendarme!*" In an ideal world, the waiter will come to the table and politely explain, "Excuse me, monsieur, but I believe you mean to say '*garçon.*' '*Gendarme*' is the French word for policeman." Ace, who lives in this ideal world, will then stare absently at the waiter for a moment and say, "Just the man I want. There seems to be some holdup in the kitchen." In the real world, unfortunately, few waiters listen closely enough to be able to tell Ace that he has said *gendarme* when he really means *garçon*—thus the empty-house effect.

Not long ago, a young woman who had just seen and heard Ace in action for the first time told him, by way of a compliment, that he was the only person she had ever met who "makes up his own jokes." According to his prescription, a worthy joke—which he prefers to call "a good story"—should be "elegantly phrased and elegantly delivered." Across the years, Ace has written countless jokes, gags, and good stories, which he and other people have brought to life on radio and television, but the best sort of Goodman Ace stories are delivered in person. Ace needs only a chair, a cigar, and, because he is inclined toward both shyness and garrulousness, a slight nudge. He goes to work like a slow-moving roller coaster. The cigar acts as a metronomic device, measuring phrases, coaxing his audience, often sending a loose flutter of ashes tumbling down his shirtfront. In a way, the ashes belong to the delivery. They make the listener suspect that Ace doesn't know where he is going with a story, but he always does. Eventually, one comes to suspect that the ashes fall on cue. Because he chews a cigar as much as he smokes it, moist shreds of tobacco occasionally fall with the ashes, staining his neckties—lovely silk neckties from Sulka and Alexander Shields. "Two experts told me that I absolutely have to give up cigars and ketchup," Ace said recently. "My doctor and my dry cleaner." He will obligingly tell Goody Ace stories to any attentive audience, but he prefers to work with groups of two or three listeners. In a clutch, of course, he will work completely alone, entertaining only himself—a tough audience but an earnest listener. A good story, elegantly phrased and elegantly delivered, ends with the cigar back in his mouth, tucked between cheek and jaw and rotating in a small circle, priming for the next go-round. Ace never runs out of good stories, because when his supply runs low he makes up another one.

Ace's timing is delicate, diffident, subtle, and smooth, and so is he. He has a soft, pale face with high cheekbones and light-blue eyes. In his sixties, when his face was rounder, he wore his gray hair in a crewcut and, with his thick-framed eyeglasses, looked very much like a country doctor. Now he has grown thinner, his hair is white and is long enough to be kept neatly parted and combed, and the roundness of his face has receded into folds, which disappear completely when he smiles. It is a lambent, ear-to-ear smile—he has impressively large ears—and the way it fills his face reminds me exactly of my grandmother's smile. This is more than a coincidence, because my grandmother is in fact Goodman Ace's sister May. To be more precise, my grandmother is actually my father's stepmother, which technically makes her my step-grandmother and makes Ace my step-great-uncle. Whatever. This fortuitous arrangement enables him at critical moments to deny any blood kinship with me. As it is, the most accurate description of our relationship would be to say that we are insufferable friends.

"Easy Aces," which hit the big-time radio circuits in Chicago in 1931, went off the air in 1945, and its sequel, "mr. ace and JANE," was last heard from more than twenty-five years ago. Today, a lot of people who, as the phrase goes, "remember radio" react with surprise when told that Goodman Ace is still alive and still making up his own jokes, many of which find their way into a monthly column he writes for the *Saturday Review.* In a way, Ace's radio career has come full circle. For the past five years, he has appeared several times a month on a National Public Radio network show called "All Things Considered"—at a pay scale, given inflation, slightly below what he earned when he first went on the air, in Kansas City, a half century ago. If Ace would consent to travel the television talk-show circuit, more people would realize that his sense of humor is as fertile as ever. For a number of reasons, however—a dash of vengeance, a dollop of vanity—he refuses to appear on television. "They used to call up and ask me to come on the talk shows, and I always told them no," says Ace. "Finally, one day the Carson show phoned, and I said, 'I'm sorry, but I don't go on television because I don't look like this.' The woman who had called said fine, thank you, and about a minute later she called back and asked, 'What was that you said about not being yourself? Is this Goodman Ace? Who are you?' I learned a long time ago from Groucho Marx: 'Don't complain and don't explain.' People don't listen to what you say anyway. It's all just noise."

Although Ace enjoyed great success writing for television—he is thought of as "the dean of television comedy writers"—he wistfully regards radio as a medium that died prematurely, without the chance to designate an appropriate heir. In his opinion, radio's greatest legacy—the imagination of the listening audience—was immediately forsaken by television. "The networks made a mistake thinking that anything that worked well on radio would be ten times as good on television," he says. "In radio, the best thing you had going for you was that little one-inch screen inside your brain, and when the mental picture flashed, you saw what you wanted to see. Radio demanded a lot more imagination, and it was cheaper. You could have a fellow in jeans and a dirty sweatshirt say to a girl in jeans and a sweatshirt—with a proper cue for music to the sound man—'You're the prettiest girl at the dance,' and the music played. Now, on television that scene would cost thousands of dollars. The Japanese lanterns alone would run into big money."

Radio comedy, in its classic form, lived a very short life— slightly more than a quarter century. It extended from the mid- twenties—when an influx of vaudeville performers coincided with the networks' willingness to offer listeners something more daring than potted-palm music—until the early fifties, when Tallulah Bankhead's "The Big Show" made a last-ditch effort to resist the inevitability of television's superior commercial appeal. Ace began his own radio career in 1928, and he was the head writer on the ill-fated Bankhead show. When this show died, in 1952, after two seasons on the air—with thirty thousand unfulfilled requests for seats in the studio audience—the natural next step for Ace was writing for television. The era that he left behind became per- functorily known as "radio's golden years," an instant wellspring of nostalgia. (Television, of course, soon gave radio loyalists good reason to feel nostalgic about what had been lost.)

Today, there's no particular reason for anyone under thirty to know or care much about the Cliquot Club Eskimos, Jack Benny's underground vault, Fibber McGee and Molly's hall closet, Jane Ace's malaprops, Joe Penner's constant refrain "Wanna buy a duck?", Kay Kyser's Kollege of Musical Knowledge, Fred Allen and Jack Benny's "feud," what "I'se regusted" means, or why Henry Aldrich was always bleating "Coming, Mother!"—and very few of us do. I happen to know a bit about these things, because at a certain point in my life it made sense to find out. I was born in 1950. Seven years before that—the year that the thirteen-hundredth episode of "Easy Aces" was broadcast—my father's father, a widower, had married Ace's widowed sister, May. When my brothers and sisters and I were growing up, in Oklahoma, we regarded Grandma May's brother, Uncle Goody, and his wife, Aunt Jane, as an aloof, almost mythical show-biz couple who lived in New York City and allegedly palled around with people like Groucho Marx, Fred Allen, Jack Benny, Perry Como, George Burns, and Gracie Allen. My parents occasionally made trips to New York, and my father always returned with a fresh collection of Uncle Goody stories.

Perhaps because Jane Ace observed a policy of not straying far from home—except to go to Miami Beach or Yankee Stadium—the Aces never made guest appearances in Tulsa. Without ever having met her, I grew up with the correct impression that Jane Ace probably did not look or act like anyone's great-aunt. My idea of what an Uncle Goody might be like took shape over a period of years during the fifties and sixties as, week by week, I watched his name roll with the credits at the end of the "Kraft Music Hall," starring Perry Como. Ace wrote the Como show, along with Selma Diamond, Mort Green, Jay Burton, George Foster, and others, for a twelve-year stretch, during which he was the highest-paid writer in television. And the writing on the Como show was generally thought to be as graceful as any on the air.

Once, when neither of us knew what he was talking about, I bragged to a friend that my uncle wrote the Como show, and my friend told me right back that nobody *writes* a television show. Television, the unmagical magic of our lives, was just something, apparently, that was *beamed in* from *out there*. And so, in a way, was my distant great-uncle. Goody became palpably more real when, in later years, he sent birthday checks accompanied by warm, funny letters. I met him briefly in New York when I was twenty, and again a couple of years later, by which time we had become something like professional colleagues. When a piece he had written about Sid Caesar for *Esquire* appeared without his name in the table of contents, I wrote to ask him why. He sent back an ill-typed letter that said, in part, "As for your remark about my name not appearing in the table of contents: I don't care. I don't coo when I'm billed. In fact, I won't buy a magazine that will publish what I write. Besides, what's in a name? Particularly a name that doesn't appear in a table of contents? We'll have to be content to table this discussion until we meet again."

What I came to learn was that this short-order performance was typical of a gifted man who is, in a fragile way, a captive of his own comic imagination. This struck me most boldly the first time I heard him speak of his father, Harry, with whom he had a frustrating relationship. We were walking down Park Avenue toward the Friars Club, where we have lunch together once every couple of weeks. The time was early autumn, near the anniversary of Ace's father's death, and he remarked that he planned to light a memorial candle that evening to commemorate the event. Then he said, "You know, my father died of cancer when I was a teenager." We walked a bit farther, and he added, "He had it before it became popular."

In 1919, at the age of twenty, Goodman Ace left the employ of the Wormser Hat Store to become the drama and movie critic of the Kansas City *Post*. In the process, he scuttled what probably would not have been a very satisfying career as a haberdasher. Although Harry Truman would later prove that haberdashery in Kansas City could serve nicely as a sort of playing fields of Eton, Ace suspected that Wormser's was not his own hot ticket. The pay wasn't bad—forty dollars a week, plus a twenty-five-cent commission on every out-of-style hat sold—but whatever excitement it offered was Ace's own invention. His friend Manny Shure, who years later joined him in New York as his secretary and sidekick, worked with him at the time. Whenever one of them had a customer trying on a hat before the mirror, he would motion to the other, saying, "Uh, *Mr. Wormser*, could you please step over here for a moment to look at the hat on this gentleman? I'd say it fits very well, wouldn't you?" They sold a lot of hats that way.

The year before Ace went to work for the *Post*, his father died. This unhappy event had one lucky consequence: as the main source of support for his mother and his two sisters, May and Sally, he became exempt from the military draft, and that was just as well for someone who might back into an airplane propeller. Instead of fighting in the First World War, Ace joined the Civil Service. He did this perhaps out of a sense of patriotic duty or perhaps because he assumed that working the 4 P.M.-to-1 A.M. shift at the downtown post office in Kansas City would be more fulfilling than his previous job, as a roller-skating messenger boy for Montgomery Ward. Somehow Ace sandwiched the post-office job between classes at Kansas City Polytechnic Institute, where he was enrolled for a while in a journalism program. Given his previous school career, which was checkered, it's unclear why he went back for more. A decent formal education probably would have ruined him at this point, but he didn't have much patience with the liberal arts while he attended K.C. Poly. He wanted to be a writer. At this stage in his life, he had read most of Shakespeare and Ring Lardner, seen a lot of vaudeville, worshipfully studied Chaplin's early films, and admired the drama criticism of E. B. Garnett, the reviewer for the Kansas City *Star*. Armed with these standards, Ace began to write a column for the school paper. He called it "The Dyspeptic," a catchy title for the work of a nineteen-year-old. The columns, which were pastiches of acerbic observations of the life at K.C. Poly, have disappeared. The last time Ace remembers seeing them was during his interview for the job at the *Post*, when he showed them to the paper's young managing editor, a fellow named Dick Smith.

"I had no reason to think they were going to hire me, but my cousin Hy White told me to go over there to talk to Dick Smith, so I did," Ace says. "He took one look at me and said, 'You're kind of young to be a drama critic, aren't you?' And I said, 'You're kind of young to be a managing editor, aren't you?' And then we both laughed—except him."

Before taking the job, Ace discussed it with his mother, explaining that he was reluctant to leave Wormser's, because it would mean taking a cut in pay. "But she understood that I would be happier doing something that I liked," Ace recalls. "She said, 'Don't worry, May's working now, and I know you like to write, and we'll get along fine.' That's the attitude she always had. If I liked what I was doing, that was good enough for her. She was a beautiful, soft-spoken lady. I was close to her all through the years, even after I moved to New York and she stayed in Kansas City. One time, when she came to visit us in New York, she had been suffering some bad headaches. I took her over to my eye-ear-nose man. He made me leave the room while he examined her. Afterward, as we walked home, I asked her what the doctor had told her. Very quietly, she said, 'He says all my teeth have to come out.' I asked, 'What did you say to that?' And she said, 'I took out both plates and handed them to him.' And my mother never even wrote for radio."

Once he was satisfied that his mother was satisfied, Ace decided to go to work for the Kansas City *Post*—twenty-five dollars a week, no commissions. In those days, the Kansas City *Post* was a rather surly—one might even say yellow—sheet. In this respect, it accurately reflected the personality of one of its co-owners, Harry H. Tammen; the other was Frederick G. Bonfils, and the two men also owned the Denver *Post*. Bonfils had cultivated the stern mien of a tight-lipped riverboat gambler, in contrast to Tammen, a boisterous man with a squat, hammered-down look. Wherever Tammen went, he carried the threat of minor catastrophe. Once, during a meeting with Woodrow Wilson at the White House, he accidentally started a fire in a wastebasket. Another time, he was knocked down by an automobile in San Francisco, and became the first auto-pedestrian casualty in that city's history to claim that the mishap had been his own fault. Tammen, however, was hardly as solicitous when it came to business. The *Post* always seemed to be offending someone, and Tammen loved that. At one point, after Ace had been on the paper for a couple of years, his pan of a certain movie prompted a man who owned three movie houses in Kansas City to retaliate by pulling his ads out of the *Post*. When Tammen heard about it, he phoned the man and said, "If we don't have your ads back by the home edition, we've got a boy with smallpox who's going to take a walk through all your theaters." The ads came back.

When Ace began his reviewing chores for the *Post*, Kansas City had two legitimate theaters, three vaudeville showcases, and two burlesque houses, all of which Ace covered, some more diligently than others. The main vaudeville showcases and the legits usually

changed shows every Sunday, and Ace soon found that after busy
Sundays spent running back and forth between the Orpheum and
the Shubert and the Gaiety, and Mondays spent reviewing what he
had seen, his work week was finished. To balance things out, he
began to augment his criticism with a daily column called "Lobbying." It started out ostensibly as a collection of amusing things
that he had overheard in theater lobbies, and soon expanded to
include interviews with visiting actors. When, inevitably, it turned
out that neither actors nor the people who hung around theater
lobbies consistently said funny things, Ace was forced to make up
the jokes that found their way into the column. By default, he had
become a humorist.

At some point during his early years at the *Post*, Ace abandoned
his family's surname, Aiskowitz. Anglicizing one's last name has
meant different things to different people. In this case, it meant
placing at a safe distance certain less-than-soothing memories.
Ace, who was born January 15, 1899, says that he can remember
certain details of his own birth—"The doctor picked me up and
slapped me once, and lo and behold, there I was, one minute old,
with a strangulated hernia and no Blue Cross"—but he manages
only a highly selective recall of the rest of his childhood and
adolescence. As periods of childhood and adolescence go, his
didn't last very long, abbreviated by the imperative to earn a living
and support his mother and sisters. "As far as the family name
was concerned, I liked the fact that it ran from 'A' to 'Z,' " he
says, but the decision to make the change didn't require much
deliberation. His colleagues on the newspaper had already found
it convenient to diminish Aiskowitz to Ais, and from there it was
only a short orthographic segue to Ace—one that deprived posterity
of a radio show called "Easy Aiskowitzes."

Radio came to Kansas City in 1921. During its first few years, Ace
stayed too busy with his reviewing chores to pay much attention,
but when vaudeville performers began to turn up on the air and,
conversely, when radio performers like Freeman Gosden (Amos)
and Charles Correll (Andy) began to show up in Kansas City with

vaudeville adaptations of their radio routines, it became his business to pay attention. He wrestled briefly with the problem of where to get the money to buy a good radio, and solved it when an obliging theater owner rigged a lottery drawing that enabled him to win a nice Atwater Kent.

Curious as it may now seem, even as late as 1930 an apparently serious debate existed over whether radio ought to become a medium for commercial advertising. That year, Merlin Aylesworth, the president of NBC, told Congress that radio should not resort to "direct advertising," which actually meant only that a sponsor should refrain from mentioning the price of his product, and soon, of course, such strange sophistries disappeared altogether. For a while during the mid-twenties, however, the direct-advertising stricture meant that sponsors simply lent their company names to programs—titles like "The General Motors Family Party," "The A. &. P. Gypsies," and "The Voice of Firestone" proliferated— and many small stations enjoyed the luxury of not worrying about advertising revenues, because the stations existed in the first place merely to publicize the well-established enterprises that owned them.

In 1922, Bonfils and Tammen sold the *Post* to Walter S. Dickey, a manufacturer of clay sewer pipes, who already owned a morning paper, the Kansas City *Journal*. As a publisher, Dickey could be as eccentric as Bonfils or Tammen. One of his edicts forbade the use of the word "concrete" in his papers—as in, for instance, "concrete example"—concrete being a looming threat to his clay-sewer-pipe empire. Dickey eventually merged his papers into one, the *Journal-Post*, and not long afterward the paper set aside a small warren adjacent to the city room, covered the walls with burlap, and established a radio-transmission line to KMBC, a local radio station. A *Journal-Post* staff member read the news over the line every day at noon—an arrangement that provided the paper with publicity and the station with a news service. The station was managed and partly owned by a man named Arthur Church. Church knew a few things about radio, but mainly he knew a two-word phrase that he uttered any time someone suggested an idea for a fifteen-minute program. The phrase was "Ten dollars." When Ace recommended two weekly programs—a chatty movie and theatre guide called "Ace Goes to the Movies" and then a Sunday-morning show in which he prefigured Fiorello La Guardia's later leap to stardom by reading the funnies to children—Church came across with a perfunctory twenty bucks.

At this point, Ace was living in marginal debt at the lavish and fabled Bellerive Hotel, and he had no trouble finding ways to spend an extra twenty per week. Although he initially became involved in radio to earn more money, the chore soon turned into pleasure, and so was to be mildly mistrusted. Ace had been careful to respect a distinction between business and pleasure. During his early years at the *Post*, he made it a policy to know actors well enough to write about them in "Lobbying" but not so well that a presumption of friendship existed. There were occasional exceptions—among them Jack Benny, Groucho Marx, Fred Allen, Portland Hoffa, George Burns, and Gracie Allen, people whose talents impressed him greatly. In the autumn of 1927, Benny sent Ace a note that said, "Opening next week in New York. Please send jokes. Will pay." Ace had never seen New York, but he did some digging and learned that Benny, the m.c., would appear second on the bill, preceded by a Chinese magician. Benny's opening gag, as Ace wrote it, called for him to saunter onstage and, arms folded against his chest, chin resting in the palm of his hand, mutter, "My, how vaudeville's changed—it used to take Japs or better to open." The joke was in character for Benny and apparently went over well the first night, because he sent fifty dollars, along with the message "Your joke got lots of laughs. If you have any more, send them along." Ace returned the check, accompanied by his own message: "Your check got lots of laughs. If you have any more, send them along." "I definitely could have used the fifty," says Ace, "but I didn't want to ruin my amateur status with my friend Jack. And through our long years of friendship we maintained that nonprofit relationship."

Notwithstanding the low-budget limitations of early radio, the medium loomed as Ace's deus ex machina. In 1922, he had precipitated minor guerrilla warfare with a retail clothing merchant named Jacob Epstein by marrying his daughter Jane. She was wispy, pretty, blond, and blue-eyed—a fairly frivolous young woman with a sophisticated sense of humor and an as yet undiscovered gift for reading overlapping dialogue. The wedding was by common standards a low-profile affair: the guest list consisted of the bride and groom, a rabbi, and Ace's friend Manny Shure. Jacob Epstein managed to conceal any pleasure that his daughter's marriage may have brought him. He had done reasonably well in the clothing business, and apparently hoped for a son-in-law who would care enough about the difference between gabardine and worsted to accept a small store as a dowry. When Epstein first heard that Ace had a job with the Kansas City *Post*, he said, "Oh, really? Where's your newsstand?" The marriage successfully withstood Epstein's assaults and lasted fifty-two years, until Jane died, although Ace now concedes that his relationship with his wife wasn't without its tribulations. "Oh, we occasionally disagreed," he says. "For instance, I don't think Jane's admiration of 'Kukla, Fran and Ollie' was as enthusiastic as mine." Whenever anyone greeted Ace in public and asked, "How's Jane?" his standard response was "Fine—if you like Jane."

In 1929, after seven years of marriage, Ace still hadn't checked into the clothing business, but Jane was on the verge of breaking into radio. It happened, as such things will, pretty much by accident. One Friday evening, "Ace Goes to the Movies" was supposed to be followed by a CBS network show with Heywood Broun. Goody was at the microphone and Jane was seated in the studio waiting for him to finish his show, and when it came time to switch to the network, Broun was nowhere to be heard. The only thing to do was to keep talking, and since Ace had already exhausted what he had to say about the movies in town that week, he began to improvise. "I'd like for all of you to meet my roommate," he said, and motioned to Jane to join him at the microphone. Then he steered the conversation toward their bridge game of the previous evening—auction bridge, the predecessor of contract bridge, being the local rage at the time. A few days earlier, a Kansas City housewife had killed her husband during an argument over a bridge

game, and the Aces were able to milk that for a few laughs. The
jokes were all quite droll. "Would you care to shoot a game of
bridge, dear?" Jane asked, and Ace remarked that the dead man
had been buried "with simple honors." When Ace accused Jane
of not playing a hand correctly, she said, "I notice that whenever
we lose, you're always my partner." She added that she didn't
really like bridge, because she thought it was unlucky to hold
thirteen cards. When Ace asked her why she didn't finesse, she
said, "I hate to finesse. It makes me nervous." The Aces did this
for fifteen minutes without a script, and somehow the dialogue
managed to flow spontaneously, and fortunately someone was listening. Don Davis, a local advertising man, called and offered the
Aces a contract for a thirteen-week show, to be sponsored by a
chain of drugstores. The figures sounded reasonable: twenty-five
dollars a week for Goody, fifteen for Jane. They signed.

To earn ten dollars per week more than his wife, Ace had to
write the stuff that they broadcast. A precedent was established.
"Easy Aces" grew out of Goody's imagination, but Jane was in-
disputably the star of the show. She delivered the laugh lines; his
were the straight setups and the softly muttered "Isn't that awful?"
that trailed in the wake of her malaprops and misquotations ("Time
wounds all heels"). Her radio persona thrived upon logical illogic;
he matched that with a sort of tolerant plaintiveness. The Aces
certainly didn't "own" the wise-husband/goofy-housewife shtick—
George Burns and Gracie Allen, among others, operated a variation
on the theme in their vaudeville acts—but the Aces were the first
to make it work on radio, because they made it work in a special
way: through the ear. Their success had almost as much to do with
their limitations as with their abilities. Gracie Allen, for example,
who had the instincts of a dramatic actress, felt comfortable on the
vaudeville stage, and managed to adapt first to radio and then to
television. Jane Ace bore no pretensions as an actress. She had a
natural gift for reading comic dialogue, and she felt most comfortable displaying it within the cozy confines of a broadcasting
studio, with a microphone and other radio actors as her only com-
panions. When "mr. ace and JANE" went off the air, in 1949, she
didn't leap for television stardom, as she certainly could have if

she had wanted to. Radio had been her métier, and, rather than undermine her success in that medium, she more or less retired.

When the Aces' first thirteen-week contract with the drugstore chain ran out, so did the drugstore chain. Arthur Church, who had become the Aces' manager, helped them find an interim sponsor. About this time, the Aces got a call from John Rich, an account executive with Blackett-Sample-Hummert, a large advertising agency that was based in Chicago. Rich had heard "Easy Aces" a couple of times while passing through Kansas City on business, and he believed that "Easy Aces" belonged in the Blackett-Sample-Hummert repertoire. In the radio era, before the networks understood quite what they could do or how they wanted to do it, advertising agencies performed many functions that the networks now perform for themselves. The agency operated, in effect, as an independent production company—first "creating" a show, then writing it, then engaging a sponsor, and, finally, delivering the finished package to the network. The deal that Rich offered the Aces—a thirteen-week tryout in Chicago, with all expenses paid but no salary included—struck them as less than persuasive. "I had heard that Jack Benny and Burns & Allen were getting five hundred dollars per week in vaudeville, so I asked for that, too," says Ace. "Rich said that sounded O.K. So, just like that, we went from nothing to five hundred a week, which I thought was pretty good."

Ace took a leave of absence from the *Journal-Post*, at no pay, but continued to write "Lobbying" on a daily basis. Meanwhile, John Rich sold "Easy Aces" to Lavoris, the mouthwash people, who were entitled to a standard renewal option if they liked the initial thirteen-week segment of the program. When Lavoris renewed "Easy Aces" after thirteen weeks on the air, Ace celebrated by cutting his column-from-abroad from seven times a week to three. Goody and Jane had initially decided that when they had saved twenty-five thousand dollars they would return to Kansas City and he would resume his job at the newspaper. But now the Kansas City tie was weakening, and when Lavoris renewed a second option Ace decided to write "Lobbying" only once a week. By the end of their first year in Chicago—the 1931–32 broadcasting season—Ace had settled his debts in Kansas City, put some money in the bank, and concluded that it was time to break his contract with Arthur Church. The day after he did it, the Aces signed for another year with Lavoris, for sixteen hundred and fifty dollars per week. The seductive charm of money began to take hold, and there went the twenty-five-thousand-dollar goal. Now the goal was unlimited.

Apparently, word of this prosperity quickly filtered back to Kansas City, because Ace started hearing from some of his hometown cronies, including a fellow drama critic with whom he had shared the services of the political boss Tom Pendergast's private bookmaker. The bookie operated out of an office on the twenty-second floor of the Kansas City Athletic Club, so Ace immediately understood a cryptic note he received one spring day in Chicago. It said, "Please send five hundred dollars or I'm going to jump off the twenty-second floor of the Kansas City Athletic Club." Today, when he tells this story, Ace pauses to let a few cigar ashes fall, and then he says, "So I sent my friend a check for two-fifty and told him to jump from the eleventh."

Everything went well with Lavoris until the middle of the second season, when the sponsor phoned one morning to complain that "Easy Aces" had gone on the air five minutes late the previous evening. "It caught me by surprise," says Ace. "I told the guy, 'But that can't be. This station *always* goes on on time.' And the Lavoris man said, 'I have a grandfather clock that hasn't lost a minute in fifty years.' At the end of the year, they decided not to pick up the program again. I don't know what they were mad about, other than our disagreement about that fellow's grandfather clock. Anyway, now we really were out of a job. So in the summer of 1933 we went to New York, where we expected to be met with open arms, and weren't."

In other words, there were apparently no sponsors available for radio shows. After Ace had checked fruitlessly with several agencies, an acquaintance told him to try Blackett-Sample-Hummert, whose New York office was run by Frank Hummert. "My response to that was that Blackett and Sample must be angry because we had lost the Lavoris account," says Ace, "but I was told to go see

Hummert, who was supposed to be different." In time, Ace discovered that "different" described Frank Hummert with some accuracy, but "tall," "quiet," "laconic," "gentle," "intelligent," and,
above all, "imaginative" described him more precisely. In the late
twenties, Hummert had left Chicago and opened the New York
office, where his copywriting skills and his reputation as a topnotch
"idea man" flourished. Together with his wife, Anne Ashenhurst,
who had originally been hired as his assistant at BSH, Hummert
became the most prolific and successful entrepreneur in radio. The
Hummerts devised story lines, hired the writers, took a direct hand
in the scriptwriting and casting, personally composed commercial
copy, and became the mainstays of the burgeoning radio soap-
opera industry. During the forties, the Hummerts had thirteen
daytime soaps on the air, plus five half-hour evening shows. Their
office was less an agency than a factory. Hiring the Aces in 1933
posed no special problems, because, unlike all the other Hummert
shows, this cast came with the writer built in. The Aces agreed to
go on the air fifteen minutes a day, four days a week, for thirteen
hundred dollars a week. Meanwhile, Jane began to balk, reasoning
that any act worth sixteen-fifty in Chicago shouldn't go for less in
New York. Ace won that argument by telling her, "Now, say this
aloud: 'I do not want to work for one thousand three hundred dollars
a week.'"

Having literally and figuratively arrived in New York, Ace began
to write scripts to fit the cultural setting. A word that frequently
came up in descriptions of the "Easy Aces" brand of humor was
"urbanity," and urbanity was a quality that the critics failed to
detect in—regardless of their virtues—"Clara, Lu and Em," "Just
Plain Bill," "Buck Rogers in the Twenty-fifth Century," "The Story
of Myrt and Marge," and most of the other programs that shared
the airwaves in 1933. As radio characters, the Aces were "white
bread"; the name of the show certainly contained no trace of identifiable ethnicity, and the subject matter conveyed a general ambience of blue-eyed blondness. Jane was a housewife named Jane;
Goody was "Dear" or "Mr. Ace," a toiler in a Manhattan advertising

agency. A broad assortment of radio actors drifted in and out of
the scripts, depending upon who happened to be in town, was
underemployed at the time, or had been dragged into the studio
by one of the regular members of the cast. The regulars included
Mary Hunter, their co-star, who played Marge, Jane's best friend,
and whose greatest attribute was a hearty, resonant laugh—a live
and welcome laugh track in the days before phony laugh tracks
lulled radio and television audiences into inattention. As Marge
laughed, Ace muttered whatever it was he was inclined to mutter.
The other cast members included, at various times, Leon Janney,
as Jane's brother, Paul Sherwood; Helene Dumas, as Laura, the
Aces' housemaid; Pert Kelton, as Mrs. Bell, another maid; Martin
Gabel, as Neal, Marge's boyfriend; Ann Thomas, as Miss Thomas,
Mr. Ace's Jane-brained secretary; Everett Sloane, who played many
characters, from an old judge to a psychiatrist to an auctioneer;
and Ken Roberts, who played the Aces' adopted twenty-one-year-
old son, Cokey. Later on, when "Easy Aces" had become a half-
hour show, Ken Roberts was the program's announcer and also
portrayed the Aces' next-door neighbor, a radio announcer named
Ken Roberts. This whimsical blurring of the distinctions between
real people and show-biz artifice must have pleased Ace greatly.
It gave the program a tone of amusingly transparent disingenuousness—the sort of disingenuousness reflected in Mr. Ace's con-
tention that he and his wife lived in "a typical little Eastern town
called New York City."

The stuff of "Easy Aces" was straightforward sitcom, each show
presenting an agon that proceeded toward a reasonably tidy reso-
lution by the end of the broadcast. Three nights each week, Jane
provoked some comic misadventure in the Ace household, and
Goody—or, rather, Dear—padded softly through the background,
hoping that it would all go away. In real life, the Aces were living
in high style—first at the Essex House, later at the Ritz Tower—
but they managed to avoid garishness. There was something fundamentally self-effacing about Ace, in both his radio and his real-
life embodiment. Certainly the radio Aces were relatively well-to-
do and sophisticated, but when the critics mentioned the show's
urbanity, they were actually applauding its literariness—its tend-

ency to focus less upon gags and pratfalls than upon words themselves. This didn't mean that, assured of a sponsor and the attention
of the listening public, Ace would have preferred to abandon the
strain of writing to go on the air with dramatic readings of *Wuthering
Heights*. What it did mean, I think, was that he wanted to show
just how, as Jane often malapropped when she was at a temporary
loss, "words fool me."

This helps to explain the abrupt demise of a syndicated "Easy
Aces" television series that flickered briefly in the late sixties. Ace
had agreed to write a pilot for the series, which was produced in
Canada. After he had seen several completed episodes, however,
he was eager, to the point of litigiousness, for the show to be
canceled. The actors didn't look right to him, and he couldn't stand
the direction. Whenever the script called for a malaprop, the camera clumsily zeroed in on the actress who portrayed Jane. The
spontaneity and delicacy of the humor had been sacrificed. Although this happened at a time when commercial television was
about twenty-five years old, it echoed many of the mistakes that
had characterized the medium in its infancy. By the early fifties,
the broadcasting business had, in a brief time span, completed a
strange cycle. Fred Allen, whose style of radio humor came as
close as anybody's to resembling Ace's, described the phenomenon
in *Treadmill to Oblivion*, his wonderful radio memoir. In the thirties, a group of Texaco executives decided that Ed Wynn would
do well as the star of a show to be called "The Fire Chief," but
they needed some reassurance that he was the right man for the
job. At the time, Wynn was appearing in a Broadway play called
The Laugh Parade. The Texaco people finally agreed that the best
way to predict Wynn's suitability for radio was to sit through his
entire Broadway performance with their eyes closed. So they did.
"When they opened their eyes," Allen wrote, "Ed got the job."
With the advent of television, the same philosophy (with a bit of
interpolation) still applied: anything that could work on Broadway
could move to radio, and, conversely, anything that succeeded on
radio could shift to the visual medium of television. As far as Ace
was concerned, this sort of reasoning was entirely wrong. To convert
a program from radio to television meant, in many instances, to

equip it with the sort of buffoonery that had characterized much
of vaudeville. Consequently, humor that was rooted in words rather
than in sight gags was bound to lose a bit in the visual translation.
The radio microphone, abetted by the imagination of the audience,
could actually "lie" much more effectively than the television camera, and that was fine with Ace. So much of what he saw and heard
in the world around him seemed slightly muddled, and he was
happy, after a fashion, to muddle right back.

"When we were doing 'Easy Aces,' the dialogue had to be made
to overlap," says Ace. "On television or the stage, the pauses
between two actors' lines could be filled with physical gestures.
But on radio we had to fill these pauses with 'Well, I—uh' and
'Oh, well, I was going to . . .' It took a while for Jane to learn how
to time and read those lines. In fact, I wrote a lot of 'I—uh's' and
'Oh, well, uh's' into her scripts. These pauses, with the background
muttering, were very important. I even built it into the show. Jane
would say, 'Don't just sit there muttering to yourself.' And I would
say, 'A man's best friend is his mutter.' And Jane would follow
that with 'Now, let's not drag _her_ into this.' That 'mutter' joke is
a malaprop, although someone might claim that it's really a lapsus
comicus. A lot of people mix up the two. A true malaprop is an
actual word with a meaning of its own, even though the meaning
is out of context. A lapsus comicus is a verbal boner that confuses
things that don't contain similar-sounding words. Sam Goldwyn
once said, 'A verbal contract isn't worth the paper it's written on,'
or Jane said, 'Love makes the world go round together.' Lapsus
comicus there. When Andy used to say, 'I'se regusted,' that wasn't
a malaprop _or_ a lapsus comicus, because there's no such word as
'regusted.' I finally eliminated the distinction between a malaprop
and a lapsus comicus by thinking of them both as janeaceisms.
Making up these things was easy, because wherever we went we
heard people saying weird things. Jane's father actually used to
say, 'You're getting my ghost.' I guess it ran in the family. Jane's
sister Eva once sent us a letter that ended, 'P.S. Guess who died.'

"The best malaprops are those that make a point, such as 'Be
it ever so hovel, there's no place like home.' . . . 'I was down on
the lower East Side today and saw those old testament houses.'

... 'I got up at the crank of dawn.' ... 'Living in squander.'
... 'Absinthe makes the heart grow fonder.' ... 'Familiarity
breeds attempt.' ... 'We're all cremated equal.' ... 'I refused
to tell him who I was, I used a facetious name.' ... 'The food in
that restaurant was abdominal.' ... 'Just explain it to me in words
of one cylinder.' ... 'Congress is still in season.' ... 'In all my
bored days.' ... 'Every picture I see of Abraham Lincoln makes
him look so thin and emancipated.' After saying these things enough
times on radio, Jane would get a little confused. We'd be sitting
at home and she would come up with a remark like something was
'the fly in the oatmeal—or is it ointment?' "

Eventually, "Easy Aces" left its mark on common parlance, and
the malaprop that proves a point invariably seems more appropriate
than the original phrase. Often, janeaceisms—which are, in the
first place, goodmanaceisms—creep into Ace's own everyday conversation. Rather than take for granite that Ace talks straight, a
listener must be on guard for an occasional entre nous and me, or
a long face no see. In a roustabout way, he will maneuver until
he selects the ideal phrase for the situation, hitting the nail right
on the thumb. The careful conversationalist might try to mix it up
with him in a baffle of wits. In quest of this pinochle of success,
I have often wrecked my brain for a clowning achievement, but
Ace's chickens always come home to roast. From time to time,
Ace will, in a jerksome way, monotonize the conversation with
witticisms too humorous to mention. It's high noon someone beat
him at his own game, but I have never done it; cross my eyes and
hope to die, he always wins thumbs down.

Three times a week, working a week ahead, Ace churned out an
episode of "Easy Aces." He gauged the quality of an episode by
the number of cigars he smoked while he wrote it. (According to
this standard, a two-cigar script rated higher than a five-cigar one,
which was often too labored.) Burdensome as Ace's work load
seems, it was actually much lighter than that of some of Frank
Hummert's drones. At the going rate of twenty-five dollars per
script, each writer, working at three different typewriters, would

manage to write five episodes of three different shows each week. With so many loose threads dangling, it was inevitable that story lines occasionally unraveled. Often, however, a story line could be abandoned with virtually no ill consequences.

"The plot mattered to me, but the most important thing was developing good characters," says Ace. "The malaprops were Jane's character lines, and she was the star of the show. I used to get a lot of letters from men who would say, 'My wife is as dum as your wife'—they usually spelled it d-u-m. Jane's character was not dumb. She was someone who viewed the world with a certain pristine literalness. When it came to a story line, after two shows we'd know whether we had something interesting. I once asked Amos and Andy—Gosden and Correll—what they did if they started a story line and realized that it wasn't going anywhere. I wanted to know if they just quickly dropped the plot or explained it away, and they said, 'No, we forget we ever said it.' You could get away with that, because you had a lot of things that worked consistently—running gags—to fill the breach. Like the hall closet in 'Fibber McGee and Molly.' Fibber was always promising to clean it out, and every time he opened the door you heard the most awful crash. Or Jack Benny's vault in the basement. You would hear Jack walking down a long corridor, and gates and locks and chains were clanging. Those things just worked best on radio. When they tried them on television, I thought a great deal was lost."

The casualness with which things appeared to happen at times in radio should not suggest that the Aces were tinkering carelessly with the medium. Like any serious humorist, Ace was curious to explore the uses of wit. He isolated a special style of humor and proceeded to exploit it, catching the sight and sound of the world with a rare set of eyes and ears. Although Ace's own political sympathies flowed generally along the Roosevelt mainstream, his success formula for "Easy Aces" did not call for heavy doses of social realism. (Jane seems not to have harbored any well-articulated political convictions, although she did once accuse Groucho Marx of being a Communist because of some derogatory remarks he made about the New York Yankees.) At one point during the thirties, a group of right-minded performers and writers suggested that radio was failing in its obligation to promote the civil rights of blacks. To correct the situation, it was felt, more blacks should be hired for radio acting roles, and the public should be introduced to greater numbers of black doctors and lawyers and fewer sleeping-car porters. Invoking the near-obvious, Ace wanted to know precisely how—shy of encouraging actors to speak in unflattering dialects—to inform a radio audience that a certain character was black or white. (One obvious irony was that Gosden and Correll, the actors who portrayed Amos and Andy, were themselves white.) Ace's oblique and sardonic answer to the dilemma was to make certain that all ostensible menials on "Easy Aces" sounded distinctly Caucasian. This led to the creation of Pert Kelton's character—a housemaid who addressed everyone by his first name, while she was universally deferred to as "Mrs. Bell." Earlier in the life of "Easy Aces," Helene Dumas portrayed a housemaid named Laura. In one episode, she struck for higher wages and picketed the Aces' home, chanting "Mrs. Ace is unfair!" When it came time for her to prepare dinner, Laura insisted that Jane carry the picket sign and maintain the litany. Jane complied, while Laura leaned out of a window and shouted, "Louder, Mrs. Ace! Louder, Mrs. Ace!"

If this sort of byplay was an attempt to redress gross social injustices, it would have to be regarded as an awfully shallow one. It should be remembered, however, that during this era few people seriously presumed that radio comedy should become a forum for political or social crusading. Because of its ability to attract an enormous audience, radio was the most democratic instrument of mass communication that the world had seen. The process of determining program content, however, was anything but democratic. The people who had the power wished to exploit radio primarily as an anodyne. There was very little argument over this point. For one thing, commercial radio's so-called golden years coincided with the Depression and the Second World War, and the public badly needed an anodyne. The era of loyalty oaths and blacklists had not fully dawned, and it was well past television's infancy before broadcasters were willing to treat a subject like racism in a situation-comedy context. Ace cared far less about social realism

than he did about the classic comic myths—the triumph of servant
over master, or, as he presented it, almost allegorically, the victory
of spontaneous and chaotic janeaceism over pompous Reason. When
Jane descended the stairs to carry her housemaid's picket sign,
Goody was not trying to disseminate subtle Marxist propaganda
over the airwaves. He liked to be topical but wanted most to be
comical.

Throughout the life of "Easy Aces," the Aces switched back and
forth between the two major networks, NBC and CBS. Their working
relationship with the Hummerts remained good, and the Aces made
a lot of money, having graduated to forty-five hundred dollars a
week by the time they went off the air. A small portion of this was
spent at Belmont and Saratoga. "We were horseplaying addicts,
albeit at very small sums, but we couldn't break the habit," Ace
confesses. (The Aces also kept boxes at Yankee Stadium and the
Polo Grounds, where Jane, who in later years cultivated a hobby
that Goody called "collecting injustices," was once struck and hurt
by a foul ball.) Christmastime usually meant a shower of silver
ashtrays and gold cigarette lighters from appreciative bookmakers,
until one day Goody simply quit betting on the horses. "I was
hurrying to finish an 'Easy Aces' script, because I didn't want to
miss the daily double. Then it occurred to me, What am I rushing
for? I'm not under contract to the horses."

He was, however, under contract to the American Home Products
Corporation, the manufacturer of Anacin and the sponsor of "Easy
Aces" during most of its existence. "For the first fifteen months on
the air with American Home Products, we were sponsored by a
product that they had to discontinue—a laxative that had a tendency to cake in the boxes on the grocer's shelf, or something like
that," says Ace. "I know that our maid used it and it made her
disappear. Following that, they came up with a product called
Anacin, which they had acquired from some small outfit in Missouri. The total sales of Anacin the previous year had been two
hundred thousand dollars. During the first couple of years that they
sponsored us on 'Easy Aces,' the sales went up nine hundred

percent." Ace likes to recite this statistic by way of demonstrating his contempt for the radio and television rating systems. Fortunately, Frank Hummert's mistrust of ratings matched Ace's. Hummert cared only whether a product sold well, and he once ran a full-page ad in *Variety* to make his feelings on the subject public.

It was not an argument over ratings, then, that provoked the ending of Ace's relationship with American Home Products during the 1944–45 broadcasting season. In 1943, the program schedule had changed from three fifteen-minute shows a week to one half-hour show a week, and Ace had decided to accompany this change with a musical innovation. Up to that point, "Manhattan Serenade," which was the "Easy Aces" theme song, had been the only music broadcast during the show. Now, however, Ace arranged to integrate music and plot by inserting brief musical bridges to pace the show through the half-hour. "I even hired the musicians out of my own pocket," he says. "The way it worked was that, say, Jane and I were having a discussion about the family budget or something like that. When we reached the point where I had just run out of patience and she had said something about 'the end of the fiasco year,' the musical bridge that carried us to the next scene would be 'Side by Side.' You know the lyrics—'We ain't got a barrel of money,' and so on. I liked the way it worked, and I think most other people did, too. But some dentist wrote the Anacin people and told them that he didn't like the music. Being in the pain-reliever business, Anacin must have counted on the patronage of dentists everywhere, so they suggested that we go back to the old music. This kind of provoked me, because in all the years on the air Anacin hadn't sent us a single letter saying that they liked the show. So I wrote a letter to them saying, 'I don't like the way you package Anacin these days. Before the war, you used to sell it in those little tin boxes, and now you're using this cardboard stuff and it just doesn't seem as nice.' And they thought up a clever answer to that, which was 'You're fired.'"

Ace's leave-taking from prime-time radio became a protracted affair, made final when "The Big Show," waylaid by television, went off the air in April of 1952. In retrospect, one wonders what took him so long. His entire vaudeville career, for instance, had lasted one week. In Chicago, during the winter of 1932, he and Jane had played the Chicago Theatre on a bill that included the Albertina Rasch Dancers, Ukulele Ike, and a less than memorable stair-dancing act. Goody and Jane had been hired to do five shows a day, six days a week, for twenty-five hundred dollars, with an offer to move on to the Paramount Theatres on Broadway and in Brooklyn for even more money. By the end of the third show on the first day, however, Ace was ready to rewrite the act—not because it didn't get laughs but because, true to character, he had tired of the material. Years later, in both radio and television, he shifted among various jobs as head writer—from Danny Kaye to Tallulah Bankhead to Milton Berle to Perry Como to Sid Caesar—with the apparent adaptability of a reliable journeyman relief pitcher. Looking back on "Easy Aces," Erik Barnouw, the broadcasting historian, detected a restless tone in the writing, which led him to say that Ace "appeared to be congenitally at odds with the form he was using." In many ways, Ace must have struck some people as congenitally at odds, period. In 1957, he wrote the screenplay for a movie called *I Married a Woman*, a featherweight comedy that makes semiannual appearances on Late Shows. "It was the best thing I ever wrote and the worst thing I ever saw," he declared when the movie came out, and he never wrote another screenplay. At various times, he toyed with ideas for Broadway, and once outlined a play called *The Title*, a romantic comedy about hypochondria, his favorite affliction. "The premise," says Ace, "was that the best cure for hypochondria is to forget about your own body and get interested in someone else's." Thus far, he has failed to carry through that project and has ignored a number of suggestions that he write for the stage. With Groucho Marx acting as middleman, he once had lunch at Toots Shor's with George S. Kaufman to discuss a Broadway adaptation of "Easy Aces"—Kaufman's idea. "If you write a play, I'll produce it," Kaufman said. "I'll make you the same offer," Ace responded. This congenial banter continued throughout the meal, and afterward the three stood outside the restaurant. Extending his hand, Kaufman said, "Goodbye now. I'm going over to the Cavendish Club to play bridge, and as I'm sitting there I'd like to think that you've already started on Act One." As Kaufman walked away, Ace said to Groucho, "He shouldn't tell me what to do. I'm going over to the Friars to play some gin rummy."

Spoiled by the freedom he enjoyed as the writer-director-producer of "Easy Aces," Ace cherished his independence. Being fired by Anacin in 1945 hardly descended on him and Jane as an unacceptable shock. It offered them a respite, and it gave Ace, in particular, a chance to reflect and realize that as mass audience appeal drifted from radio to television his career would probably have to move with it. These ruminations were conducted in Florida, to which, accompanied by their all-white West Highland terrier, Blackie, the Aces had made it their habit to retreat when they weren't busy working. During the early years of "Easy Aces," before summer reruns, Goody and Jane managed to create vacations by writing themselves out of the scripts for several weeks. Once encamped in Miami Beach, Jane convened a court of loyal friends and sycophants who were attracted by the fact that her beach cabaña was equipped with one of the best-stocked bars on the Eastern seaboard. Goody, who never drank, stayed busy playing cards, reading, writing at leisure, and nursing a highly developed hypochondria. Ace did his best to salve the hypochondria with humor, but the symptoms that he suffered were quite real. A chronic shortness of breath and a rapid pulse convinced him, expert medical opinion notwithstanding, that he had a grave heart condition. When he was in New York, he alternated among several physicians, who supplied him with tranquilizers and placebos and were available to conduct annual checkups on a monthly basis. Eventually, one of his doctors obligingly gave the disease a name—neurocirculatory asthenia—prescribed breathing exercises, and somehow persuaded Ace that death was less than imminent. A strong indication that Ace had largely conquered his neuroses came in 1966, when he published a collection of short humorous pieces called *The Fine Art of Hypochondria, or How Are You?*, which featured on the dust jacket a reproduction of one of his chest X rays, autographed by his various doctors.

The sojourn in Florida in the winter of 1945 did not convince Ace that he was ready to work again. Upon his return to New York, however, he received an offer that, try as he might, he couldn't really refuse. "An agency man came to see me in New York and asked me to become the head writer for Danny Kaye, who had a radio show that he was unhappy with," says Ace. "I didn't really want to get involved in writing for other people—I wasn't sure what I wanted to do—so I mentioned what I thought was an impossible price: thirty-five hundred a week. The agency said fine. That put me on the spot, so I raised the price to forty-five hundred, insisting that I'd need to hire some co-writers. They agreed to that, too. I told them I'd stay with the show as long as they didn't take it to the West Coast, and after I'd been working for Kaye about four months they naturally decided to move to Hollywood—which, as I recall, is on the West Coast. So I announced that I was quitting. Kaye couldn't understand why. He said, 'I thought when we went together to buy you a new sport coat the other day that meant you'd agreed to go to the Coast.' I told him I'd bought the sport coat because I assumed the show was moving to Florida. Somehow, that didn't convince him, so I said the real reason I didn't want to go to the West Coast was that I'd heard it was three hours earlier there than in New York, and who wants to wake up three hours earlier?"

Despite its shortcomings, the Kaye interlude taught Ace that he could certainly write for other performers, and soon after he quit the program he took a job at CBS as the network's "supervisor of comedy." In 1947, CBS established a School for Comedy Writers, with Ace installed as "dean." His students included, at one time or another, Neil Simon, Simon's brother Danny, George Axelrod, Ernie Lehman, Paddy Chayefsky, and six or seven other young funnymen-on-the-rise. The network gave Ace and his charges an office, a studio, a half-hour time slot, and the services of Robert Q. Lewis as the host of whatever weekly show they might produce. This noble experiment's most immediate dividend was "The Little Show"—prophetically named, because it lasted only six months and was destined to be little remembered, never enticed a commercial sponsor, and so did very little to brighten CBS's corporate balance sheet or standing in the ratings. Still, it offered bright satirical moments and, to a certain extent, prefigured such television programs as "That Was the Week That Was" and "Laugh-In." In keeping with Ace's belief that all successful radio or television comedy required the development of consistent characters, the writers of "The Little Show" managed to coin a number of innovative running gags—among them a studio audience that talked back—during the short time it was on the air. The stock characters included a chatty movie critic/gossip monger named Louella Pitkin, whose existence obviously owed a debt to Louella Parsons. Movie criticism was actually a sideline for Miss Pitkin—something she stumbled across in the course of her work as a theater usherette.

There was obviously a limit to CBS's willingness to underwrite comedy that came packaged with no rating and no commercial interruptions. In February of 1948, three months after "The Little Show" folded, Ace returned to the air with "mr. ace and JANE." Though the basic ingredients of "Easy Aces" remained intact, the Aces performed, for the first time, before a live studio audience. The crowd consisted largely, Ace claims, of the overflow from "Winner Take All," a game show that was broadcast from an adjacent studio. "mr. ace and JANE" finally succumbed to a low rating in May of 1949.

With his career as a radio performer at an end, Ace parted company with CBS, and as he did so he realized that the network meant to shunt aside creative radio. "If an atomic bomb ever falls on New York City," he told a friend, "I want to be on the eighteenth floor of the CBS Building, because there's no radio activity there at all." The fault, of course, wasn't merely CBS's. Time was simply running out for radio, a reality that Ace confronted when he next went to work, at NBC, where "The Big Show"—the Little Bighorn, in effect, of radio activity—had its début November 5, 1950.

"You are about to be entertained by some of the biggest names in show business. For the next hour and thirty minutes, this program will present, in person, such bright stars as . . ." was the way that Tallulah Bankhead—breathlessly, earnestly, almost convincingly

—began each Sunday-night program. The roll call the first week included Fred Allen, Portland Hoffa, Mindy Carson, Jimmy Durante, Jose Ferrer, Frankie Laine, Danny Thomas, and a triumvirate from the Broadway musical *Call Me Madam*—Ethel Merman, Russell Nype, and Paul Lukas. For Ace and his co-writers, it must have been an unwieldy crowd of talent, this herd of big-name egos, to fit into a ninety-minute format. The glitter of well-known guest stars made "The Big Show" a prestige enterprise, but, despite this aura, it had overtones of a swan song. Ace knew it, repressed the thought, and faced the challenge of writing for Bankhead. In taking the job, he had to absorb a significant cut in pay. "My friend Ben Griefer, who was also my manager, convinced me to take the job," says Ace. "He suspected it would be a winning enterprise. I thought Tallulah herself would be the biggest problem we'd have on 'The Big Show.' Before we had our first script meeting with her, I told the other writers that we had to be tough. 'Let's be firm,' I said. 'Let her know that we know what we're doing.' Naturally, she swept into the room, and her first words were 'Are you gentlemen the authors?' It so happened that none of us had ever been called an author before, so we ended up getting along very well."

Tallulah offered what Ace could work with best—a recognizable and distinctive popular image around which the program's humor could be molded. "Two other writers had been hired before I joined the program, and we had a dummy script for the first show," Ace says. "The script indicated that we were going to have Ethel Merman singing the score of *Call Me Madam*—it seemed like the entire score—along with Russell Nype and Paul Lukas. Then, after the songs, Tallulah would say, 'Thank you, Ethel. That was wonderful.' And Ethel would say, 'Thank you, Tallulah, for having me on the show.' Then Tallulah: 'Oh, thank you, Ethel. It was our pleasure.' Ethel: 'Oh, thank you, Tallulah.' I asked, 'Why do we keep thanking Ethel? She's getting paid to do this show, isn't she? Why don't we do this in Tallulah's idiom?' So I rewrote it, and it came out quite different. After Ethel had finished singing for eight minutes, we made it clear that Tallulah was seething—you know, because *nobody* takes the stage away from her—so when the applause died down, Tallulah said, 'Thank you, Ethel, and better luck next time. No, actually, dahling, it looks as if you've got another hit show that's certain to run on Broadway two years. Let's see, now. You've had about *fifty* shows that have run two years each, haven't you, dahling?' " And the gentle gibes flowed on and on.

"Our motto was 'We write to order,' " says Ace. "On 'The Big Show,' the theory was that every star had a right to say whether he or she liked what we had written, and we had a right to disagree or compromise. Tallulah simply read a lot of lines in good faith and then, in the middle of a live broadcast, would say, 'Oh, dahlings, I just *got* that one.' Then, there were always a few people who thought that we were out to get them. Jack E. Leonard, himself one of the early insult comics, used to say every time he saw me, 'Who are you writing against this season?' On one of the early shows, we had Margaret Truman singing. Each week, we took out a morning or an afternoon to talk with our guest stars. Miss Truman had a long list of particulars. She didn't want any mention of her father, the President, or her mother or the Vice-President or anything about politics at all on the show. I said to her, 'Miss Truman, you realize that we have a singer on this show, Mindy Carson. If we wanted a girl singer, we'd just have a girl singer. We know that you're going to sing, but we think you ought to talk, too.' She said, 'It's all right as long as I don't have to do anything political.' I explained, 'Nobody's going to do anything bad. Tallulah is a Democrat, and you like her, don't you? And you like Fred Allen, don't you? And I'm from Kansas City.' She liked Tallulah and Fred, and she remembered me from when I wrote for the newspaper in Kansas City, so I told her she could come in the day before the show and we'd take out what she didn't want us to say on the air. She said, 'Well, you might have to rewrite the whole show.'

"On Friday, the day before the dress rehearsal, she came in with three Secret Service guys, who I think were going to shoot the stuff out if we didn't agree to take it out. The first joke she objected to was when we had Tallulah say, 'I'm very eager to meet Margaret Truman. She must be a very bright girl. She's only in her twenties and already she's the daughter of the President of the United States.' After some complaining, we got by with that one.

She also complained about a couple of others, but eventually relented. The one she wouldn't let us use involved Phil Silvers, who was supposed to come out and pretend not to know who she was. Tallulah would tell Phil that Margaret wanted to break into show business, and Phil would offer to help get her into the chorus line at the Copacabana. Margaret was supposed to say, 'Oh, that would be wonderful!' Silvers would then say, 'What's your address?' She would tell him 1600 Pennsylvania Avenue. And he would say, 'Is that an apartment house or a hotel?' And so on. Unfortunately, Margaret Truman vetoed the whole routine, because she didn't want us mentioning 1600 Pennsylvania Avenue on the air. When I asked her why, she said, 'I don't want any cranks knowing my address.' "

Let's assume, for the sake of argument, that Ace's recollection of his encounters with Miss Truman accords identically with the truth. Or let's assume that it doesn't. No matter. Either way, it is a Goody Ace original. "The Big Show" lasted two seasons on radio, and Ace spent the next fifteen years working as a head writer on television—an occupation that gave him a chance to collect many more such stories, raw nuggets of truth that he has refined and burnished until they shine with a comic luster that beckons credulity. When television began, the best writers and many of the not so great ones earned salaries that now seem unsoundly generous. Ace spent most of the years from 1955 to 1967 as head writer on Perry Como's variety show. At his high point, he earned ten thousand dollars a week—a figure that made him the best-paid writer in the business. Whenever he is asked to describe the differences between writing for radio and writing for television, Ace says, "Well, in television you only write halfway across the page. It doesn't mean much to anyone else, but it does double a writer's overhead." Having explained typewriter margins, Ace then enumerates the ways in which working in television for men like Milton Berle (1952–55) and Sid Caesar (1963–64) lacked the cozy ambience that "Easy Aces" had offered. Several years ago, in one of his columns for the *Saturday Review*, Ace contended that his ten-thousand-dollar salary carried with it a great number of "nondeductible tangible intangibles." "First, writing for a medium in which 'Batman' could be No. 1, there is an immediate loss of dignity," he argued. After deducting items like dignity ($1,655), integrity ($22.80), coercing guests to read their lines as written ($1,225.30), mollifying the network ($1,190.25) and sponsor ($965.30), he calculated that he netted $16.40 each week.

Ace was well paid during those years not simply because salaries were inflated but because he accomplished for Berle and Como and Caesar what he had for Tallulah Bankhead on radio: he imbued their comedy with a subtle flavor that matched their personas as performers. The comedy was far more delicate than random gags. Lester Gottlieb, a television producer who watched Ace work on "mr. ace and JANE" and, later, on the Como show, says, "Goody gave Perry a *tone*. It was an established fact that, man for man, Goody Ace was the best guy you could get to work on a comedy-variety show. If you wanted a writer who suggested hitting somebody with a pie, you hired someone else. Among all those television writers, Ace was the one who understood the English language and made it a habit to read something other than *Variety*."

Ace recalls the Como show with palpable fondness. "Working for Perry Como was the closest thing to not being in television at all," he says. "Perry was totally relaxed, utterly unflappable. Instead of a big monologue, he would tell three jokes, and you knew that whether a joke worked or not, immediately afterward Perry was going to sing 'Ave Maria' and the joke wouldn't matter. Most of the lines we wrote weren't for Perry but for the guests. Perry just wanted it all to go smoothly. I think I wrote a lot of things like 'And now, in a gayer mood, we take you to Latin America, where we hear the gentle rhythm of Perez Prado's orchestra.' No matter what the joke was, Perry assumed that the audience wouldn't get it. He was very nice about it, but he just had the feeling that most people who watched television were studying to be morons."

The idea that working with Perry Como was "the closest thing to not being in television at all" explains precisely why Ace stayed with Como for so many years. Ace wanted to be both part of and apart from the world of television. He convinced himself that he could justifiably earn ten thousand dollars every seven days if he tithed by writing pungent television criticism each week for the *Saturday Review*. The term "medium" struck Ace as a highly appropriate description of his place of business. He said at one point, "Television is called a 'medium' because most things on it are rarely well done."

In a situation comedy called "Himself," which he created in 1965, Ace set forth his proposals for the way television should ideally work. "Himself"—a pilot episode was written but never produced—recounted the tribulations of a weak-signal, one-camera television station in the basement of the Commerce Hotel on Main Street in the mythical town of Euphoria, Missouri. The proprietor of the station would have been named Alfred Benton Collins if the show had been sold to ABC, or Nathaniel Benton Collins if NBC had bought it, and so on. As a comic hero and highly independent station operator, Collins steadfastly refuses to align himself with the meganetwork that wants to swallow up his cottage industry. Naturally, he calls his station ABC or NBC or CBS, as the situation requires, and when the network begins to flex its muscles, Collins challenges his adversary: "How long you folks been using those initials? I've had mine for sixty-five years." Ace's version of ABC/NBC/CBS is a scaled-down parody of the networks. For instance, when Collins schedules public-affairs panel-discussion programs, he won't permit more than one panelist at a time. "We don't want any violence on this station. We run this station the way television should be run—like radio," he explains. "We have all the problems in Euphoria that the big cities have: pollution, unemployment, crime, high prices. The only thing we don't have is a race problem. Believe me, though, we're still working on it. We had a black couple from Three Forks who came and looked us over, and they finally said they wouldn't mind working here, but they didn't want to live here." In Euphoria, the late movie begins at six o'clock in the evening, and the test pattern comes on at eight. Whenever a caller or visitor asks, "Are you Mr. Collins?," he answers succinctly, "Himself." Collins, the hero of "Himself," bears more than a coincidental resemblance to Goodman Ace, himself. They are both single-minded entrepreneurs who believe that mass communications would work much better if the mass could be scaled down to the level of a room of one's own.

These days, the cottage of Ace's own cottage industry is his apartment in the Ritz Tower—four spacious rooms of white walls and black-and-white tiles. The living room leads to a terrace that offers a view of Park Avenue below and Central Park to the northwest. Ace often used to sit on the terrace to read and work—a habit he sustained until a few years ago, when flocks of pigeons began to roost there. "Shoo, pigeons!" didn't get rid of the birds, nor did pigeon repellents, plastic windmills, or signs that said "No Pigeons Allowed," so he finally gave up and retreated indoors. The apartment contains the same furniture that it has had for twenty years —off-white leather upholstery, a vague flavor of Art-Deco-in-decline, the aura of a stage setting. On one of the armchairs, there is a green cushion with white lettering that says, "LAUGHTER IS THE MUSIC OF THE HEART." A white grand piano stands in one corner of the living room, and atop the piano are a ceramic vase filled with artificial roses, a thirty-year-old photograph of Jane Ace, an unframed photograph of Groucho inscribed "Dear Goody, Here Is Me. Groucho," and an ineluctably stubborn pile of unanswered mail. When Jane died, in 1974, an extraordinary flood of condolences arrived, and Ace somehow managed to respond to each one personally. Because he does some of his funniest writing in personal letters, it's encouraging that, although he can't answer all of his mail, he does maintain pet correspondences. My sister-in-law, for instance, for whom he has developed a fancy, often receives postcards from him marked "Confidential."

Several years ago, Groucho Marx published a book called *The Groucho Letters*, a compendium of his correspondence with, among others, T. S. Eliot ("Dear Tom . . ."), James Thurber, Fred Allen, E. B. White, and Goodman Ace. Not long after the book appeared, Groucho phoned Ace to say that the publisher had

liked Ace's letters best—the book happened to contain more from
Ace than from most of Groucho's other pen pals—and that he
should consider compiling his own collection. For many reasons,
not the least being Ace's failure to keep copies of his letters,
he wasn't interested in the idea, and he became especially impatient when Groucho said, "No copies of your letters! Do you
realize that I got a twenty-five-thousand-dollar advance for writing this book?" Ace said, "Groucho, if you think that publishing
a book of letters that people have written to you makes you a
man of letters, you're mistaken." At which point, Groucho hung
up. When Groucho called again, several days later, Ace wouldn't
let the matter rest. "And another thing, Groucho," he said. "I
read your book *Groucho and Me*, and I thought the writing in
it was pedestrian." Groucho asked, "What does that mean?" Ace
said, "It means that the author should have been hit by a truck."
At which point, Groucho hung up again.

Ever since Ace began in radio, he has upheld the conviction
that very few people write funny things after one o'clock in the
afternoon. Each day now, after he finishes working in the morning,
he leaves his apartment and walks two and a half blocks to the
Friars Club for lunch. If the Friars Club was once a haven for the
quickest, cleverest minds in show biz, it is not quite that today,
and Ace likes to regard himself as the leading loyal dissident on
the premises. During lunch, the Friars Club is always filled with
people, but as far as Ace is concerned the empty-house effect
prevails much of the time. One day not long ago, when he and I
were seated at a large table in the center of the main dining room,
Ace heard a fellow-Friar, a retired judge, say that someone was
"as honest as the day is long."

"Excuse me, Judge," Ace said. "I just heard you say that, and
I write for a magazine, and I was wondering if I could use that
line. I just wanted to know, though, did you make that up?"

"I don't think so. Why?" asked the judge.

"Because I'd like to credit you with it," said Ace.

"Well, I've been saying it a long time. Would that be all right?"

"I don't see why not," said Ace. "By the same token, Judge,
would you say a man is as crooked as the day is short?"

"Well, I never heard of that."

"But you could say it?"

"Yeah, I suppose so."

"But you wouldn't be able to say it after December 21st, when the days start getting longer?"

"No, I guess not," said the judge, completely baffled.

There was a bit more of this interrogation, but before I was obliged to spill my water glass on my dear great-uncle he realized that he had filled his camaraderie quotient for the day and that it was time to go upstairs for a cutthroat game of pinochle. After he plays cards, Ace usually hangs around the Friars a while longer. If he allows himself to be caught off guard, members approach to ask semiprofessional—that is, nonremunerative—favors. Would he mind ghostwriting a letter for someone who wants to send his grandson a big Bar Mitzvah check and wishes to enclose a few sage words as well? Does he have any jokes that might make a hit at the Hillcrest Country Club, out on the Coast? Could he help somebody's son-in-law find work writing for television? No one is too bashful to ask. When Mike Denicoli, the resident Friars Club barber, mentioned recently that he needed a slogan to advertise his services, Ace came up with "Hair Cut While You Wait."

Around four o'clock on a typical afternoon, the sleeping pill that Ace took before bed the previous night begins to work, and when he wakes from his nap in a Friars Club armchair it is time to head home to catch the evening news. After dinner, he somehow manages to spend the evening watching television. His favorite private eye is James Garner on "The Rockford Files." ("He has great style and something the others lack—humor.") Ace also has a weakness for "The Mary Tyler Moore Show." In the process of admiring Mary Tyler Moore and James Garner he has seen enough television so that he can distinguish among the indistinguishable Barettas, Kojaks, and Delvecchios of the airwaves. I don't know whether to attribute my insufferable friend's capacity for watching television to infinite forbearance or to boundless optimism. Perhaps it is warped nostalgia. "I saw something on television the other night that made me laugh," he said not long ago. "And I thought to myself, Gee, I wish I'd written that. Then, about five minutes later, it occurred to me: Hey, I *did* write that."

1 9 7 7

(Goodman Ace died March 25, 1982. Four years later, almost to the day, my wife gave birth to twin boys, one of whom is named after his great late great-great-uncle.)

Supers

Being a Brennan brother requires a high degree of professionalism. There are five Brennan brothers—Peter, Joseph, Patrick, Michael, and George—and all five live and work in luxury apartment houses on the East Side of Manhattan. Familiars know Peter as Pete, Joseph as Tony, Patrick as Paddy, and Michael as Mickey. George's wife and his brothers and three sisters often call him Georgie. All five brothers are supers—building superintendents. The job comes with free rent and three or four dull headaches a day. A number of people in this line of work prefer to be called "resident managers" or some other title that sounds bureaucratically lofty. Calling the Brennans supers suits them fine. Their late father, John, was a super. "We've been supers since we were in short pants," Pete, the eldest brother, likes to say. Collectively, the Brennan brothers have seventy years of supering experience. In their hierarchy of values, only one thing ranks above the nobility of supering, and that is fraternity itself.

"If you met our father, which it's a shame you can't, you'd see why we're brothers this way," Pete said not long ago. "He had a belief that you only have each other. It's very rewarding to be brothers—especially if you're close."

The boys' mother, Bridget, lives with Paddy, at 1100 Park Avenue. Some years ago—my wife was pregnant at the time—Mrs. Brennan told me, "I hope your wife has a boy. Someone to take care of you." Mrs. Brennan was born in Crossmaglen, County Armagh, Ireland, as was John Brennan. Both arrived in America in 1929. The next year, they married and settled into an apartment at 125th Street and Park Avenue and started turning out baby supers. John Brennan died in 1957. On important occasions, the

Brennan boys wear specially designed gold rings. Each ring depicts a pair of outstretched hands—one belonging to John and the other to Bridget—which arch toward a central shamrock. Five white enamel inlaid triangles, each one containing the name of a Brennan brother in gold, surround the shamrock.

John Brennan loved to take things apart. His idea of fun was to dismantle something that worked perfectly well and try to put it back together. He particularly enjoyed fiddling with the television set. He would go to the roof of the six-story tenement that the family lived in for several years, at Ninety-seventh and Lexington, and jiggle the antenna. Mickey and Paddy had the job of monitoring the situation in the living room. Mickey would sit behind the set and control the fine tuning while Paddy watched the screen. An intercom rigged from a telephone enabled them to communicate with their father, aloft. Inevitably, this ritual developed a certain tediousness. The day that Mickey and Paddy both fell asleep on the job was the same day that their father, who was not a wispy man, fell into the chimney and was stuck there for a while.

Just about any domestic-repair challenge aroused John Brennan's interest and provoked his natural goodwill. Rewiring a neighbor's doorbell gave him pleasure; accepting money for the favor did not. If the utility company turned off a friend's power, he would turn it back on by running a line from the landlord's circuit. In time, he retired from active duty and supervised his sons' progress. "He used to make us take down the lights in the house—there's nothing wrong with the lights, just take them down and put them back up again," Mickey has said. "Take all the plumbing out from under the sink and put it back together. Take the faucet out and put the faucet back in. Remember, there's nothing *wrong* with the faucet. Take the *brand-new washing machine* apart—completely down to the bottom—and then put it back together. Take the whole shower down. This was a regular thing with him. It was to make you mechanically inclined, learn a trade. It was supposed to make you a super."

The Brennan sisters are Joan, Greta, and Barbara. Greta is married to a West Side super named Mike Norton. Norton's sister, Mary-Ann, is married to a Park Avenue super named Donald

Simkowitz. Pete Brennan's eldest daughter, Betty, recently married
a young man named Christopher Lynch, who used to work as a
doorman in Pete's building, on East Fifty-seventh Street. A while
back, Pete had to let Lynch go. Now Lynch is a super in another
apartment building down the block. Two of Lynch's brothers, Jimmy
and Tommy, are supers, and a third brother, Danny, is a handyman.
The Brennans get along fine with Norton, Simkowitz, and the Lynches,
who are fluent in the language of the building-service trade—
plumbing, No. 6 oil burners, boilers, standpipes, security, union
politics, the weird lady with all the birds in Apartment 9-F—and
who are nice guys who will grab a check when it comes their turn.
Nice guys like Norton, Simkowitz, and the Lynches have only one
glaring character flaw: they are not Brennans.

Michael Pemenidis, a professional real-estate manager, who formerly worked for Douglas Elliman–Gibbons & Ives, and who knows
the Brennans well, once gave this assessment of their supering
talents: "A super is like a castle keeper; when the king is away
hunting, somebody has to watch his house. If we were living in an
occupied city, there would be an underground network of supers
telling you where to get what you need. And you would definitely
want to have a Brennan or two on your side." I don't know exactly
how Pemenidis defines the term "occupied city." I do know, however, that a creature from an alien world broke into my apartment
a few years ago and that I mentioned the incident during lunch
the next day with the Brennans. Within a week, thanks to specific
guidance from George Brennan, I was able to install a security
system that has preserved domestic tranquillity ever since.

Bernie Goldenberg, a co-owner of Chelsea Hardware and a large-
scale vendor of building-maintenance supplies, thinks so highly
of the Brennans that he keeps a photograph of Paddy, George, and
Mickey taped to a shelf behind the counter in his place of business.
The photograph was taken a few years ago during the annual Patrons
Night dinner, an event sponsored by the New York Building Managers Association. Every year, Goldenberg buys five large tables'
worth of tickets for the event—a banquet featuring the sort of
entertainment that generally qualifies it as a stag affair—and insists
that all five Brennan brothers come as his guests. "Bernie says

we're a good-luck charm," Paddy Brennan once explained. Bernie Goldenberg says, "The Brennans are topnotch supers. They run no-nonsense buildings. If you're working for a Brennan and you're no good, you're not going to last."

The Brennan brothers look blood-related, but they are by no means identical. Straight and narrow noses run in the family, along with broad cheekbones, sharp and solid chins, gray and hazel eyes, sanguine complexions, and brown-to-reddish-brown hair. Pete is forty-nine years old, Tony is forty-six, Paddy is forty-four, Mickey is forty-three, and George is thirty-seven. The three middle brothers have the most in common physically, although Tony is crewcut and crisp in manner and looks like an outdoorsman, while Mickey is slightly rumpled and looks like an indoorsman. At five feet eleven, Paddy is the tallest. Pete, who is five-seven, is the shortest. The one who least resembles the others is George: his features seem thicker, his hair is light brown, his jaw is square, and he is built compactly, like a home-plate umpire. Periodically, Paddy and Pete grow mustaches, enjoy them for a few months, and then shave them off. Pete's mustache comes in flecked with gray. He has the darkest hair among the brothers; he wears it in a pompadour, and the wave has a solid streak of natural white. A vain man might ask a hair stylist to give him one of those if he wanted to look "Continental." None of the Brennans looks Continental, and none has ever displayed a grain of pretentiousness.

Each brother is a generalist and a specialist. Tony, for instance, in addition to having the all-around mechanical know-how and administrative ability that an effective super must have, happens to have particular skills in refrigeration-system maintenance and repair. More than once, I have heard one or another of his brothers say with pride, "Tony is very well known in the cooling line." George, in addition to having the all-around mechanical know-how and administrative ability that an effective super must have, has great proficiency in electrical work and locksmithing. Mickey and Paddy excel at oil-burner and boiler troubleshooting. Pete really knows plumbing. In all, the Brennans hold forty-six government-issued licenses, certificates, and permits: electrical, refrigeration, oil burner, air-pollution-control, fire-sprinkler, standpipe, locksmithing, exterminating, scaffold-rigging, steam-fitting, and others. Despite the Brennans' distinguishing traits, it is common to hear one of them describe ways in which two of his brothers are identical. Pete has told me that Tony, the most cerebral Brennan (his middle name is Anthony), is a lot like their father and also a lot like Paddy, who is the most relaxed Brennan. Pete has also said that George and Tony have the same way of giving a worker an order: they tell him once, concisely. George has explained to me how Mickey and Tony, the two natural leaders in the family, frequently remind him of each other. George and Tony talk alike. Paddy and Tony both hunt; Tony genuinely relishes the hunt, while Paddy likes to sit in the woods with a paperback novel and, if he remembers to bring it along, his rifle. Pete and Mickey used to work together. So did Tony and Paddy. For several years before Tony went to work in his present building, Paddy was the super there. For a couple of years during the early sixties, the five brothers, moonlighting, owned and tended a bar at Ninety-third and Lexington called Brennan's Pub. The effect of all this is that the Brennans come off seeming like most large families, only more so: the individuals are genuinely individuals, but they are also quite similar, in significant and insignificant ways.

A Brennan rarely shrinks from an opportunity to, as the brothers say, "put forth the super's point of view." Two of the brothers, Mickey and George, shrink less readily than the others. Comparing notes keeps them busy when they are not otherwise busy. One of George's fundamental beliefs is that no place on earth holds greater potential for peril and human tribulation than a luxury apartment house on Park Avenue. Basically, Mickey goes along with this, although he thinks that Fifth Avenue is marginally rougher territory. Mickey is the superintendent of a hundred-and-sixty-unit co-op at 1025 Fifth Avenue. George has eighty tenant-owners on sixteen floors at 1070 Park Avenue. Paddy manages a nineteen-story co-op with eighty-three apartments a block north of George's building.

These three brothers, the three youngest Brennans, eat lunch together most weekdays and discuss some of the harsh facts of life.
If a life-threatening or property-threatening emergency arises—
this happens to a Brennan once, maybe twice, a week—the one
involved is excused. Sometimes George or Mickey or Paddy prefers
to order in and have a sandwich at his desk, and that is O.K.,
too, provided it doesn't become a habit. Pete and Tony join when
convenience permits. According to the evidence, Tony is the busiest Brennan: his building, at 180 East Seventy-ninth Street, has
a staff of twenty. Monitoring their progress prevents him from
keeping a regular lunch date. Pete's crew, at 227 East Fifty-
seventh, is relatively small—only eight men—but Pete doesn't
like to travel, and that makes his attendance sporadic. During an
interruption in his supering career several years ago, Pete drove
a city bus. Ever since, he has mistrusted public transportation.
Once a year, he musters the faith to board the subway. On St.
Patrick's Day, he rides an uptown Lexington Avenue train from
Fifty-ninth Street to Eighty-sixth Street to watch the parade. (Going
home, he takes a taxi.) The Brennans' favorite lunch spot, the
Bantry Bar & Restaurant, happens to be on Eighty-sixth, east of
Lexington. This is where, shortly after noon on a weekday, it is
not unusual to encounter a quorum of Brennans.

The Bantry management appreciates the Brennans' patronage
and would hate to lose them as customers. Across the many years
that I have known the brothers, one of my proudest moments occurred when a bartender at the Bantry, knowing that I was waiting
to meet Mickey, and mistaking me for a shop steward in Local
32B-32J of the Service Employees International Union, asked me
to help a friend of his find work as a doorman. At the time, I was
occupying a booth in the rear. The Bantry has natural charm. It
is not the sort of place that needs Muzak renditions of "I've Gotta
Be Me" or "Moon River" to set a tone. There is a buffet line ("You
know the meat's always fresh here. It's a quick turnover," Mickey
assures a first-timer), a long bar, and balkanized seating arrangements. The Brennans always settle in the rear, where a lot of other
supers, and hardware and household-cleaning-supply salesmen as
well, tend to congregate. I was seated there with them not long

ago when the subject turned, as it frequently does, to the trials and atrocities of supering. All the brothers except Tony were present. Three adjacent tables had been lined up. One of them had not been wiped clean since the previous guests departed. When Pete arrived with his sandwich, a counterwoman who was carrying a rag accompanied him.

"Now we've got a fellow-worker in trouble," Paddy said as the woman wiped the table.

"I just said could I have a few extra napkins, and she follows me over here," Pete explained.

"Oh, gee, I hate a man who complains," Paddy said.

"Speaking of complaints, it's getting to be ridiculous," George said. "I mean the complaints to the super. The funny thing about a complainer is that when the building's spotless they want to know why we didn't clean the sewers, why aren't we doing the Sanitation Department's work, how come the sidewalk's dirty across the street, how come there's a mess in Central Park."

"If I showed you the folders we keep on complaints, you'd cry," Mickey said. He sounded as if his feelings had been bruised several times. "You know the kind—the ones who tell you there's garbage in the halls. With lipstick, they're writing 'Clean Me' on a window or a mirror. They send in a complaint—'I have no intercom.' I wanna tell 'em, 'Of course you have no intercom. Your dog keeps eating the intercom wire, that's why you have no intercom.' "

George said, "One of my favorite stories: I had a boss over, a guy from the management office. While he was there, a lady called down and said she had a complaint. What is the complaint? The floor is dirty. Now, I know it is *not* dirty, so I put the boss on the phone. He gets on, she tells him the floor is dirty. He says, 'I don't know how that could be, I was just up on your floor and the carpet looked spotless.' She says, 'Well, it's not *dirty* dirty, but I didn't hear the vacuum.' Can you believe it? I love it. It's brutal."

"They'll put a matchstick beneath an ashtray to test you," Mickey said. "They'll stick a straight pin in the rug to see if it gets vacuumed."

"I got an emergency call at two A.M.," Pete said. "A lady says get up here right away. I put on some pants and go up there. Guess what it is? You'll never guess. A roach. A roach on the floor. Dead. She couldn't sleep with it there. That's the emergency. I had to pick it up and flush it for her."

"I got up with a water bug the same way," said Mickey.

"I had it with a praying mantis," said Paddy.

"I had a tenant, she sent me water bugs in an envelope," said George. "Water bugs in an envelope! I still can't believe it."

Momentum builds quickly once the Brennans get going. They sound as if they were fighting a flash fire. The idiom and inflection are, naturally, New York Irish. A Brennan says "What's up?" or "How's things?" but never "So, what's new?" or "What's happenin', babe?" It takes practice to close your eyes in a room full of Brennans and know which one is speaking. Brennanese is full of locutions such as "My porter-doorman took a heart attack." Pete and Paddy have voices that sound raspy, whiskeyfied; Tony has a clipped manner, like a man defending his home against an aluminum-siding salesman; George and Mickey give the impression that they have studied dialogue from vintage suspense movies. When George is speaking to someone in a position of authority, he rarely uses a contraction, and he never drops a "g" at the end of a gerund or a participle. He would probably make an excellent prosecution witness. Mickey's diction runs more along the lines of Lieutenant Kelly, Homicide Division. He chain-smokes, and has perfected the short, quick, conspiratorial puff.

"The job's definitely getting harder, no question about it," Mickey said, and the others nodded. "It's a shame someone doesn't round up the statistics on supers—you know, the diseases, the divorces, the murders, the suicides. You got supers going crazy. That's the pressure of the job. The health goes. You're in the building all the time, and a lot of the wives just can't take it. You see a lot of supers flipping out, giving up. It's the pressure. Too much pressure."

"And no tenant wants to hear our problems," George said. "They always hit you with the apartment. 'Hey, you got a beautiful apartment on Park Avenue.' Yeah—and I have to *shop* around the corner, too, but on a super's salary. The pressure is constant. You're in the limelight. And you have to explain to your kids why we don't have a pantry, a maid, piano lessons, dancing lessons. I tell them, 'You don't need that. You have a mother for all that.' "

"A lawyer's or a doctor's time and advice are his stock-in-trade, and it's the same with a super," Paddy said. "You've got to be a father to the men who work for you. And you know how many tenants call you up just so they have somebody to talk to? Lots."

Pete said, "What is it you say, Georgie—you got to be a what to them?"

"You have to be a social worker, you have to be a singer, a dancer, and a comedian. You have to do flood control, police work, and emergency first aid, with some babysitting on the side. You have to be show-biz."

Each Brennan brother has established a precedent. Mickey was the first to enter the residential-building-service trade, as a doorman; Tony was the first to become a super, but his supering job at that time was in a commercial building; Pete was the first super in a rental apartment building; Paddy was the first to become a super in a high-rise apartment house; George was the first to dare to hire an all-Irish crew. In addition to their seventy years of supering, the Brennans represent fifty-five years of doormanning, elevator operating, handymanning, and portering. In 1956, when Mickey and Pete entered the trade, they worked at the Queen Anne, an apartment house on East Seventy-seventh Street near Third Avenue. While Mickey was a doorman, Pete was a porter. A few months later, Tony and Paddy went to work at a high rise in the next block, on East Seventy-sixth. Tony was a doorman, and Paddy ran the front elevator and worked as a relief doorman. After a year or so, Paddy went into the Army. This was during the early stages of the war in Southeast Asia. Paddy now wishes that he had been sent to Vietnam. Instead, he spent most of his tour at Fort Benning, in Georgia. While Paddy was away, Mickey took his place at the East Seventy-sixth Street building. After Paddy was honorably discharged, Mickey enlisted in the Army. I have never heard him express any regret over not being sent to Vietnam, although he and his brothers did once march together in a parade to support our fighting boys there.

Four of the brothers—all except Tony, who, after *his* Army tour,

went commercial, downtown—did their supering apprenticeships
in the same residential building, on Sutton Place South. This piece
of fate, they believe, accounts for the good fortune that they have
subsequently enjoyed. They also attribute part of it to their experiences with a man whom Tony and Paddy and Mickey encountered in the early days on East Seventy-sixth. The super in that
building was a man named Sullivan, a friend of John Brennan's,
but the brothers' main attention was not focussed upon him. An
elevator operator named Sam Wade became their true mentor. Sam
Wade was an elderly Irish Jew who kept milk biscuits and lollipops
in a cabinet in the lobby. He wore white gloves, and he was
exceptionally tactful and helpful—particularly for someone who
didn't actually care for dogs or children. Although he did not
smoke, he always carried cigarettes and a lighter. Few contingen-
cies found him unprepared. Confronted with adversity—four-year-
olds who insisted upon being addressed as "Mister"—he remained
serene. At the end of a workday, he enjoyed home cooking and
classical music. "He would put a Beethoven album cover in the
elevator car, propped against the wall," Mickey has recalled. "The
tenants would see that and say, 'Sam, I didn't know you liked
Beethoven.' He'd say, 'Oh, I love Beethoven. But records are so
expensive.' He'd go home loaded with Beethoven albums. Beethoven
and food. Women were always trying to feed him. Now, there was
a man who could take home a hot meal every single night."

The Brennans have great confidence in their own expertise. It
is Mickey's opinion, however, that "there are very few real supers
left out there." A real super manages day-to-day details and can
maintain his cool in the face of fire, flood, heart attack, or leaking
methane. A few years ago, Mickey wrote an article about the
Brennan clan for the *American Irish Observer*, a monthly newsprint
publication. Of superintending, he said this:

> We all started at the bottom which is the only way to learn
> exactly how a building should be run. When you start as a
> porter and work your way up through the lines, then, and only
> then, can you fully understand every aspect of the business.
> It is not an easy business to learn, and the only way to fully

grasp it is through experience in every area. Only so much can be learned from books and hearsay and passing on what was learned by others. It's like everything else in the world today, to experience is to understand.

That day at the Bantry, Mickey ordered a roast beef on a roll. Before he had eaten half, he lit a cigarette. "Lots of times, I get calls from my managing agent asking me to give a hand to a guy who can't handle the job," he said. "See, a lot of the boards of directors in these co-op buildings are getting very foolish. They get a guy in there who doesn't know diddly squat, but he's willing to do work that should really be done by a handyman, and that means the board can knock out a job slot, so they take this guy on, and by the time they realize their mistake it's too late. A mistake like that is a time bomb. You might not see it for five or ten years, and then one day the building falls down. You don't want to be nearby when that happens, either. You could get injured. They're finding this problem in a lot of these buildings where the boards think they're saving a few bucks. So we get a lot of calls from our own managers when there's an opening for a super. If we recommend a guy—if management knows that a guy is a friend of the Brennans, that he hangs around with the Brennans—they'll go with the guy. They know we'll pull him through. Management says to itself, 'There's no way the Brennans'll let this man sink.' "

Mickey paused and nodded a friendly hello to two men who were seated at a nearby table. Soon I gathered that their last name was Lynch and that it was their brother who was then engaged to marry Pete Brennan's daughter Betty.

One Lynch pointed to some empty chairs at his table and said, "See, we reserved spots, but you don't want to sit with us."

"You're not in the family yet," Mickey said.

"We're not looking forward to it, either," said the other Lynch.

"Unless there's a dowry involved," added the first Lynch.

"Did you hear that tone?" Paddy said. "There's gonna be a fight."

"We're not dangerous," said No. 2.

"And you're outnumbered," said Paddy.

It was agreed that the fight should be postponed until after the nuptials, and Mickey picked up where he had left off. "There has to be constant supervision of these workers," he said. "There's no telling what you'll get with some of the clowns they're pulling in off the street these days."

George said, "Did I ever tell you about the Spanish guy we sent up to change a washer? He goes to change the washer, but he forgets to turn the shutoff valve first. So when he removed the faucet handle he had water gushing out of there. He had to stand there for two hours with his thumb plugging it, until the tenant-owner came home. It was like he had his thumb in the dike. The thumb turned raw. Unbelievable."

"And what's a guy like that gonna do in a real emergency?" Mickey asked rhetorically. He was laughing now—a choppy, nervous laugh, like his style of smoking.

"If we go to an apartment and we smell a gas leak, we don't even ring the bell," George said. "The bell alone could produce a spark that would set off an explosion. Then, there's the burial detail. A lot of times, you get stuck with the burial detail. You have to deal with the police department, the ambulance, the morgue people, and, on top of the corpse, you got a lot of collectible effects that belonged to the deceased. I had a woman in my building once dead three days with an electric blanket on. Don't ask what that was like."

"Now, that's a job for the handyman," Paddy said. "Watching the corpse."

When Paddy's brothers go on at length about the indignities and dangers of their profession, his contributions are usually muted. A while back, Paddy encountered some health problems that permanently altered his outlook. "When that stuff happened, I decided it was time to tune out the harsh music," he has said. "Since then, I've felt much better." The Neil Simon comedy *The Prisoner of Second Avenue* is Paddy's favorite movie. Its message, as he has interpreted it, is that it is a super's lot to be blamed for everything that could possibly go wrong in a high-rise building, and particularly those acts of God over which the super has no control. If you want to argue that life's basic imperfections—square tomatoes, the high cost of parking a car, the decline of manners—are the

super's fault, you will not get an argument from Paddy. Being a
super since he was in short pants has taught Paddy not to take the
harsh parts personally. He has worked at his present job for almost
seven years. I once heard him say, "I got the one building in a
million that actually appreciates a super. A tenant told me the
other day, 'You are the best super on Park Avenue.' I told him,
'I'll have to go along with you on that.' I got no gripes."

While Mickey and George elaborated on various nuances of the
burial detail, Paddy had a conversation with a young salesman who
had pulled up a chair and joined the Brennans. The salesman's
name was George McGuire, and he worked for Zip Chemical, a
vendor of household cleaning supplies. Like Bernie Goldenberg,
of Chelsea Hardware, whenever there are large social gatherings
of supers the owners of Zip Chemical like to buy tickets and
distribute them to their favorite clients. Mickey once invited my
wife and me to a dinner dance that was sponsored by the Albert
B. Ashforth Resident Managers Club. The Ashforth real-estate
company is the managing agent of Mickey's building, and Mickey
was the financial secretary and entertainment chairman of the club.
To make certain that it was an entertaining evening, he invited his
brothers and sisters and their spouses, certain brothers and sisters
and spouses of those spouses, and a number of other relatives and
friends. The Brennans et al. filled four large tables. Tickets cost
thirty-five dollars a couple. Zip Chemical picked up the tabs for
a couple of other tables.

George McGuire, the Zip salesman, was polite and solicitous.
Paddy said, "How about some coffee, George?"

"I can't drink it anymore," George McGuire said.

"I didn't say, 'Do *you* want a drink?' I said, 'How about some
coffee?' "

"You want some?" McGuire asked.

"I could use a light cup."

After polling the other brothers, George McGuire departed. When
he returned, a few minutes later, he carried three cups of coffee
on a tray. By that time, the main conversation had threaded from
death among the tenant population to death within the super population (specifically, the effects upon supers of exploding aerosol

cans), then to living and breathing but nevertheless ineffectual supers, and then to the media and how, historically, certain of their elements have maligned supers.

George Brennan said, "Remember that story in the *Post* a few years ago? They interviewed some guy who was drunk. He was stoned to the mickey. They went out of their way to find a drunk super."

"Johnny Carson was a guy who was always giving supers a hard time," Mickey said. "Remember, he had jokes like 'Christmas must be coming. I don't need a ladder to get out of the elevator.' Oh, that Carson was a stiff."

"You had Carson in your building, didn't you, Mickey?" Pete asked.

"No, I had David Susskind. A long time ago."

"He was a stiff, right?" Paddy said.

"No, Susskind was no stiff. He always left a nice tip."

"You had Joey Adams, right?" one of the brothers asked. "Who was it—Joey Adams? Joey Bishop?"

"I had Joseph E. Levine," said another brother. "Now I got Norman Vincent Peale and What's-His-Name, the 'Love Boat' captain."

"One of my tenant-owners is Ruth Gilbert, who was on with Milton Berle all those years," said a third brother. "Also, John Daly, from 'What's My Line?' And Jean Carroll, the comedienne —she used to be on 'Ed Sullivan.' She's the widow of Buddy Howe, the agent."

"I had Virginia Graham," Mickey said. "You know what I found with her? The same way she is on television, that's the way she is in person." Mickey rendered an arresting impersonation of Virginia Graham's voice. "You know, it's 'Hi, dahling.' She's very comical. Whenever the men went up there to fix things or to make a delivery, she'd say, 'Give me a second to get dressed, dahling. Oh, don't peek!' During the strike a few years ago, no one else came down with hot soup and coffee for the boys on the picket line. But she did. That showed me something. *Class*."

"All my tenants are class," said Paddy.

"It's simple, Pat," Mickey said. "The time they appreciate you is when you're a Brennan and you go into a building where they already got rid of two or three bums."

"I got no complaints," said Paddy.

Each of the Brennans is a Thirty-second Degree Mason, a member of the Scottish Rite, a loyal Shriner, a Knight of Columbus, and a dues-paying member of Local 32B-32J of the Service Employees International Union, A.F.L.-C.I.O. The Scottish Rite meets once a month or so, the Masons meet the third Tuesday of the month, the Shriners the first Thursday, the Knights the fourth Wednesday, and the union the first Friday. Outside these official councils, the Brennans see a great deal of one another. Family gatherings arise naturally and frequently; members of a less happy family might say that they occur inexorably. Among the Brennan brothers, sisters, spouses, and offspring, there are forty-five birthdays and wedding anniversaries on the calendar. Generations overlap and proliferate, and there has been a consistent string of christenings across the years. A number of ex-officio Brennans turn up at these festive events, and the Brennans go out of their way to return the favor. One Saturday evening some months ago, for instance, Brian Mynes, a friend of Mickey's since boyhood, threw a party for himself to honor his graduation from Fordham University. He rented the gymnasium and cafeteria of a parochial school on Park Avenue— one that George Brennan's children happen to attend—and invited five hundred people. Most of them came, and many brought friends. George was the only Brennan brother who couldn't make it that night. Mickey contributed to the affair by hiring a hurdy-gurdy man and his monkey to work the crowd and by persuading G.I. Joe the Hotdog King, a former sidewalk vendor (he now works as a doorman in Mickey's building), to emerge temporarily from retirement. Before Brian Mynes was a college graduate, he spent twenty-five years as a sandhog and a merchant seaman. On occasion, between subway-tunnel-construction projects and trips around the world, he manned doors and operated elevators. His brother Jimmy is a super in a co-op on the West Side. Jimmy is also the producer, director, cameraman, and occasional moderator of a cable-television program called "The Irish Circle Show." I happened to tune in to an installment of "The Irish Circle" one Sunday afternoon a few years ago when the Brennan brothers were guests. It was difficult to judge who seemed happier—the Brennan brothers, so pleased to be celebrated, or Jimmy Mynes, so proud to have all of them on his cable-TV program.

I went to the Bantry Bar for lunch one day not long after the brothers were simultaneously inducted into the Shriners. Mickey arrived that afternoon with a small photograph in a wooden frame, which he propped between the ketchup bottle and the mustard pot. It showed the five brothers and three wives (Tony's wife had been sick the night of the induction, and Paddy is no longer married) posing with their Shrine lodge's potentate, or leader. Every man in the photograph wore a tasseled fez. Along with the photograph, Mickey had brought a recent copy of the official publication of the Valley of White Plains Ancient Accepted Scottish Rite of Free Masonry. Another photograph of the Brennans was published in the newsletter. Unfortunately, the caption had the identities mixed up.

"That happens all the time," Mickey said. "They line us up shortest to tallest and then they list our names alphabetically."

"With the Shriners, the potentate insisted on having a picture taken," George said. "Out of thirty-five new members, we were the only ones he made a big fuss about."

"They really believe it's the first time in the history of the Shriners that five brothers came up together," Pete said. "Also, when we took the Thirty-second Degree together from the Masons they said the same thing."

"The potentate wanted to have his picture taken *only* with us," Mickey added. "Even though there were quite a few other guys inducted, and two of them were brothers, you can't beat five at a time."

The Brennans don't require the intervention of a potentate to encourage fraternizing. Any time a Brennan brother gets the urge, he can accomplish wonders with just a phone call. When a Brennan is in a jam and needs assistance, whether or not the trouble is related to supering, he calls a Brennan. And a Brennan responds, maybe bringing along another Brennan or two or three. In a crisis, a Brennan doesn't dally, nor does he keep score. He simply moves. "Since I met Georgie, my life has gone faster than ever," George's wife, Barbara, has said. George once had to pass up a festive evening on the town—a supers' ball planned by the Douglas Elliman real-estate organization—because of a fire in the subbasement of his building. The fire erupted the night before the ball, but twenty-four hours later George was still mopping up. Also, his tuxedo had suffered some smoke damage. When the fire started, Paddy, who lives a block away, had run over to assist.

"There used to be a tailor's shop in the room where the fire broke out," George told me a few weeks later at the Bantry as he recounted the drama. "It's where the tailor did his pressing. As soon as it started, I turned off the gas meters down there. Otherwise, the whole building could have blown. We should get a commendation for that from the Fire Department, but the tenant-owners will never know about it."

"When you get through with that commendation, you can get me some new shoes," Paddy said.

"How about nineteen dollars instead?" Mickey suggested.

"Eighty dollars," Paddy said. "I don't spend anything less for my feet."

"You don't want something like that fire to happen if you're in the middle of a degree ceremony with the Masons or the Shriners," Pete said. "But we do get emergency calls."

"I was taking a course in boilers one night and my wife called me about a leak," George said. "If I couldn't have got away, one of the brothers would have covered for me."

"Hey, talk about an emergency, I had the Mother Superior from Marymount stuck in the elevator there the other day," Mickey said. He was referring to a Catholic girls' school that is around the corner from his building. "The Mother Superior wasn't strong enough to open the door to help herself out. She was very cute, but then she got a little nervous. I cut up my hand getting her out, but it was worth it. Now she prays for me every day."

●   ●   ●

The members of the world's most perilous profession maintain a distinction between a "dress super" and a "working super." As the titles imply, a dress super does his best to look like a white-collar manager and to avoid circumstances that could result in his having to send a jacket and a necktie out for dry cleaning. Tony is the only dress super in the family. His building, at Seventy-ninth and Third Avenue, has a hundred and ten apartments, and his staff of twenty comprises twelve doormen and elevator operators, one handyman, one handyman-porter, one package-and-security man, one porter, and four relief workers who rotate among jobs. Despite Tony's skill at delegating authority, he is hardly deskbound. He stays in motion, on and off the job. In the autumn, he stalks deer, with a bow and arrow or with a rifle. He subscribes to the *American Hunter* and reads articles with titles like "Do It Yourself: Yukon Moose Hunt" and "How the Experts Fool Fall Turkeys." I phoned him once during the week before Christmas to ask whether I could drop by for a visit, and he discouraged me by saying, "I don't have time. I'm busy hustling. This is my money time of the year. I've got to be loose. In a big building, you're dealing with a lot of personalities, if you know what I mean."

Later that day, I went to see Mickey Brennan. When he greeted me, he was seated at his desk and was drinking a cup of coffee. I was surprised to find him in repose, and even more surprised to see him wearing a blue suit, a white shirt, and a solid-blue necktie. When I asked him why he was disguised as a dress super, he said, "How I dress depends on how I feel. Today, I didn't feel like doing any work."

Mickey's desk is made of steel that has been painted black, and its surface is protected by a large sheet of glass. Under the glass he has put the business cards of contractors who do work or would like to do work in the building. I saw "Alter Steel House of Windows," "Leonard Morena Tile and Plaster, Inc.," "Henrik Berkovitz, Expert Carpenter," "Felix McCloskey, Painting and Decorating," "Jimmy—For Expert Finish Floor Waxing," "Fonde Plastering and Tile Corp.," "Pioneer Fence Co., Inc.," and "Martin Elevator Co.," among many others.

"Normally, a tenant comes to me and wants to know how much a paint job costs, I give 'em the names of three painters and say,

'You pick 'em,' and that's that," Mickey told me. "But I made a mistake here the other day. I had a tenant-owner, a lady who needed a plaster job on her ceiling. The whole ceiling was coming down. I look at it, I say, 'You know, don't do a patch, do the whole ceiling.' She says, 'How much would that cost?' I say, 'I don't know, maybe eight, nine hundred dollars.' I give her the name of a contractor, he comes to take a look, and he quotes her a price of eleven hundred dollars. So you know what she says? She says, 'Mr. Brennan kept three hundred dollars for himself.' " Mickey quoted the woman in a high-pitched, mocking tone. Then he shook his head. "It's getting rougher."

The implication that any Brennan would accept undeserved or tainted income Mickey finds offensive in the extreme. Pete Brennan once explained to me, "If you're taking something from an outside contractor—I mean a kickback—you can't get rid of him. If the managing agent for the building comes to me and says, 'I want to change the plasterer,' or the painter, the plumber—anyone—I say, 'Fine.' Then the plasterer can't go to the managing agent and say, 'Hey, you're throwing me out of the building and I was taking care of your super.' He can't do that, because I won't take nothing."

The price of such honor is that none of the Brennan brothers has accumulated sufficient assets to retire and go live in County Armagh. A super who belongs to 32B-32J might start out at two hundred and ninety dollars a week and then, depending upon seniority and other considerations, can earn as much as five hundred and fifty dollars a week. People who live in well-maintained New York City apartment buildings generally assume that a super's salary is supplemented at Christmastime by gratuities that amount to an extortionist's daydream. According to the Brennans, this is a pathetic misconception. In Mickey's building, a complicated system for accepting gratuities has evolved. Each year, two weeks before Christmas, every tenant receives a letter expressing heartfelt season's greetings from the building staff. This letter includes a list of the employees and their positions. (Otherwise, some residents might not ever get to know the help by name.) When a tenant decides which employees are worth a tip and how much, he or she puts the money in separate envelopes and gives them to a designated member of the building staff—usually a doorman, never the super. Each employee then signs a book, stating that he has received envelopes from certain tenants—and no one can ever complain that the super has pocketed his tip. An employee might well complain, however, that, considering a tenant's lack of munificence, the super might as well have pocketed the tip. One Christmas, before Mickey took over 1025 Fifth Avenue, a tenant there made the mistake of sending down neckties rather than dollars for the members of the staff. Eight or nine men, all of whom already owned neckties, went upstairs and tied their gratuities to the tenant's doorknob. In turn, the tenant felt underappreciated. Mickey knows the devils that would drive a man to decline the gift of a necktie, but he forbids his men to retaliate in a hostile manner. Confronted with an undertipper or a nontipper, he adopts a Gandhi-like bearing. "A lot of the tenants, the ones that skunk you, they think you're going to be mad," he told me. "But I never change my attitude toward them whatever. I give them a big smile and a hello and it kills them. Drives them right up the wall. That friendliness makes them crazy. They go up the wall."

Mickey's philosophical beliefs hold that a super should average about fifty dollars a tenant. Reality, however, clashes with dogma. "I'll tell you the truth. Some of these tenants, I'd rather give *them* the money so they'd leave me alone. It's three dollars. It's worse than stiffing you altogether. It's unbelievable. They stiff you so bad they make you feel sorry for them. The real rich—I've got only one or two of those. Georgie and Paddy have them on Park Avenue, but not here. The *real* rich are used to service, and they know how to take care of you. The one who complains that the building's filthy, the help is never nice to him, nothing goes right—he dollars you. Some of them stiff you completely. The whole thing is crazy. Sometimes a doorman will outdo a super. Figure that one out. There's tenants I've never been inside their apartments in four years—they give a hundred. The stiffs hand you an envelope the week before Christmas, along with a list of five jobs they want done. Sometimes they forget to put anything in the envelope."

Mickey doesn't refer to the room where he keeps his desk as an office; he calls it the shop. The shop is the size of a comfortable

living room. It has cinder-block walls and a concrete floor that
have been painted battleship gray. Organized disarray prevails.
Screwdrivers, mallets, and wrenches hang from pegs along the
walls. A large wood-surfaced workbench occupies the center of the
room. Several metal vises are mounted on the workbench. Fan
belts hang from hooks in the ceiling, which is twelve feet high.
Steve Somlai, a muscular, hale fellow in his late forties, who is
the building's handyman, came into the shop. He stood on a metal
ladder and began rummaging among the fan belts.

"I need four L-seven-twenty belts, Mike," he said. He speaks
with a German inflection and has a peripatetic manner. "Order me
seven-twenties."

"Right," Mickey said. Within seconds, Steve had descended
the ladder and trotted out.

"He never stops running," Mickey said. "From now to five
o'clock, he'll be running. But a lot of it's lost motion."

A young woman who was a member of the building coöperative's
board of directors dropped by to discuss the floor tiles in the
elevators. There are two passenger elevators, each one serving
eighty apartments. Both elevators had newly installed polished oak
parquet floors. Apparently, several tenants had complained that
the parquet tiles somehow violated the building's aesthetic consistency. The co-op's directors had decided not to replace these
tiles, however, because the elevator floors had already been torn
up four times in an effort to reach a consensus. Mickey's demeanor
during this conversation was deferential. He said "Yes, Ma'am"
several times and nodded rhythmically. After the tenant had left,
he said, "She's the new young. They want to spend the building's
money to make it look nice. Then you get the old old. They don't
want to spend. You can take a survey in this building. You'll be
lucky to get two people to agree on anything." Mickey's attitude
toward the tenant-owners who are, in effect, his employers is a
mixture of formal respect, amused tolerance, and awed bewilderment.

Mickey once took me on a tour of his building—through the
boiler room, through the storage rooms and the bicycle room and
the package-delivery room, along the dimly lit ground-floor cor-

ridors, past the eclectic modern furnishings in the lobby, up the interior fire stairs, back downstairs by elevator, and into a courtyard filled with magnolias, rhododendrons, pansies, forsythia, ivy, and linden trees and guarded from invaders by a tall fence topped with razor wire and axle grease. This was not long after the building had received a cosmetic overhaul, including fresh paint and a scrubdown of the wallpaper in the public areas. In one of the storage rooms, awed bewilderment overcame him. It was an ugly, musty hole that brimmed with old, moldering luggage, including many steamer trunks. "They save stuff that they never want," he said. "You're not supposed to have nothing down here but luggage. But the stuff they keep—I can't believe it. A tenant sees one of the men throwing out an old sink one day, the tenant decides he has to have it. He sticks it down here and forgets about it. So we end up with everything, including the kitchen sink. Get a look over here. This guy's saved every copy of *Playboy* going back to the Year of the Flood."

As we sat in Mickey's shop that pre-Christmas afternoon, several building-staff members came in to report on their progress. They all seemed to know what they were doing, and everyone had a cordial attitude. The drop-ins included Steve the handyman, a doorman, an elevator man, a porter, Steve the handyman again, an outside painter who had been hired by a tenant, and Steve the handyman once more.

"You notice I got the League of Nations working here," Mickey said. "I've been that way for a long time. Georgie's finding out just now that that's a good approach. He's been to seven grievance arbitrations against men who worked for him. I've never been to any. Georgie usually wins, but who needs that headache? He's got all Irish in his building. I've got everybody. You get all one thing, eventually they'll band together and turn against the super. You get all Puerto Ricans or all Irish in here, you couldn't run this building. Here, I'll give you a dime to call up Georgie's building and ask for King Billy. Whoever answers will tell you whether he's in or out. You know, William of Orange, the curse of Ireland— King Billy. That's what the men call Georgie when he's not looking."

On one of Steve Somlai's visits, Mickey said, "Tell this man

about your Christmas tips, Steve. Tell him about your favorite
tenant. You know which one I'm talking about. She give you any
newspaper coupons lately?"

Steve shook his head in a resigned way. "Don't forget the empty
jars. She gives me those. She's got a whole closetful. That's a fire
hazard, Mike."

Mickey explained the situation. An elderly tenant regularly asked
Steve to come to her apartment to do repairs, and when he finished
she tipped him with grocery-discount coupons that she had clipped
from the newspaper, or, if she didn't have any of those around,
she might offer a banana or an orange or a box of cornflakes or
half a roast-beef sandwich. Now, apparently, she had branched
into empty glass jars. When Steve turned his back, Mickey whispered to me, "He doesn't know how to say no."

Mary Ann Brennan, Mickey's wife, stuck her head in at the
doorway. She is a slender, attractive blond woman whose maiden
name was McCall. "My family doesn't go in for the Brennans' sort
of clannishness," she told me not long after I met her. "We're
secure. We know who we are. We don't need each other to constantly remind us."

George Brennan's wife, Barbara, has said, "Before I married
Georgie, everybody warned me there were no secrets in the Brennan
family. They were right. But I actually believe that they are among
the best supers—the Brennans are."

Mary Ann Brennan is reserving judgment. She had come down
to the shop to ask Steve Somlai to repair something in the family's
apartment.

"I don't bother to ask Mickey, because it never gets done," she
said.

I asked her what was broken.

"Ask Mickey," she said, smirking.

Mickey shrugged.

"O.K., I'll run through it for you," Mary Ann said. "The children's bedroom window doesn't open, so in case of fire there's no
way those poor, helpless children could get out. There's no doorknob on the closet in my children's room, so God forbid the baby,
Jimmy, should get locked in there. He'd probably asphyxiate. I

don't even want to think about that. I just want it fixed. The faucet hasn't worked for a year and a half. We need a new flushometer in the toilet bowl. It makes noise all night unless you get out of bed and jiggle the handle. I know there's some other stuff, but those are the main things right now. My mother-in-law lives with Paddy. Paddy never fixes anything in his apartment. My mother-in-law pays the handyman to fix anything that needs it. In Pete's and Tony's apartments, if anything goes wrong it stays that way."

I looked at Mickey for confirmation or denial. He was staring at the ceiling, at the fan belts. He was smoking a cigarette. He looked down, he smiled, and he shrugged again.

Midmorning one St. Patrick's Day, Peter Brennan and I met at his building, on East Fifty-seventh Street. It is an unspectacular building—red brick, twenty stories, leaded windows, a few Art Deco flourishes—whose main virtue is its proximity to the Sutton Theatre. We stood at the door, beneath a gray canopy, and chatted—about the weather (looked like snow) and about Pete's clothes: a black chalk-striped suit and a white shirt. If it had not been for his bright-green necktie and a green shetland sweater, he might have looked as if he were on his way to a wake. These were definitely not the clothes he wore when he had to drain a hot-water line or change the oil in a boiler compressor. We rode an elevator down to the basement, and I followed Pete to his shop, a room ten feet by twelve. Its shelves and cabinets contained linoleum adhesive, powder abrasives, furniture wax, floor wax, wax remover, grease remover, steel wool, waterproofing, glass panes, glass cleaner, grout, paper towels, drainpipes, drain traps, gallon cans of paint (floor enamel, tile enamel, flat wall latex, deck latex), paint remover, light bulbs, light fixtures, sledges, wrenches, saws, brushes, screwdrivers. Pete's building was undergoing a metamorphosis from rental to co-op. He explained some possible implications—how housekeeping decisions, for example, could allow for a margin of creativity.

"Work that you'd do with the landlord's money you might not necessarily do with a co-op's money," he said. "Say I go into an apartment and there's a place where the plaster on the wall's been getting wet from the shower," he said. "You use a shower long enough, you're gonna get loose plaster. You can have fresh plaster or you can have tile. Now, if you're a halfway decent tenant that doesn't give me a hard time, you get the tile job. If you're breaking my chops all the time, you get the plaster job. Sometimes, in a co-op, you start doing some of these jobs and when the bills come in the tenant-owners don't want you to do the big jobs anymore.

"My responsibility in this building is to avoid the outside contractor. I've got three doormen, a relief doorman, a porter-doorman, a regular porter, a handyman, and a standby man. I do the repairs myself—the major things. If a guy goes up and just plunges out a toilet, I wouldn't put that in the classification of handyman's work. We use outside contractors here sometimes, but my job is to avoid that. Without exaggeration, I would say that I save my boss thirty to forty thousand dollars a year.

"People say, 'Oh, you're a super, how great.' But they don't realize how sick you feel when you've been in a building eight years with a tenant, saying 'Hi' to the tenant every day, and he says, 'Hi, Mr. Brennan,' and then one day he dies. That hurts. And all along everybody thinks, Oh, that job's so easy."

I knew that Pete had been experiencing some bad luck. One morning, he had gone to the basement and there in the laundry room had found his night porter seated in a chair with some bullet holes in him. By chance, this happened the day that John Hinckley shot President Reagan, so the shooting on Fifty-seventh Street brought Jimmy Breslin and some other newshounds around to Pete's building. Then, a few months later, a tenant had apparently met the wrong stranger in a bar and invited him home, with fatal consequences. After these mishaps took place, the other Brennan brothers told me that while none of it was Pete's fault it wouldn't do him any good, professionally speaking. In his supering career, Pete had established certain procedures and policies. ("I've learned that whether a tenant is right or wrong, agree with him. I get invited to lots of parties here, but I never go. It's not personal, it's just policy.") Still, it had never occurred to him that he needed to devise a homicide policy. By the time of the second murder, however, he had a system for dealing with the hardworking reporters who lined up outside his building: he wouldn't let them inside. "After James, the night porter, died, I went down to the precinct to take a lie-detector test," he said. "That was strictly voluntary. After the tenant got taken out, the police sealed the apartment. Then a cleaning crew comes in. That's an outside contractor's job."

Talking about these matters dampened Pete's mood. It improved, however, when his two sons, Joseph and Peter, showed up and announced that they were ready to go to the St. Patrick's Day parade. We walked west along Fifty-seventh Street to Lexington Avenue and then headed for the I.R.T. station at Fifty-ninth Street. It was time for Pete's annual subway ride. He gave Peter money to buy three tokens. "We're only going one way," he said. "It's a cab ride home."

The first train that pulled in happened to be an express traveling on the local track. "That's a break," Pete said. "It saves me having to make two extra stops." He stood the whole way and before long emerged safely on Eighty-sixth Street, opposite the Bantry Bar. A raw, nasty wind blew from the west. What seemed like a modest number of spectators huddled in clusters on the sidewalks between Lex and Park. Pete walked toward Park. "This weather's gonna kill a lot of people," he said. For a few moments, I thought he meant that the combined effects of drink and overexposure would be literally deadly, but then he said, "I mean it'll keep the crowd down. Lots of people won't come in, because they heard snow."

We hadn't gone far when, just as the St. Joachim Drum and Bugle Corps, of Cedarhurst, came by playing "Take Me Out to the Ballgame," we encountered Mickey and George and Paddy Brennan. Mickey wore a blue suit, and Paddy had on gray slacks and an off-white Irish cable-knit sweater. "How much more Irish can you get?" he said. George wore a brown camel's-hair topcoat and a gray motoring cap.

With a cigarette clenched in one corner of his mouth, Mickey passed out lapel pins to the others and said, "Here. Here's for the blood you gave."

"What?" Pete said.

"You're all blood donors now."

"I can't afford any more medals," Pete said. "I ain't got room."
"When did we give blood?" Paddy asked. "I don't remember
giving blood."

"You *gave*," Mickey said.

"Oh, yeah, yeah. Right, right," Paddy said.

Soon the Brennans were joined by their friend Brian Mynes. The
brothers have always admired Brian's capacity for bold innovation
—especially his shameless willingness to wear a jade shamrock
in his left earlobe. On this day, he also wore a camel's-hair topcoat.
A brass object attached to a yellow-white-and-black ribbon dangled
from his breast pocket. It was a commemorative subway token.

"It's the Monsignor Temple's Meritorious Medallion, in honor
of Peter Brennan," Brian Mynes said. "I was going to ride one of
the horses in the parade today. I had it all rented for forty bucks,
but then they told me I had to rent a uniform, too, and that was
an extra sixty. Maybe next year."

The Brennans had gathered in front of a Chembank Card machine
across the street from Gimbels and the RKO Twin Theatre.

"Our old neighborhood always shows up right at this spot," Paddy
said. He described the territory—from the "G" in the Gimbels
sign to the canopy of 115 East Eighty-sixth Street, and, on the
downtown side, from the Chemical Bank to the "Park" sign just
west of Barnes & Noble. The New Jersey Gaelic League, the Suffolk
County Police Emerald Society, the Don Bosco High School Band,
and the Mother Cabrini High School Band went by in the parade.

George Brennan surveyed the crowd and offered a play-by-play.
"All walks of life," he said. "All walks of life. See that fellow,
he's with Con Ed. Over there, he's got a leather-goods store in the
Village. He's a lawyer, did real well when Frank Hogan was D.A.
All walks of life. There was a lot of talent in this neighborhood.
You know Frankie Reilly? He's a piper with the Fire Department's
Emerald Society Bagpipe Band. And his brother Pat Reilly used
to play with the Paddy Noonan Band. You know Paddy Noonan,
the accordion player. And Terry Flynn's a big man with the State
Liquor Authority. And Joey Flynn, his brother, is a dancer. They're
all from the neighborhood."

Several overmedicated teenagers went by, saying unflattering

things about the Queen of England. I noticed that neither George
nor any of his brothers was drinking, and I asked him why. "It's
a workday," he said. "If I get an emergency and I go fix something
and the tenant-owner smells alcohol, then I'm branded a boozer
for life. Plus, I'm shorthanded today. My handyman took sick this
morning. I had to drive him to Doctors Hospital. See, you can
never relax on this job, *never*. Not at any time. Like, take those
two guys over there." He pointed toward a pair of middle-aged men
who were watching the parade and, at the same time, watching
him. "Now, those are two guys who should never drink, *ever*. They
work for me. That's Jack, and the other one's Mike. I'm down here,
and you might think I'm watching the parade, but I'm also keeping
an eye on them. I want them to stay straight. Mike did some work
for me on my house upstate. He's a very talented man. He lifts
houses. He lifted mine forty inches. That's a hard job, you know.
You have to be a talented man. Otherwise, you could crack a house
in half. Look at him. He's looking over here."

It began to snow—lightly at first, and then not so lightly. This
was definitely long-underwear weather. After about an hour of
parade-viewing, Pete, Paddy, and Mickey retreated to Mickey's
apartment. A while later, George and I headed that way, too,
moving into the snow squalls and in the opposite direction from
the Irish Dancing Music Association of America, the Saffron Kilts
Pipe Band, of Babylon, Long Island, and the National Board Ancient Order of Hibernians Ladies Auxiliary. At Mickey's, there
was a smorgasbord—cold cuts, pigs-in-blankets, sliced cheeses,
chips and dips, hot meatballs. In the kitchen, atop the stove, two
briskets, five tenderloins, cabbage, and potatoes all boiled together
in an enormous pot. Friends and family had been dropping by for
some time. Most social gatherings at the Brennans' adhere to an
open-door policy. Guests wander in and out and back again. There
are a number of regulars, whose first names or nicknames I have
come to know—Joe, Ackie, Dougie, Kathy, Carol, Nessa, Nora,
Bill, Phyllis, Fiona, Louie, Ace, Jimmy, Pete. Usually, there are
a few Jimmys and Petes. The Brennan brothers named their children after themselves and one another and their friends, and their
friends did the same. Mickey and Mary Ann have five children—

Alfred, Michael, Veronica, Jimmy, and Brian. George and Barbara
have three—George, Bridgette, and Bobbi-Anne. Paddy has a son,
Patrick, who is called P.J. Tony's wife is Gloria, and their children
are John, Gloria, Joseph, Anthony, and Jason. Pete's wife is Eileen,
and their children are Joseph, Peter, Betty, Eileen, and Loretta.
Once, Pete was trying to explain an incident to me and he said,
"We thought maybe it involved one of the kids. Like maybe it's
my son Joe, who's named after my brother Joseph, which is Tony."
When a conversation takes a turn like that, I sometimes lose track.

Tony was seated at the kitchen table, along with Pete Martin,
a cousin from the Brennans' mother's side, and Mike Norton, the
Brennan brother-in-law who is a super on the West Side. They
were talking about Abercrombie & Fitch, where Tony had worked
as an engineer for many years.

"First, I was residential, then I was commercial, then I went
back to residential, where I am now," Tony was saying. "Abercrombie & Fitch was, you know, a place for the aristocrat set.
These very upper-crust customers shopped there."

Mike Norton said, "Did they use to have a catalogue? That was
a very old store, I remember. They had a catalogue, right?"

"Right," Tony said.

"It was the oldest mail-order catalogue, right?" Norton said.

"I don't know about that," Tony said.

"Yeah, I think it was."

"Maybe you're thinking of Sears," Tony said. "We weren't like
Sears. I used to see Frank Sinatra come in and order shirts by the
dozen. If he liked one, he'd say O.K., a dozen of those. And those
were twenty-five-dollar shirts. I did great there. I used to be able
to get these goose-down jackets—the ones that the customers returned because they had a tiny flaw. I'd get them for three bucks.
Real goose down. I had a closet full of those. I got them for all
the brothers. I saw a lot of stuff in that store. We had a guy one
day shoot himself in the gun department. He bought and paid for
the shells and took a shotgun off the rack and loaded it with his
shells and leaned on the trigger. Bought his own ammo. He was
all over the store. And Montgomery Clift used to come in there.
He wasn't in good shape. He used to come with a valet who would
help him stand up while he shopped."

Norton said, "He was very close friends with Elizabeth Taylor. She was with him after he had a bad car accident."

"I think he was married to Dinah Shore," Pete Martin said. "Wasn't he married to Dinah Shore or some singer?"

"I think she was married to someone else," Norton said. "George Montgomery?"

"Montgomery Ward?" Tony asked.

"*That's* the catalogue I'm thinking of."

The Brennan brothers are union men at heart—they have accumulated eighty years of membership in Local 32B-32J—and yet, without much soul-searching, they would say that a correct list of their priorities looks like this:

1. Brennanism
2. Superdom
3. The union

In 1980, the brothers found themselves at odds with the leadership of 32B-32J. The focus of the disagreement was an election campaign for the chairman of District Five. The district runs from Fifty-ninth Street to 110th Street and from the East River to Fifth Avenue, and its chairman occupies a seat on the union's board of directors. The incumbent was a man named Vernon Sampson, who had been the District Five chairman for fourteen years and had developed the habit of running for reelection unopposed. Roughly eight thousand union members are qualified to vote, and about two thousand usually do. The district chairman would run on a slate. When you voted to reinstall Sampson as chairman, you were also voting to install Rocco Petruzzi as recording secretary and Eddie Mathews as district-board member.

The Brennans entered a complaint—it was what ultimately put them at odds with the leadership of their union—that they were being subjected to taxation without representation. There were no supers on the union's governing board. In the spring of 1979, the doormen, elevator operators, handymen, and porters in 32B-32J had staged a strike that lasted eight days. Tenants in Manhattan's

most comfortable apartment buildings had to resort to opening their
own doors, punching their own elevator buttons, hauling their own
garbage to the curb for collection, hailing their own taxis, and
deciding who among them would sort the mail. (Shortages of mail-
room volunteers never arose.) The residential-building superintendents' contract with the Realty Advisory Board on Labor Relations,
a landlords' association, had an expiration date that was not the
same as the contract that covered other building-service employees.
During the 1979 strike, therefore, most supers were forced to cross
the picket lines of their fellow union members. Similarly, to this
day, strike or no strike, if a super disciplines or fires a worker and
the matter winds up in a formal arbitration, a union delegate usually
represents the worker at the arbitration hearing, while the super
is represented by management. The Brennans felt that if they
elected one of their own to the union leadership they could straighten
out these odd alignments.

Rather than designate one of themselves to run against Vernon
Sampson, the Brennans persuaded their pal Jimmy Mynes to take
on that job.

"We were supposed to run a whole slate of guys against Sampson,
but we didn't know the rules and we just ran Jimmy," Mickey said
after the election campaign. "We couldn't run for this ourselves
—on a slate with Jimmy—because, you know, we're the Brennans.
Like, everybody's afraid of us."

There were other complications. One of the election-fitness re-
quirements was that you had to have paid your dues—or some
such nitpick. George, Mickey, Pete, and Tony had been marginally
negligent in this regard. Paddy was paid up, but Paddy despises
conflict. In a tavern very early one morning, the Brennans got the
idea that Jimmy Mynes would make a fine candidate. Jimmy, who
at the time was feeling too good to object, more or less agreed.
"Jimmy's a fanatic," George explained. "Jimmy pays his dues a
year in advance. By the time he sobered up, it was too late to back
out. We'd already had the election posters printed."

To the Brennans' regret, the election campaign turned un-
friendly. The boys went to meetings of various superintendents'
organizations—SURE (Supers United in Realty Education), the

Scandinavian Supers Club, the Douglas Elliman Resident Managers Association, the New York Building Managers Association —and George often addressed these gatherings. At night, they would post Jimmy Mynes campaign signs around upper Manhattan, and quite often the other side would tear the signs down. The other side would put up Sampson posters, and the Brennans would cover them over with Mynes placards. Mickey and George contend that they were tailed by big bruisers. "For days, I had a guy following me, he weighed at least two hundred and forty pounds," George has said. Mickey believes that his bruiser was even bigger. The Brennans invested a lot of energy in the campaign. George said, "I went to see three hundred and fifty supers, and I called up two hundred and fifty more. But a lot of them were non-English-speaking." The campaign lasted four weeks. When the votes were counted, Jimmy Mynes had lost, but he had received thirty-eight percent. Originally, the Brennans had expected to pick up less than ten percent, so they took heart at the outcome. "We shook the industry," George said when it was all over. "We were talked about from one management company to the next. They all knew us. There was a spy here in my very own building. He was telling the union about my every move. I finally told the guy I knew who he was. He got very quiet, and he has been ever since."

There are times when George gets going on the subject of the union and you can almost feel his temperature slowly rising. George believes that he has been penalized for his dissident activities: for a time, whenever he had to attend an arbitration hearing, the hearing tended to be scheduled on his day off—that sort of thing. Even when, in the spring of 1982, 32B-32J and the Realty Advisory Board signed a new contract, just as another strike appeared imminent, the result failed to satisfy George entirely. "I was surprised," he told me, reacting to the settlement. "I thought both sides would let a strike go on for two or three days, just to make everybody look good." The union members won an increase in their life-insurance coverage, full pay for unused sick days, an extra holiday, an improved dental plan, and sixty-five dollars a week in raises over the three-year term of the contract. The supers got all those things, along with nine dollars a week more over the life of the contract. "The settlement's good, I guess," George said. "Of course, right now it means a thousand bucks less in my pocket. If there's a strike, the supers get paid days off, overtime. If it runs two weeks, we make about a grand on the deal. But they settled. That's good. Naturally, the extra money probably puts us in another tax bracket, but I really thought it was going to be worse."

A few days later, I sat with George in his office and listened to his fresh dispatches from the front. He wore a cream-colored short-sleeved polyester shirt, light-brown slacks, brown loafers, and a cowboy belt with a large brass buckle—a working super's clothes.

"Something's always doing in this business," he said, sitting forward in his chair, resting his wrists on the edge of his desk, looking me straight in the eye. "It's the craziest business in the world. You can lose your job and everything—your livelihood, your address, your home—with thirty days' notice. In a co-op, someone bangs on my door, I have to respond. A lot of guys like to be opening supers—they go into a building that's just opened, they wait for the first tenants to get settled, and then they leave. That's the way they want it. They like that, because in a new building a lot of stuff takes a walk. New refrigerators, ovens, light fixtures—it all walks. That's what an opening super's around to prevent. It's more hours, but the advantage is you're not dealing with anybody but the head boss. In a co-op, everybody's a boss, every tenant-owner's a boss. If I told you some of the things supers get fired for—for not smiling at certain tenants—you wouldn't believe it."

At that moment, I smiled at George, and he smiled back. When he smiles, he often arches his eyebrows and nods. It is an I-know-it-pal-and-so-do-you expression, a mixture of self-confidence and circumspection. His approach to supering is systematic. He has a system for recording workers' hours and vacations and days off; a system for accepting a tenant's delivery from the dry cleaner; a system for storing tenants' spare keys (in brass-riveted manila envelopes); a system for storing ice cream in case Gristede's delivers a tenant's groceries after he has already left for the weekend;

a filing system (every letter, every complaint, every proprietary lease, payroll records); a system for painting the plumbing pipes (yellow for steam lines, orange for hot water, green for cold water, brown for sewer lines). A red leather-bound logbook is kept at the concierge's desk, in the lobby. Tenants' complaints, requests, regrets, and ideological convictions are recorded in it. The entries for a typical three-day stretch run like this:

2E—gate on C-D-E staircase on first floor is insecure. Door is always left open. Lock is loose. Gate door is not aligned correctly. Dr. B. wants the situation corrected.

10B—toilet keeps running

8D—dining room window needs to be loosened

11A—toilet running

15B—toilet running continuously

16B—thinks she has a leak inside the newly plastered wall of the bathroom

6E—pull string for light in maid's bathroom came out. Please fix today.

16B—sometimes get cold water in hot water

15E—Mrs. W.'s radiator is making unbearable noises

—chair at the concierge desk is in a most deplorable condition.

A great deal of George Brennan's pride and the co-op's money has been invested in the security system. A concierge in the lobby operates a console that has two video screens and contains controls for the boiler, the fire alarm, the intercom, the elevators, and cameras and microphones inside the elevators. "You're known by your security," George said. "Security makes or breaks a super. We have a doorman working twenty-four hours a day, but a doorman's a *greeting*, not a bouncer. With our system, if the doorman misses you the deskman gets you. I didn't install the system myself, but I made some suggestions, and I supervised the installation. I'm an experienced electrician, and I studied locksmithing. I attended the Jewish school of locksmithing in Brooklyn. That's not what the school is called. That's what I called it. It was set up in

Williamsburg. Locksmithing used to be an all-Jewish profession, but now the Greeks are coming in pretty strong. I learned key-cutting and troubleshooting there. They've got courses in safes, car doors—whatever you want to know. I think the security system in this building is very effective. If you come to this building as a visitor, you tell the man on the desk where you want to go and he calls up the tenant-owner. If you're O.K., you get into the elevator and the man on the desk controls where you're going. There's a camera in there. He can let you out or he can lock you in there—if he has a reason. If you're coming down in the elevator and you want a taxi, you can call down to the man on the desk and he'll tell the doorman and by the time you hit the street there will be a taxi waiting. We've had no robberies since I've been here. We had a near-miss with a maid. Plus a few umbrellas gone. I was getting annoyed. We were constantly buying new umbrellas for the doormen. I had a man on the door, Jim Murphy, a former homicide detective. One day, a hand reaches in and snatches two umbrellas, and Jim ends up going all the way to Eighty-sixth and Second Avenue to catch these two youths. When he got back, I gave him hell. I said, 'What are you running off for?' He said, 'You told me to keep an eye on the umbrellas.' He was a great guy. One time, a fellow came by and tried to get in and Jim didn't like him. The guy tried to walk right past Jim. He was well dressed, but he didn't look right to Jim. Jim said you're not going anywhere. The guy tried to anyway. Jim threw him against a wall. The guy had a gun in his belt. Jim threw him up against the wall again. I thought we were both goners. But the guy just left. He knew Jim meant business. Jim told me that if the guy was going to use the gun he would have, but since he didn't intend to he didn't try to. Jim was a quality human being."

When I asked George what special traits he looked for when he hired someone, he said, "You don't want thieves, drinkers, or guys with hand problems. You know what I mean? A guy who can't keep his hands to himself if the lights in the elevator go out. Don't laugh. I've heard the complaint." A tour of George Brennan's building is a great pleasure, because it is such a well-kept, attractive, and orderly-seeming place to live and to work, and yet his description of life there approximates a series of bulletins from a war zone. According to George, true professional supering is unavoidably rooted in a siege mentality. Evidently, George regards himself as a defiant mercenary in a foreign land, hunkered down in the island fortress with inadequate ammo supplies—forced to cope with raids from the outside, guerrilla tactics by subversives among his none-too-trustworthy minions, and lack of support from the native population, whose leaders have engaged his services to protect themselves from democracy. A stroll through the premises—from George's office to the boiler room, the storage rooms, and the lobby, then up to the residential floors, each of which has been individually and handsomely decorated—is accompanied by this rat-a-tat delivery:

"Every time you look, a man's taking a bulb home. I don't mind, but when he takes a dozen, then it's a problem. . . . You'll find most supers don't educate their elevator men about what to do during a fire. You're supposed to shut it off and leave it on the first floor, for the firemen. Right? But some of the guys they're pulling off the street to work these days—forget it. . . . Here's where we store the candles and emergency lanterns. Blackout, power failure, national disaster. We're prepared. You've got to be ready for a crisis. But I can't go by a tenant's definition of a crisis. To a tenant, a crisis could be 'I got an odor in the garbage can.' You've got to do flood control, be a policeman, protect people's kids. I've got collections of valuables here that should be in museums under security, but they're here without alarms, and I'm supposed to be watching over them. Where does the price of the job go with the responsibility? . . . Here's where we keep the extra keys, locked over here. I had a tenant-owner once took a heart attack. Tried but were not able to get inside in time to help him. Otherwise, we might have saved him. And this particular party I'd asked him I don't know how many times for a key. But by the time we got the four locks on his door undone it was unfortunately too late. . . . This is where the deliveries come in. No deliveryman goes upstairs. The cold things we put in the refrigerator. You make a mistake with ice cream only once. Then you learn. . . . I used to keep a talking parrot down here in the office. Had a new man on the door one night. He hears voices downstairs. Panics. He gets paranoid, running up and down Park Avenue. He hails a cop car. They come in with their guns out. They were going to storm the parrot. . . . We're getting a big problem with these do-it-your-selfers. They come up with the price of the apartment but then they try to do their own renovations. They take all the debris and leave it in the hallway. This building has a specific alteration agreement. No work before nine in the morning, no work after five o'clock. They will take the cheapest contractors they can find. From Connecticut. From New Jersey. It doesn't matter. Anywhere they can get these guys. They come in and these guys are bums. Out-of-staters. I've seen jobs done, I'll tell you the truth I'd be afraid to sleep in that place. I saw one guy tie up all the electrical pipes, all the riser pipes, with string. I said something about it to the tenant. Thanked me at the time. Then he went to the board of directors. Said I was trying to shake down the contractor. . . . Had a plumber punch a hole in the waste-line pipe. Tried to glue it back in with putty. The manager called. He said So-and-So called him, do I know what she wants. I said nope, she hasn't spoken to me in two years. Why? Because she had a lousy plumber in there doing a bad job. You put a stop to a job and the tenant-owner hates you. You bring in the right guy and it double-costs her and somehow it's my fault. How come it's my fault? She's the one brought the bum in in the first place. . . . A lot of them are coming from *Jersey*. Imagine. . . . Tenant-owner calls me up, says, 'I'm going to sue the building.' She had her whole kitchen redone. What happened? She had a carpenter do the work. I had nothing to do with it. I don't know where she got him. The guy took all the lamination off the butcher block. She didn't want a sheen on the butcher block. He sanded it off. Now all the butcher-block coun-tertops are buckled. Tears are streaming down her face. She thinks it's something we did in the building. She went away for the week-end. She thinks we had a bad leak or something. You should have seen that butcher block. . . . Window washer's supposed to come by. I left a note. The tenant wants to know where's the window washer. I left a note with the man on the front desk. Someone threw away the note. She's got a schedule problem. She's a stew-ardess. Husband's a root-canal specialist. One of the tops around. . . .

Christmastime, they kill you with the by-the-ways. They call and
say could you come up, I want to see you about Christmas. You
go up and they say, Oh, by the way, could you just take a look at
this, that—who knows? They hand you ten dollars and a list of
forty different jobs. I heard one the other day. Tenant gives the
handyman a ten for Christmas and says, 'Oh, yeah, by the way,
could you check the smoke alarm?' So he checks it, and naturally
the batteries are dead. He goes out to get new batteries. The
batteries alone run six or seven dollars. The handyman makes three
dollars on the deal. Don't get me wrong. They don't have to pay
it. It's a gratuity. In fact, I quit counting on it. I really try not to
think about it. It's embarrassing. They call and if you don't come
up immediately they're ready to stiff you. Yeah, they stiff you. It's
embarrassing."

An isometric map of midtown Manhattan has been mounted on
one wall of George's office, and next to it is a bulletin board. Some
interesting documents have been attached to the bulletin board.
There are copies of George's certificates of membership in Electrical Workers Local No. 3 (lapsed), the Ancient Accepted Scottish
Rite, the New York Elevator Constructors Masonic Club, the Kis-
met Temple of the Imperial Council of the Nobles of the Mystic
Shrine, the New York Building Managers Association, and the
Hudson Council Knights of Columbus; a refrigeration certificate of
instruction; a locksmith's license; a standpipe license; a certificate
of instruction from the New York City Department of Air Resources;
and a permit for the use of Hilti Fastening System's .22-caliber
gun for adhering Sheetrock to metal studs. There is an article from
the *Irish Advocate* that traces the lineage of the surname Martin—
the Brennan brothers' mother's maiden name—and points out that
New York City's finest supers are maternally descended from
Strongbow the Viking. Also, there is a photograph from an old New
York Yankees yearbook which shows George and his son, George,
Jr., out at the ballpark. The caption says, "Thurman Munson gloves
foul fly in accepted fashion." George and George, Jr., were at the
ballpark that day thanks to a friend who provided front-row freebies,
and George, Jr.'s head is visible between the late great Yankee
captain's glove and his chin.

In one drawer of his desk George keeps a black-plastic album filled with clear-plastic pages. "When contractors come to the building to do work and they ask whether I'd like one of their cards, I say yes. I say to them, 'See, I'm putting this in the front of the book. And if all goes well it stays there. But if things don't go right it moves farther and farther back in the book. And finally it moves into the wastebasket.' "

A few moments later, there was a knock on the door. George said, "It's open," and a painting contractor who had been doing work in the building entered. He asked George about a tenant who was apparently interested in having some work done in her apartment, and George, in turn, called the concierge and asked him to get in touch with the tenant, a Mrs. Miller. "The contractor's here and he wants to come up and see how big the job is," George said. After checking with the tenant, the concierge called back to say that Mrs. Miller didn't want the painter just then. When George heard this, he reacted with dismay. "Brutal, just brutal," he said, hanging up the receiver and then calling the tenant directly. "*Mrs. Miller?* It's Mr. Brennan, the super. Mrs. Miller, I have the painter in my office right now. He doesn't want to paint today, he just wants to see what materials he'll need for tomorrow. Could he come up?" A pause. "Fine. He'll be right up." He hung up the phone and said to the contractor, "Just the living-room ceiling and a little wall." When the contractor was gone, George said, "Never leave it to someone else."

The phone rang. It was Paddy Brennan calling to say that he and Donald Simkowitz, the Brennans' brother-in-law's brother-in-law, were getting ready to walk to lunch at the Bantry, and that they would pick up George on the way. George tidied his desk. He closed a box of index cards, and he called my attention to a bronze statuette of a monkey examining a human skull. "Darwin in reverse," he said. "Come on. We'll go out the back way. But first I want to show you something." We stepped into an adjacent room that was the size of a large walk-in closet. It had glazed yellow brick walls. Along one wall were three large barrels—floor wax, wax stripper, and soap. Six mops and three brooms hung upside down from brackets on the opposite wall. Above each bracket was a piece of embossed plastic tape printed with an employee's name. A hasp and a padlock secured each mop and broom. "With the name tapes, I can feel the mops, see if they're wet," he said, smiling and arching his eyebrows in a familiar way. "With the padlocks, no one can say he didn't do his work because someone stole his mop or broom. Each man gets one key to his padlock and I hold one key. You lose your key, you go home without pay. Nobody's lost one yet. Check out the mops. You can see who's a pig. You can see who's halfway clean. If it looks rusty, it means they let the mop lie too long in the pail. You can tell by looking which ones I'm concerned about. This cuts out all the nonsense."

We left that room, walked down a corridor, climbed a short flight of stairs, and emerged on a sidewalk about twenty-five yards from Park Avenue. Someone had left a huge empty cardboard shipping crate—big enough to hold a subcompact automobile—at the top of the stairs. The box partly obstructed the sidewalk. George regarded it with great disdain and said, "Tenant ordered a Magic Chef. Told Magic Chef to take away the carton. Magic Chef took it and left it for the super. Terrific. Brutal."

By the time we reached the corner, Paddy Brennan and Donald Simkowitz had, too. We strolled together down Park Avenue and then crossed at Eighty-sixth Street, heading east, toward the Bantry.

"I imagine Georgie gave you the lowdown," Paddy said. "Did he tell you the one about the handyman that took the heart attack under the kitchen sink?"

I said that he hadn't. Paddy hesitated. "I don't want to say the super's name, because he's still in the trade," he said. "But this really happened. This super has a handyman working on a job, unclogging a sink, installing a new trap, and he wonders what's taking the handyman so long. So he goes up there and he sees the handyman took a heart attack, he's lying there right under the sink. So the super naturally just moves the handyman out of the way and finishes the job. He'd promised the tenant it would get done that day."

"What happened to the handyman?" I asked.

Paddy looked at me with the sort of patience that adults usually reserve for small children. "The handyman died," he said. He was grinning. "But that's not the point."

"What's the point?"

"The point is, *the job got done*."

1 9 8 3

Winging It

THIRTY THOUSAND TUNES, IF TIME PERMITS

Like the scalpel or the food processor, the violin is a tricky instrument: in the wrong hands it can make a mess. A census of
violins would probably turn up about ten thousand on the island
of Manhattan. Three belong to Rubin Levine, who uses them to
earn a living. All of Levine's violins were made in Germany. One,
a Heberlein, he reserves for intimate gatherings in small quarters.
Often, however, he finds himself in situations that lack intimacy,
and the Heberlein is insufficient. Levine lives near Times Square
and communes with nature along Broadway in the Forties and
Fifties. Fortunately, another of his violins, whose brand name is
Schuster, can be hooked up to an amplifier. If Levine should be
concerned about overcoming interfering noises—if, say, he should
decide to entertain stalled motorists on a windy day—he would
rely upon the Schuster. Twenty years ago, Levine bought this violin
from a member of Local 802 of the American Federation of Musicians, an organization to which, since 1940, he has sporadically
paid dues. The third violin, whose acoustical system is entirely
natural, is about sixty years old. Its manufacturer is Roth. It has
a slightly warped neck and belly, a worn fingerboard, many nicks
along the purfling, and aluminum-wound steel strings. Most violins
have gut strings, which nowadays are often wrapped with metal
thread. The gut makes delicate nuances ? possibility. Steel strings
militate against delicacy. A virtue of steel strings is their ability
to penetrate the general din. Levine plays all three violins with a
French-made bow, which he obtained after a complicated negotiation with the same fellow union member. Together, the bow and

the Schuster required a cash commitment by Levine in the very
low three figures. The Heberlein cost about the same. For the Roth,
Levine paid eighty dollars, which at the time seemed extravagant;
the seller, however, was a hardship case, and Levine, while he is
no sucker, has been known to perform gratuitous acts of kindness.
In any case, buying it has paid off.

Musically, Levine is linked less to the nineteenth-century French
and German traditions of virtuosity than to the mid-twentieth-cen-
tury traditions of the Catskill Mountains. A magical bond exists
between Levine and all his violins—especially the Roth. It enables
him to produce an effect that is grating but also harmonious, that
immediately repels but ultimately attracts. In Levine's hands, the
instrument transcends its mundane violinness: a Bach partita rep-
licates the sound of an I.R.T. local slowly rounding a curve; a
concerto by Mozart evokes a scalded alley cat; something by Pa-
ganini reminds a listener of something back at the house that needs
oiling. Levine practices his scales and his fingering technique every
day, and he performs almost every night. "We're always striving
for a per*fec*tion, for a *tone*," he says. His ability to inspire and
amaze himself inspires amazement. A foot patrolman attached to
the Midtown South police precinct said not long ago that he was
convinced that Levine, although he often seemed to be holding
back, had talent that would make a mother proud.

During mild weather, Levine is a street musician. It is true that
he has played six hundred weddings, five hundred bar mitzvahs,
six years in Las Vegas nightclubs and casino lobbies, aboard several dozen Caribbean ships, onscreen in two feature-length motion
pictures, a thousand nights in a Rumanian steak house, more
weekends in the mountains than he can remember, more weekends
in Atlantic City than he cares to remember, naked in a steam bath,
and at twenty-eight thousand feet in an airplane flying from New
Orleans to LaGuardia. His essential musical self, however, is that
of a sidewalk serenader. On a warm and sunny summer day, as
many as fifty street violinists may be at large in New York City.
Most of them perform somewhere along Fifth Avenue or in the
parks. Levine's milieu, Times Square, is too hostile for the average
street performer. Knowledgeable critics have told me that quite a

few of the ostensibly serious street violinists out there decorate their playing with fake double-stops, acciaccatura, and other hollow embellishments. Levine fakes nothing. No street performer plays a violin more loudly than Levine. None claims to have a more extensive repertoire. None ad-libs as compulsively. None is more hopeful.

Levine's habit is to station himself, his violin, and his open violin case near some Broadway theater entrance before curtain time, during intermissions, and at the end of a performance. To do this requires nerve, fortitude, and a willingness to be elbowed by people with briefcases and squash racquets who are rushing for the theater door or for taxis. The sidewalk outside the Ambassador Theatre, on West Forty-ninth Street, is one of Levine's favorite spots. Until a few months back, it was the home of *Dancin'*, a musical that had virtually no plot and very few words and thus attracted a lot of tourists, many of whom spoke little English. Most tourists, foreign or domestic, have never before caught an act like Levine's.

Steady theatre patrons have become familiar with Levine. His face is memorable. It is rubbery and susceptible to gravity. Parts of it droop. He has large ears that are slightly pointed, a wide, thin mouth, and a straight and substantial nose. Adrift in a musical reverie, he closes his eyes—dark-brown eyes—and purses his lips in a satisfied way. His countenance poises there, as if a piece of chocolate were slowly melting on his tongue. In a crowd of short people, Levine might appear to be tall. He is five-six, but he seems more like five-eight. This is because he almost always wears a hat. As a rule, it is an olive-and-brown houndstooth-check fedora, which he has adorned with small treasures: a bronze clef sign; a red plastic Big Apple; a fake half-cigarette that is painted to look as if it were aglow. Levine does not smoke. For this and other reasons, he is in vigorous good health. He has broad but slightly rounded shoulders and a solid, trim physique. Unless he removes his hat, he does not look his age. What hair he has left is pale gray. Levine is sixty-five years old.

No one who has spent thirty or forty seconds in Levine's company would mistake him for anything but a native New Yorker. On occasion, he performs while wearing a red bandanna, a waxed handlebar mustache, and a red felt vest festooned with lapel pins, stickpins, and tie tacks. He does this, redundantly, to encourage the impression that he is exotic. He says that he was born to English royalty but that as an infant he was kidnapped by Jewish gypsies and sold to his mother. Levine's birth certificate says that he was born in Brooklyn. He grew up in Bedford-Stuyvesant. His mother, Tillie, had a pretty voice and excellent recall of lyrics, and his father, Aaron, played flute and clarinet in a klezmer band. His brothers Nat and Danny and a sister, Ruth, played the piano. (Nat was also a drummer.) Another brother, Bill, played the violin. Rubin is an alumnus but not a graduate of Boys' High; when he was sixteen, he and the school principal agreed that it would serve both their interests if he would spend his mornings and afternoons somewhere else in Brooklyn. In 1957, he got around to taking the high-school-equivalency examination and did quite well. Outside of music, Levine has had brief careers selling automotive supplies, jewelry, and reversible gloves. He tried marriage once, during the nineteen-fifties, but terminated that arrangement when, as he once explained to me, he and his wife "became unpopular with each other."

For several years, Levine has resided in a hotel on Forty-ninth Street, not far from the Ambassador Theatre. Not long ago, I happened to be standing in the hotel lobby when one of the desk clerks, Alex Bryant, a tall young black man who moonlighted as an amateur music critic, ventured a lengthy and persuasive exegesis of Levine's musical style, his main point being that making a violin sound consistently like a dyspeptic woodland creature implies a greater artistic risk than trying to mimic Menuhin or Zukerman or Stern. This disquisition was interrupted when Levine entered the lobby. In each hand he carried a brown paper shopping bag. He wore his houndstooth fedora, brown cotton slacks, soft-soled black leather shoes, a light-green cotton sports jacket, and a blue T-shirt that was inscribed "Take a Bath with a Friend." Levine excused himself to go upstairs for a few minutes. The hotel where he lives has certain house rules. The management prefers that guests pay cash in advance. Also, it frowns upon loiterers. There were no chairs in the lobby, and only two tables. A plastic fern rested on one tabletop. Next to it was a stack of brochures promoting bus tours of Niagara Falls. A hotel guest, a young woman who seemed to be on time for an appointment with someone who was not, paced impatiently. When Levine reappeared, he was carrying his violin case. Something about the young woman, who was dressed in maroon slacks and a white turtleneck sweater, gave Levine the urge to entertain; he has a habit of playing anywhere at any time, without provocation. There are occasions when he neglects to adapt his music to his surroundings. A few months ago, while performing at an Episcopal wedding on Park Avenue, he inadvertently broke into a lively number called "Chussin Kalah Mazel Tov." Afterward, the mother of the bride, a woman who had been taught how to speak without moving her jaws, told Levine how much she appreciated his high spirits. Now Levine placed the violin case on the front desk and opened it. The Roth was inside. Without waiting for anyone to utter a request, he removed the violin, rested it upon his left collarbone, clamped it there with his chin, drew his bow, and proceeded through the first bars of Mozart's Piano Sonata No. 17. He played with the legato grace of an apprentice meatcutter carving his maiden shell steaks. The woman paused in her pacing and then slowly walked toward Levine. When he lowered his bow, she and Alex Bryant applauded.

"Oh, you never heard a violin before," Levine said. His tone was a mixture of anticipation and surprise. His voice is slightly nasal. For emphasis, he raises it an unnatural octave every second or third sentence. The effect is of listening to someone who speaks in italics. "Luck-*kee*. I have a wide range. From the ridiculous to the slime. I can play until you stop me."

"Oh, please, play," the woman said. She spoke with an English accent. Hearing her inflection inspired him to render "God Save the Queen." Actually, he only started to play "God Save the Queen"; he didn't finish. Levine has frequently said that he knows thirty thousand melodies. The idea is to cram as many as possible into a single performance. Levine realizes that it isn't feasible to play all thirty thousand in one set, but he seems not to mind trying. Everything that he plays he abbreviates—usually radically. It is

possible that he knows only the first third of thirty thousand melodies or that thirty thousand is a slight exaggeration. At any rate,
no one has ever volunteered to spend several consecutive days
in a room with Levine in order to confirm the true scope of his
repertoire. The only song that he regularly carries through to its
conclusion is "Happy Birthday." Several times a night, Levine
greets random citizens with "Happy Birthday." Whenever he hits
one whose birthday happens to be that day, he collects a nice
reward.

"Notice the delicacy," Levine said as he shifted to "Country
Gardens." He added, "Or, rather, the lack of delicacy."

"Do you play this as a hobby or professionally?" the Englishwoman asked.

"You really know how to hurt a guy," Levine said.

"Isn't that a fair question?"

"That's not a question. That's an indictment. Maybe an incite-
ment."

"I mean, do you play in an orchestra?"

"Why? Whaddya have in mind?"

The Englishwoman stuck around long enough to hear bits of
"Scarborough Fair" and "Rule, Britannia," and then friends of hers
arrived. They stood in the lobby—a group of eight—and discussed
whether to have dinner at Mamma Leone's or Broadway Joe's.
Ignoring their conversation, Levine continued to play.

A pair of Oriental men in business suits entered the lobby. One
was quite tall. "Excuse me," Levine said to them. "Are you Japanese or Jewish?"

"Chinese," the tall man said. His suit was black, and his companion's was gray.

"Oh, *Chi*-nese," Levine said.

"Taiwan," the man in the gray suit said.

"Very good," Levine said, smiling. "See if you recognize this."
He played "Alishan Girl." Both men nodded and, in a faint way,
smiled back. "A girl in Foochow taught me that," Levine said.
When Levine had done what he could to "Alishan Girl," he segued
briefly into "Sukiyaki," saying, "This is a new service we've installed in the hotel lately. Music of the wrong ethnic group."

By now, the Taiwanese men were trying to get Alex's attention. For the moment, however, Alex had his attention fixed upon Levine.

"Mr. Levine," he said, leaning across the front desk. "You are an absolute genius."

"I'm not in tune," Levine said, unapologetic. "But have you noticed that people don't notice?"

A CLUSTERED AFFAIR

The Friends of State Assemblyman Angelo Del Toro, a Harlem Democrat, have witnessed a selfless display of Levine's gifts. They have heard his violin, and they have seen him more or less formally attired: tuxedo, black waffle-sole shoes, formal dress shirt with black ruffled front and cuffs, no tie. For fund-raising purposes, the Friends of Assemblyman Del Toro convened one night at an Italian restaurant in the East Sixties. Levine took along three other musicians: Ron Wasserman, a bass player; Danny Barrett, a cellist; and Paul Germano, a violinist. The four had not rehearsed. Before they got started, Levine outlined strategy: "We'll try to be loose. I'm the leader the first half-hour. Then anybody can take over." When I arrived, the restaurant had already become crowded. Three members of the group—Germano had wandered away for a while —were playing what I later decided must have been "Wave," by Antonio Carlos Jobim. They rendered it in a syncopated style that effectively obscured its identity. Also, they played in a shifting variety of keys. Levine stood opposite a table where two Friends of Assemblyman Del Toro were seated. The guests, unabashed politicians, looked comfortable. One of them wore a dark business suit, a pink shirt, and a bright-red tie. He smoked a pipe. He was black and had gray hair. The other pol, a chunky coffee-complexioned man with a Ronald Colman mustache, wore a gray suit and a blue-and-white checked tie. When the combo finished the Jobim tune, Levine turned to the pols and said, "What else don't you want to hear?" They didn't answer. Probably they didn't intend to be rude; this was an event where sober attempts at musical appreciation were periodically being subverted by thoughtless intruders saying things like "Have you met Mario Cuomo? Shake

hands with Mario Cuomo." Levine began to play "Bésame Mucho,"
and the bass and cello players more or less accompanied him.
When he had finished, he said, "What would you like to hear us
kill next? How about 'La Bamba'?" The black pol said, "How about
The Pirates of Penzance?" Somehow, Levine injected a Latin rhythm
into Gilbert and Sullivan. When he had polished them off, the
other pol asked for some Viennese waltzes. As the group played
"The Blue Danube," Paul Germano rejoined them, just in time to
blend into "Adiós Muchachos." They concluded the set with "La
Paloma." Most of the crowd had gravitated into an adjacent room,
where there was a bar. In a loud voice, Levine said, "How'd you
like the way we cleared this room? Pretty effective, huh? There
was some heavy improvising."

Levine introduced me to Barry Deutsch, who had come to this
event because of his friendship with the combo leader rather than
with Assemblyman Del Toro. Deutsch, a large man with a heavy,
thick-featured face and wavy white hair, had already done recon-
naissance work in the next room. "There's a lot of people in clusters,
Ruby," he said. "It's a clustered affair." Levine and his group
went in there to work. Deutsch and I found a table where two chairs
were vacant. I asked him how he happened to know Levine, and
he proceeded to tell me the professional life story of a friend's
cousin who's a big agent out on the Coast. The combo played "The
Godfather," "September Song," and the Mozart theme of *Elvira
Madigan*. I offered to go to the buffet table to get us both something
to eat, and Deutsch promised to save my chair. When I returned,
someone else was sitting at my place. A pair of crutches was
propped against the chair. Deutsch turned his palms up and gave
me a what-am-I-gonna-do look. I ate lasagne standing while the
combo played "Spanish Eyes" and "El Toreador."

Now the musicians took a break. Deutsch went to the buffet
table to reload, and Levine said to me, "You realize, of course,
that Barry is very well connected. He's the concierge at an apartment house on the East Side. Oh, and that building—don't ask.
Myriads of inducements and various flagellations. The King of
Sweden once visited there incognito, and, oh, what goes *on* there!
From the sleazy to the snoozy."

More tables had been crammed into the restaurant than comfort
permitted. This did not discourage Herman Badillo, the former
congressman and former deputy mayor, who squeezed his way
around the room shaking hands. Levine managed to engage him
in a conversation, which I couldn't overhear. Afterward, I asked
Levine what they had talked about.

"He felt that it was necessary to pay homage to me," Levine
said. "I told him if he was going to be that way I'd have to play
his favorite song. He asked whether I know 'What Are You Doing
the Rest of Your Life?' Come *onnn*. Of *course* I know it. I told him
we have an arrangement that calls for four mariachi players but
tonight we'll wing it. I said, 'Here's what we'll do. We'll ruin the
beginning, we'll louse up the middle, we'll play it out of tune so
everybody will be at home, and we'll bring the whole group together
at the end on a note of discord.' "

Levine ate some food that Barry Deutsch had brought him.
When he rested his fork, he said, "Have you noticed that there's
a very subtle thing going on here? The owner of this restaurant
calls me whenever someone is having a party and makes a request for classical music of a high order. And you see what we're
accomplishing. We're doing this thing for them, and they're responding. You heard—we played the *Carmen* suite for them,
'La Cumpasita,' 'Adiós Muchachos,' 'The Breeze and I,' a little
Cuban number. I think the main reason for this event was a way
of getting Herman Badillo and Mario Cuomo to come down and
hear us play."

Ron Wasserman, the bass player—the only student at the Manhattan School of Music who is also an acolyte of Levine's—came
over and asked how soon the group should get back to work. It
didn't seem urgent. A pianist was playing a medley of show
tunes—"Mame," "Hello, Dolly!," "Side by Side," "Oh, What a
Beautiful Mornin'," "Pack Up Your Troubles"—while the Friends
of Assemblyman Angelo Del Toro enthusiastically clapped and sang
along. "Look at the bartenders," Wasserman said. The bartenders
were too busy clapping to pour drinks.

Levine shielded his eyes for a few moments and then waved
as if shooing away a housefly. He said, "Yeah, time to go back

to work. Cancel the piano player. Look at these people. They
hate it."

ELIGIBLE VIOLIN, STROLLING

At least once a week, Levine goes through the motions of looking
for work. Until recently, Local 802, the musicians' union, had
its offices above the Roseland Ballroom, on West Fifty-second
Street. On Wednesdays, around midday, the dance floor became
the union's informal hiring exchange. One Wednesday, I met Levine at his hotel, and we headed for Roseland. The first block
of our walk took us past the Colony Record Shop, a Chinese fast-
food place, a Korean salad bar, the On Parade restaurant, a General Nutrition Center, and a Chock Full o' Nuts. The Korean salad
bar occupies the site of what was until 1974 Jack Dempsey's steak
house. Levine worked at Dempsey's on and off for ten years,
strolling the aisles. At one point, the restaurant manager, Jack
Emil, asked him to go outside and play, thinking that this would
draw crowds of potential patrons. In 1971, when the movie version of *Fiddler on the Roof* opened across the street, at the Rivoli
Theatre, someone from United Artists hired Levine to stand in
front of the theater dressed as if he had just landed in town from
Anatevka. Serially, he would play the entire score of *Fiddler*. He
could run through the whole thing in two and a half minutes—
three if his mood was largo di molto. Now, in frequent atavistic
moments, melodic bits of *Fiddler* leap from Levine's violin as if
they were dying to get out of there. Levine credits Jack Emil with
the bright idea of opening the violin case to see what would land
inside. A career was born.

The key personnel at the Colony, On Parade, and Chock Full
o' Nuts know Levine well. At the Colony, he regularly spends the
late, late hours in the sheet-music department, expanding his ho-
rizons. He is familiar with the Colony's vast inventory and can
assist customers. For this, he is compensated with a forty percent
discount on recordings and sheet music, plus all the free shopping
bags he can handle. At On Parade, a couple of doors uptown from
the Colony, Levine has a nice bowl of soup every day. He advises

friends and strangers to do the same. The Chock Full o' Nuts at Fiftieth and Broadway attracts some overflow from an Off-Track Betting parlor nearby. Levine makes an occasional bet, and has been known to extend short-term loans to OTB patrons who need a stake to get even. Between Fifty-first and Fifty-second, we passed Circle Magic, where accessories for parlor magic tricks are sold. There is one particular effect that Levine performs flawlessly. If both his violin and his running commentary upon his violin playing fail to please an audience, he can fall back on his ability to make a red silk handkerchief disappear.

Inside Roseland, about a hundred men and a few women were gathered on the dance floor. The musicians were mostly middle-aged and beyond. They stood in small groups, in the dim glow of yellow, green, red, and blue overhead lights. A canvas tarpaulin protected the floor. One member of Local 802 sat at a table on the stage. Speaking into a microphone, he made occasional proclamations about union business. This man wore a dark-brown jacket, a green-and-maroon plaid vest, and a checkerboard-print necktie. He had slicked-back dark hair, a black-dyed mustache, and a tight jaw, and he looked as much a part of the scenery as Roseland's plastic palm trees. About every fourth member of the crowd wore a toupee or smoked a cigar, or both. A fellow who was carrying a brown vinyl briefcase and wearing a greenish topcoat and a matching fake-fur Russian cap approached Levine and said, "What's in the bag today, Ruby?" Levine, who was holding a shopping bag from the Colony, smiled and shook his head. The union members are accustomed to seeing Levine arrive at the hiring hall with items that he is willing to sell. For a long while, he made a practice of showing up with large quantities of vitamins, which he had bought at a price well below retail. His supplier was an acquaintance who could obtain them at a price even further below retail. Levine believes in vitamins. He is partial to E, although he also thinks highly of B and C. He will tell a friend whom he suspects of being vitamin-deficient, "I'm gonna make you healthy if it kills both of us." When he runs low on vitamins, he compensates by being well stocked with some other interesting commodity, like pipe cleaners or small tape recorders or golf shoes.

An invisible announcer—not the one on the stage—periodically paged union members. A page often meant a booking. Someone whose name was called would go to one of four phone booths in a dark corner to the left of the Roseland stage. There were also bookers working on the floor. A short, white-haired man passed by. Levine squinted at him. "Who's that?" he said. "Oh, it's Nat. He's a booker. Watch this." He walked up to the white-haired man and said, "Nat, whaddya got? How about this—you want to put me down as an eligible violin, strolling? Nat, put me down I'm available to do a single show, all by myself." Nat, the booker, nodded and, although Levine had not asked about his health, said that he was feeling better. Then he moved on. As Levine mingled with the crowd, I asked him how the hiring exchange worked, how the bookers found musicians, and how he, in particular, lined up a job. "It's very simple," he said. "The bookers know my style, and they do everything in their power to avoid me." In self-defense, Levine has a rather derisive attitude toward certain bookers. He saw one now, a red-faced man who was wearing an open-necked shirt. He approached him, grabbed the man by the sleeve, and said, "Stanley! Give me anything! Please, I'm desperate! Give me a tentative job and cancel on me." Not all bookers have well-developed senses of irony. Stanley, the booker, had a do-I-need-this expression on his face. A neatly attired man called Danny, who lives in Sea Gate, in Brooklyn, asked Levine whether he thought a violin and a trumpet could work together on the street. Levine said that he doubted it—they'd probably clash—and added that several musicians had said that they didn't want to play with him because he was too good. For a while, Levine fell into a conversation with Irwin Cooper, a drummer. They discussed Levine's failure to buy some oceanfront property in Miami Beach that had been available in 1947. When Cooper asked Levine how he was doing, he said, "Fine. Working with my own hammer and chisel." Joan Wile, the mother of Ron Wasserman, the young bass player, happened to be in the crowd. While Levine was talking to her, an elderly man in a gold tweed driving cap, a brown corduroy jacket, and blue trousers approached. Levine interrupted himself and said, "Say hello to Frank Gregory, the greatest violin-maker in—"

"No *kidding*," Joan said. "My husband makes violins."

"Your husband makes nice children is what he makes," Levine said.

"No, I mean my second husband," she said. "Yes, he's the treasurer of the Southern California Association of Violin Makers. What's your name? I'll tell him I met you."

"Frank Gregory," said Frank Gregory.

"He can make a violin from a cheesebox," Levine said.

"Are you a member of the Southern California Association of Violin Makers?" Joan asked.

"He's a member of the Southern California Association of Cheese Makers," Levine said.

Gregory motioned for Levine to follow him. Several chairs were lined against a wall on one side of the room. A violin case rested on one of the chairs. Levine explained to me that Gregory wanted him to test a violin. I must have had a puzzled look on my face at that moment.

"Tell this man why I have to test your violins," Levine said to Gregory. "He doesn't understand."

"What's there to tell?" Gregory said. "You're my official expert on sound, that's all."

"Why?" Levine asked.

"Some people, when they play . . ." Gregory paused thoughtfully. He has a broad, flat face, a thin gray mustache, and a great-avuncular demeanor. "Some people, when they play . . . they project. The sound projects. With Ruby, it pro*jects*. There are other fiddle players that—I mean, you just don't hear anything. You see motion, but the motion doesn't connect. In other words, you've got to know how to draw a tone out of a fiddle."

When I asked Gregory to evaluate Levine's playing, he paused once again—a lengthy pause. At last, he said, "Well, he's a violin player in *his* category, let's put it that way. What's his category? Well, the work that he does—that's his category. In that category, he's very good. He's appreciated. He has originality. His bowing technique, his way of holding the violin—it's a unique process that he has. Perhaps a little unconventional."

Gregory's analysis caused Levine to become quite animated. "Leonard Rose, the cellist, saw me one day on Fifth Avenue," he said. "He stopped to watch. I said, 'Hello, Mr. Rose.' He was embarrassed that *I* would know who *he* was. He watched for a while, and he said, 'You hold the bow wrong, you hold the violin wrong, but you get a beautiful *sound.*' "

On Gregory's violin, Levine played "On the Sunny Side of the Street" and then briefly ran through something that might have been turned out originally by one of the Bachs. Concluding with several repetitions of the first phrases of *Fiddler on the Roof*, he nodded at Gregory, who closed his eyes and nodded back.

"You know you're not listening to Heifetz or Perlman," Gregory said. "You're listening to Levine."

SOME ITEMS

Some items that have been deposited in a storage room on the premises of Local 802, that belong to Levine, and that he occasionally inspects for inventory purposes: several shopping bags from the Actors' Fund Bazaar, containing mostly clothing (shoes, trousers, shirts); several suitcases, the pasteboard-and-plaid-weave variety, containing more clothing, including a pair of white boxer shorts that once belonged to Cyril Ritchard; piece of brass electrical-insulation pipe ("You don't throw away things like *this!*"); two sheets of sandpaper; some Norwegian kroner; lighter fluid; incense burner; suspenders; shoe polish; horsehair shoebrush; fuses; glue; liquid dye; bubble bath ("I'm not a bubble-bath user, how'd *that* get in there?"); brass lock; "Alleged Good Luck Candle," manufactured in Maspeth, Queens; lots of sheet music; books (*B.C.: It's a Funny World*, by Johnny Hart; *Self-Realization and Self-Defeat*, by Samuel J. Warner, Ph.D.; *Body, Mind, and Sugar*, by E. M. Abrahamson, M.D., and A. W. Pezet); pair of galoshes; roll of adhesive tape; bundle of personal mail; receipt for Blue Cross premium, paid in 1973.

Some items in Levine's living quarters: vitamins; more sheet music; more books (*Swimming for Total Fitness*; *Adolescent Sexuality in Contemporary America*; *Abnormal Psychology and Modern Life*); two tennis racquets; three briefcases; Styrofoam-cooler lid; small portable TV-radio; batteries; stuffed toy python; winking-eyeball toy eyeglasses; tennis ball; cardboard boxes (one resting atop a lampshade); King Karol shopping bags; Colony Record Shop shopping bags; magnets; duck call made of nickel; honey-dyed mink stole that cost ten dollars; bass guitar; chromatic harmonica; rolls of cash-register tape.

Some items that Levine had on consignment recently at the H/J Unique Trading Company, a buy-and-sell establishment at Eighth Avenue and Fifty-third that is the home of a zillion buyables, some of which you might not actually need (lawnmower, Purple Heart, foundation garment), owned and operated by Herb (né Herbert) Cohen and Julie (né Julian) Cohen, who are not related (Herb is the one whose daughter attends grad school at City University; Julie is the one who once bought a wooden leg from a man for five dollars and later resold it to him for seven, who once almost bought a palomino mare from a fruit vendor but decided not to because there wasn't room for a horse in the shop, who looks like Bud Abbott, and who when the *News* inquiring photographer asked him recently whether legalized gambling on football, baseball, and basketball made sense to him replied "Yes"): three wristwatches; three gold rings; gold chain; pair of headphones; dictating machine; clothing; marble-and-brass desk calendar; binoculars; transistor radios; bowling ball; bowling shoes; sheet music (*Milton DeLugg's Accordion Folio of Popular Songs*; *The Pagani Edition School of Velocity for the Piano Accordion*, by Pietro Deiro; *Accordion Collection of Lawrence Welk Recorded Hits*, arranged by Myron Floren; *Charles Magnante's Accordion Method, Book 1*; *Charles Magnante's Accordion Method, Book 2*); one accordion.

A thought from Rubin Levine: "I'm not a hoarder. Everything has its use. The name of the game is fun and games. If it's fun, let's keep doing it. You want a cough drop? Here. It'll make you cough like crazy."

SOME ADDITIONAL THOUGHTS, INSIGHTS, ENCOMIUMS

Herb Cohen, of H/J Unique Trading: "Ruby Levine's got a lot of friends. He's played Vegas and he's played the entire Borscht Belt.

He got borscht all over himself. He's played on cruise jships and he's played for people in Connecticut. He's got tips from nothing to eleven hundred dollars. He's got a lot of very poor friends, he's got a lot of rich friends, he's got a lot of friends that nobody would ever want to meet. The man who owned the Golden Nugget casino once gave him his silver belt buckle. Basically, the man liked what he heard, and he decided not to worry about his pants falling down. That says a lot about Ruby."

Kenneth Sipser, mathematics educator: "He's well defined. Whatever you see, that's what he is."

Nathan Pitt, advertising man: "He does not seem to be driven by the same demons that drive most of us. He has a habit of not relating to his environment in a very specific way. He speaks articulate Yiddish—particularly if he's having a conversation with somebody who is Irish. I used to spend my free time fishing off the bridge in Far Rockaway. I mentioned one day to Ruby, just in passing, that I needed a fishing rod. The following week, Ruby showed up with seventeen of them. He said, 'Ten dollars.' I said, 'For which one?' He said, 'For all seventeen.' "

The Honorable Leonard Yoswein, Justice, New York State Supreme Court, Administrator of the Second Judicial District, Kings County and Staten Island: "I know Ruby through Nat Pitt. He was once married to a close friend of Nat's wife. He once got me a gray flannel suit for five dollars that I wore for five or six years. It fitted me perfectly. I think he found it at a police auction. He's a great klaberjass player. He's more artistic at that than with a violin."

Seymour Axelrod, unpublished poet, retired city employee, regular patron of the On Parade restaurant (where he often orders mashed potatoes and a glass of seltzer): "Somewhere in him there is spring. A very pristine quality. His eyes are painted with watercolors, you know, and you can see them trailing off into sunlight. There's something so tender at the bottom of him."

Max West, financial planner: "He's a very good cardplayer. He has card sense. We used to play a lot. He almost never lost. We'd stay up around the clock. Once, I won, and he suggested that I was cheating. He introduced me to horseplaying. When it comes to haggling, he could be a big man in the Casbah. He resents anyone who calls what he does on the street panhandling. He calls it busking. He says, 'What's the difference if I give a concert *in*side Carnegie Hall or *out*side Carnegie Hall?' "

AT SAMMY'S

Two nights a week, Levine takes his violin to Sammy's, a Rumanian restaurant on Chrystie Street, near the Bowery. Strolling among the diners, playing fragments from his collection of thirty thousand melodies, he does his best to encourage gratuities. He tells jokes. He says, "For my opening number tonight, I would like to play Mendelssohn's Violin Concerto." A pause. "Oh, would I *love* to play that concerto." Another pause. "But I'm operating under a slight handicap. I have no talent." Instead, he says, he will play a slightly less austere composition, "This Can't Be Love Because My Wallet Is Missing." He says, "A guy the other night asks me to play 'Far, Far Away.' I say, 'I'll play on Delancey Street.' He says, 'That's not far enough.' So I'm gonna play 'The Flight of the Bumblebee,' which will be followed by the flight of the people." A few of the jokes tread on the boundary between propriety and vulgarity; most go blindly crashing over the border and into the thickets.

Levine canvasses the entire room. He tries to play "My Yiddishe Mamme" for some tourists from Chile. This fails to move them. He switches to "La Cucaracha." Bombing a little more, he walks away saying, "It's one of those nights. It's always one of those nights." Some patrons are apparently too busy wrestling veal chops to pay attention to Levine. Some are not worldly enough to know what it takes to persuade Levine to go serenade that red-faced guy three tables away, the fellow wearing the nubbly gold sports coat that evidently was once living-room draperies. Some patrons love Levine's violin-playing and his palaver but forget to tip. A young married couple have come to Sammy's to celebrate the wife's twenty-sixth birthday. Levine says, "What's your favorite song? I'll kill that for you. If you can stick me with a song, I'll give you back the money which you're not thinking of giving me in the first place."

People go to Sammy's to commit premeditated excesses. Between courses, they tell one another, "This is unreal." Sammy's serves what its management calls Jewish-style food. The chef is black, born in Grenada. He has yet to make a pilgrimage to Rumania. His interpretation of Jewish-style food involves ample doses of garlic. A garlic sausage called karnatzlack can be ordered either as an appetizer or as a main course. The menu says of it, "Guaranteed for 10,000 Miles." Every diner is entitled to free side dishes of half-sour pickles in brine and broiled bell peppers in vinaigrette sauce. A bowl of mushroom-barley soup costs two dollars and fifty cents—two ninety-five if you have it with the unborn chicken eggs. The bottle of seltzer goes next to the jar of liquefied chicken fat. The nearest hospital is Beekman Downtown.

An entertaining thing to do while recuperating between courses and bracing for a visit from Levine is to read the writing on the wall. The walls are covered with Masonite. Much of the Masonite is covered with Polaroid snaps of busy eaters. The rest is covered with business cards that have been attached by satisfied eaters: Audrey Furgatch, Sea Grove Realty, Glen Cove, N.Y.; Steve Yablon, President, Mr. Taxi, Inc., Tenafly, N.J.; Herb Blau, Herb Blau, Inc., Parking Lot Specialists, Philadelphia; L. "Lymey" Bressler, Marty Walker, Inc., Clothiers and Haberdashers, 1400 Broadway; Monty Koffer, Monty's T.V. Service, Melville, N.Y.; S. Lapidus, Lapidus Mobile Decor, Long Branch, N.J.

A party of eight sits at a round table in the center of the room. The party's food has not yet arrived. Levine plays bits of "Fascination," "It Ain't Necessarily So," and "The Ride of the Valkyries." He has tried the red-silk-handkerchief trick and the Brahms violin concerto, but he has yet to collect. It occurs to him that he should perhaps reassess the situation, so he retreats momentarily. He says, "How'd I do? I don't know yet. So far, they gave nothing. But they love me. They just gave nothing. I don't care. It's a challenge. I'd rather try to be funny before they eat. After they've eaten, they're gonna laugh anyhow. Wait. I'll give them another chance." Back to the table he goes. He holds his violin in his left hand and his bow in the right, high in the

air, and he shuffles laterally, as if he were wading a river and
the water was chest-deep.

"HARDENED CRIMINALS.
I'M PLAYING.
TEARS ARE RUNNING
DOWN THEIR FACES."

One evening in the early autumn, Levine asked me to meet him
at On Parade. A few doorways shy of the destination, I encountered
him heading in the opposite direction. "I have to go get something at the hotel," he said. "I'll meet you in the restaurant.
A friend of mine, Larry, is there. A heavyset kid. You'll see
him. I'll be back in a few minutes." I had no trouble recognizing Larry. He was seated opposite Levine's violin case, in the
booth nearest the front door; he was in his early twenties; and
he looked as if he had been planted by the management as proof
that On Parade was the place to take your big appetite. This
possibility occurred to me because I was aware of an arrangement
that Levine has with the restaurant's owners, Pete Patsatsis and
Steve Avlonitis. Whenever Levine happens to pass On Parade, if
he is not hurrying to an engagement elsewhere he stops, as if
startled, and looks in the front window. There is a nice view of
two well-stocked glass-walled pastry coolers. After staring inside
for a while, he enters the restaurant as conspicuously as possible.
The idea is to entice passersby to do likewise. Some do. When
Levine comes to On Parade for a bowl of soup—something he does
almost every day—the chef always sends over an extra dish of
croutons.

Sustaining a conversation with Larry presented a challenge.
He was preoccupied with the back pages of the *Post*. The pro-
basketball season had just opened. Soon Levine returned and handed
Larry what looked like a substantial wad of greenbacks. Larry said,
"Hey, thanks a lot, Ruby. Next week. O.K.?"

On Parade has mixed motifs—Greek and nautical. A plastic
grape arbor and plastic ferns hang from the ceiling. A sign says
"Welcome Aboard." A wall clock has been mounted on a ship's

propeller. A plastic lobster on a platter hovers above one booth, not far from a harpoon, a pair of oars, and life preservers inscribed "Captain Pete" and "Captain Steve." I examined the décor while Levine and Larry examined their faith in the New York Knicks and the New Jersey Nets. When I asked whether they followed other sports, Levine said, "We follow anything and everything. Football, basketball, baseball, boxing, cockfighting, cockroaches, fire trucks. If it moves, we bet on it." Because Larry was in a hurry—he said he had to go make some important phone calls—he and Levine quickly discussed some pending business. There was the matter of a portable tape player that Larry wanted to buy as a gift for Levine—the lightweight kind that straps to the waist and comes with stereo headphones. First, however, he wanted Levine to buy it at the Colony, since he qualifies for a deep discount there; then Larry would reimburse him. They also made a date to see a certain movie that was showing at a theater on Eighth Avenue—it had to do with cowgirls or coeds on a pleasure trip to one of the Scandinavian countries. After Larry left On Parade, Levine said, "You know, I bring in a lot of customers. For Larry alone, they should make me a partner. I'm glad you got to meet him. There are a whole lot of people I'd like you to meet. I'll introduce you to my detractors, my protractors, my contractors, the whole schmeer. I'd like to introduce you to my parents, but they're not around anymore. I sneaked in, you know. My mother had shut down the factory after my brothers and sister were born. I'm not supposed to be here. But I had the good fortune to pull through. My mother was in her forties already. My mother used to say to me, 'Don't forget. I'm your best mother.' "

On Parade's headwaiter, Gus Theodosis, came to the table to ask whether we wanted anything to eat, and to help Levine pursue one of his scholarly interests: besides the extra croutons, Levine also receives free lessons in Vulgar Greek. After some incomprehensible repartee, Levine ordered bowls of split-pea soup for both of us. A thirst for knowledge impels Levine to enroll occasionally in courses at institutions of higher and mid-level learning. Last year, he studied anthropology and Spanish at Hunter

College. At the Network for Learning, an adult-education emporium, he has done advanced work in massage and elocution. He
also attends public lectures—on politics, nutrition, taxidermy,
career planning, whatever else sounds interesting. If the scheduled
program fails to stimulate him, he can always open his violin case
and entertain and enlighten himself. Levine is a great admirer of
the Zen philosopher Alan Watts. "I have a couple of Alan Watts
lecture tapes I want you to hear sometime," he said. "A week
before he died, I was supposed to go hear him speak. But I was
involved in a pinochle game and I was a loser, so I didn't get
away in time. I'll never forgive myself. Do I believe in Zen
Buddhism? *Sure.* I believe in Martians, too. Listen, I spent six
years in Vegas—I believe in *any*thing. I played country music
for Howard Hughes in Vegas, at the Desert Inn. He tipped me
six hundred dollars. Oy, Vegas. I did some incredible things
there. Oh, *yeahhh.* You know about that guy who used to take
the old ladies out to Vegas and bury them in the desert? I met *him*
in the casino about the third week I'm in Vegas. I had no *idea*
who he was. He befriends me. He's trying to wine and dine me.
And I'm taking him around. I introduce him to this lady who's
running a gem shop. She recognizes him from one of the detective
magazines. A couple of days later, I go fishing at Lake Mead, I
come back to my room, at the Hi-Ho Motel, and as I'm putting my
key in the door three F.B.I. guys are pointing their guns at me,
telling me to freeze and put my hands in the air. I say, 'Hey, easy,
look at my hands, they're in the air.' They frisk me. See, nobody
knows how many women this guy schlepped out into the desert. I
had some explaining to do there. Part of the problem might have
been my violin. You know, a violin is a scary thing—it's magical.
People see a violin, it's like an icon. They think either I'm religious
or else there's a gun in there. So the F.B.I. gets me on file. They
would have anyway. All the top criminals in the world—I played
the violin for them. I played for Meyer Lansky at Sammy's. In
Florida, in 1947, I was with a guy named Max—an executioner
for Murder, Inc. Hands like baseball mitts. He could throttle
you with either one. Quite a guy. Loved flowers. Loved children.
Loved dogs. Loved to kill. He thought he was my bodyguard.

Somebody looked at me the wrong way, he was ready to . . . I'd
say, 'Max, wait!' I played at parties down there. Don't for*get*, I
know all the Irish, all the Italian, Yiddish, all the hip tunes. I
know them. I know stuff like 'Ace in the Hole.' All the gangster
tunes, all the Mafia tunes—like 'Mala Femmina' and 'Tarantella.'
I play 'em all. Hardened *crim*inals. I'm playing. Tears are running
down their faces."

When Gus Theodosis returned to report that there was no more
split-pea soup, Levine reacted as if he had just heard alarming
news—say, an underdeveloped nation devastated by mudslides.
"You're *kid*ding," he whined.

The waiter suggested chicken-and-rice soup. This option seemed
to appal Levine.

"Oh, God, I'm sorry," Levine said, shaking his head.

I tried to make him feel better by saying that I wasn't really
hungry.

"It's not *you* I feel sorry for," he said. "I *dream* about that split-
pea soup."

After some coaxing, Levine settled for a cup of the chicken-
and-rice. He finished it quickly. It was time to go to work. On his
way to pay the check, he passed an acquaintance who had just
taken a seat at the counter. "Whatever you do," Levine told him,
"don't order the split-pea soup."

It was a quarter to eight—fifteen minutes before curtain time—
and the carillon at St. Malachy's, the Actors' Chapel, on West
Forty-ninth, was playing an ecclesiastical hymn that for some reason sounded exactly like "There's No Business Like Show Business." As Levine approached the Ambassador Theatre, heading
toward the music, a young woman who was wearing a trenchcoat
and carrying a briefcase stopped him. She said, "Excuse me, but
could you tell me where that music is coming from?"

"That's St. Malarkey," Levine said.

The young woman stepped back, as if examining Levine from
a different angle might explain something. Then she nodded
emphatically—pointing her chin in the air, lowering it to her
chest—and continued walking toward Broadway.

At the Ambassador, Levine found a spot near the side entrance

and removed his violin from its case. He was wearing his houndstooth fedora, a green cotton sports jacket, and a peach-colored T-
shirt that bore a closeup photograph of Morris the Cat. Before
addressing the violin with the bow, he said, "This is ri*dic*ulous.
*No*body's *lis*tening." Then, as the theatergoers arrived, he began
to play amelodically, as if tuning his instrument. He did this for
twenty or thirty seconds, during which it occurred to me that he
had at last achieved the pinnacle of discord. He had a cheerful
look on his face. In a loud, stagy voice, he said, "Now for my
second number. That first number doesn't do a thing. Every orchestra in the country plays that for its first number. I tried it. It
goes *no*where." The church bells at St. Malachy's continued to
chime. "Wait. I got a ringing in my ear. Does anybody else have
that? I went to the doctor. I said, 'Doctor, I got a ringing in my
ear. What should I do?' He says, 'Don't answer.' Great doctor.
Henny Youngman's doctor. For my second number, that beautiful
French tune 'Assassination.' Used to be called 'Fascination.' Now
I play it."

For the next twenty minutes, Levine chattered and played, played
and chattered. His technique is to play just enough of a tune to
make recognizable that which is being disfigured. Then he comments upon his act of transmutation.

"Did you happen to see those motions I was making while I
played, with the fingers and arms and hands? Do you know that if
you can't play, those motions mean *nothing*? Now, here's another
song you're not gonna like."

The unwritten agenda for the evening called for Levine to make
two appearances at the Ambassador—before the first act and
during intermission, forty-five minutes later—and then to work
his way down to Shubert Alley, with stops at the Biltmore (*Who-
dunnit*), the Imperial (*Dreamgirls*), the Majestic (*42nd Street*),
and the Broadhurst (*Amadeus*). From there, he would cruise back
uptown to the Broadway Theatre to serenade the homeward crowd
from *Evita* ("Evita, come back! Evita, where are you going? Look,
Evita! Look at the way they're walking out on me! I'm emptying
the whole theater. Help, Velveeta!"), back down to the Uris, and
finally to the Circle in the Square, where the manager, William

Conn, makes Levine feel welcome by allowing him to perform
in the lobby.

" 'Sunrise, Sunset'? Nope, that's one I don't know. You stumped
me. You're entitled to twenty-eight requests. Also, you get the hat.
Take my hat. Anything you want. Take a quarter. No, wait. I'm
not finished. I got eighty numbers. Wait! Hey, is anybody listening
at all? I know a lot of music. I know every piece of music that was
ever written. I just can't *play* any of it. Actually, I happen to be
a very fine player. I just *sound* bad. Now, as the applause fades
with the people . . ."

Between these theater engagements, Levine conducts vital
peregrinations. He takes a brief detour into the Colony Record
Shop, he stares into the window of On Parade, he visits Circle
Magic, where he converses with the proprietor, Sy Sussman (a.k.a.
Sy Sands: "Sy Sands is my name, deception's my game; nice to
meetcha"), he drops by the lobby of the Edison Hotel to make
calls from one of the pay phones. Levine likes the telephone,
because he is such a fluent talker. As a telephonist, he employs
a range of gifts as vast as those he brings to the violin. Once
during a long-playing conversation, I listened mutely on my end
as he dilated upon these topics: the creative genius of the rock
star Meat Loaf, differential calculus, his plans to leave his body
to an all-women's medical school, how long he can hold his breath
underwater, old left-wing politics, the mating habits of the squid,
nuclear disarmament, Reggie Jackson, the high caliber of the
clientele at Smith & Wollensky's, the wisdom of Al Capp, mores
in Spanish bordellos, mosquito control, the literary art of Rafael
Sabatini, fresh underwear, foreign-currency exchange rates in Rio
de Janeiro, and how to bet the last race at OTB. Now, just before curtain time:

"What was *that*? That was 'The Pink Panther.' *Every* kid's supposed to know 'The Pink Panther.' My lucky night. I get kids don't
know music. But you're cute. You've got professional dimples. Uh,
good evening, sir. I've been hired to keep this sidewalk clear.
What a job I'm doing. That last song was 'Love Story.' 'Love
Story'—because I can *feel* it. Not too well, but I get some sort of
secondary subliminal indication that it's true love. . . . What'm I

talking? You people can see I'm not a well man. You can't see? I obscure it from you. Where have I *failed* you? What have I done *right?*"

Inside his violin case there was a mashed white carnation, a dollar bill that Levine had put there himself, and some quarters. Levine looked down and said, "Who threw in the dollar bill? Oh, *I* did. Well, then a wee bit of Scottish music in honor of your generous contributions." He played "Scotland the Brave" and danced a couple of steps at the end.

"Look at this. I'm getting independently poor. Wait a minute. I didn't finish yet. You're sleeping at my show? No, if you enjoy not watching me, that's also O.K. But take your money back. I don't want your money. I'm looking for contri*bu*tions. Wait. I really haven't started yet. Let me at least do my final number. Is anybody listening at all? Who would like to buy a violin cheap? I'm just practicing. Wait. *Who* put the dollar in the violin case? Not *my* dollar, the other dollar. That's a down *pay*ment. I'll come to your house. I'll give you lessons. Give me another chance. Wait. Let that man through. He's a contributor!"

A young couple—he had brown hair, a mustache, and a three-piece suit; she had black hair, a little too much makeup, and a beige leather coat—were standing close enough for Levine to hear him call her Diane. Levine played "My Diane." She seemed not to notice. "You know that song?" She shook her head. "You don't know *that?* Here. You win the violin. Anybody doesn't know that deserves the violin. Who's your favorite composer? Who's your favorite decomposer? *Beethoven?*" He played twelve notes of Beethoven's Fifth Symphony, and then extended a monologue with bits of "The Godfather," "Tzena, Tzena," and the score of *My Fair Lady.*

"Now, for my last number . . ."

It was eight o'clock, and the sidewalk was almost empty. The violin case contained two singles and about three dollars in change. Levine's mood was bright. Two Japanese couples approached, and Levine moved into his Nipponese standards—"Sukiyaki" and "Sakura." When he finished, he smiled and bowed. They smiled and bowed. As they entered the theater, having neglected to tip,

Levine smiled and bowed again and said, "Thank you. O-hi-o."
He played "Hi-Diddle-Dee-Dee."

"You remember that one. A great number. 'Hi-diddle-dee-dee,
an actor's life for me.' From *Pinocchio*. All right, my next offering
is 'Zip Up Your Doodah.' O.K. What else don't you want to hear?
Anybody!"

1 9 8 3

The Initiator

Speculating on the hyperkinetic brain of Gordon Manning, a staff consultant to NBC News, the commentator John Chancellor said not long ago, "It's like a Gatling gun in there, and every once in a while one of the projectiles it fires hits the target. I think Gordon's comfortable with that style—just spewing out ideas. On the other hand, you couldn't express the sorts of ideas Gordon is forever coming up with unless you had, to begin with, a journalistic sense of the importance of the ideas. He isn't just a booker or a fixer. Gordon Manning isn't Arnold Toynbee, but neither is he the William Morris Agency. He's somewhere in between."

Officially, Manning is retired from NBC News, where until a year ago his title was "vice-president, news projects"—a designation vague enough to suggest that what Manning did on the job defied concise definition. The retirement amounted to a bookkeeping formality; Manning, at seventy, immediately became a consultant and has continued to show up at NBC News five days a week and to occupy an office at Rockefeller Center. He spends his time reading, thinking, talking on the telephone, writing memos and letters, and inducing in the people around him alternating currents of admiration and exasperation. There is no shortage of witnesses who, having worked with Manning—not only at NBC but at CBS and *Newsweek*, where he also spent extended stretches of his career—are eager to volunteer opinions on just who Gordon Manning, sui generis, is and just what it is he does. Devoted readers of the novels of Richard Condon, who is a friend of the real Gordon Manning, have across the years encountered in them a variety of characters named Gordon Manning. *The Whisper of the Axe* features Gordon Manning as an Army psychiatrist. In *A Trembling Upon*

Rome, Gordon Manning is an English cardinal. The Gordon Manning of *Prizzi's Family* happens to work for a television network but in other ways fails at verisimilitude. In *Prizzi's Glory,* Condon's forthcoming novel, the Republican Party selects Gordon Manning as its Presidential candidate. Although in *The Abandoned Woman* a Captain Manning (formerly of the Irish Guards) manages to make love to the future Queen of England, these fanciful Gordon Mannings do not wind up in the embraces of femmes fatales. "Basically, Gordon's above that," Richard Condon has explained. Nor do Condon's Gordon Mannings ever get bumped off by the mob. It is in this respect that art is most clearly influenced by life—by the novelist's knowledge that the flesh-and-blood Gordon Manning tends toward perpetual motion, a habit that would deprive a hit man of a hittable target. Manning's friends understand that he has cultivated interesting acquaintances the world over and that his essential charm resides in his resourcefulness as a go-between.

"There's nothing very profound about Gordon," Benjamin Bradlee, the executive editor of the Washington *Post*—who has been a friend of Manning's since they were both editors at *Newsweek,* in the late fifties and early sixties—has said. "He has a very good sense of himself, and that gives him a good sense of what's important. He was always more interested in, say, getting in to see President Kennedy than in talking to him. The inside flavor—that's what he would want to carry away. But the challenge was to get inside. He energizes people, and he has a primitively fertile imagination. By 'primitive' I mean that I don't think he wants to know the philosophy of nuclear-weapons strategy. But he can figure out how to line up the guy who knows. He's a pragmatist, not a philosopher. He's high-energy, short-term."

Steve Friedman, the former executive producer of "The Today Show," said recently, "Gordon is a journalist—but he's also a guy. You go to his house and he challenges you to boccie. He cheats at boccie. He mixes it up. Is there anybody who doesn't like him? Yeah—the same people who think of television news as a business. Gordon thinks of it as an adventure. Gordon is not very businesslike. You don't have to worry about Gordon smoking a pipe and talking about theory. He's a guy."

• • •

Shortly before nine o'clock on a Monday morning last December
—the morning of the opening of the United States–Soviet Union
summit conference in Washington, the third face-to-face meeting
between Ronald Reagan and Mikhail Gorbachev—I found Manning
in the lobby of the Hay-Adams Hotel, across Lafayette Park from
the White House. He was seated at a small writing table and was
talking on the telephone. He speaks in a clear, top-of-the-morning,
let's-get-rolling voice—answering a phone, he barks "Manning!"
as if he were a city editor calling to attention a young reporter
named Manning—and with a well-oiled glibness, a cascade of cold-
sober, deadpan wisecracks that mesh with his working style, which
inclines toward the peripatetic. The former CBS News correspondent Hughes Rudd, whose trademark was a curmudgeonly demeanor, used to complain that Manning had "the attention span
of a hummingbird." For the most part, however, Manning's running
patter generates bonhomie. One of Manning's favorite encomiums
is "Bravo, mon coco!" On a day when things roll right, he can be
counted on for a dozen "Bravo, mon coco!"s. The phrase originated
with a friend, a television cameraman who lives in Paris. Manning
happened to be at poolside on the French Riviera one day several
years ago when the cameraman's dachshund demonstrated its swimming skills. The master hailed the dog with "Bravo, mon coco!"
—a spontaneous piece of poetry that Manning, without bothering
to adjust the phrase for gender, has been repeating left and right
ever since. Manning has a terrific memory for names, from chairman to water boy, and a greeting from him is a gusty fanfare. A
stroll through a familiar crowd in Manning's company is like being
in the orbit of a professional herald. One comes to suspect that if
Manning were to bump into, say, Pope John Paul II in an airport
terminal he would hit him with a "Hey! Holy Father—Rome, Italy!
Gordon Manning, NBC News. How the hell are you?" and then
quiz the pontiff about his recent ski trip and his favorite restaurants
in Warsaw.

At the moment, however, cooling his heels in the Hay-Adams
lobby, Manning seemed mildly chagrined.

"The Russians stiffed us for dinner last night," he said after hanging up the phone. "Now we're waiting for them to show up for breakfast."

Specifically, he was waiting for Albert Vlasov and Nikolai Shishlin. Both men are deputies of Aleksandr Yakovlev, the Communist Party propaganda chief and Politburo member, who is one of Gorbachev's closest advisers and has been described as the General Secretary's alter ego. During a reception at the Soviet Embassy in Washington in 1984, Anatoly Dobrynin, then the Ambassador to the United States, had introduced Manning to Shishlin, and Manning had not failed to grasp that Shishlin was someone worth getting to know. Eventually, in the summer of 1986, a meeting was arranged between Manning and Yakovlev. This took place in the course of one of Manning's most ambitious undertakings of recent years—an unrelenting effort to persuade the Soviet leader to sit for an exclusive interview with Tom Brokaw, the NBC anchorman. During Manning's first encounter with Yakovlev, some encouraging byplay occurred when the Russian, who had been wounded in the Battle of Leningrad and was later decorated with the Order of Lenin, referred to Manning as "too young to remember the Second World War." When Manning replied, "Mr. Secretary, while you were defending Leningrad against the Nazis I was on a United States naval-supply ship in the Pacific, transporting Hershey bars, razor blades, condoms, and hair tonic to our fighting men," Yakovlev rose from his chair, grasped Manning's right hand in a stevedorelike grip, and declared, "We are brothers-in-arms."

More than a year later, on the eve of the Washington summit conference, NBC News broadcast a freshly taped one-hour interview—Brokaw asking the questions, Gorbachev responding. As television-news scoops go, this was a grand accomplishment. It does not detract from the telegenic charms of the principals—the adroit, well-prepared, all-American anchorman and the supple-brained Soviet General Secretary—to say that if it had not been for Gordon Manning there would probably have been no interview. Although Gorbachev had the wisdom to recognize the strategic value of an hour of American prime time just as he was about to travel to Washington to sign a nuclear-arms-control treaty, this wisdom manifested itself only after Manning had spent two and a half years bird-dogging the Kremlin. (Months after the broadcast, Manning received a 1987 George Polk Award for foreign television reporting—official acclaim for his roles in bringing about the Gorbachev interview and also a week-long series of NBC News broadcasts from China earlier that fall.)

Manning's courtship of Gorbachev belonged to a continuum. In 1984, for instance, after months of subtle and not so subtle importuning, he received permission from the Communist Party Central Committee for "The Today Show" to broadcast for a week from Moscow. Yuri Andropov, then the General Secretary, died several months before the broadcasts. Nor did his successor, Konstantin Chernenko, ever consent to sit before the NBC cameras. When Gorbachev surfaced, Manning pursued him with every plausible stratagem. Anatoly Dobrynin was an old friend, and when Yuri Dubinin succeeded him as Ambassador, Manning made a new friend. Whenever influential Soviets happened through New York, Manning met with them for drinks, took them to dinner, invited them to his home. During the first two and a half years Gorbachev was in power, Manning went to Moscow half a dozen times, carrying proposals and revised proposals. He dispatched scores of telexes to his friendly acquaintances on the Central Committee. He sought the intervention of trusted emissaries—Americans who were headed to the Soviet Union on official or unofficial missions. He worked the room in Geneva, the site of the first Gorbachev-Reagan summit, in 1985, and also in Reykjavík, in 1986. He dined with the right people, drank risky quantities of Armenian brandy to lubricate the gears, and, on a couple of occasions, thought he had a deal, only to see it slip away.

"It wasn't a perfunctory, 'You're overdue with your insurance premium please remit' sort of process," Manning later said. "It was a series of continued personal contacts and riding the news waves—developments in the arms negotiations, changes in the war in Afghanistan, *perestroika*. You always bait hooks in this business, and sometimes you catch fish."

"I think Gordon has the world's largest Rolodex," Paul Greenberg, the senior executive producer of NBC News, who worked with

Manning at CBS as well, said recently. "It wasn't that the other networks weren't also trying to get to Gorbachev. I'm sure people at every network said, when Gorbachev came to power, 'We should get the first interview with this guy.' And everybody else in the room said, 'Sure, you bet.' Everybody sent a telegram to Dobrynin. They all thought they were on top of the situation. But they couldn't have been doing anything like what Gordon was doing."

"It wasn't that he beat the bushes harder than anybody else for two and a half years," said Les Crystal, a former president of NBC News. "He beat them for ten or twelve years." In the spring of 1987, Sandy Gilmour, the Moscow bureau chief for NBC, had a conversation with Valentin Lazutkin, the director of foreign relations for Gosteleradio, the Soviet state network. Some months later, Gilmour told me, "Lazutkin and I started talking about Gordon, and he told me, 'Well, I can say this, I can say that I truly love this man. He is very down to earth.'"

In the minds of certain enlightened Soviet bureaucrats, it seems, to be down to earth is to approximate sainthood. When Manning began to campaign for the Gorbachev-Brokaw interview, he entertained a vision of the General Secretary and the NBC anchorman in a casual setting: on the patio, say, of a dacha in the Lenin Hills (with Raisa Gorbachev dropping by for a chat along the way)—touches that would imbue the exercise with a resonant person-to-person tone. The setting that the Soviets had in mind, however, was the Cabinet Room in the Council of Ministers Building, inside the Kremlin, and that is where the interview took place. At its conclusion, Gorbachev chatted with his American guests while he autographed copies of his book *Perestroika*. At one point, he asked a translator for the English spelling of Gordon Manning. Then he took a copy of a coffee-table collection of photographs of Moscow and presented it with the inscription "To Gordon Manning—the *Initiator*. Gorbachev." When Brokaw said, "You know, Mr. Secretary, it is Mr. Manning who has been sending all those telexes," Gorbachev replied, "I finally said, 'Enough, let's go ahead and do the interview.'"

● ● ●

In the lobby of the Hay-Adams, a few minutes passed, and then Nikolai Shishlin and Albert Vlasov arrived—two amiable professional Socialists in dark business suits. Shishlin had gray hair and looked like a relative of Zbigniew Brzezinski. Vlasov, who wore eyeglasses with thick black frames, had white hair and a significant cowlick, and bore an impressive resemblance to my Cousin Jack, who lives in Oklahoma City but started out near Kiev. It was in Manning's capacity as an upper-echelon talent scout that he had invited Shishlin and Vlasov to breakfast. Along with Joe Angotti, the NBC News executive with over-all responsibility for the network's coverage of the summit, Manning, Shishlin, and Vlasov headed for the dining room. NBC planned to broadcast nine hours of summit coverage over four days, including half an hour that afternoon, when the plane bearing Gorbachev would arrive, and a half-hour program that evening.

As a waiter distributed menus, Manning proceeded to the immediate priority. "Now, tonight, Nikolai, we need somebody of weight and importance to go on with Brokaw. We have a ten-thirty P.M. special on the air. That's prime time. Karpov you mentioned" —referring to Victor Karpov, the Soviet arms-control negotiator.

"We will try," said Shishlin. "But I am afraid tonight he will negotiate."

"All right, then," Manning said, and, referring to a memorandum that he had prepared in New York, he began to recite other names—Marshal Sergei Akhromeyev, Chief of Staff of the Soviet Defense Ministry; Anatoly Dobrynin; Yuri Dubinin; Aleksandr Bessmertnykh, the First Deputy Foreign Minister; Valentin Falin, the chairman of the Novosti Press Agency; Georgi Arbatov, the head of the U.S.A. and Canada Institute—as potential guests, he hoped, for "The Today Show."

Shishlin, who was consulting a pocket-size directory that listed all the members of the Soviet delegation and their hotels, replied, "I think we will be seeing all of them at the airport, for the General Secretary's arrival."

"You don't think Dobrynin would go on with Brokaw, do you?" Shishlin was convinced that that would not happen.

"O.K. Wednesday, for our morning program," Manning said. "We talked about three generals."

Vlasov recommended General Gely Batenin, an arms-control expert on the staff of the Central Committee.

"Now, Albert, on Thursday, again for 'The Today Show,' we'd like you on there. Hope you're not going to be bashful."

"Is very difficult," Vlasov said, shaking his head. "Very difficult."

The waiter arrived with food, and as Shishlin studied his order—bran cereal, bacon, eggs—Manning said, "There you are, Nikolai. Good old American breakfast. I bet you don't get that over in—"

"O.K.," Shishlin said, smiling. "I will taste."

There were a few more items on Manning's agenda. NBC was interested in preparing a story about Gorbachev's mail from American citizens. Would it be possible to get copies of some of those letters? Of more immediate concern, might Gosteleradio be able to provide film of the quarters that the General Secretary and Mrs. Gorbachev would be occupying at the Soviet Embassy, and would they consider sharing it with NBC? Vlasov and Shishlin doubted that (risky security). Joe Angotti mentioned Larisa Chicherova, the secretary in the NBC News bureau in Moscow—a Soviet woman who was eager to visit the United States but hadn't been able to obtain a visa in time for the summit. Vlasov would see what could be done about a future visa.

Angotti said, "There's a little joke in the Moscow bureau that Larisa doesn't do any actual work for the bureau—she spends all her time translating Gordon Manning's memos to you and the General Secretary."

The check arrived, Manning grabbed it, and it was time to go. When Vlasov rose from the table, so did Manning. As they shook hands, Manning looked Vlasov in the eye and said, "Albert, I want you to say to yourself, 'I am not bashful. I am not shy. I am going to appear on American television. I am going to do this for Gordon Manning.' "

• • •

Manning wore out half a dozen briefcases during the four days of the Washington summit—a Gordon Manning briefcase that week being a legal-size white envelope imprinted with an NBC logo, bound by rubber bands. Gathering the memo that he had been referring to at breakfast, he shoved it into an already overstuffed envelope. After a three-minute detour to his room, upstairs, he reappeared in the lobby wearing a coffee-colored topcoat and a brown houndstooth-check wool slouch hat. Manning has black hair, a bit gray at the temples, and he brushes it straight back; a pink complexion; bulldog jowls; blue-gray eyes; and a straight nose that seems custom-designed for his half-lens reading glasses. He walks with a turned-out, slightly hoppety gait—an aftereffect of surgery in 1978 and 1981 to replace arthritic hip joints. When someone asked Manning whether his prosthetic hip joints set off security alarms in airports, he said no—the joints happen to be made of plastic—"but the metal plate in my head does." The slouch hat makes Manning, who is five-nine, look like a tallish gnome.

The weather in Washington that morning was sunny, chilly, and crisp. NBC had a temporary broadcast installation on the Ellipse, a half-mile walk from the Hay-Adams, and Manning and Angotti headed there now. The newsroom was a double-width trailer situated next to a two-story tower, which contained the anchor booth— a cubicle with a Plexiglas wall that afforded a full-frame view of the White House. The trailer had the mobile-newsroom usuals: blond Masonite paneling, gray acrylic carpeting, chrome-and-vinyl armchairs, wide folding tables, plenty of telephones and computer terminals.

Manning made himself at home and put in a call to WRC-TV, the NBC station in Washington. He began the conversation without preliminaries: "O.K., let's review the bidding now. I've got Vitaly Zhurkin to sit with Brokaw this afternoon. When do I pick him up and when does he go on the air?" After he finished that call, he went to work trying to track down Zhurkin, a deputy in the U.S.A. and Canada Institute, to confirm his availability. He phoned Zhurkin's hotel: no luck. Then he called his own office, in New York, to retrieve from his Rolodex the phone number of the Soviet press office in Washington.

While Manning was on hold, John Fritsche, an NBC News senior unit manager, came into the trailer and mounted a large plastic clock on one wall.

"Uh, excuse me, sir," Manning said, putting a hand over the telephone mouthpiece. "Is that my wristwatch you're delivering?"

"Hey, Gordo!" said Fritsche. "Congratulations on Moscow. Great coup!"

All week long in Washington, Manning was forced to endure that sort of thing—old friends accosting him on the street, grabbing his lapels, telling him, in so many words, "Bravo, mon coco!" Later that morning, when he and Angotti stopped by the Washington headquarters of Gosteleradio, on the back lot of the CBS News building, the blandishments interfered with his work. Manning and Angotti had gone there to speak with Genrikh Yushkiavitshus, the vice-chairman and American operations chief of Gosteleradio. From Yushkiavitshus, a long-time friend, Manning hoped to get his hands on some footage of the interior of the Soviet Embassy—the same stuff he had asked Vlasov and Shishlin about at breakfast—as well as copies of Gosteleradio's own transmissions from the summit. He found Yushkiavitshus in a trailer, in the company of a couple of backslappers whom Manning knew from his CBS days. The atmosphere was friendly, but Manning would not have been heartbroken if the CBS people had removed themselves from the room and allowed him to speak with Yushkiavitshus in private. This did not happen, however, and Manning left the trailer empty-handed.

A limo and driver were at Manning and Angotti's disposal, and from the CBS News building, on M Street, it took them northwest, toward WRC. Along the way, Angotti told me that, independent of Manning, he had come close to arranging the Gorbachev interview himself. "I had the whole thing set up, almost," he said. "I was working through a Western European peace group called the Alerdink Foundation."

Manning remonstrated with a series of throat-clearing noises.

"O.K., Gordon," Angotti said. "But I had some great fun. I went to a lot of terrific parties in Holland."

Inside WRC, Manning found his way to the office of Margie Lehrman, a producer for "The Today Show" who is based in Washington. She was meeting with Marty Ryan, the program's executive producer, and two other producers, Ron Steinman and Cliff Kappler. Manning sat down on a sofa and began tossing out the names of possible interview guests: Vitaly Zhurkin; Fyodor Burlatsky, a political scientist and a columnist for *Literaturnaya Gazeta*; Yevgeny Primakov, the director of the Institute of World Economy and International Relations; Z. I. Chernyshev, the Soviet Chief of Protocol.

"What about some of the bigger guys?" Marty Ryan said.

"I was after Yuli Verontsov, the chief arms negotiator, but I haven't heard on that yet," Manning said. "Or else Aleksandr Bessmertnykh, the First Deputy Foreign Minister." In a pinch, he said, he could probably get Boris Piadychev, a deputy spokesman for the Foreign Ministry. For the broadcast the next morning, Manning had lined up John Chrystal, an Iowa banker and farmer—a nephew of the late Roswell Garst, whose farm, in Coon Rapids, Iowa, Nikita Khrushchev had visited in 1959. Every two years for nearly thirty years, Chrystal had been visiting the Soviet Union, and he had known Gorbachev since his days as Secretary of the Central Committee for Agriculture. "Chrystal is scheduled for a six-thirty A.M. pickup at the Hay-Adams," he said. "And I have a six-thirty pickup at the Madison Hotel to go get one of the Russians."

"Gordon," Ryan said, "who in the delegation is a big shot?"

O.K., well, for Wednesday, Manning could deliver Gely Batenin, the arms-control expert on the staff of the Central Committee, who was recommended by Shishlin and Vlasov. And Valentin Falin, the chairman of the Novosti Press Agency, was available for Thursday.

A television set in the office was tuned to a live Cable News Network broadcast of a news conference that was being held by Marlin Fitzwater, the White House press secretary, and Gennadi Gerasimov, the chief spokesman for the Soviet Foreign Ministry. "Let's get Gerasimov for Wednesday," Ryan said.

Cliff Kappler mentioned Eduard Shevardnadze, the Soviet Foreign Minister.

Manning said, "You know, last night over at the Madison"—

one of three hotels that the Soviets were occupying for the week—
"ABC had five good-looking young women, two of whom spoke
Russian, working the lobby."

"And we had one English-speaking consultant," Marty Ryan
said.

"One vapored-out seventy-year-old English-speaking consultant," Manning said.

"One vapored-out seventy-year-old English-speaking consultant
with bad hips," Cliff Kappler said.

"Get me the Shevy man for Thursday morning," Ryan said. "You
won't fail, Gordon. I know it."

Manning slipped into an office down the hall to make a few calls.
At one point, Joe Angotti entered the room and said, "Have you
done anything on Zhurkin yet?"

"I'm trying to get him."

"Well, skip it. Because there are no head winds. The plane's
coming in at four-ten"—twenty minutes ahead of schedule—"so
there's less time to fill."

Freed of an immediate task, Manning decided to take a ride
downtown and recirculate through the Madison Hotel lobby.

"Stanley, what are your instructions?" he asked the limo driver
along the way.

"Not to leave your side, Mr. Manning."

"Bravo, mon coco!"

It was late in the lunch hour when we arrived at the Madison
Hotel, and the dining room was sparsely populated. We took a
table next to a window, Manning ordered gumbo and chicken salad,
and before the food arrived he excused himself to scour the premises.

"That's Yevgeny Velikhov, the Soviet Star Wars guy, in the
back," he said when he returned, nodding toward a table that was
on the opposite side of the room and was partly hidden from view.
"But I don't see anybody else."

Ben Bradlee sat at a table a few feet away, having lunch with
a friend. When Manning had entered the dining room, Bradlee
gave him a big hello, clapped him on the shoulders, and congrat-
ulated him on the Gorbachev interview. "Ya done good, Gordo,"

Bradlee said, smiling broadly. "You've come a long way since covering sports, interviewing the Splinter. Come see me."

Invoking the Splendid Splinter—Ted Williams, of course—Bradlee had referred to Manning's journalistic wellspring: wire-service sportswriting. Manning comes from the school of born reporters, the endlessly curious, world-is-my-oyster variety, the foot soldiers who might have answered the call to the priesthood if it hadn't been for the celibacy part and so answered the call to newspapers instead. He did most of his growing up in Waltham, Massachusetts, and Lancaster, Pennsylvania, spent three years after high school working at a variety of jobs, entered Boston University at the age of twenty-one, and graduated in 1941. His senior year, he became managing editor of the *Boston University News* and a reporter for what was then called the United Press Associations, which he joined full time after graduation. The U.P. motto was "A deadline every minute," and the enforcer—the wire service's New England manager—was Henry Minott, a little man who actually wore a green eyeshade. "Henry was the best teacher I ever had," Manning told me. "He used to say, 'Plan for the things you can plan for so you're ready for the things you can't plan for.' He was relentlessly competitive. His criteria for what made a story were: Who cares? Why do they care? And why do they care now? There were fourteen people in the Boston bureau, and we covered all of New England but Connecticut. The Associated Press had three bureaus working the same territory. We were a guerrilla army of journalism. All out of college. No overtime, no expenses. Henry had us all quivering. Of course, you got beat a lot, but you couldn't help it. You sank or swam under Henry."

The job of a U.P. utility man in Boston was to rewrite the dispatches from northern New England and to cover shipwrecks, politics, crimes of passion, and the local gods: the Red Sox and the Bruins. "Writing sports was the way to show if you had any flair or style," Manning said. What felt good was when the U.P. bosses in New York, informing editors around the country what to watch for on the night wire, would herald an item like "Gordon Manning in Boston. 'How Ted Williams Sees Dizzy Trout's Fastball,' 300 words."

In 1943, Manning enlisted in the Navy. He was married soon thereafter, to Edna Currier, a woman who has proved to be exceptionally companionable and extraordinarily forbearing. The Navy sent the Mannings to San Francisco, where the first of their four sons was born. When the war ended, Manning would have loved to work for the San Francisco *Chronicle*, but a lot of other people had the same idea, and he returned to Boston, to the U.P., and became New England sports editor. After leaving the U.P. for the second, and last, time, in 1946, he moved to Washington, where he briefly edited a publication called *Sportfolio*. From there he went to New York, where he worked on a number of sports magazines. For a while, he was a writer and editor on a Cowles weekly called *Quick*. When, one day, a fellow editor appeared at Manning's desk holding a can of marshmallow fluff and asked him to rewrite a recipe on the label for a feature in the magazine, Manning told himself, "I've got to get out of here." *Collier's* had commissioned him to write an article on Yogi Berra, and now he took a job there as a staff writer. Within a year, he became managing editor—a position he held until 1956, when he left *Collier's*, which was about to fold, and joined the staff of *Newsweek*.

Kermit Lansner, who eventually became, along with Manning, a co-executive editor of *Newsweek*, remembers Manning's arrival: "Then, suddenly, this character appears on the scene—this wisecracking little fellow named Gordon Manning." The late fifties and early sixties at *Newsweek* have become, in Lansner's memory, "an idyllic time." Originally, Manning was hired as a senior editor, with responsibility for the back of the book—cultural and scientific reporting, reviews, and the like. When the Washington *Post* bought the magazine, in 1961, Osborn Elliott was promoted to editor-in-chief and elevated Lansner and Manning. Their job was to oversee the entire editorial content, front and back of the book. Ben Bradlee ran the Washington bureau. "It was such an exciting place to be, because we worked for No. 2," Bradlee recently recalled. "That hones your sense of competitiveness." By all accounts, Manning contributed amply to the camaraderie. In a memoir that Osborn Elliott published some years ago, he tells about a round of golf that he, Manning, and Bradlee played in Ponte Vedra, Florida, in 1962:

As Bradlee was addressing his ball for an approach shot to the green, Manning cried out: "Watch out, Bradlee, there's a rattlesnake behind you!" "Goddamn it, Manning, cut the bullshit," said Ben. But just then we all heard the unmistakable buzzing of a rattler. Bradlee jumped a mile. His old caddie took an iron from his golf bag, and with one graceful swoop knocked the head off the snake. "That was a pretty good shot, Sam," said Manning. "What club did you use?"

A stickler for accuracy, Manning told me, "Oz gets that story wrong. I'd been needling Bradlee all the way around the course, trying to upset his game by pretending I was a TV sports commentator—you know, talking into my 3-wood, which I was holding like a microphone. But I didn't 'cry out' to Bradlee about the snake. I said it very softly. I said, 'You know, Ben, there's a rattlesnake right behind you. There's really a snake. You might want to get out of the way. Looks to me like a pretty big rattlesnake, Ben.' We were down around the green, pitching up. That rattler came out of the canebrake. Bradlee told me to shut up and went ahead and hit the shot. But Oz is right about one thing: I did ask the caddie what club he used."

Most of Manning's colleagues at *Newsweek* learned to adapt to certain idiosyncrasies that have never really dissipated—what Lansner calls "a relentless, terrierlike quality to his way of editing." A galley proof that had been subjected to a Manning edit would often come back to the writer decorated with little taped-on scribbled queries. He was quick with praise but also quick to second-guess. Because each issue of *Newsweek* closed on a Saturday afternoon, Manning, who had settled his family in Westport, was in the habit of spending Friday nights in Manhattan. Late one Friday in the spring of 1964, word of a major earthquake in Alaska arrived—an act of God several magnitudes more stirring than the San Francisco earthquake. With the spirit of Henry Minott whispering in his ear, Manning issued orders to the overnight desk: "Get the San Francisco bureau chief and our L.A. people up there. Hire photographers. Also, place a person-to-person call to Lowell

Thomas, Jr., in Anchorage." From a previous job, he knew Lowell
Thomas, Jr., a documentary filmmaker who later became lieutenant
governor of Alaska, and he also knew "the oldest trick in journalism: when there's a natural disaster, you place a person-to-
person call, and the instant phone service is restored the phone
company honors that." He went on: "Four o'clock the next afternoon, I got a call from Lowell Thomas, Jr. This earthquake did
tremendous damage. Thomas told me about his family, what happened, and we got the story, plus photographs."

The *Newsweek* offices are at Forty-ninth and Madison. Only six
blocks away, at CBS, the fact of the earthquake somehow eluded
everyone. Not until Saturday morning did Fred Friendly, who a
few weeks earlier had become president of CBS News, learn that
the earthquake had happened. Friendly, whose initial response to
CBS's second-rate coverage of the disaster was a rage that could
have been measured with a seismograph, later referred to the episode as his Bay of Pigs. Never again, he vowed, would he endure
this kind of embarrassment. Determined to hire a "hard news"
person for CBS, Friendly soon found his way to Manning. Thus
did Manning's career in print journalism end and his career in
television news begin. The offer from CBS came at a time when
Manning was feeling frustrated with news-magazine journalism,
because of "the way time erodes the news value of a story." He
believed that in going to television he was returning to his deadline-
every-minute roots.

Manning's first title at CBS was vice-president and director of
news. As a practical matter, being in charge of hard news—what
Bill Leonard, a former president of CBS News, has described as
"today's story today, tomorrow's story tomorrow"—meant oversee-
ing everything but documentary programs. He ended up staying
with the network more than ten years, during much of which he
was the executive in charge of the "CBS Evening News." In 1966,
Manning helped create a half-hour Saturday edition of the "CBS
Evening News." This idea was not immediately embraced by everyone at CBS, the assumption being that nobody would tune in.
Manning put Roger Mudd in the anchor chair and hired Heywood
Hale Broun (of the windy diction and the blinding madras jackets)

as the resident sports poet. Political conventions, the war in Southeast Asia, space shots—the high-pressure stuff that CBS News was learning to cover better than anyone else—became the stuff that Manning thrived on.

According to Roger Mudd, "The fact that Gordon didn't know anything about television when he came there was the best thing about him. Gordon's greatest contribution was his ability to rise above the technocracy of TV—the long lines, the microwaves, the satellite dishes, the trucks and switches and charters—and to think almost exclusively about substance. He was very tough when he had to be, but basically he loved what he was doing and just lacked the antagonistic approach that so many television executives have. He never succumbed to the feeling that there was anything he couldn't do."

Manning's tenure at CBS coincided with the so-called Cronkite era, the generation during which the "CBS Evening News" came to dominate nightly news programming. "In the corporate sense, Gordon was fearless, which is why he could come up with ideas," the CBS correspondent Morley Safer has said. "At CBS, Gordon was the guy whom you could expect to say, 'How come nobody's ever done Chou En-lai yet?' " The how-comes and why-don't-we's and shouldn't-we-be's gushed from Manning—occasionally to the consternation of his deputies, one of whom once complained, "Gordon's question mark is our command."

When Manning arrived at CBS, he didn't even have a passport. By the time he left, he had made numerous trips to Southeast Asia (including one six-week ordeal in 1970, during which he recovered the bodies of four CBS employees who had been killed in Cambodia); had seen China, India, the Middle East, and all of Europe; and had produced special interviews with Marshal Tito, in Belgrade, with Anwar Sadat, in Cairo, and with Aleksandr Solzhenitsyn, in Zurich.

"Going to CBS brought about Gordon's transformation from a provincial," Kermit Lansner says. "The old Gordon used to think it was an affectation if you were interested in international affairs. Knowing anything about Charles de Gaulle meant you were affected. He used to say he didn't like foreign food. He never ate veal, because his father told him if the veal had been healthy it would have grown up to be a beef."

Successfully transcending these prejudices, Manning developed an appetite for travel that was almost, but not quite, insatiable. On one occasion, he petitioned Friendly for relief. "Gordon came to me with a complaint," Friendly recalls. "He said, 'I've been working too hard and traveling too much. If I don't start spending more time with the kids and Edna, I'm afraid she's going to divorce me.' And I said, 'I can live with that.' "

Walter Cronkite—who has sailed with Manning often, in the Caribbean and off the New England coast; who in 1971, on three hours' notice, boarded an overnight flight to Paris with Manning in a long-shot quest for an exclusive interview with the leaders of the first official permanent diplomatic delegation from the People's Republic of China to the United States in almost a quarter of a century; who went to Switzerland with him when Manning arranged the first Western television interview with Solzhenitsyn, in 1974, shortly after he began his exile from the Soviet Union—has described Manning as "the greatest traveling companion since Boswell." Osborn Elliott remembers attending a convention of news executives with Manning some years ago in Las Vegas: "I was slated to have breakfast with Gordon, who was also staying at Caesar's Palace, and he called up at seven A.M., waking me up, and said, 'Oz, we have a date for breakfast this morning. I just thought you might be wondering why they have mirrors on the ceilings of all the bedrooms here.' I said, 'Yeah, Gordon, I was really wondering about that. Why is it?' He said, 'That's so you can shave in bed.' "

The notion behind Manning and Cronkite's spur-of-the-moment junket to Paris—the inspiration of a CBS producer named Sandy Socolow—was for them to film an interview with the Chinese diplomats before the diplomats departed for New York. Upon landing in Paris, Cronkite, who had a bad cold, went to the hotel and took to his bed. Manning proceeded to the local CBS bureau and drafted a letter, an interview request, to Huang Hua, who was one of the senior New York-bound diplomats. (Huang Hua had previously been the Chinese Ambassador to Canada and had been named

China's representative to the U.N. Security Council. Manning had met him in Ottawa, while trying to arrange to get a CBS News team into the People's Republic in advance of Richard Nixon's first visit.) He visited the Chinese Embassy, bearing a friendly entreaty to Huang Hua, and got the door slammed in his face by a less than friendly subordinate. As a fallback, he had already bought all the remaining seats in the first-class cabin of the Air France flight that his sources had told him was supposed to deliver Huang Hua and the chief delegate, Deputy Foreign Minister Qiao Guanhua, to New York. At Orly Airport, Manning and Cronkite became aware of a second plane, at an adjacent gate, that was receiving lower-echelon members of the Chinese delegation. There came a moment in the passenger lounge when it seemed unclear whether Huang Hua and Qiao Guanhua would board Manning's Air France flight or the other. Turning to Cronkite, Manning said, "If those guys get in the other plane, we're done for," and Cronkite replied, "I knew we never should have come here. This was a terrible idea."

However, Huang Hua and Qiao Guanhua did board the right Air France plane, whose steward Manning had prevailed upon to stow camera equipment under one of the seats in first class. Before the plane even pulled away from the gate, the steward informed Manning that there was a problem in the galley and he couldn't serve breakfast. With an additional gratuity, Manning encouraged the steward to serve the Chinese dignitaries non-stop champagne instead. Finally, Manning went forward and greeted Huang Hua and Qiao Guanhua, who reacted with alarm, as if under the impression that Manning was announcing a hijacking. Huang Hua, recognizing Manning, reassured his companion, saying, "I know him. He works for Walter Cronkite." At which point Manning gestured broadly, and magically produced Cronkite. A friendly negotiation ensued, and the Chinese agreed to give Cronkite an in-flight on-camera interview. When the plane landed in New York, the assembled press corps had to make do with a brief prepared statement by Qiao Guanhua. "It was one of those moments in journalism when this is a little boy's game and you're delighted," Manning said. "I'm coming off that plane with the film that those other guys all wanted."

Early in 1974, Manning was replaced as senior vice-president
and director of news at CBS and given a less exalted, executive-
producer position. He stayed on with the network a little more than
a year (long enough for his pension to vest), during which he
arranged the Solzhenitsyn interview. Along with Eric Sevareid, he
also created a series of one-hour "wise owl" interviews—conversations with the likes of John McCloy, George Kennan, Robert
Hutchins, and Willy Brandt. Manning's decision to resign altogether, in 1975, did not dismay certain CBS executives, whose
affection for him was limited. An ostensible factor in his fall from
grace was his role in the hiring of Sally Quinn as a co-anchor of
the "CBS Morning News"—an inglorious episode for all involved.
(Quinn later wrote a book, *We're Going to Make You a Star*, in
which she told about having fantasized going on the air and saying,
"Good morning, I'm Sally Quinn and we are not prepared to do
this show and I don't know what I'm doing up here.") In reality,
the Sally Quinn business played a minor part in Manning's departure, which had its roots in complicated intramural facts of
corporate life at CBS. In 1966, Fred Friendly—protesting the
network's decision to televise reruns of "I Love Lucy," "The Real
McCoys," and "Andy of Mayberry" rather than George Kennan's
live testimony during the Senate Foreign Relations Committee hear-
ings on the Vietnam War—resigned as president of CBS News.
That same day, Manning was approached about succeeding Friendly
but, out of personal loyalty, he said he wasn't prepared to discuss
the idea. It was not that he did not wish to be president of CBS
News; it was a matter of circumstances and timing. This infuriated
the network group president who had made the approach—who
believed that Manning's loyalty was misplaced. Manning saw in
the network group president a flawless representative of a subcul-
ture that he had a habit of referring to as "a bunch of salesmen
from Hoopletown." Nine years later, the chief salesman from Hoopletown brought about Manning's removal as head of hard news.

Manning had not seen it coming, although some of his friends
felt that he should have. Only months before, he had gone to China
as the escort of William Paley, the chairman of CBS, and his wife,
Barbara. Every day, he had breakfast, lunch, and dinner with the

Paleys, who seemed to share Walter Cronkite's view of Manning as an ideal traveling companion. Unfortunately, the trip, which was supposed to last two weeks but stretched into more than a month, turned out to be fateful: in Beijing, Mrs. Paley became ill with what at first appeared to be bronchitis and later turned out to be terminal lung cancer.

"Nobody who's ever been close to Paley—at his best a very good fellow, at his worst something else—has stayed close for a long time," Fred Friendly later said, analyzing the consequences of Manning's close relationship with the company chairman. "That's just something we all learned: when you get too close to Paley, it turns to ashes. And Gordon was certainly as close to Paley as anyone else in the news division."

Whatever personal affection Paley felt for Manning did not impel him to veto the decision to demote Manning. Years later, Walter Cronkite asked the network group president to explain what Manning's sin had been. The answer was "He pressed too damn hard."

When Manning arrived at NBC, in mid-1975, as when he had arrived at *Newsweek* and CBS, aspects of his legend had preceded him. "There were two basic accounts of who Gordon Manning was," Joe Angotti has said. "On the one hand, he was this wonderful, beloved fellow who had been running CBS News. And on the other we had reports about this maniacal little guy who does nothing but write memos. All the things we'd heard turned out to be true in one way or another. We were bewildered by him at first. He was just a flurry of activity constantly in motion."

Officially, Manning was "executive producer for specials and politics," and his immediate task was to coördinate coverage of the 1976 Presidential campaign. The centerpiece of NBC's Election Night set (and again in 1980 and 1984) was a mammoth Manning-inspired apparatus, a fourteen-by-twenty-four-foot Plexiglas map that would illuminate in blue any state that was won by the Republicans, in red any state that went to the Democrats, and in white any state that was not yet decided. Several years ahead of computer-generated graphic simulations, it required its own air-conditioning system. It wasn't just a piece of glitz. It rendered literally the Big Picture.

Excused from responsibility for day-to-day news coverage, Manning was able to exercise his talents as a superbly connected gadfly. In 1977, he conceived and produced a special program titled "Human Rights: A Soviet-American Debate," and won a Columbia-DuPont award. He did the diplomatic advance work for "The Today Show" 's week of broadcasts from Moscow in the fall of 1984, and then turned his attention to Vietnam. A satellite ground station was installed in Ho Chi Minh City, and, in April of 1985, ten years after the last American soldiers had departed, NBC broadcast the first live pictures ever from Indo-China to the West. He brokered NBC News's week of broadcasts from China last fall, and lately has been trying to get permission for NBC News crews to work in North Korea while the 1988 Summer Olympic Games take place in Seoul.

In the spring of 1985, Tom Brokaw and a camera crew went to La Libertad, a mining town in south-central Nicaragua that is the birthplace of President Daniel Ortega, to gather material for an "NBC Nightly News" segment. They had not been long in La Libertad when they became aware of the presence of a reporter from TASS. It occurred to Brokaw that he might like to capture the man from TASS on film, and so, along with an assistant, Marc Kusnetz, he introduced himself.

"And where is it you are from?" the Soviet asked.

"NBC Television," Brokaw said.

"NBC? I see. Well, do you know Gordon Manning?"

"Of course," Brokaw said.

"*The* Gordon Manning?"

"Yes," Kusnetz said. "There's only one."

"Thank God," the Soviet said.

For a couple of years in the early eighties, Manning was the executive responsible for "The Today Show."

"His job, rather than telling me what to do, was to protect me from the fools who were running this place," Steve Friedman, the former executive producer, has said. "Gordon threw himself in front of the train many times." When Friedman decided, in 1980, that he wanted Richard Nixon to sit for a five-part series of interviews during the Presidential race, he enlisted Manning. "This was before Nixon made his comeback. I didn't go to Leonard Garment. I didn't go to Nixon's P.R. guy. One day I went to Gordon. Lo and behold, three months later, we ended up in Nixon's town house, with Teddy White doing the interviewing."

This is not to say that Manning has never delivered a body he wished he hadn't. In 1977, he engineered Gerald Ford's oral memoirs, with John Chancellor as the interviewer. "I think Gerald Ford went to sleep on the air before I did, but I went to sleep shortly after that," Chancellor has said.

Nor did Manning reveal himself to be an ideal producer, a buttoned-up master of the control room. Because it happened almost twelve years ago, Tom Brokaw has a mellow recollection of the night he and David Brinkley co-anchored a one-hour special on the death of Mao Zedong. Manning was, in theory, presiding in the control room.

"It involved what are called lashups from all over the world," Brokaw said. "And it was chaos. Things didn't come up on the satellite when they were supposed to. I was trying to read names off the TelePrompTer that I wasn't sure how to pronounce. At one point, Brinkley, in order to interview Eugene Rostow, had to walk, on camera, from one end of the set to the other. And Gordon was the executive in charge. During a break, I got up from my chair and went into the control room to tell him, 'We are crashing and burning. This is a disaster,' and I found him on the phone to Joseph Kraft. It was one of those conversations where he's saying, 'Well, look, Joe, it's always a pleasure. Best to Polly. And lunch when you get back to New York. O.K., Joe.' If it had been anyone but Gordon, I would have had a meltdown."

During lunch at the Madison Hotel, while Manning was recounting for me some of his biography—starting with Henry Minott, he fast-forwarded here, backtracked there, and had arrived back at the pursuit of Gorbachev—Bradlee, on his way back to the office, stopped by the table once more.

"Hey, Gordon, you still sending memos on matchbooks?" he asked.

A written message from Manning—commonly known as a Gordogram—is a to-be-treasured artifact bestowed on just about anyone who has sustained an acquaintance with him for more than, say, four hours. I've been on friendly terms with Manning ten years longer than the minimum, and during that time I've received Gordograms imperfectly typed on hotel stationery, handwritten in block-letter scrawls on postcards and magazine-subscription blanks, and scribbled in the margins of newspaper clippings—never yet on a matchbook, but once on a cocktail coaster.

"The matchbooks are fine if they aren't already printed with advertisements to go to welding or drawing school," Bradlee said.

"You know, John Chancellor claims I once sent him a long memo on one of those toilet-seat sanitary covers," Manning said. "But I think he made that up."

Gordograms emanate from Manning's ruminations while he is shaving, from conversations with interesting fellow passengers, from this story in *The Economist* or that one in the Hong Kong *Daily News*. A newspaper that has passed through Manning's hands looks as if it had been messed with by a kindergarten collage class. Some of Manning's associates claim to have received Gordograms on sugar-cube wrappers. Once, when Manning was convalescing from hip surgery and couldn't defend himself, Roger Mudd showered him with a hundred or so empty Sweet'n Low packets that he had inscribed with mini-memorandums of his own. Paul Greenberg says, "Gordon's killed more trees than Chernobyl." The Gordograms that circulate among the "A" list at NBC tend to be about what worked or didn't work on last night's broadcast, or they are proposals for special kinds of debates; special kinds of programs; So-and-So who could make a contribution to "The Today Show"; possible stories (the man in Baraboo, Wisconsin, who does mating dances with whooping cranes; the rumor he had heard—and, in March, 1984, passed along to anyone who might want to follow it up—"that Ronald Reagan conducts a lot of his life by astrology").

"I would always read the first sentence, then I would check to see whether anybody else had got it," Steve Friedman, who, having left NBC, has been forced to subsist on a low-Gordogram diet, has said. "If no one else had got it, I read it. If anyone else was on the list, I didn't read it, because I knew somebody else would respond. I often got seven a day, thirty-five or forty a week. I once got one that started out on hotel stationery, in longhand. The next two pages were napkins. Then page 4 was typed. Those were the ones you knew were sent only to you."

Tom Brokaw says he reads Manning's memos—not all twenty-eight pages sometimes, but he reads them. The final day of NBC News's venture to China last autumn happened to be Gordon and Edna's forty-fifth wedding anniversary. Aboard a flight from Beijing to Shanghai, Brokaw toasted the Mannings and presented them with a handsomely bound collection of China memos.

"They took up an entire seat on the plane," Brokaw said. "You know, when we were in China we had some disagreements with the Chinese, and we became involved in these contentious sessions. And quite often, to make a point, the Chinese would bring out one of Gordon's memos. They had them all neatly arranged in plastic folders. The Chinese treated this stuff as if it were a communiqué from the Congress of Vienna. They would say, 'But Mr. Gordon Manning, in his memorandum of such-and-such date, represented to us that'—whatever. And we would leave those meetings, and Gordon would always berate me. 'See, Brokaw! The Chinese take my memos seriously. Brokaw doesn't even read them! But the Chinese . . .' "

Steve Friedman says, "Gordon will be pounding out memos as long as his fingers are nimble enough to type. And after that he'll write them in crayon. Three weeks after he dies, we'll still be getting them. Maybe from the hotel he's staying in."

Lunch done, Manning wandered out of the Madison Hotel dining room, saying, "Let's go look for some Comrades." At that moment, a fleet of limousines had gathered at the hotel's main entrance, on Fifteenth Street, to receive the V.I.P.s whose presence was expected when the General Secretary's plane arrived at Andrews Air Force Base. In the milling crowd, Manning spotted a couple of

pals—Aleksandr Aksyonov, the chairman of Gosteleradio, and
Sasha Petrov, his interpreter. He also greeted Boris Piadychev, a
deputy spokesman for the Foreign Ministry, and Genrikh Borovic,
who looked like a professional wrestler but was actually an agitprop
playwright and Soviet television personality. Nobody had much
time to chat, so Manning decided to ride back to the NBC studio
at the Ellipse. He had calls to make. He began trying, fruitlessly,
to track down Victor Karpov, the arms negotiator, still hoping to
book him for a special broadcast that evening with Tom Brokaw.
He checked in with Marty Ryan, of "The Today Show."

"Now, this is for tomorrow morning, right?" Manning told Ryan.
"That would be Tuesday. One Russian you want, correct? O.K.,
we possibly have Bessmertnykh or Yuli Verontsov. For Wednesday,
the general who speaks English. And then, Thursday morning,
Gerasimov—unless we get Albert Vlasov. O.K., I'm at the Ellipse
now. I'm here, and if you have any legwork for me keep me posted.
Bravo, mon coco!"

Manning had a few Gordograms to get out. In a room equipped
with eight computer terminals, he chose one of two manual typewriters and began to write letters to Victor Karpov, Aleksandr
Bessmertnykh, Yuli Verontsov, Yevgeny Primakov, and General
Gely Batenin.

Brokaw wandered over. "Gordon, do you know anything about
Dobrynin?"

"They gave me a flat no. So I'm trying to get Karpov."

"For ten-thirty tonight? Great."

A few minutes later, Brokaw was back. "Gordon, if you can't
get Karpov, how about Gerasimov?"

"I can get him!"

"What about Arbatov?"

"I can get him!"

Brokaw beamed and, patting Manning on both shoulders, said,
"Gerasimov was in great form at his news conference today. Let's
get him."

"Gerasimov fought me hard on the Gorbachev interview, you
know," Manning said. "I saw him last night. I grabbed him by
that alpaca coat of his and looked him in the eye and said, 'We

couldn't have done it without you, Gennadi.' He smiled. There
were two smiles. His and mine."

All three networks had planned special news coverage at four-
thirty, when Gorbachev's plane was due to arrive. At that hour,
Manning led me to the mobile control booth, one trailer away from
the makeshift newsroom. He sat in the rear, about twenty feet away
from a bank of more than a dozen illuminated television monitors.
Several screens showed Brokaw straightening his necktie and chat-
ting casually with Brent Scowcroft, his first interview guest. "A
minute to airtime," the assistant director said.

" 'A minute to airtime,' " Manning said. "I like that."

There was an opening telephoto shot of Gorbachev's plane as it
approached Andrews Air Force Base, a quick cut to the crowd of
dignitaries assembled on the tarmac, then a cut to Brokaw and his
guest at the studio. NBC failed to televise the actual touchdown,
and Manning said softly, "I would've stayed with the plane." The
camera caught Secretary of State George Shultz conversing with
Eduard Shevardnadze. To the tune of "Some Enchanted Evening,"
Manning sang to himself: "Shultz and Shevardnadze . . ."

When the broadcast was over, Manning had more work to do:
letters to finish; phone calls to make; a briefing list that Robert
Wright, the president and chief executive of NBC, could study
before a meeting with Gorbachev later that week. (Wright was one
of a handful of American media executives who had been invited
to a rather cozy gathering at the Soviet Embassy. Manning would
also attend. It was a provocative session during which Wright,
seated directly opposite the host, posed a question about human
rights and Gorbachev replied, "I did not come here to be interviewed. If you want an interview, I will ask you questions.") I
decided to go back to my hotel for some rest. Manning and I agreed
to meet again at eight-thirty that evening in the lobby of the Hay-
Adams.

At eight-thirty-five, we were on our way from the Hay-Adams
to the Madison Hotel, once again to troll for Soviets. The sidewalks
teemed with pedestrians and police officers. At the corner of Six-
teenth and K Streets, waiting for a light to change, we heard a
familiar chorus of rapidly approaching sirens. For no apparent

reason, the lead vehicle—a District of Columbia police car, with
a strapping black cop behind the wheel and a crewcut, mustached
Russian (obviously) security agent riding shotgun—halted briefly
as it reached the intersection. It seemed that something the Soviet
security agent had said or done had provoked the D.C. cop. One
could easily read the lips of the cop, who, defying the howl of the
sirens, was treating his startled passenger to a lesson in American
slang. When the motorcade moved again, a ZIL limousine shot
past us. Manning thought he had spotted Pavel Palashchenko, one
of Gorbachev's primary translators, inside the ZIL. "Hey, that
might be the big guy," he said.

A dark-haired young pedestrian who wore a Walkman stood next
to us.

"You K.G.B.?" Manning asked him.

The pedestrian shook his head, indicating that he hadn't heard
the question. He removed his earphones. "What's that?"

"You in touch with the Russians?"

A canvass of the glittering lobby of the Madison—it glowed with
ormolu and chandeliers and was filled with red and white
poinsettias—didn't turn up any of the faces Manning was hoping
to see, so he found a house phone. When he tried the room of
Nikolai Shishlin, he got no answer. This rankled him: Manning
had just done his Russian friend a favor. Only two hours earlier,
Shishlin had phoned and said, "Gordon, my friends are thirsty.
You could find us perhaps some Scotch?" and Manning had arranged for a case of Dewar's to be delivered to the Madison. Getting
through at last to Albert Vlasov, he said, "Albert, I'm really in
very desperate shape. Nikolai told me he would call me back in
twenty minutes—that was two hours ago—and I haven't heard
from him, and I'm down in the lobby now. Albert, we have had
no Soviets on the air yet. It is to your advantage to help us out. . . .
O.K., thank you. I'll be here."

Moving around the corner, toward the elevators, Manning spotted
Gennadi Gerasimov, the Foreign Ministry spokesman, and his deputy, Boris Piadychev. With no coaxing, Gerasimov acknowledged
that he would be available for an interview that evening. At the
moment, he had a shopping bag full of packages and wanted to go
to his room. As he departed, Manning began to sweet-talk the

handsome, gaunt-looking Piadychev. Soon Piadychev was asking, "What will be the general area of questions?"

"The agenda for the summit talks. Where do we go from here. The general scope of things. The I.N.F. treaty."

"Hmm." Piadychev wanted to think this one over. "When does this go on the air?"

"Tomorrow morning," Manning said. "This is live."

"Live?"

"I will pick you up at six-thirty," Manning said.

"Six-thirty? This is so early. We Russians are lazy. We like to sleep."

"Hey, Boris, this is summit time. The good old summit time."

Not long after this conversation broke up, an NBC errand runner named Steve Plotka entered the lobby carrying a large package wrapped in shiny red paper—Nikolai Shishlin's case of Scotch. Manning had meanwhile moved back to the house phones. Bending over to rest the whiskey on the floor, Steve Plotka succeeded in splitting his trousers along the seam. While he contemplated what to do about that problem—his solution was to remove his jacket and tie the sleeves around his waist—an assistant manager of the hotel appeared and brusquely explained that no packages were allowed in the lobby, that it would have to go back outside. Steve Plotka retreated through a revolving door with the Scotch and was greeted by explosives experts from the Secret Service and the District of Columbia Police Department. Some other Secret Service guys were milling in the lobby, along with what looked like a claque of K.G.B. agents—men who wore tiny receivers in their ears and seemed to have done their shopping at Banana Republic. For reasons that eluded me, the K.G.B. men suddenly began to dash in and out of the lobby. At a pay phone now, Manning was saying to someone at NBC, "I've lined up Gerasimov for tonight. . . . Two minutes? Well, hell, you've got to give him more than that. I'm killing myself down here. . . . What plane crash? . . . Well, this is a summit special. The news comes on at eleven o'clock. That's when you report the plane crash. This is a Soviet-American summit. This is our fourth broadcast and our first Russian."

Two men, one of them wearing press credentials that identified him as a representative of *Pravda*, approached Manning. "Mr. Manning," the *Pravda* man said. "Who are you looking for? Perhaps we can help."

"I don't need anyone," Manning said, waving them away. "I'm on a call to the outside."

The Soviets retreated. A minute later, however, Shishlin materialized and introduced Manning to the solicitous Soviets, one of whom, a prematurely white-haired man with a dark William Powell mustache, turned out to be General Gely Batenin, the very person Manning was hoping to put on the air. His companion from *Pravda* was Gennadi Vassiliev, a political columnist. The group found some easy chairs in the lobby, and Manning settled down to business. "Now, Mr. General, let me tell you the plan and we'll see if it suits you," he said, and then he turned to Vassiliev and asked, "Does the General speak English?"

"Yes, he speaks English, but he is sometimes in need of help."

"Perhaps you would like to come on the air with the General," Manning proposed.

That prospect suited Vassiliev. The United States government was picking up the out-of-towners' hotel and meal tabs, but the Soviets had only limited pocket money. A little coast-to-coast television exposure seemed like a nice extra perk.

"Who will be his partner?" Vassiliev asked.

"He'll be alone," Manning said. "Oh, who will interview him? Gumbel. Bryant Gumbel."

"Gumbel," said Vassiliev.

The General nodded in recognition and said, "Ah, Gumbel."

Manning needed to collect a few biographical details. "And the General is a war hero?" he asked the man from *Pravda*.

"Too young. He is the one to keep your eye on for the future."

"And, Gordon," Shishlin interjected, "because ABC and CBS and CNN have all asked me to appear with them, and because of our long friendship, I have decided I will speak only to NBC."

"You're on," Manning said.

Gennadi Gerasimov had returned to the lobby from his room, wearing his gray alpaca topcoat and a faintly supercilious, bemused smile. Gesturing toward him and then toward the other Soviets, Manning said, "You gentlemen know Mr. Gerasimov?"

At six-thirty Wednesday morning, Manning told Vassiliev, a driver would be waiting in front of the hotel to pick up General Batenin.

"And your first name?" Vassiliev asked. "It is . . .?"

"Gordon. G-o-r-d-o-n."

"Gordon Manning," Nikolai Shishlin told the man from *Pravda*. "My best friend."

1 9 8 8

Wall Power

Hundreds of buy-low, sell-high manipulators circulate in the marketplace where antique prints, maps, and books are traded, but none of them much resemble a buy-low, sell-high manipulator named W. Graham Arader III. Arader advertisements identify him as a purveyor of "16th to 19th century paintings, Early American engravings, watercolors and prints, important natural history color plate books, maps and atlases, autographs and manuscripts." This order of priority reflects Arader's ambition to become a buyer and seller, in the grandest style, of American and European paintings —an ambition that has not yet become a reality. The reality of the moment, and one thing that distinguishes Arader (pronounced "uh-*raide*r"), is that he buys and sells more original prints, usually copper engravings from rare color-plate books, than anyone else in the world. He goes about his business in a manner that irritates and ingratiates in roughly equal measure. What Arader, like all successful art dealers, mainly offers clients are his imprimatur and his personality. He is abrasive and solicitous, argumentative and engaging, unscholarly yet imposingly knowledgeable, charming when he absolutely needs to be and flatly rude when it suits him, which is often.

"He's certainly not the little old print dealer in the musty room," Thomas Armstrong, the director of the Whitney Museum, who is a friend and satisfied client of Arader's, said recently. "The personality is quite lively. It makes the whole situation very interesting. There's that bombastic presence of Graham's. I don't think he's got anything he wouldn't sell. Which, ultimately, is the kind of dealer you want to work with. At heart, he is a dealer. I think he truly loves the material, but he can always get more."

"Graham Arader is a primitive person," says Michael Zinman, a collector in Ardsley, New York, who when he is not trading rare maps and books with Arader trades heavy industrial equipment throughout the world. "He thinks in a primitive way. He's the only guy I know who lives stream-of-consciousness. Graham is a perpetual enthusiast. Whatever is on the platter at the moment—he lives in that eternal present. He's not an intellectual. He's a throwback to some other form. Whatever the primal force is that propels Graham, most of us have that force harnessed."

A few years ago, Zinman obtained a colored copy of something called the Champlain map—a document published in 1613 as part of the great French explorer's *Les Voyages du Sieur de Champlain.* The map's border depicted several native vegetables and fruits that Samuel de Champlain discovered on his travels through New England and Quebec—Nouvelle France, in his nomenclature—and the map itself signified the first attempt to show the proper latitude of New England. Colored copies are extremely rare, and Zinman paid $6,500 for his. "I had it restored," Zinman recalls. "Graham was in my office one day, and when I showed it to him he was beside himself. He said, 'Michael, this is a magnificent map. This is one of the most beautiful maps I've ever seen. Michael, you've got to sell it to me. You've got to.' He said, 'Michael, if you sell me this map I'll hang it over my bed. I'll sleep beneath it for the rest of my life. I mean it, Michael. You've got to sell it to me.' He asked me what I paid for it, and I told him, and he offered me ten thousand. He swears he's going to hang it over his bed, so I say O.K. The next morning—*the next morning*—at ten o'clock, the phone rings and there's Graham's voice shouting, 'I *sold* it for *twenty-seven five!*' I've never laughed so hard in my life. Was I angry? No, why should I be angry? When he said he wanted to hang it over his bed—at *that* moment—he meant it. Then, as soon as he got into his car to leave here, that moment was gone. The next day was another moment. There really is no guile with Graham Arader. I'm convinced that if he had to shoot someone he'd feel more anguish shooting me than shooting anyone else, but he would definitely shoot me. He'd say, 'Mike, I hate to do this, I really hate to do this, but I have to do it. I'm not asking you to understand, but I have to.' He tells you what he's going to do and he does it. In that sense, he's far more honest than, say, the auction houses, which make a great fuss about all their presumed—if you will— ethics. And I believe he truly loves what he sells."

Rick Watson, an American-born bookseller in London, says of Arader, "Over here, he's viewed as a large, loud, brash American full of enthusiasm and energy that he doesn't seem to have any natural way of discharging. Graham has been not solely but largely responsible for educating a new generation of collectors—introducing them to a field—and also for bringing about a reappraisal of values in those things that he sells. People say Graham's a philistine, he's interested only in making money, but if he were interested solely in making money he'd be in the stock market or in real estate. I think he has a genuine love of the objects he deals in."

When I told Watson about Michael Zinman's copy of the Champlain map, he smiled, and said, "It reminds me of that line from *The Maltese Falcon* where Sydney Greenstreet says, 'Well, Wilmer, I'm sorry indeed to lose you. I want you to know I couldn't be fonder of you if you were my own son. But, well, if you lose a son it's possible to get another.' "

Dave Davis, a psychiatrist and collector in Atlanta—overstating the case somewhat, perhaps, for colorful effect—said not long ago, "Graham Arader is probably the most successful map dealer in the history of the world, and I personally know every major map dealer in the world. He is the standard-bearer of the industry. His competitors do not love him, because he's like the doctor who advertises. His ego is exciting and stimulating, but it's not relaxing. Being with him for any extended length of time is like being stranded in Six Flags. I *like* Graham, you understand, but I would rather have *three* gears, myself."

Self-promote Arader does. Each month, the inside back cover of *The Magazine Antiques* carries a sumptuous-looking spread in which readers are informed that the firm of W. Graham Arader III is "building America's major corporate art collections and counts 100 of the Fortune 500 companies as satisfied clients." A couple of years ago, Arader ran full-page ads in a number of publications devoted to antiques which demonstrated his lack of confidence in the light touch. "W. Graham Arader III Is Searching" said the overline. The text began, "Capitalize on the decade's strongest collecting trend and dispose of old family maps, prints and books discreetly. America's leading print dealer, W. Graham Arader III, is seeking important inventory materials for which he will pay excellent dollar value. Arader, who has paced the booming prints market for a decade, is the country's acknowledged authority in the field. Let him help you turn print materials into liquid assets. Your entire collection or a single piece can become an excellent investment profit." And so forth.

"Graham is not friendly to his competitors," says Henry Taliaferro, the resident expert in the map department of Arader's New York gallery, on upper Madison Avenue. (Arader also has galleries in Philadelphia, Chicago, San Francisco, Atlanta, and Houston, and his staff includes specialists in rare books, autographs, paintings, and twentieth-century prints.) "He sees his competitors as adversaries. He inspires them to jealousy. He's successful. He has the finest stock. He goes to auctions and consistently outbids them. And Graham doesn't do what he could to assuage them when he wins."

Arader is now thirty-seven years old. He has a high, flat forehead, a strong jaw, a small mouth, broad cheeks, brown eyes, and thinning brown hair. He has a barking laugh, a voice that can blast through walls, and an ability to invade another fellow's personal space from several feet away. He is six feet tall, well past two hundred pounds, and somehow nimble. He walks on the balls of his feet, arms swinging—more the swift linebacker than the defensive tackle. On a typical workday, he wears chinos, a polo shirt, a V-neck sweater, and scuffed brown leather running-around shoes. For Arader, dressing up means putting on a uniform that does not vary: gray suit, white shirt, red club tie, wing tips. Sometimes he remembers to brush his hair and sometimes he forgets. In circumstances where a high premium is placed on civility, he radiates the aura of a congenitally disobedient child who must strain every drop of protoplasm to behave properly. His dominating presence in the world of rare maps, prints, and books suggests what the

Metropolitan Museum of Art, say, might be like if George M.
Steinbrenner III were placed in charge.

Clarence Wolf, a Philadelphia seller of rare books, who regards
Arader as a former friend—he has yet to forgive Arader for dragging
him into an unpleasant lawsuit a few years ago, and believes that
"Graham is his own worst enemy"—has said, "I've got to give
Graham credit: he has done something that nobody else has. He's
touted as being the biggest print dealer in the world, and I suppose
he is. To get into this business at the time he did and to be able
to create what he's created, that's amazing. The thing that is his
most overriding concern in any facet of his life is winning. I mean,
he *cannot lose.* He's obsessed with the idea of winning, and not
being beaten. Here's a guy who's got all this energy, a real genius
at what he does. He's done something that very, very few people
have done. It's unfortunate that he couldn't do it in a more prescribed and acceptable fashion."

By now, Arader has grown accustomed to hearing himself described in such terms. A while back, the magazine *Art & Auction*
referred to him as "the self-anointed emperor of the auction room"
and "the man the book trade loves to hate." Remarks like the latter
grate—"Ten of those a year and I'm out of business," Arader
complains—but not enough to inspire contrition. The name-calling
achieved a fortissimo in the late fall of 1985, after Arader attended
an auction at which a large collection of watercolors by Pierre-
Joseph Redouté, possibly the most gifted botanical artist who has
ever lived, was sold. Redouté, who was born in 1759 and died in
1840, was a painting instructor to Marie-Antoinette. Not only could
he paint sublimely but he was fast on his feet; after the French
Revolution, Empress Josephine became his patroness. His two
greatest works, *Les Liliacées* and *Les Roses*, record the botanical
life at Malmaison and other imperial gardens. "Every one of his
drawings was perfect, and was perfectly reproduced," one art historian has written of Redouté. The four hundred and eighty-six
original watercolors for *Les Liliacées* were created between 1802
and 1816, and were reproduced in a stipple-engraved edition of
two hundred. A full eight-volume edition of *Les Liliacées* sold at
auction in London last spring for $258,000. At one time or another,

Arader has owned more than thirty complete copies of either *Les Liliacées* or *Les Roses*, or Redouté's other masterpiece compendium, *Choix de Plus Belles Fleurs*. Individual plates from these books trade for prices ranging from $600 to $12,000, in a market that Arader vigorously stimulates.

The watercolors, which were painted on vellum and bound in sixteen volumes that weighed a total of three hundred and twenty pounds, had been bought from Redouté by Empress Josephine for either 25,000 or 84,000 francs. (Historians differ.) After her son, Prince Eugène de Beauharnais, inherited the collection, it spent more than a century in Bavaria. In 1935, the Prince's heirs sold his library, and a New York art-and-book dealer named Erhard Weyhe bought *Les Liliacées*, for $16,000 (49,000 Swiss francs), and immediately placed it in a vault. There it remained until his family decided, in 1985, to sell it. Eighteen of the watercolors had fallen into other hands along the way. The sale of the four hundred and sixty-eight remaining was an occasion that Sotheby's spent many dollars over many months to publicize.

"This is the best work of the best flower painter who ever lived," Arader said again and again as the auction approached, making it publicly plain that he had no intention of letting *Les Liliacées* elude him without a fight. "The great oil paintings of the seventeenth century—those are gone. The best watercolors of birds, Audubon's originals—the New-York Historical Society has them, they're gone. The great portraits of Indians—they're gone. Buying Redouté's watercolors is my only chance."

Arader's guile was guileless. Weren't these, after all, Empress Josephine's watercolors? And weren't Arader's two young daughters named Josephine and Lilli? He believed that success was foreordained, but he wanted to make sure.

"Redouté really got his juices simmering," Dave Davis, the Atlanta psychiatrist, has said. "He was on the phone at all hours of the night. His mood was even more bombastic than usual. He was spouting his numbers over the telephone. And the longer he talked, the more outrageous he got. The numbers would never come out right."

Several strategies were contemplated and rejected. The plan that

Arader settled upon involved a degree of hocus-pocus but had the
virtue of being technically legal. He decided to syndicate the
collection—subdivide it into a hundred shares (four watercolors
per share), sixty-nine of which he was willing to sell. Arader's
finder's fee would be the watercolors that remained after the shareholders, participating in a round-robin "breakup" procedure that
would last for hours, had picked their way through the lot. The
price per share would be one percent of what Arader bid at auction,
plus a premium of fifteen-hundredths of one percent. A prospectus
that Arader published revealed that he was willing to bid as high
as $8.8 million for *Les Liliacées*. That meant that after Sotheby's
had received its ten percent commission and Arader had tacked
on his syndicator's premium a share could end up costing more
than $110,000. There was the further possibility that Arader, flushed
with auction fever, might get carried away and bid ten or eleven
million. Unloading the sixty-nine shares would seriously test his
skills as a promoter. Other potential bidders loomed—among them
the Bibliothèque Nationale of France, the Getty Museum, and the
Morgan Library—but if Arader prevailed he not only would have
the satisfaction of owning what he knew to be the best of the best
but also would earn for himself a few million dollars.

At ten in the morning on November 20, 1985, Arader stood
against a wall in an auction room on York Avenue as John Marion,
the chairman of Sotheby's North America, announced that he would
accept for *Les Liliacées* a minimum opening bid of $5 million. A
Sotheby's employee named Jane Wyeth, acting on Arader's behalf,
bid that amount. Less than two minutes later, it was all over. No
other serious bidders had materialized. Exploiting the free publicity
provided by Sotheby's, Arader had apparently scared everyone else
away. The price to the syndicate, $5.5 million (including the ten
percent commission to Sotheby's), came nowhere near the previous
record for a single book—a distinction that belongs to the *Gospels
of Henry the Lion*, which was bought by the West German government for $12 million at a Sotheby's auction in 1983. Nevertheless,
when Sotheby's totted up its sales results in 1985–86 it turned out
that Arader had offered more in a single bid than anyone else that
auction season. "It worked. It's unbelievable. I scared them all

off. I pulled the bluff," Arader told the press. He had bought the best of the best cheap.

Even after his fellow shareholders had claimed their watercolors —a share had ended up costing $63,253—Arader remained in control of the Redouté market. He owned a hundred and ninety-two of the lilies himself, and he retained in his inventory several others, which shareholders eager to recoup part of their investment had consigned to him. To keep the market percolating, he exercised his natural abilities. A few weeks after *Les Liliacées* was broken up, I watched Arader at work in his home, in Villanova, Pennsylvania. He was explaining to a not indigent young matron, who wore a cozy nutria jacket (and whose acquaintance with Redouté was brand-new), exactly what he had to offer her. Arader was an earnest, persuasive pedagogue. "What makes Redouté great is the fact that these drawings were on vellum, and, of course, the quality," he said. "The thing that would make it easier would be if you saw other watercolors. Then you'd realize that there is no comparison; his contemporaries weren't twenty percent as good as Redouté. Now, here are the ones that are literally imprinted on the minds of people who *know* watercolor, who *know* Redouté. What do you like? I mean, what are your *feelings* about these?"

"I do love this pineapple thing," the woman said. "What are you selling it for?"

"A hundred and eighty-five thousand. It's a lot, but it's time-less. . . . That one? That's ten thousand. I'll sell you that, but a weedy little thing for $10,000—that's not what Redouté is about. He's about the flair, the color, the way it sits on the page."

A week later, during the 1986 Winter Antiques Show, at the Seventh Regiment Armory, in New York, I watched him as he teased a slender, elderly white-haired dealer. "O.K. You ready for some serious pain?" Arader said as he prepared to remove one of Redouté's parrot-tulip paintings from a protective album. "O.K. This is it—the *best* watercolor of a flower that ever existed. And I got it."

Insincere flattery in the antique trade is not so different from insincere show-biz flattery—plenty of *loved*-it-*ab*solutely-*loved*-it twaddle gets tossed around. Arader has a way of making his insincere flattery seem definitive, even documentable. When he says that something is "the most fabulous thing I've ever seen"—on a hyperactive day, he might utter the phrase fifteen or twenty times—he means it. He spouts superlatives for all occasions. He enjoys making pronouncements about other art-and-antique dealers: Stuart Feld, of Hirschl & Adler, is "the greatest dealer in American paintings in the country"; William Reese, a book dealer in New Haven who specializes in Americana and Texiana, is "the finest young dealer in the country, a person I admire greatly"; So-and-So, on the other hand, is "the most incredible scumbag in the art-and-antique business." At the Winter Antiques Show, not long after the white-haired dealer had wandered away, perhaps in pain, Arader introduced me to a ceramics dealer who possessed "the finest eye in the business." Arader had just sold the ceramics dealer two Redouté watercolors. Ten minutes later, he introduced me to a fop in a full-length scarlet frock coat who "knows more than anyone in the business," and, ten minutes after that, to a woman from Sotheby's who was "the most straightforward, honest person working for an auction house anywhere in America." Arader removed from his briefcase four maps that he had bought that day from Michael Zinman—four maps for $20,000. One was a John Smith map of Virginia—"the most incredible mapmaking project of the seventeenth century." He described a husband-and-wife pair of clients as "the country's leading collectors." He mentioned an appointment the next afternoon with his "best customer—Numero Uno by a factor of two."

While gossip of just about any variety arrests Arader's attention, his taste inclines toward gossip about people who have accumulated, through whatever devices, vast amounts of money. All Arader clients are "valued clients." The title of "most valued client" belongs to whichever client he happens to be addressing at the moment. When Arader wants to convey the impression that he is profoundly interested in what a client is saying, he rocks on his heels, tilts and bobs his head, and exclaims, "Oh, *really?*" and "I *see-ee-ee.*" Some of his clients belong to the breed of magnificoes

whom if they don't like the way your ears look you are supposed
to oblige by falling on your sword. "I feel like I'm these people's
servant," Arader likes to say. "I'm their *footman.*" Others are
agreeable single-digit millionaires who seem eager to believe in
the beauty and value of the things he has to sell. Arader once
invited me to accompany him to an appointment with a Major Figure
in the World of Publishing—*if* I was willing to pose as an employee.
"Well, then, don't come," he said when I declined. "I understand.
It's a shame, though. You'd get to see me when I'm really excited."
The world as Arader has established it in his peculiar vision is
populated by ten thousand people spread across the territory between Bar Harbor and Honolulu who have the resources and the
predisposition to share his understanding that the greatest Early
American art—the finest paintings by Stuart, Catlin, Cole, Church,
Trumbull, Peale, Sargent, Remington, Moran, Bierstadt, Durand,
and others; the most coveted eighteenth- and nineteenth-century
views of American cities—has all been carted off to museums or
to the private collections of the mega-wealthy. The ten thousand
potential clients between Bar Harbor and Honolulu have to be
served in other ways. It is not too late for them to acquire "collections" of beautiful things, but they need a Graham Arader to
guide them along the way.

Arader's logic came to him in a logical sequence. He grew up in
Philadelphia, the eldest of four children. His mother, Jean, is a
painter. His father, Walter G. Arader, who describes himself as
"a boutique investment banker," ran a successful printing company, which he sold in the late sixties; was once Secretary of
Commerce of Pennsylvania; and now sits on the boards of a dozen
corporations and good-works enterprises, including the University
of Pennsylvania and the Pennsylvania Academy of Fine Arts. During the mid-sixties, Walter Arader began to collect maps: first sea
charts, then individual maps from famous atlases—Blaeus, Or-
teliuses, Mercators. Maps that cost Walter G. Arader $100 or $200
are now listed in the catalogues of W. Graham Arader III for prices
ranging from $4,000 to $12,000. Walter Arader also gardened and

kept bees. When Graham applied to Yale, he sent along a quart jar of the family-label honey, accompanied by a letter that said, "Please don't accept this as bribery but as an example of student achievement." Yale's admissions officers, imagining whatever, accepted him. The headmaster of the Hill School, which Graham had attended for four years, suggested that a year in England, before Yale, could do some good. He spent it in Dorset, at the Canford School. There were frequent trips to London—to discotheques, gambling clubs, Fortnum & Mason's, the British Museum, and booksellers and map dealers, where he carried out buying assignments from his father. He was instructed to find a Speed map of the world for less than $125, or a Speed map of North America for $100. For himself he bought county maps, mainly of Dorset.

Arader had spent much of his adolescence on the tennis court at the Merion Cricket Club, the squash court at the Hill School, and the court-tennis court at the Philadelphia Racquet Club. For three years at Yale, he played No. 1 singles on the varsity squash team, and his senior year he was its captain. He belonged to the Fence Club, an *echt*-preppie fraternity, and also to the Elizabethan Club, which had one of the finest collections of Shakespeare folios in the world and quaintness beyond necessity: free tea and sandwiches every afternoon (cucumber sandwiches on Tuesdays only), and, in warm weather, croquet in the backyard. As a freshman, he had found his way to the map room of the Sterling Memorial Library and to the Beinecke Rare Book and Manuscript Library. Sterling had two hundred thousand maps, including twenty thousand rare ones, and the Beinecke had important atlases and manuscript maps, among them the Vinland Map, Martellus's and Ruysch's maps of the New World, George Washington's copy of the Faden atlas, sixteenth- and seventeenth-century atlases by Blaeu, De Wit, and Ortelius. The curator of the Yale map collection was Alexander O. Vietor—a distinguished collector in his own right, of charts and marine Americana—and he became Arader's mentor. His curatorship lasted from 1946 until 1978 (he died in 1981), and during that time he greatly expanded Yale's collection of Early American maps of discovery. Vietor was a gentleman and a gentle preceptor. He found Arader's avidity endearing. For Arader, getting plunked down in the middle of Yale's map collection was the equivalent of matriculating at a vocational-training school for merchant princes. A former Yale librarian has said that Arader was the only undergraduate he ever saw in the bibliography room of the Sterling Memorial Library, and he saw him there often. No one who paid any attention misapprehended Arader's motives. He had what a curator at the Beinecke Library recently recalled as "a thoroughly commercial autodidacticism."

On trips back to England with the Yale squash team, he bought more maps and books. He visited Maggs Brothers, a Berkeley Square establishment that makes deliveries to Buckingham Palace. When John Maggs, of the fifth generation of Maggses to run the firm, showed him a hand-colored Christopher Saxton map of Dorset—dated 1579, the earliest map of that English county—Arader said, "How do you know this is original color?" In the London book trade, a raw young American who challenged the bookseller to the Queen about original color was a presumptuous young American. Inevitably, he was becoming a dealer; the London book trade had the choice of liking him or not liking him. He bought county maps—by Saxton, Speed, Norden, and other seminal English mapmakers—and books about racquet sports. When he paid $250 for a sixteenth-century Italian book by Antonio Sciano, the first book on tennis ever printed, he phoned his father with the exciting news. Walter Arader lectured his son about the dangers of overdrafts and the folly of impulse buying. Three months later, Graham sold the book in Philadelphia for $2,500. From his dormitory room he sold antique maps—a novelty in the early seventies, when what other Yale students were selling from their dormitory rooms was definitely not maps. Senior year, he won the Adrian Van Sinderen prize, given "to stimulate book collecting among undergraduates, to encourage bookbuying, book-owning, and book-reading both as a hobby and as a fundamental part of the educational process." He majored in economics and, summers in Philadelphia, ran a tree-surgery business. His senior thesis was a comparison of the barriers to entry into the Connecticut and Pennsylvania tree-surgery industries. He sent questionnaires to

tree surgeons in both states, and a friendly professor ran the re-
sponses through a computer. Arader wrote a passable thesis and
then took out advertisements in tree-surgery journals that said "Buy
the Yale Report on Tree Surgeons." He sold five hundred copies,
at $25 each.

The money had a purpose. For $100 he could buy a Nicolas
Sanson 1650 map—the first to show all five Great Lakes; $150
would get him an Ortelius map of North and South America published in Antwerp circa 1570. Or the same money could buy Delisle's 1703 Carte du Méxique et de la Floride, the first to delineate
accurately the Mississippi Delta. The Sanson, if it is in excellent
condition, now sells for $5,500, the Ortelius for $6,500, the Delisle
for $9,000. Shortly before Arader's graduation, in 1973, Vietor
wrote for him a letter of introduction to Thomas J. Watson, Jr.,
recently retired as the chairman of IBM. Watson was interested in
maps of Penobscot Bay. Arader concocted inside his brain a fantasy
in which Watson played Andrew Mellon to his Joseph Duveen. He
went to London, Amsterdam, and Paris and spent $10,000 on early
maps that showed Penobscot Bay. He had graduated and was living
at his parents' house, on the Main Line. The day the phone rang
and Arader's mother answered, heard a man's voice say he was
returning a call to Graham Arader, and told the man, "I'm sorry,
but you shouldn't be calling on this number, you're going to have
to call again, on the children's phone," was the day Arader and
his parents agreed that he should move himself and his business
elsewhere.

Today, when Arader recounts this incident he invariably raises
his voice, grabs his listener by the arm, brings his face in for a
closeup, and says, "*Watson* thought he was calling some *big-time*
map dealer, and in*stead* he gets some lady telling him to use the
goddam *children's* phone. That was the end of it. I went insane.
My mother said, 'Well, *I* didn't know.' I could have killed her. In
all the years since, I've never been able to sell Watson a thing,
although God knows I've tried."

Twenty-four hours later, Arader had packed most of his books
and maps and headed for New Haven, where he planned to live
with a girlfriend who was still an undergraduate. He had begun to

cultivate clients among a number of physicians and psychiatrists around New Haven and in Fairfield County. The girlfriend's dorm room, he figured, would work for the time being as his corporate headquarters. This arrangement lasted less than twenty-four hours, after which he moved into an attic room above a used-book store. He repatriated to Philadelphia and established a stable mailing address. He was receiving catalogues from the leading European dealers and from the auction houses, and he was buying maps of North and South America, New England, Pennsylvania, the mid-Atlantic states, Dorset—places he knew, because he had been there. If he paid $3,200 for a 1770 map of Pennsylvania—a map that happened to have been Thomas Penn's copy—he would price it at $8,000 and, one way or another, find a buyer. It was mainly a matter of hustle. In the fall of 1974, Walter Arader lent him $150,000, and he began to travel the antique-show circuit. The shows were held in Charlotte, Atlanta, Houston—the polite provinces. He had a station wagon and would drive for three days and then stand up inside an exhibition hall for four days. Also in 1974, he printed his first catalogue.

To anyone who met Arader during the early phase of his career it was obvious that he understood maps in a visceral way. What made a great map great—he grasped that. He enjoyed conducting impromptu seminars on original color—how pigments look when they've oxidized for three or four hundred years, how paper that is old can blot counterfeit new color, absorb it in dense concentrations. It came out sounding not so much pedantic as passionate. The map market was circumscribed, the mechanics weren't all that complicated. If he could buy well, he knew, he could sell better than anyone else. To novices he could sell decorative maps—he could take Blaeu, Mercator, and Ortelius atlases, remove the bindings, and thus create hundreds of antiques that looked exciting mounted, framed, and hung on walls. Getting his hands on the best material was the key, and he went aggressively after rare, significant maps, the upper five percent of the market. For bedtime reading he tried memorizing passages of I. N. Phelps Stokes' *Iconography of Manhattan Island* and the *Dictionary of American Biography*. His strategies were simplistic. Maps were historically

interesting, and maps were *pretty*. If Arader thought that visual
maps were undervalued, then he could persuade a not unintelligent
clientele—unsophisticated, perhaps, but not unintelligent—that
they were valuable. And so they were. He calculated, correctly,
that if he skimmed three auction catalogues a day and fifty major
reference books a year, if he read *Forbes* and *Fortune* and *Town
& Country* and *W*, if he went to antique shows and auctions, if,
above all, he bought the best material in the best condition, and
if he remained reasonably patient at certain moments, he could
obey his instincts and he would make money.

With his energy and his inventory, he could establish values.
Why couldn't a map be treated as a commodity? At one point,
inspired by the Hunt brothers, who at the time were in the early
stages of their grotesque and calamitous scheme to control the
world silver market, Arader decided that it would be fun to corner
the international map market. He got as far as discussing this idea
with a few friendly collectors. It was a provocatively plausible
notion—supply was finite, nobody was mining more rare maps—
but in too many respects it was unwieldy. There also existed the
potential for close encounters with the Justice Department. No law,
however, could prevent Arader from printing catalogues and in-
flating prices, and that is exactly what he did. If other dealers
listed a map for $7,000 or $9,000, he would say, "We'll sell it
for sixteen five." Which was less risky than it sounds—less risky,
certainly, than trading pork bellies or soybeans—because his personal energy alone could influence future prices. Other dealers,
seeing Arader's catalogues, would say, in effect, "Oh, well, now
we have to raise our prices, too."

By the late seventies, Arader was the leading map dealer in
America, and he was regularly trading with the principal dealers
in Europe. A map run—the aggressive-spending fervor of a newly
hooked collector—seemed to last one and a half to two and a half
years, Arader had learned. To keep expanding, to generate the
sort of enterprise that he hopefully envisioned, he had to diversify.
The world map market peaked in 1980. A London dealer once
explained, "There was inflation, and there was Graham Arader."
Not long thereafter, Arader, as he puts it, "just got bored with

maps." Making the rounds of antique shows, he had begun to
cultivate clients who didn't necessarily have an interest in maps
but were attracted to the Early American natural-history renderings
by Audubon, Catesby, and Wilson; John Gould's birds; the images
of Native American life by Catlin, Bodmer, and McKenney and
Hall; the illustrations of the voyages and explorations of Cook,
Wilkes, and La Pérouse; the lyrical views by Currier & Ives and
Louis Prang. Prints were less scarce than maps, and they were a
lot less difficult to sell. Their aesthetic appeal as wall furniture
generally surpassed that of maps, and they made fewer intellectual
demands. Women tended not to buy maps, but they loved botanical
prints. Selling prints appealed to the side of Arader that was impatient, that demanded instant gratification. He could muscle in
on the high end of the interior-decorating business. If you ran a
corporation in Pittsburgh and Arader somehow got the word that
you were redesigning your headquarters or thinking of earmarking
funds for art acquisition, you could count on him to show up at
some point, peddling eighteenth- and nineteenth-century views and
maps of Pittsburgh, of Pennsylvania, of the Ohio Valley. This was
a perfectly legitimate way to spend the shareholders' money, Arader
would aver. As with maps, he did not intend to dabble in these
markets, he intended to reinvent them.

His earliest catalogues of prints featured Brookshaw fruits, Audubon birds, Bodmer and Catlin Indians, Redouté flowers, and
American-naval-battle scenes. Arader's decision to diversify produced consequences for him that were thoroughly gratifying, but
for a lot of map collectors and dealers it produced sudden adversity.
"It just died," Arader says. "*Internationally*, the map market died.
The excitement that I put into it was what had been keeping it
going. So when I lost interest there was no energy behind it. German
and English maps you couldn't give away." He stopped issuing
map catalogues and did not issue another for four years, until Henry
Taliaferro joined the firm.

In 1977, Arader had bought a house in King of Prussia, a suburb
about twenty-five minutes west of Independence Hall. The house,
which is listed in the National Register of Historic Places, is two
hundred and thirty years old. George Washington slept either there

or at a place down the road on his way to Valley Forge. It is one
of the few two-story houses in a settlement of contemporary ranch-
style dwellings, and it is the only one with a fancy name to match
its fancy pedigree: Ballygomingo. A Philadelphia writer once described Ballygomingo as "rising proud as an ocean liner amidst a
sea of sampans." The house has a stone-and-stucco exterior, mul-
lioned windows, and twenty-four rooms, filled with eighteenth- and
nineteenth-century American and English furniture. For several
years, Arader slept upstairs and ran his business downstairs. He
hung selections from his inventory on the walls and installed rows
of oak-and-brass portfolio files in a wing that contains a gallery
and a library. In 1980, he bought a house in Houston and converted
it into a gallery. This was followed by other new outposts, in New
York (1981), San Francisco (1982), Atlanta (1983), and Chicago,
Omaha, and Winston-Salem (all 1984). He has since closed the
Omaha and Winston-Salem galleries. In 1979, he bought Sessler's
bookstore, a downtown-Philadelphia institution, on Walnut Street.
The previous proprietor was a woman named Mabel Zahn, whose
career at Sessler's is said to have spanned seventy years. Among
people in Philadelphia who read books and among the book trade
beyond Philadelphia, Mabel Zahn was legendary. Current books
were sold in the front of the store, and from her office in the back
Mabel Zahn dealt in rare books and autographs. Walter Arader,
who became a partner in the purchase of Sessler's, told his son
when they first contemplated the venture, "If you discovered a cure
for cancer and if you brought about universal racial harmony *and*
you closed Sessler's, in Philadelphia you would be remembered
for closing Sessler's." Today, Arader operates a business on the
site formerly occupied by Sessler's, which, with some temerity, he
refers to as Sessler's—but he has, in effect, closed Sessler's. His
rare-book expert, Karen Nathan, has an office and a four-thousand-
volume selling stock upstairs. Downstairs has, after a thorough
remodeling, been transformed into an art gallery and filled with
prints, maps, and paintings.

    In the backyard of Ballygomingo, in the summer of 1983, Arader
married a woman from Atlanta named Vallijeanne Hartrampf and
known as Valli. Her father, Carl Hartrampf, is a more-than-

prosperous plastic surgeon, a fifth-generation Atlantan, and the
son of a lawyer who ran the largest collection agency in the Southeast. Carl Hartrampf had been an occasional Arader client (Georgia
maps) for several years before Valli met Graham, on a blind
date; they were married four months later. She has light-brown
hair, green eyes, a well-trained smile, soft features, and a quick-
to-the-point Southern voice that leaves a vapor trail of finishing-
school politesse. At one time, she worked as promotion director
of the Atlanta Historical Society, and at the firm of W. Graham
Arader III she is officially in charge of promotion and print advertising. According to her husband, "she also decides whom
to hire and fire and which clients I should really pursue, on the
basis of whether or not she really likes them." Ballygomingo con-
tinues to be Arader's main office, but he and Valli now live ten
minutes away, in Villanova, in another house with a stately name:
Oakwell. A Lutyens-style granite castle built in 1920, Oakwell
was originally a wedding gift from a natural-gas baron named
Bodine to one of his children. It shares eleven acres with huge
maples, beeches, conifers, and, of course, oaks—a backyard
laboratory for an erstwhile tree surgeon. The first time I visited
there, I arrived shortly before a potentially important client was
due to drop by. "When I'm with Mrs. T., try to make yourself
scarce," Arader told me. At Oakwell, this posed no problem:
there were twenty-five rooms to drift through, each one capable
of deepening my sensation of scarceness. It seemed sufficient to
comfortably contain the Arader brood—the two girls, Lilli and
Josephine, and a son, Walter Graham Arader IV, who was born
in 1986—and a triumphant assortment of English and American
antique furniture, Oriental rugs, silver, paintings, prints, armillary
spheres, powder horns, antique globes, maps, reference books,
and rare books. It struck me as less majestic than, say, the Duke
of Devonshire's country estate, but still nice. The next time I went
to the house, a few weeks later, I noticed that there was even more
furniture on the premises and that the pictures had been moved
around. Some of the prints and paintings had, of course, been de-
accessioned. This reminded me of the art dealers' rule—"Never
fall in love with a picture." Arader, I realized, regularly falls in

love with fine things, but the concept of love does not get confused
in his mind with the concept of eternity.

I was once with him at Christie's in New York when he encountered a print dealer named Paul McCarron. Arader greeted
him in a friendly way, then turned to me and said, "Paul sold me
the finest image of a watercolor flower arrangement that I've ever
seen. It really was."

" 'Was' means that you sold it, I take it," said McCarron.

"The next hour. I owned it one hour. But I loved it."

Arader is a trustee of the Yale Library Associates and is a member
of the Young Presidents' Organization, the Philadelphia Racquet
Club, the Merion Cricket Club, the Union League of Philadelphia,
CINOA (Confédération Internationale des Négociants en Oeuvres
d'Art), and the Appraisers Association of America. For several
years, he belonged to the Antiquarian Booksellers' Association
of America—the A.B.A.A.—but in December of 1983 he was
dropped from the rolls, against his wishes. Arader's disagreement with the A.B.A.A. grew out of a disagreement between
him and E. R. Schierenberg, who is a Dutch bookseller and the
principal in a firm called Antiquariaat Junk. From Amsterdam,
Schierenberg had sent Arader, in King of Prussia, a five-volume
set of John Gould hummingbirds. Arader had decided that they
were unsatisfactory, and Schierenberg had decided that the manner
in which Arader chose to return the books—casually packaged,
shipped third-class, uninsured—was offensive, and had filed a
complaint with the A.B.A.A. The association's governors, taking
into account grievances that had been lodged against Arader
previously, examined the evidence (including an ungentlemanly
letter from Arader to Schierenberg) and concluded that Arader
had violated one of the stated purposes of the A.B.A.A.—"to
further friendly relations and a cooperative spirit among members."
When the governors sent Arader a letter telling him that they
had accepted his resignation, he replied that he had not resigned. When the governors explained that it wasn't a voluntary
matter, he sued them, alleging a conspiracy to restrain trade

and to deprive him of his right to earn a living, and demanding reinstatement.

"These things that he was alleged to have done weren't necessarily immoral," Clarence Wolf, who was a member of the A.B.A.A. board of governors and, at the time, a friend of Arader's, has said. "He just didn't subscribe to the principles that the A.B.A.A. stands for. Then, when he sued, it got really nasty."

Although the A.B.A.A. governors based their expulsion of Arader on the association's bylaws, he felt that he was actually being punished for having become too successful as a print dealer. The lawsuit, which dragged on for almost a year, proved far less successful than most of his deals.

"These are some of the most distinguished booksellers in the world, and Arader called them liars and thieves," said a lawyer named Lawrence I. Fox, who represented the A.B.A.A. in the litigation and was himself a defendant. "This guy was totally disrespectful. He was like an errant child, and he definitely wasn't getting his way."

Arader's case did not receive much of a boost from one piece of evidence—a letter he sent to Schierenberg at a time when Schierenberg, unbeknown to him, had already complained to the A.B.A.A. In one lively paragraph Arader wrote, "The reason that I sent the books back to you sea mail is that you lied to me when you said that the set was good. The set of Hummingbirds was terrible. In fact there were only six prints that weren't foxed [discolored by decay]. I didn't like being lied to and did not feel like sending the books back air mail which would have been much more expensive." In the next paragraph Arader accused Schierenberg of trying to induce him to commit an insurance fraud. He quickly reversed direction, however, and concluded with this masterstroke: "I am sorry that our relationship has fallen to this level and hope that this incident can become a thing of the past. Right now I am spending over $500,000 a month for inventory and I feel strongly that you could help me. At times I am in a desperate need for material and need as many dependable sources as I can find."

When Fox took Arader's deposition, there were several illuminating exchanges. One occurred when Fox asked Arader about a certain English book-and-print seller:

> FOX: He sells similar materials that you do?
> ARADER: Not similar. Grossly inferior quality.
> FOX: Is there anyone that you believe is comparable to your selling quality?
> ARADER: No.
> FOX: Nobody?
> ARADER: Nobody.
> FOX: Here and in Europe?
> ARADER: Anywhere living.

To this day, Arader occasionally says that he is ready to kiss and make up with the A.B.A.A., but then he remembers the $150,000 that the litigation cost him—he ended up both losing the case and having, eventually, to pay all the A.B.A.A.'s legal expenses—and he changes his mind.

A few months ago, in London, I was having a conversation with John Maggs, the proprietor of Maggs Brothers, when Stephen Massey, the head of the rare-books-and-manuscripts department of the New York branch of Christie's, happened into the shop. "Arader —is he good for the trade or bad for the trade?" Maggs asked Massey.

Without hesitating, Massey—who, on another occasion, had told me he thought Arader was "a good guy"—said, "Well, he's bad for the books that go through his hands. But he's made them rarer."

"What bothers me about Graham is that he cuts up books," a book dealer from Los Angeles said recently. "That is not the book trade. You can't collect *prints* that way. If you want to collect *prints*, then you must collect things that were made as prints in the first place, not plates removed from books that a dealer has destroyed. What offends me is such a dealer's failure to appreciate that a rare book has a numinous presence beyond the physical borders of the book itself."

In the face of such an argument, many dealers seek refuge in euphemism. "We don't talk about 'breaking books,' we refer to 'freeing maps from atlases,' " a map dealer told me. "If you can find a bookseller who has never broken a book, I'll be amazed. There's an awful lot of hypocrisy about that."

Fewer than two hundred copies of the double-elephant-folio edition of Audubon's *Birds of America* were printed, and perhaps fifty or sixty complete sets have survived in their original bindings. The notion that breaking, and selling plate by plate, a double-elephant folio—"freeing" it into hundreds of decorative objects—ipso facto constitutes vandalism has had vigorous adherents since the beginning of the century, when the practice began. Arader has owned and broken one complete set. Sotheby's or Christie's will gladly sell Audubons by the plate when the opportunity arises. What tends to offend certain book dealers and collectors is the large scale on which Arader breaks varieties of books—and, of course, his less than oblique manner. Bill Reese, the book dealer in New Haven, who is on cordial terms with Arader, recalls a time when he watched Arader at the delivery counter on the second floor of Sotheby's in New York, claiming a book that he had just bought at auction. The book was a first edition of John Smith's *Generall Historie of Virginia, New-England, and the Summer Isles* (London, 1624). Five editions of this book were issued, and each contained four maps—two of Virginia, one of New England, and one of Bermuda. (Each of the maps had been previously published by Smith in several revisions.) Arader had found a buyer for the New England map and planned to keep the others, for the time being.

"He had the book open on the delivery counter and was pressing down on it hard, vigorously massaging the gutter. I said, 'Graham, what are you doing?' He said, 'What do you think I'm doing, Billy? I'm testing the strength of the binding.' Then—*r-r-r-r-ip!*—he razors the son of a bitch out."

The 1624 edition is rare but not extremely rare; more than fifty copies exist in libraries. Arader, accused of vandalism in this instance, would invoke the "democracy" defense—democracy for the second-string rich, engineered by competitive commercial instinct—which says that removing a book's binding makes it possible to share the contents with a wider population, permits many

more people to own an expensive beautiful object that was once
part of an unwieldy, much more expensive, less displayable beautiful object. Pursued to the extreme, this logic could justify, as a
blow for egalitarianism, the dismembering of a Brueghel canvas
into forty nicely framed vignettes. The idea that there is a social
interest (what the French call *droit moral*) in preserving works of
art in their original state would, one assumes, tend to prevent
depredation of that degree. On the other hand, in the United States
there happen to be no federal laws to prevent it. Until there were
federal laws protecting bald eagles, a lot of bald eagles were shot
and stuffed. Or, as Robert A. Weiner, a lawyer I know who specializes in art law, said not long ago, "Tearing up books isn't nice.
It's an offensive practice. Is it illegal? No. But it's not nice."

Many of the billionaires and triple-digit millionaires whom Arader
most desires to bump into—the first-string rich—he can bump
into at the Winter Antiques Show in New York. Arader has plied
his wares there since 1976. One weekend afternoon during the
1986 show, I happened to be standing at his booth when a middle-
aged couple came by. They didn't stay long. The man looked at
the watercolor original of a Redouté peony and said to his wife,
"A hundred and fifty-five dollars"—a misreading of the price tag
that was wishful by three decimal places. After his wife pointed
this out, the man said, sotto voce, that he thought they would be
better off shopping elsewhere. When such confusions occur, Arader
makes no effort to conceal his pleasure. After the couple left, he
told me, "A Mexican diplomat came around here a few years ago
and picked out something like $45,280 worth of prints and maps.
He had an entourage—wife, kids, toadies, mistresses. He gets all
the stuff together and then, with a grand flourish, reaches for his
wallet and starts to pay me $452.80. I know what's happening,
but I decide to string him along. I say, 'Um, that's fine, Mr.—uh,
Rodriguez, if you want to leave a deposit. That will leave a balance
of $44,800,' or whatever. Now Mr. *Rodriguez* realizes what's hap-
pening, and he's a diplomat, so he has to figure out some way out
of this. So he takes one little $250 map and says, 'I tell you what.

I will think about these other things and will give you a call in the morning.' Of course, what happened was that the next day he sent a messenger back with the map and we had to refund the two-fifty. That happens about twice a year."

In Arader's booth that day were a Ruysch world map, printed in Rome in 1508 ("the first obtainable map to show any part of America" said a label on the back of the cardboard mat), for $85,000; Sir Robert Dudley's "A Particular Chart of the Northeast Coast of America," Florence, 1646, a copper engraving from his *Arcano del Mare*, the first marine atlas entirely drawn on a Mercator projection, for $6,500; Juan Oliva's 1615 "Sea Chart of the Mediterranean," hand-colored on vellum, for $25,000 (part of a thirty-plate atlas for which Arader had paid $132,000); Cellarius celestial charts, part of a series of twenty-nine spectacularly illuminated maps that were first published in Amsterdam in 1660 and were reprinted in editions issued in 1661 and 1708, priced from $4,000 to $6,500; Redouté prints; aquatint and mezzotint botanical engravings from the Robert Thornton *Temple of Flora*, the most famous English botanical-plate book ever produced; Audubon double-elephant-folio birds (white pelican, Carolina paroquet, wild turkey) and quadrupeds (American bison and white-tailed deer); prints from the American edition of Catlin's *North American Indian Portfolio*; John Gould birds; Brookshaw fruits; paintings by Catlin, Moran, Alfred Jacob Miller, and Berninghaus; file cabinets filled with prints. On top of one file cabinet was a first-edition copy of Mark Catesby's *The Natural History of Carolina, Florida, and the Bahama Islands*, and on top of that was a pile of matted McKenney and Hall portraits. I was admiring these last—lithographs of Native American chiefs executed in the mid-nineteenth century—and I asked Arader a question about them.

"I'm bored with those," he said.

"Why?"

"I've seen them. I've had them too long."

"Are they rare?"

"Common as dirt."

They were priced at around $750 apiece. To a customer who cavils about price, Arader is able to produce a snappy response without much trouble. If a young burgher in a chesterfield studies a $2,400 Bodmer hanging on Arader's wall and remarks that Bodmer prints were much cheaper twenty years ago, when he had one decorating his dorm room at Dartmouth, Arader replies, "Well, twenty years from now they'll be saying the same thing."

To justify his prices, Arader regularly pontificates on a subject that he refers to as "connoisseurship." Until he was five years out of Yale, he says, he "didn't understand connoisseurship." He likes to quote from a monograph published in 1961 by the late Charles Montgomery, professor of art history at Yale, citing, in particular, one poetical passage that includes the statement "Nothing opens the purse or closes the eye so quickly as the desire to get a great bargain." The quotation concludes, "Whereas in the joy of a treasure one soon forgets a high price paid, in the possession of the second-rate one remembers only its cheapness." Arader's voluble, high-speed palaver tends to color Montgomery's eloquence with a Fuller Brush man's inflection. Nevertheless, he has been able to convert his boilerplate plea for connoisseurship into a purse-opening lever. As a practical matter, what Arader seems to mean by "connoisseurship" bears less relation to the root of the word—a certain subtle knowledge that feeds instinct—than to the simpler notion of buying only the most salable merchandise, the no-dings no-chips variety. "If you buy a Bierstadt, there had better be a mountain in it!" I once heard him exhort an acquaintance over the telephone. "And a stream, too. You have people who pay $10,000 for a Bierstadt and because one just sold somewhere for $650,000 they think they've got a bargain. But $10,000 gets you a Bierstadt of a *butterfly*. You haven't bought anything!"

Often Arader sells art that he happens not to have in his inventory. "I really *need* this map," I once heard him tell a caller. "I sold it twice last week and I have only one copy." Or he will plead, "I need a roseate spoonbill right now fairly desperately. I need a mallard fairly desperately. But if you love everything you have and it's part of your home decoration or your office decoration and you don't want to sell it, I understand. . . . Oh, *really*? O.K., I'll call her. Give me her number. . . . Fine. . . . That's right. Buying or selling. . . . O.K. Bye."

Where he bought material, when he bought it, what he paid—
Arader has phenomenal recall of those details. He also keeps track
of where it goes after it leaves his hands. If his memory were to
fail, he could always refer to a computer printout that lists, item
by item, what every one of his clients has bought. When you ask
Arader about his inventory-management tactics, he says, "I've got
masses of stuff. It sells when it sells." Once, in a bold moment,
I asked him what it might all be worth. He replied, "Five million
to twenty million, depending on my mood," and I realized that my
question was not only impertinent but clumsy. "Things are valued
how they're valued," he said. "And who's creating the value? I
am. I sell the stuff, so I'm creating the value. So are auction houses,
other dealers, collectors. It's pretty shaky. It involves factors such
as 'Do you like me?' and 'Do you enjoy buying from me?' and 'How
well do I serve you?' As a dealer, I try to do all the things that a
good slave can do. I'll give you reference books. I'll frame your
print nicely. I'll come to your house and hang it. I'll help your
kids get into boarding school."

Arader employs about sixty-five people, thirty of them in sales.
When he hired Henry Taliaferro, in 1984, his object was to restore
the map department to its former, full-throttle vigor. Taliaferro, an
equable, genteel Texan, had previously been a competitor; with a
partner, he had sold maps and books in Austin. "Before I came
here, I didn't know all the specifics, but I knew enough to know
that Graham had the best clients and the best stock," Taliaferro
once told me. "For instance, for someone who knows maps, the
chance to write a catalogue on portolans"—hand-drawn sea charts
dating from between the fourteenth and seventeenth centuries,
usually the work of Italian, Catalan, or Portuguese draftsmen—
"is a wonderful prospect, but only by working for Graham, at least
in this country, could I find the maps. Only Graham has the imagination to go out and buy the things he buys and create the market."

The Arader salespeople are granted considerable autonomy. A
salesperson in New York is free to pursue a client in, for instance,
Chicago or Atlanta, provided that the salesperson has cultivated
the client. At one time, Arader traveled regularly to Houston; he
no longer does. He sells to clients all over the world—he is re-

sponsible for half the company's sales volume—but he has no desire to run the satellite galleries himself. He has set foot in his San Francisco gallery twice, Chicago once, Atlanta half a dozen times. "Things function more smoothly when he's not around," Hollie Powers Holt, who manages Sessler's, has said. "But we sell a lot more when he is around." Walter Arader once told me that he was particularly fond of Hollie Powers Holt, who has worked for Graham for nine years, because "she's very ethical and Graham needs all the ethical encouragement he can get." The employees who tend to get along best with Arader are the ones who don't take rudeness personally. When I had spent several months sporadically observing Arader in action—he had evidently begun to wonder to what effect—he told me that if I had been working for him he would have fired me long ago. Arader hires and fires with equal relish. His catchall standard for firing is "dishonesty or sloppy treatment of a customer." (In my case, the ground would have been dilatoriness.) One of his pet forms of interoffice communication is the hortatory memorandum. Such missives issue from Ballygomingo at irregular intervals—at times daily, at other times only weekly or monthly. The memos, dictated, transcribed, and dispatched full of typos, sound remarkably like Arader himself, fulminating in his free-associational quintessence.

The buoyantly self-aggrandizing compliment to an employee:

"First of all, CONGRATULATIONS to Sharon for making a $200,000 sale last week. Incredible! This is the company record for a single sale and I am delighted to have passed my record on to such a deserving woman. Keep up the good work. You're terrific.

"Sharon is succeeding because she is seeing her clients and going after the big hitters. She made this sale by traveling to Houston and visiting a major collector there. You must travel if you want to sell. You must call on your clients and love them to death."

The strategic graceful gesture, clarified:

"It is the tradition of great booksellers and art dealers that they take their clients to lunch and/or dinner on closing a big sale (over $5,000). I authorize you all to follow this tradition but only when the client has *paid* for the object that he is buying."

The unveiled threat:

"No one may purchase anything from my inventory for more than $100 without getting my permission first. No one may purchase anything for their own account while I am paying for their time. You must offer me whatever you see for sale while you are working for me at an antique show. . . . Any source that you learn about while you are working for me may not sell you anything unless you offer it to me first. If there is a deviation from these rules, you will be immediately fired and all benefits ended. My sources are the most important part of my business. . . ."

The dire snowball:

"We had a poor September with sales of $290,000, which is $326,000 behind budget. This is why I am so in debt. Bluntly, if I have two months in a row like this I will have to start letting people go. I would say at least six or seven people. Three months like this and I would have to close at least three offices and fire another ten people. Four months and I would be close to out of business but could probably hold on to three or four offices. By five months I would be selling real estate and putting most of my material up for auction. And at six months I would be out of business."

The window of self-awareness:

"My biggest mistake in building my business and the mistake that I regret most was my temper. I got mad at people and ended relationships. One mad customer can wipe out the positive comments of 100 satisfied ones. Try to stay civil, friendly with ALL collectors and dealers in your area. But keep the information about the business strictly confidential. You can be very friendly without giving away our business secrets. I don't want anyone knowing our personal victories or defeat[s]. Sell the products, gossip about *other* people, and listen."

Personal grooming and hygiene tips:

"If you smell, you aren't going to sell. Your hair must be clean, your breath must be fresh, your teeth must be clean. If you smoke, you should take a bath, wash your teeth and put on a fresh change of clothes before you attempt a major sale. . . . No employee should eat garlic, onions or anything that smells before attempting a major

sale. I would rather have you cancel the appointment than have
the client smell what you have been eating. This may be unfair,
but it's America. People who smell just aren't going to make it
with 50% of all collectors. Why? Because smelling you is no fun.
And when the buying experience isn't fun, the client goes elsewhere."

Art auctions provide free, democratic entertainment. Just because
Chippendale-carved mahogany hairy-paw-foot wing chairs from
Granny's attic now sell at Sotheby's for $2.75 million (minus the
upholstery) and nice-to-look-at van Gogh flower paintings go for
$54 million (pleasantly framed) that does not mean that anyone
with sufficient curiosity and feigned insouciance cannot still go to
Sotheby's or Christie's and unobtrusively watch everything—the
way the auctioneer smiles with the corners of his mouth turned
down when things don't go quite right, the way the cool-guy bidders
just barely arch their eyebrows when they raise a bid. Anyone can.
Arader does his best to enliven the atmosphere. Usually, he takes
a spot in the back, where he can pose and move his elbows around.
This forces members of the crowd to turn in their chairs periodically
to observe him, to acknowledge that his presence has altered the
chemistry of a high-dollar ceremony. "When dealing with Graham
in a bidding situation, there are two possibilities," a client who
came to know Arader the hard way—by bidding against him
unsuccessfully—told me. "One, you can say, 'Why should I bid
against this guy? He obviously intends to crush me.' Or, two, you
can say, 'Maybe I'll just run up the bid anyway and break it off
in him.' "
   "There are two sides to Graham," Clarence Wolf says. "When
he is in an auction, for Graham that's sort of like theatre-in-the-
round. That's the very essence of Graham Arader. That's when he
really comes to fruition. I think Graham is a real gladiator in the
auction ring and, in my experience, a relentless bargainer when
it comes to buying privately. When he's buying something privately,
he tries to browbeat you and wear you down. His great auction
records give him entrée into private situations."

When Sotheby's was selling James Rosenquist's painting *F-111*, in the fall of 1986, Thomas Armstrong asked Arader to bid on behalf of the Whitney Museum. "I thought he had a lot of savvy about auctions," Armstrong said. At the last minute, Armstrong decided to bid himself, and from Arader's point of view that was no tragedy. The Whitney was equipped to spend no more than $1.2 million, and the painting ended up selling for more than $2 million, so Arader was spared losing in front of a large audience. A dealer bidding for a client customarily collects a fee, usually ten percent, but Arader performs this service for one percent or, often, no fee at all, because he enjoys being known as a buyer; because even if he doesn't buy the object in question there is still the challenge—if the item is a print or a book—of finding it cheaper somewhere else later on and selling it for less than the auction price to the client, who will then admire Arader for being crazy and wonderful; and because it permits him to cross swords with the big auction houses, Sotheby's and Christie's. Sotheby's sales during the 1986–87 auction season totaled $1.3 billion, an increase of $600 million over the previous year. Christie's, during its 1986–87 season, took in $900 million, compared with $573 million in 1985–86. It invigorates Arader to imagine himself in mortal combat with these two institutions—particularly Sotheby's. Once, after a sale at Sotheby's, he approached Alfred Taubman, the chairman of the holding company that owns the auction house, and said, "Congratulations, Mr. Taubman. You did pretty well today. And I did *real* well."

"Sotheby's wants bidders to pay retail prices; they're trying to put us out of business," Arader frequently complains, and he delights in any opportunity, as he sees it, to get even. David Redden, head of the books-and-manuscripts department at Sotheby's in New York, to his credit bears no resentment toward Arader for having accused him, during a map auction a few years ago, of conjuring a phantom bid. The episode unfolded this way: the bidding on a certain atlas of seventeenth-century portolan charts started at $80,000, Arader raised that to $90,000, the auctioneer announced a bid of $100,000, the bidding ran up until Arader was at $120,000, the auctioneer acknowledged a bid of $130,000, and Arader, at peak volume, answered back, "Where's the bid, David? I don't see the bid. You're running it up on me, David! You're lying, David. There's no bid. You took that off the wall! I caught you, David! Where's the bid? Where's the bid?" It was a dramatic moment, witnessed by about a hundred startled people. As Arader advanced toward the platform in a menacing manner, Redden abruptly halted the action, explaining that there seemed to be some confusion. When the bidding resumed— Redden agreed to start all over again—Arader bought the atlas for $120,000, plus ten percent to Sotheby's. A dealer who was present has said, "Everybody loved it, including people who don't like Graham."

Arader's most triumphant moment at Sotheby's—the auction of Redouté's *Les Liliacées* watercolors, and the subsequent syndication bonanza—whetted his appetite for more. In the succeeding months, he syndicated a lithographed edition of Audubon's *Viviparous Quadrupeds of North America* and two first-edition copies of Catesby's *The Natural History of Carolina, Florida, and the Bahama Islands.* One advantage of these syndications, beyond their immediate profitability, was that they enabled Arader to assemble a roomful of his most valued clients and address all of them at once. And the message that he had to convey was: Sotheby's will sell it to you retail, I'll sell it to you wholesale.

Last January, a London book dealer named Julian Browning attended an auction in Monte Carlo and paid $100,000 for a hand-colored first-edition copy of *Hortus Eystettensis*, the work of an early-seventeenth-century German botanist named Basilius Besler. Only three other copies with original color were thought to exist. The copy that Browning bought had ten badly stained plates (ten out of three hundred and sixty-seven), and its binding was in poor condition—factors that, despite the book's rarity, made it less than desirable to most dealers and collectors. Because Graham Arader has so little in common with most dealers and collectors, Browning ended up owning the book only a short while. Three weeks after the sale in Monte Carlo, he flew to New York and resold *Hortus Eystettensis* to Arader for $120,000.

Hortus Eystettensis had been in Arader's possession for three days when the 1987 Winter Antiques Show opened in New York. He had already devised the terms by which he intended to syndicate the book: thirty-six shares, ten prints a share, $11,000 a share. Arader also had another syndication in the works—a collection of watercolor-and-gouache paintings of flowers by an eighteenth-century German artist named Barbara Regina Dietzsch. The Dietzsch was being offered in seventeen shares, four watercolors a share, $60,000 a share. During the show, Arader, without provocation, would drag any seemingly promotable browser into a corner and bring out the books. "This you've got to see!" he would say. "You've *got* to see it. Believe me, you'll thank me a thousand times for showing this to you."

A group of three married couples from Philadelphia came into Arader's booth with the intention of saying hello. They had been there less than a minute when Arader reached into an oversized briefcase and removed the Besler book, saying, "This is a great deal. Only three hundred copies of this edition were printed. A dealer around the corner is selling individual prints with *new* color for $1,800. Mine, with original color, will end up costing you $1,100 apiece. Now, look at this one, and this. Oh, wouldn't you kill to own that? I would. *But*—neither of us has to."

None of the Philadelphia visitors pretended to be familiar with what Arader was offering to sell them. The conversation went like this:

"Which one's sixty?"

"This is four for sixty?"

"What's ten?"

"This one—eleven for ten or ten for eleven?"

"How many shares?"

"Seventeen of the sixty, thirty-six of the eleven?"

"And what is this stuff?"

"We don't *need* any more art," one of the husbands said.

"These are incredible," Arader said, now grasping the Dietzsch volume. "And I guarantee you, you're not happy with any of it, I'll buy 'em back."

"How do I know they're incredible? You haven't even shown me what they are."

"Hey, you want to see what they are? Here." He dropped the book on a portfolio cabinet.

"Look at the way he throws that down. He just threw a million dollars down the drain."

One of the wives, sensing that an opportunity might be slipping away, said, "Could you write it down for me? Can I go now? How many shares are you selling?"

"How many do you want?"

Another member of the party told Arader—"strictly *entre nous*"—that she was going to Russia soon on some risky business.

Arader said, "I've got a good friend in Omaha who's best friends with Anatoly Dobrynin. If you want me to call him, you're in."

The Dietzsch-syndication breakup took place at Ballygomingo on a Sunday in late February, and the *Hortus Eystettensis* was broken up on a Saturday in late April. That Saturday evening, Arader and his wife, and an employee named Joseph Goddu, after driving at an unhealthy speed from Philadelphia to Kennedy Airport and arriving just in time to catch their flight, were on their way to London, where, less than forty-eight hours later, another copy of *Hortus Eystettensis* was due to be auctioned at Sotheby's.

"It's the greatest sale of flower books ever—*ever*," Arader, for once innocent of hyperbole, told me when he suggested that I accompany him to London to witness the sale. Over more than thirty years, Robert de Belder, a Belgian diamond merchant, horticulturist, and book collector, had managed to amass what a Sotheby's catalogue described as "the greatest private collection of botanical books in the world." During 1986, the four-thousand-title library was sold to Bernard Quaritch, Ltd., the London booksellers. Quaritch had invested three years in a quiet effort to find a permanent home for the books—two of them on behalf of de Belder and a third after buying the library. The purpose was to find an owner likely to keep the collection intact. Arader was not among the parties approached by Quaritch.

Rick Watson, the Quaritch employee who was responsible for

cataloguing the de Belder collection, explained the firm's strategy, saying, "This company has existed for a hundred and forty years. We exist for the purpose of continuing to exist. In a pinch, we can get our hands on the odd 10 million pounds. De Belder was a customer of ours for thirty-five years. We have not exactly sent out flyers saying 'Amazing Opportunity!' We find patience to be a commercial asset. But that appears not to be American thinking at the moment."

Failing to find a single buyer, Quaritch finally decided to auction off the prize items in the collection.

"How many lots will there be? Almost four hundred," Arader, now in London, said as his taxi moved through inexplicably slow Sunday-morning traffic, heading from Heathrow Airport toward Sotheby's sale room, in Mayfair. "How many am I going to bid on? Maybe all of them. A bargain I will buy. I'll pay a pound for anything. I want to spend about two or three million dollars. This is big. That's why we're here."

Sotheby's had granted Arader a million-pound line of credit, interest-free, with no payments due for sixty days. "A lot of Americans won't be here, because the dollar's dropped ten percent in the last three months," Arader said. "It's rough sledding. I think I made $15,000 last week in the commodities market, hedging the pound. I bought a million pounds forward, for payment June 20. I needed to own those pounds at a sure dollar fifty-eight."

Arader still had on the blue dress shirt and khaki trousers he had been wearing the previous day in Philadelphia. He looked rumpled and not well rested. His in-flight slumber, he reported, had been interrupted by an altercation with a fellow passenger. The other passenger had been unable to avoid jabbing his knees into the back of Arader's seat, and Arader had been unable to resist offering to damage the man's kneecaps. Valli said, "When Graham goes on these marathons, he doesn't get scrappy, he gets dangerous."

A copy of the auction catalogue sat in Arader's lap, and he turned now to the page that described de Belder's colored copy of *Hortus Eystettensis*. One passage said:

THE HORTUS EYSTETTENSIS IS WITHOUT DOUBT ONE OF THE GREATEST FLOWER BOOKS EVER PRODUCED IN ANY COUNTRY. COPIES WITH CONTEMPORARY COLOURING ARE NOTORIOUSLY RARE: THIS OUTSTANDING EXAMPLE IS PROBABLY THE FINEST IN EXISTENCE. IT CONTAINS AN ORIGINAL WATERCOLOUR OF AN AMERICAN ALOE DATED 1626 WITH AN UNRECORDED DOUBLE-SHEET ENGRAVING OF THE SAME BY WOLFGANG KILIAN DATED 1628. THIS MAY, THEREFORE, HAVE BEEN THE COPY OF KILIAN, THE PRINCIPAL ARTIST OF THE WORK.

Arader had a contrary opinion of the de Belder specimen. When Sotheby's brought it and a hundred or so other books from the collection to New York for display a few weeks earlier, Arader had studied the *Hortus Eystettensis* and convinced himself that its plates were not colored in the seventeenth century.

"This is not the exact same book you just bought and sold?" I asked him.

"No, it isn't," he said. "It's the exact same book, but without seventeenth-century color. You need to go to Quaritch and get them to look you in the eye and say that it's original color. But they can't say it.* You've got to say to them, 'I notice that the copper in the green pigment does not oxidize through the paper.' The de Belder copy is in far superior condition to the one I bought, but it's not original color. This might have been colored in the nineteenth century, but not in the seventeenth. The only original-color copies are in the British Museum and Eichstätt, West Germany. Plus the one I bought, which was unsalable as a book because it had ten bad plates and the binding was terrible. No book collector would have bought that as a whole book. That's where I make the market for books like that."

*But they can, and do, eloquently—as witness the comments of Rick Watson, of Quaritch, cited below. (See p. 357.) Moreover, after this Profile originally appeared in *The New Yorker*, a second gentleman from Quaritch rang me to state forthrightly that Arader's comments about oxidation were nonsense and that a study would soon be published which would reveal the de Belder *Hortus Eystettensis* to be not just "original color" but one of the earliest colored copies in existence.

"You have no intention of bidding on this?"

"I *had* an intention. I was going to bid up to 150,000 pounds, but that was before I became convinced it's not original color. So I'm going to bid considerably less, because there's so much other stuff I want. What I'd like to see happen is for this Besler to go for a lot of money to some sucker that Sotheby's develops that I've never even heard of."

It was ten-thirty when Arader arrived at the entrance to Sotheby's, down an alley off New Bond Street. In the sale room, the de Belder books reposed within an L-shaped arrangement of floor-to-ceiling shelves at one end of the room. Upon handing a guard a wad of ten-pound notes, Arader was immediately set up with a private viewing area—four chairs and a ten-foot-long green-baize-covered table—at the opposite end of the room. Henry Taliaferro, who had arrived in London for a map auction the previous week, and Joe Goddu began ferrying books, many of them taller than a robust toddler, by the armload.

Valli took a seat next to her husband, and looked over his shoulder when Taliaferro brought around the Besler. Arader conducted a brief hands-on tutorial in original color. "Do you see the difference?" he said. "Does your eye see the difference?" When the natural pigments in copper engravings oxidize over time, they tend to penetrate the surface of a page and leave traces on the reverse side. Examining the Besler, Arader was convinced that he was looking at an application of modern color, which, instead of oxidizing, had bled through the paper.

"Look at that!" he said. "Did you see that color yesterday, in the prints we sold? If you looked at all my folds—where the paper had been hung and folded to dry—all my folds were white, because they started breaking and leaving white. And all the folds in the pages of this book are darker, because the newer color got stuck in them. O.K.? Look at that. You didn't see that color yesterday. O.K., that's some oxidation there, but it's also bleed. Oh, I feel great! This is going to go for a lot of money and, at best, it's early-nineteenth-century. That's why you get some oxidation of some of the colors, but the green is what should be oxidized."

A few minutes later, Arader was shown a copy of a mid-seventeenth-century florilegium by Johann Theodor de Bry. "Now, *that's* oxidation," he said, his tone hushed, as he turned the pages. The estimated selling price of the de Bry, according to the catalogue, was eighteen to twenty thousand pounds. "*That's* oxidation. Oh, *wow!* This is what it's all about."

"I love this thing," Valli said. "Love love love love love love *love* it."

"*All-l-l* about. This is one of the two really great early-seventeenth-century books in the sale. We can sell it complete or we can break it. It should stay complete if we can swing it."

Henry Taliaferro, arriving with more books, asked, "Did you look at the de Bry?"

"Yeah. We died. Just died," said Arader.

"So what did you decide to do?"

"Uh, forty," Arader said, meaning he would bid 40,000 pounds for it.

"It's *so* cool," Valli said. "Isn't it, Henry?"

"Sh-h-h!" her husband cautioned. "Keep it down."

The sale room was populated with perhaps thirty other potential buyers and curiosity seekers: beady-eyed, bushy-headed gents with continuous eyebrows, G. B. Shaw beards, corduroys, and hearing aids; stout ladies in Glen-plaid skirts; young Oxbridge-looking women in gray blazers, herringbone-tweed skirts, and patent-leather pumps; well-dressed Italians with reading glasses dangling from chains around their necks. Like the well-oiled gears of a piece of antique factory equipment, they methodically un-shelved books, laid them on the baize-covered tables for examination, stood on stepladders to reshelve them, occasionally fell off the ladders.

As the books kept coming, the dialogue between Arader and his wife perked along:

Valli: "Watercolor drawings of fungi. That might be cool."

Arader: "No." A pause. "No, you're right. They are cool."

Valli: "No, they're clumsy."

Arader: "How much? Nine hundred of them. So we pay two bucks apiece. Bid a thousand pounds."

Arader (regarding a nineteenth-century monograph on corn): "I don't like this."

Valli: "Oh, really? Those prints have got a lot of wall power. I thought you'd like that."

Arader (on *A Catalogue of Willows, Indigenous and Foreign, in the Collection of the Duke of Bedford* &c.): "I'll bid 400 pounds. Write 'Boring' in the catalogue."

Valli: "*The Flora of Java.* We don't want another one of those, do we?"

Arader: "We sure don't."

Arader (on a collection of six hundred and four watercolors and twenty-eight pencil-and-wash drawings, French, mid-nineteenth-century): "This is what we should be selling. I don't think there's any question. This is incredible. They're *good*, honey. This is good, solid stuff."

Valli: "Maybe we should sell it complete."

Arader: "Nah."

Arader (on *The Wild Flowers of Southern and Western India*): "Now, here's a cool book. You're gonna like this, honey."

Valli: "No, I don't. They're big and sloppy."

Arader (studying Maria Sibylla Merian's eighteenth-century work on the entomology of the Dutch colony of Surinam, *Dissertatio de Generatione et Metamorphosibus Insectorum Surinamensium*): "The *ultimate* bug book. You're gonna lose it when you see this one. Look at that. Isn't that the coolest? Perfect oxidation. Look at this one, honey. You up for this? Look at these, honey. Don't miss this. Don't miss this."

Henry Taliaferro: "There's not a dog in there."

Arader: "How many plates, angel? Seventy-two? So we pay 500 each. We bid 22,000 pounds. We won't get it, but we'll try. No —some rich guy'll get it. Boy, that's a great book."

Arader (suddenly noticing a middle-aged man standing a few feet away): "Who's that guy over there? O.K., watch him and see if he's writing down what we're saying. I don't want that guy *around*. If you heard me say I'd bid 50,000 for something and you didn't like me, you'd go up to 45,000, wouldn't you? These English dealers love to see me lose. They love to run me up. They say things like 'I nearly had a stroke doing it, but I gave that Arader a real caning.' "

The fatigue factor in this exercise—fatigue combined with nervous energy and a dash of paranoia—had to be reckoned with. After about three hours, Arader was working his way through certain books with the celerity of a brushhogger. He was capable of opening a book to a single page, saying "A hundred pounds" or "Two hundred pounds" or "Stringy stuff," and dismissing it. He said, "Lot 169 I'm not excited about. And 160 I'll take a pee on, too. Yeah. Right. I'm *really* bored. Lot 159 has a lot of green. It's neat, but it wouldn't sell. Brilliantly framed, it would sell."

The auction was to be held in two evening sessions, on Monday and Tuesday. The longer Arader spent looking at books, the testier he became, and I decided to excuse myself and poll various members of the London rare-book-and-map trade for their opinions of Arader. Everyone I approached had something quotable to say— even those noncombative souls who wished not to be quoted.

"Controversy and Graham Arader are never very far apart. I think he seeks it, doesn't he?" a reticent curator at the British Museum said.

"He's a McEnroe young man, really," said John Maggs. "He's the big bruiser. His type of business is almost like brokerage. It's a different world altogether. He strikes me as a high-powered doorstep salesman. He is the great American image. He's the dream incarnate, isn't he?"

"Before Graham turned up, the American print trade wasn't exactly a back-street trade, but you had to find your way around," a map-and-print dealer named Robert Douwma said. "He's given prints a place with antiques; he's appealed to a much wider public, not just to collectors. Basically, he's changed prints and maps into status symbols for a larger group of people."

"He's sort of a mythical figure by now. I heard he'd sued Nancy Reagan," said a print dealer in Bloomsbury, who was misinformed.

"The typical map-and-book people don't behave brashly," said Jonathan Potter, a map dealer in Mayfair. "Graham doesn't fit in at all, and I think that's the nicest thing that some dealers might say about him. The people in this business don't build up enemies, and Graham has done that, just through his manner. But, for all his personal traits, he's done wonders for the map business. As far as I'm concerned, if he comes over here and shouts about antique maps, that's great."

When I went to see Rick Watson, of Quaritch, and mentioned that Arader had impugned the authenticity of the color of the de Belder copy of *Hortus Eystettensis*, he reacted with a combination of outrage and delight. "This book was a record of a garden that existed in Eichstätt, in Bavaria, for only thirty years and was then destroyed," he said. "To attack the authenticity of the color of this book, you would have to be a botanist who knew the plants in cultivation in Bavaria in 1612 and what they looked like when they flowered. The expert in this area is William T. Stearn, the retired senior principal scientific officer of the botany department of the British Museum. Stearn says this is the *only* copy in existence which is demonstrably original coloring based upon Wolfgang Kilian's original watercolors—colored either for him or by him. Kilian, to color the engravings, had to refer to the original paintings of the plants. The de Belder copy contains an original watercolor by Kilian as well as an uncolored, signed and dated, engraved plate of the same image. Neither appears in any of the other copies. We think this was Kilian's own copy. Stearn spent many years looking for a reliable copy, and when he found the de Belder copy he went berserk over it. If Graham is going around saying this isn't original color, he's absolutely nuts."

The sale of the book at Sotheby's on Monday evening confused rather than resolved the debate. Roy Davids, the auctioneer, a slender, pink-faced man with black-framed eyeglasses, spoke in a flat, evenly modulated tone. Both nights of the auction, he began the bidding without a speck of ceremony. A tote board behind the platform displayed prices simultaneously in pounds, dollars, Swiss

francs, lire, deutsche marks, and guilders. The pound was selling
for a dollar sixty-eight. At the front of the room stood a dozen or
so Sotheby employees in black tie. The air of formality that they
lent to the event enabled Arader—who had shown up in chinos,
a blue button-down shirt, no necktie, and no jacket, and had
perched himself on a bookshelf at the back of the room and was
resting his feet on the seat of an empty chair—to be even more
conspicuous than usual.

As each item came up for sale, it was displayed on a large red-
felt-covered rotating easel. Lots 1 through 7 went for prices ranging
from 1,100 to 13,000 pounds. Arader's first buy was Lot No. 8,
the collection of more than six hundred nineteenth-century French
watercolors and pencil-and-wash drawings. He bid $32,000, nearly
quadrupling Sotheby's highest estimate ("That *cost* me," he said),
and the crowd uttered its first pregnant murmur of the evening.
Arader smiled genuinely for the first time in a couple of days. He
smiled again a few minutes later when a three-volume collection
of Early American hand-colored floral engravings sold for $5,700
—more than twice the high estimate. Some friends from Philadelphia who happened to be in London had stopped by to watch
the auction. Arader turned to them and said, "I've got one of those
in our catalogue, in better condition, for $2,800."

That was a portent of things to come—prices that seemed not
merely high but in many instances laughably so. The *Hortus Eystettensis* was the twenty-third item to be sold, and the bidding had
barely begun when it became clear that the catalogue estimate—
$250,000 to $330,000—was out of touch with reality. Or else
reality had lost touch with itself. The book sold to Nico Israel, a
well-known Dutch dealer, for slightly less than a million dollars:
the record for a botanical-color-plate book. Israel's avidity throughout the auction made it clear that he was bidding not for himself
but for some extremely well-heeled mystery client, and Arader was
thrown by this turn of events—filled with conflicting emotions.
Only two days earlier, when he disposed of his copy of *Hortus
Eystettensis*, selling it plate by plate (he kept sixty plates for
himself), he had received $330,000 for a book that cost him
$120,000. And now another copy of the book—one whose au-

thenticity he seriously doubted—had sold at auction for more than eight times what he had paid. Two uncolored copies of *Hortus Eystettensis* were auctioned next, one of them a first edition, which went for $219,000. A reporter later described the spectacle as "reminiscent of tulipomania."

I said to Arader, "Too bad you didn't wait three days to sell your Besler."

He said, "Hey, now I've got thirty people who'll kill for me. It's a good investment."

He bid successfully for a late-eighteenth-century collection of watercolor drawings of British ferns, paying 6,500 pounds ("That's stealing it; I was willing to go to 15,000"), and for 7,000 pounds (3,000 less than he was prepared to pay) he bought a collection of nineteenth-century watercolors by Priscilla Susan Bury. When the bidding concluded for the evening, Arader had acquired only fifteen of the nearly two hundred items sold. He was in no danger of straining his million-pound line of credit.

Again and again, toe to toe with Nico Israel, he had been outbid. Once, when Israel bought a book for 20,000 pounds, Arader quietly approached the underbidder, a young Oriental woman with shoulder-length hair, and offered her the same book, from his stock, for ten percent less than the auction price. Otherwise, there was not much that Arader could do but marvel, wonder, and mutter to himself, "Rich people. Rich people. Europeans. This is *retail!*"

Israel, an elfin, diffident, white-haired man, was so intent on taking home certain items that he didn't bother to raise his head during much of the bidding. He stared down at his catalogue and nodded each time he upped the price. Perhaps mesmerized by how effortlessly he was spending his client's money, Israel did let one item slip away, and Arader got it. This was the de Bry *Florilegium* (according to Sotheby's, "an exceptional copy")—the seventeenth-century classic that Valli Arader loved loved loved loved loved loved loved. The catalogue estimate was 18–20,000 pounds, and Arader had vowed to go as high as 40,000. His eyes narrowed as the bidding dashed past 40,000, and at 75,000 he was wincing. When Israel bid 88,000, Arader at last shook his head, indicating to the auctioneer that he was dropping out. Then, quickly, he

changed his mind and got back in, at 90,000. Nico Israel, for no
evident reason, failed to respond to this bid, and so Arader bought
the book. With the commission to Sotheby's, it had cost him more
than $165,000, but he was glad to have it.

When an eighteenth-century German study of plants and insects
("contains the first observations and depictions of pollen tubes,"
said the catalogue) went for 3,000 pounds to a buyer whom the
auctioneer identified as "Junk," Valli whispered, "Who's Junk?"

"He's the guy who got me kicked out of the A.B.A.A.," said
Arader.

"Let me at him."

"No, honey. The last time I talked to him it cost me $150,000."

After the final item of the evening was sold—an early nineteenth-
century Dutch work on trees, bought by Arader for 3,000
pounds—he said, in a final burst of hubris, "Lemme go talk to
Nico. Get him off my goddam back. Jesus!" A crowd swarmed
around Nico Israel, who had a quivery, cryptic smile on his face
and seemed rather dazed by what he had just perpetrated. Israel,
it turned out, had something he wanted to discuss with Arader—
the elusive de Bry—but now was not the time.

There was some brief milling and head-scratching, and then
Arader, Valli, Henry Taliaferro, Joe Goddu, Julian Browning, his
partner, Desmond Burgess, a dealer named Tom Schuster, and I
headed for a restaurant in Piccadilly. It was a nouvelle-Italian
place. The menu included roast saddle of hare, deep-fried wing
of skate, and a salad of warm liver and crisp lettuce. We gathered
around three tables that had been lined up together, not far from
a table where two couples were ordering dessert. "Don't be bullied
by Felix into ordering the rhubarb crumble," I heard one of the
men at the next table say to his companion. The conversation at
our table did not stray from what had just happened at Sotheby's.
The theories were simple and complicated: Nico Israel was buying
for Quaritch; Israel was buying for de Belder; Israel was buying
certain lots for himself and certain lots for de Belder; Israel and
Sotheby's had some sort of side deal working; Israel was not actually
spending any *real* money.

The same conversation was rehashed the next evening, after a
repeat performance by Israel. In all, the proceeds of the de Belder

sale exceeded $10 million—"beyond our wildest dreams," according to Rick Watson—but only a fraction of it was Arader's money. For $185,000, he bought the Maria Sibylla Merian study of the insect life of Surinam. And he managed to pay for some of his troubles in London by selling the de Bry to Israel. "Boy, why did you buy that book? You will never be able to sell it," Israel said, and Arader agreed to let him have it for 125,000 pounds, thus turning an overnight profit of more than $40,000.

Directly and indirectly, Nico Israel was putting money in Arader's pocket. Israel paid $300,000 for "an exceptional copy" of Robert Thornton's *Temple of Flora*.

"Do I have any whole copies of that book?" Arader said, at the restaurant. "I've got *three* of them!"

Another bidder paid a quarter of a million dollars for de Belder's first edition of Catesby's *The Natural History of Carolina, Florida, and the Bahama Islands*—a book that Arader had bought and sold many times, whole and syndicated.

"Henry," Arader said to Taliaferro. "Call Mrs. Moore and tell her we'll buy back her Catesby. We sold it to her for $140,000, and she's been complaining that it was too much. So we'll buy it back."

For Arader, who had come to London planning to spend millions of dollars, the auction prices brought revelation and anticlimax, pleasure and discomfort. Was this indeed tulipomania, an aberration? Was it a market expanding to the bursting point? Arader's net worth seemed suddenly to have doubled or tripled—a salutary development. Perhaps it would make sense to call all his galleries and have everything sent back to Philadelphia to be repriced. On the other hand, suddenly someone other than Graham Arader was forcefully defining the marketplace—not a salutary development.

A waiter took everyone's drink order. Arader ordered ginger ale and discussed with Julian Browning how very much he would like to own Stair & Company, the antique-furniture dealers in New York and London. He talked about a collection of autographs that he had just bought for $19,000 and figured he could sell for $200,000.

The drinks arrived. Arader raised his ginger ale and proposed a toast. "To greed," he said. "Once again. No question about it."

1 9 8 7

Predilections

Among the nonfiction movies that Errol Morris has at one time or another been eager to make but has temporarily abandoned for lack of investor enthusiasm are *Ablaze!* (or *Fire from Heaven*), an examination of the phenomenon of spontaneous human combustion; *Whatever Happened to Einstein's Brain?* (portions of the cerebellum and the cerebral cortex are thought to be in the possession of a doctor in North Carolina, other parts are floating around here and there); *Road*, the story of one man's attempt to build across northern Minnesota an interstate highway that no one else wanted; *Insanity Inside Out*, based on the book of the same title, by Kenneth Donaldson, a man who, in his forties, was wrongly committed by his parents to a mental hospital and got stuck there for fifteen years; *Weirdo*, about the breeding of a giant chicken; *The Wizard of Wendover*, about Robert K. Golka and his laser-induced fireball experiments in Utah; and a perusal of Yap, a South Pacific island where stone money is the traditional currency.

Some months ago, Morris attended a meeting with executives of Home Box Office, his primary motive being, as they say in the movie business, to pitch an idea—in that case, the one involving Einstein's brain. The meeting did not go particularly well. An HBO person at one point said admonishingly, "You know, your movies are ironic. Our viewers just don't like irony."

Groping for a more tactful evasion, another HBO person said, "We're already doing a transplant movie."

"But wait a second," Morris replied. "This brain hasn't *been* transplanted—*yet*."

Unapologetically, Morris draws his films fresh from the substance of the real world, where irony has a way of running riot. Describing his work, he goes to some lengths to avoid using the term "documentary" ("the 'D' word," he will say, in a pinch), but he has not yet coined an alternative label that a Hollywood publicist might use to characterize a generic Errol Morris movie. During the past twelve years, he has directed and released three films: *Gates of Heaven*, about two pet cemeteries in northern California; *Vernon, Florida*, a series of interviews with several residents of a swamp town in Florida; and *The Thin Blue Line*, which arrived in theaters around the country last summer and fall, and which Morris has described, not immodestly, as "the first murder mystery that actually solves a murder." An Errol Morris movie features real people talking uninterrupted, mainly about literal objects or events, only occasionally about feelings or ideas: trafficking in entertaining truths as well as in equally entertaining transparent prevarications; free-associating, it often seems, as if the camera were a psychotherapist whose expensive time it would be a pity to squander on silence.

Near the midpoint of *Gates of Heaven*, which was completed in 1978, a woman with a pinched mouth whose age might be anywhere from seventy to eighty-five sits in a chair before an open doorway. She is never identified, but, it happens, her name is Florence Rasmussen. In a manner that alternates between passive and bold, accented by facial expressions that range from beatific to sinister, Florence Rasmussen soliloquizes elegiacally:

"I'm raised on a farm, we had chickens and pigs and cows and sheep and everything. But down here I've been lost. Now they've taken them all away from here up to that— What's the name of that place? Up above here a little ways? That town? Commences with a 'B.' Blue. It's— Blue Hill Cemetery, I think the name of it is. Not too far, I guess, about maybe twenty miles from here. A little town there, a little place. You know where it's at. But I was really surprised when I heard they were getting rid of the cemetery over here. Gonna put in buildings or something over there. Ah well, I know people been very good to me, you know. Well, they see my condition, I guess, must of felt sorry for me. But it's real, my condition is. It's not put on. That's for sure! Boy, if I could only walk. If I could only get out. Drive my car. I'd get *another*

car. Ya . . . and my son, if he was only better to me. After I
bought him that car. He's got a nice car. I bought it myself just a
short time ago. I don't know. These kids—the more you do for
them . . . He's my grandson, but I raised him from two years
old. . . . I don't see him very often. And he just got the car. I
didn't pay for all of it. I gave him four hundred dollars. Pretty
good! His boss knows it. Well, he's not working for that outfit now.
He's changed. He's gone back on his old job—hauling sand. *No*,
not hauling sand; he's working in the office. That's right. He took
over the office job. His boss told me that on the phone. But, you
know, he should help me more. He's all I got. He's the one who
brought me up here. And then put me here by myself among
strangers. It's terrible, you stop and think of it. I've been without
so much, when I first come up here. Ya. It's what half of my trouble
is from—him not being home with me. Didn't cost him nothing to
stay here. Every time he need money, he'd always come, 'Mom,
can I have this? Can I have that?' But he never pays back. Too
good, too easy—that's what everybody tells me. I quit now. I quit.
Now he's got the office job, I'm going after him. I'm going after
him good, too—if I have to go in . . . in a different way. He's
going to pay that money. He's got the office job now. And he makes
good money anyway. And he has no kids. He has not married.
Never get married, he says. He was married once—they're divorced. Well, she tried to take him for the kid, but she didn't.
They went to court. It was somebody else's kid. She was nothing
but a tramp in the first place. I told him that. He wouldn't listen
to me. I says, 'I know what she is.' I said, 'Richard, please, listen
to me.' He wouldn't listen. He knew all, he knew everything. Big
shot! But he soon found out. Now that's all over with. I've been
through so much I don't know how I'm staying alive. Really, for
my age . . . If you're young, it's different. But I've always said
I'm never going to grow old. I've always had that, and the people
that I tell how old I am, they don't believe me, because people my
age as a rule don't get around like I do."

   With an arresting instinct for symmetry, Florence Rasmussen
manages to contradict most of what she has to say. It seems that
she knows certain things, but then, in the next moment, she trots

out contrary information: I have roots with the earth; I'm lost in this world. People have been very good to me; I'm all alone, surrounded by strangers, my own flesh and blood treats me badly. I have a health problem that's real; I protest too much. I'd like to drive my car; but I might not even have a car any longer, might have to buy a new one. I bought my son—O.K., he's not my son, he's my grandson—a new car; well, I didn't pay for the whole thing, I gave him four hundred dollars, but anyway I want my money back. His boss— Hold on, he has a different boss. He hauls sand for a living; nope, he's got that office job now. He's not the marrying kind; he was married once. He has no children; he's been involved in a paternity suit. I'll never grow old; I'm so old people can't believe it. Even though I can't walk, people my age as a rule don't get around like I do.

Gates of Heaven gives an account of a pet cemetery that fails and one that succeeds; Mrs. Rasmussen refers to each in only a glancing manner. The first day that Morris set out as a bona fide film director with an actual film crew was the day the residents of the failed pet cemetery were being exhumed, so that they could be transferred to the other cemetery. The cinematographer Morris had engaged to shoot *Gates of Heaven* he fired that same day—a consequence of serious philosophical differences that culminated in a physical struggle for the camera. ("It's *mine!*" "No, it's *mine!*") Day Two, Morris met Florence Rasmussen, and she became the first person with whom he ever filmed an interview. The footage from that interview didn't make it into the final cut, however, because the replacement camera operator, a woman, felt compelled to engage the interviewee in a dialogue. When Mrs. Rasmussen mused "Well, here today, gone tomorrow. Right?" the camerawoman said "No. Wrong." Morris couldn't decide which made him angrier—that the camerawoman had interfered with the interview or that her notions about death and the hereafter were so misguided. In any event, he fired her on the spot and hired a replacement, who lasted three or four days.

One of Morris's techniques is to situate his interview subject in a chair (when possible, a specific chair: a lightweight canvas-and-metal-frame low-back Regista) that is a precise distance (forty-nine inches) from the camera, which is equipped with a 25-mm Zeiss high-speed prime lens—a lens of fixed focal length, which is one that cannot zoom—and is secured to a tripod, so that the camera cannot pan. When Morris went back to reshoot Mrs. Rasmussen —accompanied by Ned Burgess, his fourth, and final, cinematographer—she rewarded him with what has become the emblem of the Morris style: a seamless monologue from someone who has been allowed to talk until the truth naturally sorts itself out. Quotidian lies, the little fabrications that make the commerce of daily life possible, if not always palatable, are laid on the surface by the speaker. A muted strain of implicit skepticism—the silent voice of the filmmaker—bubbles along just beneath that. Peripheral stuff turns out to matter. "I like the idea of making films about ostensibly absolutely nothing," Morris says. "I like the irrelevant, the tangential, the sidebar excursion to nowhere that suddenly becomes revelatory. That's what all my movies are about. That and the idea that we're in possession of certainty, truth, infallible knowledge, when actually we're just a bunch of apes running around. My films are about people who think they're connected to something, although they're really not."

Gates of Heaven is the only one of Morris's films that can be said to have emerged with its original subject matter intact. *The Thin Blue Line*, which at its inception was to have been a study of Dr. James Grigson, a Texas psychiatrist who regularly testifies for the prosecution in death-penalty cases, instead became a horrifyingly satiric examination of the wrongful murder conviction and near-execution of an innocent man. *Vernon, Florida*, which is essentially plotless—a pastiche of interviews with a turkey hunter, a policeman, a retired couple who are convinced that a glass jar in their possession contains radioactive sand that grows, a wild-animal collector, a Holy Roller preacher, a worm farmer, and others—evolved haphazardly, almost desperately, from an unwieldy idea Morris had of making a fiction film based upon a bizarre insurance scam. A loquacious man named Albert Bitterling, who appears intermittently throughout *Vernon, Florida*, has held a pair of opera glasses against the the lens of a camera and photographed the night sky. In one scene, displaying the opaque result, he says,

"Of course, as you can see that picture ain't too good, it's a cheap camera, you get a cheap picture." Then, speaking literally and in metaphor, he encapsulates the filmmaker's dilemma: "Well, of course, you see, when you have a camera . . . You have a camera and you point it at a certain— Just like if you had a gun. You don't shoot, do you? Well, if you had a gun and you pointed it at something, you're liable to hit what you're pointing at, and then again you might not."

Vernon, Florida has been, as a practical matter, the least accessible of Morris's films; it was completed in 1981, but a commercial videocassette version of it has just been released. Video-cassettes of *Gates of Heaven* became available only a few months ago. *The Thin Blue Line* is the first of Morris's films to be widely distributed in theaters. A word that regularly comes up when Morris discusses the until quite recent low-orbit trajectory of his career is "disturbing." The frustration of making movies that only modest numbers of people have seen, or even heard of, has encouraged Morris to cultivate a melodramatic haplessness. In a less ironically disposed person, this tendency might be taken for neurotic self-indulgence. When Morris consents to be the interviewee—when it becomes his turn to sort the truth out—he ends up quoting Shakespeare ("But since the affairs of men rest still uncertain, let's reason with the worst that may befall") or himself ("The fact that the world is, like, utterly insane makes it tolerable"). Once, when I made the mistake of asking, in an offhand manner, how he'd been feeling lately, he said, "I've been horribly depressed, which, as you know, can be terribly time-consuming. I mean, if you're going to do it right, that is." Another time, en route to a preview screening of *The Thin Blue Line*, he said, "I hope this won't be terribly embarrassing." A pause, then: "No, actually, I remember, when I was a teenager, thinking there was no point in going on, but then I realized that life is just an endless series of embarrassments and I'd hate to miss out on all that."

The first time I met Morris was in an airport, on a day in early 1987, when he was still working on *The Thin Blue Line* and was flying to Dallas to attend a federal-court hearing. He wore a navy pin-striped suit, carried a briefcase, and could easily have masqueraded as a typical traveling litigator except that he was not flying first class. Days when he doesn't wear a suit, he dresses like a permanent graduate student—khakis, Black Watch blazer or tweed jacket, button-down shirt, dark-framed Clark Kentish eyeglasses. He has short dark-brown hair, which often looks as if it had been slept on the wrong way, and a rueful, asymmetrical smile. Although he is six-one, imperfect posture renders his presence less than imposing. Photographs make him appear either darkly handsome or dolefully goofy. Morris is now forty-one years old. He grew up in Hewlett, on the South Shore of Long Island. His father, a doctor, died when he was two, and his mother, a Juilliard graduate, who did not remarry for more than twenty years, supported him and an older brother by teaching music in a public school. Errol studied cello, read with a passion the forty-odd "Oz" books, watched a lot of television, and on a regular basis went with a doting but not quite right maiden aunt ("I guess you'd have to say that Aunt Roz was somewhat demented") to Saturday matinées, where he saw stuff like *This Island Earth* and *Creature from the Black Lagoon* —horror movies that, viewed again thirty years later, still seem scary to him. "I don't really understand how Errol got drawn to these themes that interest him—maybe that he lost his father," his mother, Cinnabelle Esterman, told me not long ago. "I remember the first time we went on a trip out West. We had to take a flight to Chicago, and a friend drove us to the airport. And I noticed that along the way, in the car, Errol was reading the *World Almanac*, studying about air crashes." In the tenth grade, he was enrolled in the Putney School, in Vermont. Part of what had drawn him to Putney was its highly regarded music program. Morris's most vivid memories, however, include having a forbidden radio confiscated because one evening he made the mistake of loudly singing along while listening to Birgit Nilsson perform the immolation scene from *Götterdämmerung*. On another occasion, for an offense that he cannot recall, a dormitory proctor deprived him of his cello.

Next came the University of Wisconsin, where he excelled academically ("the first time I did really well at anything, except elementary school") and, in 1969, received a degree in history. For a couple of years, he drifted about, earning money as a cable-television salesman in Wisconsin and as a term-paper writer in Massachusetts and "trying to get accepted at different graduate schools just by showing up on their doorstep." This strategy, which did not succeed at Oxford and Harvard, finally worked at Princeton, but graduate school soon proved to have been not such a hot idea. Morris's mistake was in pursuing academic disciplines—at Princeton, the history of science—in which he had "absolutely no background."

"I did enter Princeton actually thinking I was going to get a doctorate," he says. "I was wrong. I had big fights with my adviser. I was supposed to be concentrating on the history of physics. And, naturally, my adviser expected me to take all these courses in physics. But the classes were always full of fourteen-year-old Chinese prodigies, with their hands in the air—'Call on me! Call on me!' I couldn't do it. I reneged on some of my commitments. At the end, my adviser actually assaulted me. He was on sabbatical and had an office at the Institute for Advanced Study. I remembered thinking, This is the Institute for Advanced Study, and he's *assaulting* me. I'd written a thirty-page double-spaced paper, and he produced thirty single-spaced pages of his own criticizing it. The bile just flowed out of him. I accused him of not even finishing reading what I'd written. It turns out I *was* a problem, but at least I wasn't a drudge, and that school was filled with drudges. I remember saying to my adviser, 'You won't even look through my telescope.' And his response was 'Errol, it's not a telescope, it's a kaleidoscope.' "

In 1972, Morris moved to Berkeley, where he had been accepted as a Ph.D. candidate in philosophy at the University of California. His recollections of that experience also lack a warm glow, but something fundamentally positive did take place, which was that he discovered the Pacific Film Archive, a cinemathèque/library/revival house/symposium center, and the only place in the Bay Area with the ability to devote several days to a retrospective of, say, the cinema of Senegal. Tom Luddy, a film producer, who was then the director of the Archive, recently said, "There were a bunch

of regulars and a bunch of eccentric regulars, and Errol was one
of the eccentrics. I often had to defend him to my staff. What made
him eccentric? Well, for one thing, he dressed strangely. Remember, this is Berkeley in the early seventies. And Errol was wearing
dark suits with pants that were too short, white dress shirts, and
heavy shoes. He looked like a New York person gone to seed.
Then, I let him use our library for research, and he was always
getting into little frictions with the staff. He felt he could both use
the Archive and put it down. He would leave messes. He never
bothered to reshelve books. I found myself defending him, which
was often difficult, because he would attack me for the programming. He was a film-noir nut. He claimed we weren't showing the
real film noir. So I challenged him to write the program notes.
Then, there was his habit of sneaking into the films and denying
that he was sneaking in. I told him if he was sneaking in he should
at least admit he was doing it."

The Archive opened each afternoon at five-thirty. Among the
other eccentric regulars were a superannuated Berkeley professor
who had a habit of showing up at 5:30 A.M.; the narcoleptic who
used to come for the first show, immediately fall asleep, and remain
that way through the final feature; a disconcertingly loud laugher,
known as the Cackler; and a misanthropic woman who, with her
dog, lived in a van outside the Archive.

Meanwhile, Morris's academic career failed to thrive. "Berkeley
was just a world of pedants," he says. "It was truly shocking. I
spent two or three years in the philosophy program. I have very
bad feelings about it." His own flaw, he believes, was that he was
"an odd combination of the academic and the prurient." While he
was supposed to be concentrating on the philosophy of science,
his attention became diverted by an extracurricular interest in the
insanity plea. A quotation from "The Black Cat"—a story in which
Edgar Allan Poe writes of "the spirit of perverseness . . . this
unfathomable longing of the soul *to vex itself* . . . to do wrong for
the wrong's sake only"—had become resonant for him, and he
began to ponder the metaphysics of mass murder. In 1975, he
returned to Wisconsin long enough to have several interviews with
Ed Gein, the real-life prototype for the Norman Bates character in

Psycho and a midwestern legend. "You couldn't spend long in Wisconsin, especially with my predilection, without hearing a lot about Ed Gein," Morris says. Gein was then confined to Central State Hospital, in Waupun, a maximum-security institution for the criminally insane. Evidently, Morris was the first person in quite a while to make a special effort to talk with him. What perhaps discouraged other potential visitors was that Gein not only murdered people but also was a cannibal, a grave robber, and an amateur taxidermist. Morris found his way to Dr. George Arndt, a Geinologist and the author of a study—a catalogue of Ed Gein jokes, basically—titled *Community Reaction to a Horrifying Event*.

"I go and meet Dr. Arndt," Morris says. "Almost from the beginning, I entertain serious doubts about the wholesomeness of Dr. Arndt's interest in the Gein case. Dr. Arndt seems real excited that there's this kindred spirit interested in the Ed Gein story. I tell him I've been spending a lot of time in Plainfield, Wisconsin, where Ed Gein lived and committed his crimes. I tell him I've been to the Plainfield cemetery to look at graves. I had the names of the graves whose occupants Ed had exhumed. I noticed that those graves made a circle around his mother's grave. Dr. Arndt looks at me and says, 'You know what that means, don't you?' I say, 'No, sir.' He says, 'It's a kind of sublimation. Transference. He couldn't go down directly after his mother. He had to go down through the other graves.' He says, 'There may be underground tunnels leading to his mother's grave.' So we go in his Cadillac to the Plainfield cemetery. When we're almost there, he pulls over and starts looking around in the brush for something, and he comes up with a big thick stick. We get to the cemetery, we find the graves where the exhumations took place, and he has me put my ear to the ground near Mrs. Gein's grave. While I do that, Dr. Arndt walks around beating the ground, searching for hollow sounds. I hear nothing. Finally, I ask, 'Dr. Arndt, why didn't he just dig straight into Mrs. Gein's grave?' And Dr. Arndt gives me this look and says, *'Too devious.'* "

During his research, Morris stumbled across the provocative fact that Plainfield, with a population of seven hundred, had within a

ten-year period been home to several multiple killers, and that
Gein's depredations had antedated the others', almost as if he had
driven the town mad.

"One of the things that have always fascinated me about abnormal behavior is that we can't really explain it to our satisfaction,"
Morris says. "Almost everything I do now in my work is about
epistemic concerns: how do we come by certain kinds of knowledge? Take the insanity plea—we talk about insane acts and insane
people. When we talk about insane acts, we're saying we don't
understand something about the act itself. When we say someone
is insane, we're either saying, one, 'That person could be mentally
ill,' or, two, 'I don't *know* why that person does what he does.'
Rather than expressing a knowledge, we're expressing a *lack* of
knowledge. I wrote an essay on the insanity plea and movie mon-
sters and certain mechanistic fantasies we have about criminal
behavior. I very much wanted to write a doctoral thesis on this
stuff, and it hurt my feelings when Berkeley just sort of kicked my
ass out of there."

The demise of Morris's academic career was a protracted matter,
and he stayed at the university long enough to get a master's degree
in philosophy. All the while, he was a devotee of the Pacific Film
Archive. Tom Luddy introduced him to Werner Herzog, the German
director, whose fascination with fanatics, losers, Nazi supermen,
and dwarfs dovetailed with Morris's outside-the-mainstream preoc-
cupations. Once, making the film *Even Dwarfs Started Small,* Herzog inadvertently set a dwarf afire; the dwarf survived, and Herzog
did penance by throwing himself onto a cactus. At the time he and
Morris met, Morris's reading diet included, in addition to his academic texts, the *National Enquirer* and *Weekly World News.* For
listeners whom he deemed worthy, he had assembled an endlessly
digressive repertoire that included eyewitness tales of Geinology
and other vignettes of American dementia.

"Werner was very taken with Errol," Luddy recalls, adding that,
despite Morris's never having shot a single foot of film, "Werner
treated him as an equal."

Morris and Herzog discussed the question that Morris and Dr.
Arndt had left unanswered—whether or not Gein had disinterred

his mother—and they set a date for a rendezvous in Plainfield in the summer of 1975. The idea was that, with shovels, in the moonlight, they would satisfy their curiosity. When Herzog arrived in Plainfield, however—he had been working on a film in Alaska and was now driving toward New York—no familiar face was there to greet him. He made a phone call to California and learned that Morris had had second thoughts. A few months later, Morris did return to Plainfield, alone, and rented a room from Ed Gein's next-door neighbors. This time, he stayed almost a year, during which he conducted hundreds of hours of interviews with some of the other homicidally inclined local talent. He had no focused idea of what to do with the material. Maybe he would make a film about Ed Gein called *Digging Up the Past*, or maybe he would write a book. Although he still had a fellowship at the University of California, he didn't have enough money to transcribe all his interview tapes. Some supplementary financial support came from his family, but it was not unqualified support. "My mother was worried about what I was doing," he says. "She has this wonderfully euphemistic way of talking to me. At one point, she said, 'Errol, can't you spend more time with people your own age?' And I said, 'But, Mom, some of these mass murderers *are* my own age.' "

It didn't do Morris any good when, in order to talk to one of the Plainfield murderers, he made his way illegally into a state mental hospital, got caught, and was reported to his academic supervisors at Berkeley. In the fall of 1976, while Morris was still in Plainfield, Herzog unexpectedly returned. During Herzog's visit the previous year, his car had broken down, and he had discovered an automobile-repair shop—a grim place set against a grim, flat natural backdrop—that struck him as an excellent movie location. So now he had come to finish a film, *Stroszek*, most of which had been shot in Berlin. He asked Morris to work with him, but Morris felt that he had been abused. "Stealing a *landscape*," he complained. "The worst kind of plagiarism." On the other hand, he had never made a film himself, and here was a chance to observe a master. So he stuck around, and when the shooting was completed Herzog, afflicted with some measure

of guilt, handed him an envelope stuffed with cash. They were
in a motel room. Morris went to a window and tossed the envelope
into a parking lot. After retrieving the money, Herzog offered it
once more, saying, "Please don't do that again."

The envelope contained about two thousand dollars—more than
enough to finance a two-week trip Morris had been planning. Recently, he had read a newspaper article about an insurance investigator which mentioned, in passing, how several people in an
unidentified Southern town had tried to collect benefits after "accidentally" losing limbs. Morris had tracked down the insurance
investigator and learned that the town was Vernon (pop. 883), in
the Florida panhandle. Vernon's unofficial nickname was now Nub
City. In the hierarchy of nubbiedom, the supremely rewarding self-
sacrifice was the loss of a right leg and a left arm, because, so the
theory went, "afterward, you could still write your name and still
have a foot to press the gas pedal of your Cadillac." Morris stayed
in Vernon long enough to read some files at the courthouse, talk
to an insurance broker and several nubbies, and receive at least
one unambiguous death threat. At the Cat's Eye Tavern one night,
a citizen twice Morris's size smiled as he extinguished a cigarette
on the lapel of Morris's blazer. Morris remembers thinking that
perhaps he had packed the wrong clothes. Also, "I remember it
hurt my feelings, because it seemed that, you know, maybe the
people in Vernon didn't like me." Rarely did murders take place
in Vernon, because, someone explained, "down here, people don't
get murdered—they just disappear."

Back in Berkeley, Morris tried to write a script for a fiction
feature to be called *Nub City*. Mainly, he had a pitch line—*Nub
City* would be "about people who in order to achieve the American
dream literally become a fraction of themselves"—but the plot
elements were still gestating. Months went by and he made only
slight progress. One afternoon while waiting for inspiration to de-
scend, he was eating lunch in the Swallow, a restaurant in the
same building as the Pacific Film Archive, and he saw a headline
in the *San Francisco Chronicle* that said, "450 DEAD PETS GOING
TO NAPA VALLEY." Suddenly, he had an altogether different idea
for a film; *Nub City* would have to wait.

• • •

It was enough that in deciding to make *Gates of Heaven* Morris selected a subject that, on its surface, seemed highly likely to repel. He also insisted on making a documentary film "the opposite of how you were supposed to." That meant being static and obtrusive—using artificial light and heavy, earthbound equipment rather than the standard hand-held, mobile tools of cinema verité. After Morris hooked up with Ned Burgess, a compliant cinematographer, the making of *Gates of Heaven* progressed in a straightforward fashion. The film was shot in the spring and summer of 1977 and cost a hundred and twenty thousand dollars to make; the money came from a wealthy graduate-school classmate and from Morris's family.

Getting to know mass murderers and their relatives in Wisconsin, Morris had developed an interview technique that, reduced to basics, amounted to: Shut up and let people talk. "Listening to what people were saying wasn't even important," he says. "But it was important to *look* as if you were listening to what people were saying. Actually, listening to what people are saying, to me, interferes with looking as if you were listening to what people are saying."

The first half of *Gates of Heaven* explores the broken dream of a man named Floyd McClure, who lives in Los Altos, a peninsula town thirty miles south of San Francisco. In the opening frames, McClure describes, in a sincere but unmaudlin manner, how the accidental death of a beloved collie in his childhood inspired his vision of a pet cemetery. Choosing a site, he settled on what he calls "the most beautiful piece of land, as far as I was concerned, in the whole valley." (Never mind that the land was situated right next to a freeway; it also happened to be across the street from his house.) "A pet-cemetery business is not a fast-buck scheme, it's not a suede-shoe game," McClure says. "It's a good, solid business enterprise. And in order to have this concept it has to be in your heart, not in your billfold. And these are the type of people I wanted in business with me, in the pet-cemetery *concept*." His co-investors in the by now failed enterprise allow themselves to be interviewed, the owner of a rendering plant talks, families of departed pets have their say, Florence Rasmussen appears. Monologues tend not to parse. At one point, McClure says, "And this is the part of the inspiration of getting our little pets . . . into a cemetery. Something that we could be proud of, of saying 'My little pet did his chore here—that God has sent him to us to do a chore—love and be loved and serve his master.' And, boy, these little pets that did that . . . Like I said before—death is for the living and not for the dead."

The second half of *Gates of Heaven* focuses on the Harberts family—Cal and his wife, Scottie, and their sons, Dan and Phil —who are the proprietors of Bubbling Well Pet Memorial Park, the *final* final resting place of the displaced tenants of Floyd McClure's doomed pet-cemetery concept. Dan, the younger son, has been employed in the family business for a few years. Phil has recently given up selling insurance in Utah (his idol is W. Clement Stone, the Chicago insurance tycoon and an avatar of the Positive Mental Attitude) and has repatriated to the Napa Valley.

Cal Harberts says, "We created the Garden of Honor. And in this garden we will bury a Seeing Eye dog or a police dog killed in the line of duty at *no* cost—*if* it's killed in the line of duty. And for anybody else who wants to share this garden then we created a price which amounts to more than any other garden that we have."

Phil, who manifests what might or might not be symptoms of an incipient existential crisis—possibly a consequence of having listened to and delivered too many motivational lectures—says, "I have to say to myself: What does it mean to me? What does *this* mean to me? What is it going to mean to me? I recognize this and— A couple of things when I was instructing motivation back in Salt Lake City is that if we don't stop and ask ourselves a question once in a while to probe our subconscious or to probe our conscious . . . I used to teach it. It's a plain, simple formula. We reduced everything to a formula, memorized it, and therefore we were able to repeat it constantly. I used to call it the R2-A2 formula: Recognize, Relate, Assimilate, and put into Action! Like, I could be driving down the freeway and see a 450 SL. I could say, 'Hey, I

like that. What does that mean to me? What would I have to do
to get it? How can I do it?' And then go to work for it. And strive
for it. It kind of makes life easy. I think that's why a lot of people
don't— They get frustrated. They have emotional problems, it's
that they don't know how to cope with their—*mind.* There are three
things that I've got to do and that if anybody wants to do to be
successful, to have the desire, the want-to. Why do you go to work
in the morning? *Gee, why am I here?* Because you want to. But
that's obvious. And then the next very important ingredient is
something that a lot of people and a lot of businesses fail to delge
into. It's the activity knowledge. It would be the equation to a
mathematical problem. It would be equal to the chemist's ability
to emulsify chemicals—you know, properly, the valences. But the
knowledge of it, the whole scope. Everything in detail. And then
the third element would be, of course, the know-how or the experience. I have the inspiration to action. I don't have the activity
knowledge, but I'm getting the know-how before I'm getting the
activity knowledge. As a matter of act, I'm getting more know-how
than I'm getting activity knowledge. But they can be correlated
together. They can be overlapped."

Dan Harberts says, "As far as preparation—a hole has to be
dug, prepared. We have to make sure that the hole is going to fit
the size of the casket. Because you don't want to make it too large,
because you're going to waste space. And you don't want to make
it too small, because you can't get the thing in there."

Gates of Heaven was first shown during the 1978 New York Film
Festival, which happened to coincide with a newspaper strike. In
other words, *Gates of Heaven* sprang into a void. When the film
opened in Berkeley, that same year, a glowing review by Michael
Covino appeared in the *East Bay Express.* (Covino later retooled
the essay, and it was published in *Film Quarterly.*) More than two
years elapsed before *Gates of Heaven* was seen again, in New York
or anywhere else—before anyone paid significant attention. In the
spring of 1981, New Yorker Films arranged a limited national
distribution. The notices were favorable—in several instances,
extravagantly so. Perhaps the most ardent champion of *Gates of
Heaven* across the years has been Roger Ebert, who includes it in

his list of the ten best films of all time and calls it "compulsively watchable, a film that has engaged me as no other movie has in my twenty-one years as a movie critic." When Ebert is invited to give a speech and is told that he can screen a film of his choosing, he selects *Gates of Heaven*, which he regards as "a film about hope—hope held by the loneliest people who have ever been on film." Ebert estimates that he has seen it at least fifty times—often enough to have memorized long passages. "Every time I show this, it plays differently," he says. "Some people think it's about animals. Some people think it's about life and death. I've shown it to a group of bankers, who believe it raises all kinds of questions about success, about starting a small business. People think it's funny or sad or deadpan or satirical. They think that Errol Morris loved the people in the film, or that he was being very cruel to them. I've never yet had a person tell me that it's a bad film or a film that doesn't interest them."

Werner Herzog commemorated the Berkeley première of *Gates of Heaven* by eating one of his shoes—a poached desert boot—in a public ceremony. Though less spectacular than flinging oneself upon a cactus, this event was sufficiently momentous for the documentary filmmaker Les Blank to record it in a twenty-minute short titled *Werner Herzog Eats His Shoe*. A haze of myth enshrouds the genesis of the shoe-eating. Tom Luddy's version has Herzog, while one day arguing with Morris in a hallway of the Pacific Film Archive, saying, "You'll never make a film, but if you do I'll come and eat my shoe at the première." Herzog maintains that it happened in a more encouraging manner, as in "You are going to make a film. And the day I am going to see the film in a theater I will eat the shoes I am wearing." Morris, who claims not to recall any of the above, says the entire stunt was concocted by Luddy.

"I didn't make *Gates of Heaven* so that Werner Herzog would have to eat his shoe," he says. "It's not as if I decided to realize my potential as a human being in order to get somebody to ingest something distasteful. I specifically asked Werner *not* to eat his shoe." Morris was supposed to fly from New York to Berkeley to attend the screening and to appear in Les Blank's film. At Kennedy Airport, he boarded a plane, but when a mechanical problem forced all the passengers to get off he decided not to go. "As a result, I don't appear in *Werner Herzog Eats His Shoe*," he says. "I suppose I regret that reticence. Why be so prissy? Why try so hard to control things? I'm not even sure what that's all about. Probably, as a result of my petulant behavior, fewer people have seen *Gates of Heaven* than otherwise would have. In fact, I'm still surprised when anyone tells me he's seen it."

In the winter of 1979, Morris went back to Vernon, Florida, and for very little money he was able to rent one of the biggest houses in the county. Vernon was no less xenophobic than any other small southern town. When the locals asked Morris why he had come there and he gave vague, misleading answers, the typical response was "No, you're here because of the Nub City stuff." He spent much of his time attending revival meetings and driving around to places that had interesting names—Blackhead, Lizard Lake, the Ebro Dog Track. Although he was still enamored of the Nub City idea, he had not yet written a workable screenplay. If he were to try to make a nonfiction film about the Nub City episode, "it would turn into one of those bad investigative documentaries where people are slamming doors in your face." Finally, after several months of insisting "I'm not here about Nub City, I'm not making a film about Nub City," guilt overwhelmed him, he indeed became incapable of making a film about Nub City, and he left town.

A year later, he returned, rented the same big house, and spun his wheels some more. Now, however, vacillation carried a steeper price tag, because he had financial help from German television and from WNET, the public-television affiliate in New York. A crew of recent graduates from the New York University film school drove to Vernon in a rented van, bringing with them equipment so heavy that the van blew out two sets of tires on the drive south. When they arrived, Morris had still not decided what the film would be about. A controversy had arisen involving the firing and rehiring of one of the local police officers. Morris felt that the officer's travails were connected with "the Napoleonic ambitions of the king of the nubbies." The king of the nubbies had advised Morris to

leave town within twenty-four hours or leave in a casket. When
Morris failed to oblige, the king made what seemed a sincere effort
to run down Ned Burgess, the cinematographer, with a truck. More
or less in desperation—to get the king of the nubbies off his back,
to give the public-television people something, *anything*, for their
money—Morris began to film interviews with various interesting
citizens of Vernon, among them Roscoe Collins, the cop; Joe Payne,
the collector of wild animals (opossum, gopher, tortoise, rattlesnake); Albert Bitterling, the cosmologist with the opera glasses
("Reality—you mean, *this* is the real world? Ha, ha, ha. I never
thought of that"); George Harris and Claude Register, two geezers
who discuss how an acquaintance put a shotgun to his forehead
and pulled the trigger with his big toe ("And he said, that day, he
says, 'That'll be the last thing I ever do is to shoot myself.' Which
it was"). *Vernon, Florida* contains not a single reference to Nub
City. Rather, as with *Gates of Heaven*, the film's subjects are the
American vernacular and the malleability of truth. Morris presents
Vernon, Florida, as is—no special effects, what you see is what
you get—as if he had stumbled across, and without editorial in-
trusion had agreed to share, an unexplored settlement full of Florence Rasmussens.

Howard Pettis, the worm farmer, says, "I've never studied
no book on these wigglers. What I know about 'em is just self-
experience. They got books on 'em, but them books is wrong. They
don't teach you right. They don't teach you right on 'em. Teach
you what kind of feed to feed 'em. How to do 'em and all, there.
And it's all wrong, in my book." Henry Shipes, the turkey hunter
("I can't tell you how it feel. It's just a hell of a sport, that's all"),
sits in a chair in his living room and, with enormous relish, recounts
the gut-stirring thrills of each of a series of trophy kills. While the
viewer is not prohibited from imputing deep meanings to the images
or the monologues of Henry Shipes, one ultimately gets the feeling
that if turkey hunting stands as a metaphor for anything it is probably turkey hunting. In the film's final scene, Henry Shipes, on a
hunt, surveys a crowd of buzzards roosting on a cypress tree and
counts them aloud—thirty-five. "Listen to that sound," he says.
"That *fwoop fwoop*. Hear that sound? Getting in and out of the
trees? That flop-flop sound? Mmm-hmm. That sound'll sure mistake

you for turkeys. Listen! Hear that flop-flop? Limbs breaking. Hear
that good flop then? Listening to that gives me the *turkey fever.*
Mmm-hmm. I wish there's as many turkeys as there are buzzards."

Like *Gates of Heaven, Vernon* had its première at the New York
Film Festival—the 1981 edition. Werner Herzog called it "an
invention of cinema, a discovery of one side of cinema that all of
us have not known yet." A review in *Newsweek* said it
was "a film as odd and mysterious as its subjects, and quite
unforgettable"—unforgettable, that is, for those who laid eyes on
it. Because it had a running time of only sixty minutes, no national
distributor materialized, and not until the summer of 1982, when
it was shown on public television, did significant numbers of viewers or critics take notice. Meanwhile, Morris was, as usual, low
on funds. He was living in Manhattan, occupying rooms in a series
of not quite elegant hotels—the Carter, the Bryant, the Edison,
the Wellington—before finally settling in a building in the West
Fifties, where he still keeps an apartment. The more dire his fiscal
circumstances grew, the better he got to know a Mr. Montori, an
employee of a collection agency. Mr. Montori seemed to derive
pleasure from gracing Morris's telephone-answering machine with
one-a-day rhetorical questions like "Mr. Morris, have you no sense
of shame?" and "Mr. Morris, were you really brought up to act
this way?" Then the calls abruptly ceased. After several months
had passed, Morris phoned the collection agency, asked "Is Mr.
Montori O.K.?," and learned that his tormentor had moved on to
a more rewarding position elsewhere.

In earnest, Morris sought backing for what turned out to be some
of his most resistible film projects: *Road,* the story of the northern
Minnesota interstate-highway folly; Robert K. Golka, the laser-
induced-fireball wizard in Utah; Centralia, Pennsylvania, the coal
town where an inextinguishable subterranean fire began burning
in 1962. Morris concluded that "people who tend to be interested
in documentary filmmaking weren't interested in my films, because
they didn't look like documentary films." The theme of *Road,* in
particular—a man wants to create a complicated and expensive
thing for which absolutely no need exists—was, he says, "dis-
turbingly self-reflective."

As his debts accumulated, his stepfather advised him that the time had come to "turn yourself in to the phone company." Instead, Morris permitted himself a brief Hollywood interlude. In 1983, Edward Pressman, a producer whose credits include films by Brian De Palma, Terrence Malick, and Oliver Stone, agreed to finance the development of a screenplay about the exploits of John and Jim Pardue, brothers from Missouri who, fifteen years earlier, had killed their father, their grandmother, and two accomplices and robbed five banks, in two instances using dynamite. Pitching the film, Morris would say, "The great bank-robbery sprees always take place at a time when something is going wrong in the country. Bonnie and Clyde were apolitical, but it's impossible to imagine them without the Depression as a backdrop. The Pardue brothers were apolitical, but it's impossible to imagine them without Vietnam." Pressman underwrote a sojourn at the Chateau Marmont, a Hollywood hotel that is famous in part because John Belushi died there (not because Errol Morris wrote anything memorable while in residence). Morris enlisted Tom Waits and Mickey Rourke to portray the Pardue brothers, and got as far as writing a treatment before the project derailed.

Next, Morris was set to direct a Pressman film called *The King Lives*, about an Elvis Presley impersonator; this venture proceeded not very far before Morris was fired. For Dino De Laurentiis, Morris agreed to work on an adaptation of a Stephen King short story. Then De Laurentiis changed his mind and asked him to adapt a different King short story. Then he changed his mind again and gave Morris two and a half weeks to write a screenplay based on King's "Cycle of the Werewolf." Around the time that De Laurentiis rejected the script—because it "wasn't frightening enough"—Morris's brother and only sibling, Noel, died suddenly of a heart attack, at age forty. "I was very depressed," Morris says. His apartment in Manhattan was a couple of blocks from the Ed Sullivan Theater, from whose studios fund-raising telethons were often broadcast. He found himself dropping in. "My favorite was the Stop Arthritis Telethon," he says. "When I would go to these things, I would always see the same people in the audience, and I'd look upon them with some pity, and then I realized that I was one of them."

In 1984, Morris married Julia Sheehan, an art historian, whom he had met in Wisconsin in the mid-seventies, during his Ed Gein phase. Julia had tried to get a friend to introduce them, but the friend "made such a mess of it I actually approached Errol to apologize," she says. "I wanted to meet him because I'd heard he had been interviewing murderers. I didn't know anyone else who knew any murderers. It was quiet in Wisconsin—the sixties were over, not much was going on—so somebody who had met murderers sounded good." Morris recalls saying to her, early in their relationship, "I was talking to a mass murderer but I was thinking of you," and immediately fearing that this might not have sounded affectionate. Julia, however, was flattered: "I thought, really, that was one of the nicest things anyone ever said to me. It was hard to go out with other guys after that." They share a vivid and fond memory of their wedding, which took place in the Criminal Court Building in Brooklyn.

"They frisked us on the way in, which was very romantic," Julia says.

"We got married between two prostitution cases," Morris says. "And we celebrated with a whale-shaped cake from Carvel."

They have since become the parents of Nathaniel Hamilton Morris, and Julia has come to understand her husband well. Some time ago, she stopped in at the Strand Bookstore to pick up an order for him. The clerk who was helping her couldn't find the books and asked whether she knew the subject matter. "I don't know any of the titles," she said. "But they're probably about either insanity or murder or Nazis." Indeed, there was one of each.

"The Nazis, of course, are interesting to me," Morris once told me. "I just finished reading Joseph Goebbels' diary. You know a movie director Goebbels really liked? Frank Capra. I have this heartwarming image of Goebbels sneaking away from the office in midafternoon to go watch *Meet John Doe* or *Mr. Deeds Goes to Town.*"

What Morris likes to call his "predilections" led him, in early 1985, to Dr. James Grigson, a Dallas psychiatrist. Under Texas law, a jury cannot impose the death penalty unless it is confident that a convicted person will commit future violent crimes. To encourage juries to arrive at that conclusion, Dr. Grigson for more than fifteen years regularly appeared as a prosecution witness in capital cases. In almost every instance, Dr. Grigson would, after examining a defendant, testify that he had found the individual in question to be an incurable sociopath, who it was "one hundred per cent certain" would kill again. When Morris first went to see Dr. Grigson, it was with the idea of making a film titled *Dr. Death*. Grigson proved to be as obliging to Morris as he had been to the prosecutors he served, and encouraged him to interview several men who, helped along by Dr. Grigson's testimony, had received the death penalty. Don't be surprised if these fellows profess their innocence, Dr. Grigson warned; that, after all, is how sociopaths behave.

A number of the twenty-five or so inmates with whom Morris spoke made such a claim. One was a thirty-six-year-old man named Randall Dale Adams, who was an inmate of the Eastham Unit, a maximum-security prison in southeast Texas. In the spring of 1977, Adams had been convicted of and sentenced to die for the murder, the previous fall, of Robert Wood, a Dallas police officer. Wood has been shot five times by the driver of a car that he and his partner, Teresa Turko, had stopped in west Dallas for a minor traffic violation. Nearly a month elapsed between the murder of Wood and Adams' arrest. Adams told Morris that he had been framed, and that the actual killer was David Harris—"the kid," he kept calling him during that first conversation—who had been the principal prosecution witness at Adams' trial. Morris had not gone to Texas with the purpose of finding and becoming an advocate for innocent incarcerated men; he had gone there because of his fascination with Dr. Grigson. He didn't really believe the story Adams told him, because he had no particular reason to believe it. Nevertheless, he went to Austin three weeks later and read the transcripts of several trials. A number of passages in the Adams transcript aroused the possibility that Adams was telling the truth. After Morris met David Harris, two weeks later, in a bar outside Beaumont, his doubts about Adams' guilt and his curiosity about the case deepened.

This came at a time when Morris's film career was in another lull. Suzanne Weil, then the head of programming for the Public Broadcasting System and a generous believer in Morris and his work, had arranged a grant sufficient for him to begin his research on *Dr. Death*. (She once told me, "Errol is the one person in the world who, if he now came to me and said, 'I want to make a documentary titled *My Grandmother Remembers* or *So-and-So: Potter of the Southwest*,' I would tell, 'Go ahead.' ") Morris's main source of income at that point was free-lance employment with a private detective agency that specialized in Wall Street securities and commodities cases. Most of the agency's referrals came from law firms.

"When I worked as a detective, I felt like this well-paid conceptual cleaning lady for lawyers," he has said. "It's like— There seems to be hair clogging the drain. My job was to clean it out and find out if it was really hair. I had one particular problem: people would start talking to me and when I'd leave I often couldn't remember what they had said. I wanted to use a tape recorder, but my employer was totally opposed. So I worried about whether I was getting valuable information. I also worried about getting stains on my clothes—I had to wear suits all the time. Because I couldn't use a tape recorder, my most important piece of equipment was my can of K2r spot remover."

The owner of the detective agency, who prefers anonymity, told me that what he valued most about Morris was his talent as a listener—the talent that has served him so effectively as a filmmaker. What happened next was that Morris began to employ in his film work certain skills he was honing as a detective. As a "director-detective"—a phrase Morris used to describe himself when he was promoting *The Thin Blue Line*—not the least of his accomplishments was cultivating Henry Wade, for thirty-six years the District Attorney of Dallas County. Instead of handling the Adams prosecution himself, Wade assigned it to Douglas Mulder, one of his most experienced assistants. After gaining access to the files in Wade's office, Morris became convinced that Mulder had seriously tampered with the truth and that Adams had received anything but a fair trial.

Randall Adams and David Harris met by chance the morning before Officer Wood was killed. Adams had run out of gas and was walking along a road in west Dallas when Harris, a sixteen-year-old with an extensive criminal record, driving a car that he had stolen in his home town of Vidor, Texas, pulled over and offered to help him refill the tank. They spent the rest of the day, a Saturday, together—bumming around a shopping mall, drinking beer, visiting pawnshops, shooting pool, smoking marijuana. That evening, they ended up at a drive-in theater that featured two soft-core-porn movies. Officer Wood was shot at twelve-thirty Sunday morning—almost three hours after Harris, according to Adams' testimony, had dropped him off at the motel where he was living. That became Adams' alibi: he was home asleep when the crime was committed.

Teresa Turko proved to be a poor eyewitness to the slaying of her patrol partner, and gave an inaccurate description of the car that the killer had been driving. The first break in the case came because David Harris, back in Vidor, told several friends that he had killed a policeman in Dallas. After being arrested and leading the Vidor police to the murder weapon, a .22-caliber handgun that belonged to his father, Harris was turned over to the Dallas police. At this point, he changed his story and said that he had only been bragging—that the real killer was a hitch-hiker he had picked up and spent the day with. Which is how Adams, who had no prior criminal record, came to be charged with murder.

Initially, Adams was represented by Edith James, a lawyer whose criminal-trial experience included no homicide-defense work. She brought in as co-counsel a general practitioner named Dennis White. In one of White's previous head-to-heads with Doug Mulder, things had ended badly for his clients—two brothers named Ransonette who had made the mistake of kidnapping the daughter-in-law of a Dallas newspaper publisher. At the sentencing hearing in that case, White argued that the victim had not been harmed by her captors, and suggested a lenient prison term of five years. The prosecution mentioned a term of five thousand years. The jury, aspiring to Solomonic wisdom, said, in effect, "O.K. Let's compromise," and sentenced each defendant to five thousand and five years. Dennis White was simply no match for Doug Mulder, who is said to have once boasted, "Anybody can convict a guilty man. It takes talent to convict an innocent man."

Testifying during Adams' trial, David Harris offered a chronology of the events surrounding the murder that varied from Adams' version by approximately two and a half hours. Adams and Harris agreed that they had left the drive-in theater during a movie called *Swinging Cheerleaders*. Mulder elicited from Harris testimony that their departure had occurred shortly after midnight; Adams said they left around nine-thirty. In the D.A.'s files, Morris discovered a memorandum from Mulder's own chief investigator stating that there had been no late showing of *Swinging Cheerleaders* that night and that the final feature had ended shortly after ten o'clock.

This was the sort of serious defect in Harris's version of the facts that Mulder apparently had no intention of allowing to interfere with his prosecution of Adams—who, at twenty-eight, was eligible for capital punishment, whereas Harris, at sixteen, was not. It was also, unfortunately, the sort of discrepancy that Adams' attorneys failed to make clear to the jury. Nor were Edith James and Dennis White prepared when Mulder produced three mysterious witnesses, all of whom testified that they had driven past the scene of the crime moments before Officer Wood was murdered and that Randall Adams was in the driver's seat—the position from which the shots were fired. The three witnesses, Emily Miller, Robert Miller, and Michael Randell, all of whom were aware of a five-figure reward for information leading to the conviction of the killer, appeared in court on a Friday and impressed the jury. White, outmaneuvered by Mulder's strategy of presenting his "eyewitnesses" during the rebuttal phase rather than as part of his case-in-chief, conducted an ineffectual cross-examination. That weekend, White received a call from a woman named Elba Carr, who knew Emily and Robert Miller and expressed the opinion that "Emily Miller had never told the truth in her life." When, back in court the following Monday, White asked to question the Millers and Michael Randell further, Mulder told the judge that all three had left town or were otherwise unreachable. Actually, all three witnesses were still in Dallas. The Millers, in fact, were ensconced in the Alamo Plaza Motel as guests of Dallas County. Not until nine years later, when Morris came along and found in the District Attorney's files bills for phone calls that the Millers had made from the Alamo Plaza, did Mulder's role in this apparent deception become evident.

Toward the end of *The Thin Blue Line*, Errol Morris asks David Harris, "Would you say that Adams is a pretty unlucky fellow?" and Harris responds, "Definitely—if it wasn't for bad luck, he wouldn't have had none." Ironically, of course, Harris's reply is accurate only up to the moment when Morris met Adams. Not only did Morris discover important evidence in the prosecution's files; he discovered the absence of some important documents—specifically, the official record of a police lineup at which, according to Emily Miller's trial testimony, she had positively identified Randall Adams. Most significantly, Morris tracked down the three rebuttal witnesses themselves and persuaded them to appear on film. Emily Miller, a bleached blonde, whose childhood ambition was to be a detective or the wife of a detective, told Morris that she had failed to identify Adams in the lineup but that a policeman had told her the correct suspect, "so that I wouldn't make that mistake again." Robert Miller told him, "I really didn't see anything." Michael Randell, who had testified in 1977 that he was on his way home from playing basketball when he drove past the murder scene, told Morris that in fact he had spent that evening in an adulterous endeavor and that he was drunk "out of my mind." Each of the state's rebuttal witnesses, it therefore appeared, had committed damaging perjury. Putting David Harris on film posed a significant challenge. The first interview appointment, Morris says, Harris missed "because he was off killing somebody"—Mark Walter Mays, a Beaumont citizen, whose apartment Harris had broken into, and whose girlfriend he had abducted. Another interview had to be postponed when Harris tried to use Morris in an escape attempt from the jail where he was awaiting trial for these crimes. The climactic interview finally took place in the Lou Sterret Jail, in Dallas, by which time Harris had been convicted and sentenced to death for the Mays murder, and it included this exchange:

MORRIS: Is he [Adams] innocent?
HARRIS: Did you ask him?
MORRIS: Well, he's always said he's been innocent.
HARRIS: There you go. Didn't believe him, huh? Criminals always lie.
MORRIS: Well, what do you think about whether or not he's innocent?
HARRIS: I'm sure he is.
MORRIS: How can you be sure?
HARRIS: Because I'm the one that knows.

On a straightforward, realistic level, *The Thin Blue Line* is the story of how Adams got railroaded, the story of an innocent man wrongly accused. Its aura, however, is that of a dreadful fantasy, a mixture of the ghastly and the absurd. By any standard, it breaches the conventional definition of "documentary." Tom Luddy has said that *The Thin Blue Line* illustrates Morris's belief that cinema verité is "too mundane—that there is a way to heighten the structure of the facts." To accomplish this, Morris combines straight interviews—his unblinking talking-heads technique, from *Gates of Heaven* and *Vernon, Florida*—with artful restagings of certain incidents. The restaged episodes correspond to conflicting versions of "the facts" proposed by the people who appear in the interviews. Also, inserted throughout the film are closeups—of a gun, a mouth and a straw, a milkshake spilling, popcorn popping—that have a fetishistic quality, an exaggerated objectivity (evidence of Morris's passion for film noir). The *Rashomon*-like result is something considerably creepier than the cold-blooded murder that *The Thin Blue Line* explores.

The day before the interview with Harris, which took place December 5, 1986, Morris appeared in the courtroom of John Tolle, a federal magistrate in Dallas, who was presiding over a habeas-corpus hearing—an effort by Adams to win a new trial. In addition to Morris's oral testimony, unedited footage from his interviews with the prosecution witnesses became part of the court record. Watching these interviews—either unedited or as they appear in

the final cut of *The Thin Blue Line*—one marvels at Morris's ability
to win the confidence of so many people so prone to self-incrimination. On film, the witnessess against Adams seem to suffer collectively from the actor's nightmare—an instinctive fear of silence,
terror at the thought of forgetting one's lines. Talking to Morris,
they manage to discredit themselves thoroughly.

Under oath in Magistrate Tolle's courtroom, however, Emily
Miller and Michael Randell tried to recant their statements to the
filmmaker. Among the questions raised by Adams' habeas-corpus
motion were: Had Adams been denied due process because he had
not been effectively represented by his attorneys during his original
trial, because of certain evidence that was illegally withheld from
the jury during that trial, and because in 1980, when the United
States Supreme Court overturned his death sentence (on a technical
point involving jury selection), he received from the governor of
Texas a commutation of the death sentence to life imprisonment
rather than a new trial?

Morris returned to Magistrate Tolle's courtroom a month later,
for the second, and last, day of the habeas-corpus hearing. Doug
Mulder, by now a highly successful defense attorney, testified,
responding to unwelcome questions from Adams' appellate lawyer,
Randy Schaffer, with mumbled replies and lapses of memory. As
the hearing ended, reason dictated that the magistrate would rule
on Adams' petition within a few weeks. Tolle, however, turned out
to be an even more gifted procrastinator than Morris. The New
York Film Festival committee had expressed interest in showing
The Thin Blue Line in September of 1987, but Morris failed to
meet the deadline. Finally, on March 18, 1988, *The Thin Blue
Line* had its première, at the San Francisco Film Festival. Morris
appeared to be in buoyant spirits that day, and I asked him what
he expected to do after the screening. "Oh, I imagine the usual
lithium treatments," he said. "Followed by a period of hospitali-
zation." A month later, *The Thin Blue Line* led off the USA Film
Festival, in Dallas. Magistrate Tolle had yet to be heard from. Two
more weeks passed—sixteen months had elapsed since the conclusion of the habeas-corpus hearing—and Tolle at last rendered
his judgment: "All relief requested . . . denied." As far as Morris's

role in the case was concerned, Tolle wrote, "much could be said about those videotape interviews, but nothing that would have any bearing on the matter before this court."

A week later, Randy Schaffer filed a motion asking that Tolle's opinion be set aside, because an astonishing fact had come to light: In the spring of 1977, on the heels of Adams' conviction for the murder of Officer Wood, Dennis White had filed a five-million-dollar lawsuit against Doug Mulder and Henry Wade, alleging that the District Attorney's conduct during the trial had violated the defendant's civil rights. John Tolle then worked in the civil division of the Dallas County District Attorney's office. White's suit had been briskly dismissed by a federal judge. After the screening at the USA Film Festival, Dennis White mentioned to Morris that he recalled Tolle's having been involved in the 1977 civil suit. The records of that litigation were dredged from a file, and, sure enough, John Tolle's name was all over them: John Tolle had triumphantly represented Mulder and Wade. Somehow, not quite ten years later, Magistrate Tolle had decided that this coincidence did not disqualify him from rendering an opinion on Adams' habeas-corpus petition. Rather, he had chosen to hear the case, and had then sat on it for seventeen months before eventually ruling, in effect, in favor of his former client. The embarrassing revelation of Tolle's conflict of interest forced him to withdraw his recommendation; thus, an additional year and a half of Adams' life had been consumed by a proceeding that ultimately yielded irrelevance. Rather than start all over again in federal court, before a different magistrate, Schaffer decided to formally withdraw the writ and refile it in state court, citing new evidence that Adams had never received a fair trial.

Officer Robert Wood was murdered Thanksgiving weekend in 1976. Twelve years later almost to the day, Adams and his attorneys returned to the room where he had been convicted of the murder and handed a death sentence—Criminal District Court No. 2, on the fourth floor of the Dallas County Courthouse. By Texas statute, the judge who presides at a trial—in this instance, District Judge

Don Metcalfe, whose evidentiary rulings against Adams formed part of the basis for the writ—also presides at any subsequent appellate-writ hearing. Adams' bad luck, while consistent, was not absolute, however, and Metcalfe had since left the bench. In 1984, he was succeeded by Larry W. Baraka, a respected former prosecutor and defense attorney, whose special distinction is that he is the only member of the Texas judiciary who is black, a Muslim, and a Republican.

On the eve of the hearing, I had a phone conversation with Morris. In New York the previous day, he told me, his secretary had taken a call from a stranger who said, "An important message for Errol Morris: Stay away from the hearing in Dallas on Wednesday. You might disappear"—a forewarning that brought to mind his experience in Vernon, Florida, a decade earlier, where, he had been informed, unfortunate people had a tendency to "just disappear."

"My stepfather told my wife I should wear two bulletproof vests, so that one covers the seams of the other," he continued. "I don't mind a death threat, as such, but I do mind the idea of disappearing. That's like the 'delete' button on your personal computer—'We deleted that character.' Disappearing suggests a whole set of unsavory possibilities."

As it turned out, I couldn't be in Dallas the opening day of the writ hearing, and thereby missed a memorable striptease by David Harris. Testifying for three hours, Harris said that he had been alone in a stolen car and in possession of a stolen gun when Wood pulled him over. In a videotaped interview that was introduced as evidence, he said that he had had his finger on the trigger as Wood approached him. Judge Baraka, no quibbler, announced, "As far as the court is concerned, he's in fact telling me he did it." Randy Schaffer read aloud a letter from Harris to his mother, written in September, 1988—just two months earlier—that said, "It seems like my whole life is surrounded by 'wrongs' of some kind and it seems like I've never done the right thing when I could and should have. Absolving Randall Dale Adams of any guilt is a difficult thing for me to do, but I must try to do so because he is innocent. That is the truth."

Next, Schaffer called Teresa Turko, Robert Wood's patrol partner, as a witness. He wanted to make plain to the judge that Turko's
initial description of the killer, recorded immediately after the
shooting, differed measurably from the one she had offered at
Adams' trial. Dennis White had not cross-examined Turko about
the first statement, because, in violation of a cardinal principle of
criminal-trial procedure, Mulder had not given him a copy. Nor
would the document have come to light, of course, if Morris had
not insinuated himself into the Dallas District Attorney's good
graces and scrutinized Mulder's old files.

When I caught up with Morris, at the end of the first day of the
hearing, his mood was upbeat but not entirely sanguine. The drama
of Harris's confession notwithstanding, it did not, in a technical
sense, really help Adams. In Texas, evidence of innocence is
insufficient to win a new trial. What Schaffer had to prove was that
Adams' original trial had been "unfair" on constitutional grounds.
Even if Baraka were to grant Adams' writ, his ruling would have
the effect only of a recommendation to the Texas Court of Criminal
Appeals, a nine-judge panel, which in 1977 had unanimously
upheld Adams' conviction. Harris's testimony was useful, however,
in bolstering some of the other claims in the writ—most significantly, that Harris and Mulder had an understanding in 1977
whereby in exchange for testimony against Adams unresolved criminal charges against Harris in another county would be dropped.
(Under cross-examination at the original trial, Harris had insisted
that no quid pro quo existed—an avowal that Mulder has always
maintained. Further harm to Adams was done when Judge Metcalfe
refused even to allow into evidence the fact that Harris had such
charges pending.)

Randall Adams wore the same outfit to court all three days of
the hearing—a bright-orange jumpsuit with "DALLAS COUNTY JAIL"
in black block letters stencilled on the back; leg irons; and handcuffs, which were attached to a chain around his waist. When
Adams was escorted into the courtroom on Day Two, Morris had
already arrived and taken a seat in the front row of the spectator
section, between Adams' mother, Mildred, and his two sisters,
Nancy Bapst and Mary Baugess. Two of Mildred Adams' sisters

and their husbands had also come to Dallas for the hearing. George
Preston, a lawyer who was assisting Randy Schaffer, leaned across
a low partition that separated the spectators from the business end
of the courtroom and showed Morris a printed sheet of paper,
portions of which had been highlighted in yellow.

"This is from the Bar Association code," he said. "It regards
tampering with witnesses and suppression of evidence."

"I'd like a copy of that," Morris said.

"Our Xerox machine broke, so I had to tear this page out of the
book," Preston said.

"That page must have been missing from Doug Mulder's copy,
too," Morris said.

The first witness on Day Two was Emily Miller. Randy Schaffer
expected to score several points while she was on the stand: her
failure to identify Adams in a lineup; the intervention of the Dallas
policeman, who then pointed out to her the "right" suspect; her
subsequent perjury regarding her performance at the lineup; and
evidence that, like David Harris, she had struck an implicit deal
with Mulder—specifically, her testimony against Adams in exchange for the dismissal of an outstanding robbery charge against
her daughter.

A week after the murder of Robert Wood, at which time a twenty-
thousand-dollar reward was being offered for information leading
to the arrest and conviction of the killer, Emily Miller had given
a formal statement to the Dallas police. According to what she saw
while driving past the crime scene moments before the shooting,
the suspect was "either a Mexican or a very light-skinned black
man." That this description would divert suspicion from Adams,
an auburn-haired Caucasian, perhaps explains why Mulder never
showed the statement to Adams' attorneys. By the time of Adams'
trial, Emily Miller's description of the killer had metamorphosed
so that it matched the defendant. In Judge Baraka's courtroom,
when Schaffer presented Emily Miller with a copy of her original
statement she said that she had left her eyeglasses at home and
couldn't read it. When Schaffer then read it to her and proceeded
through a barbed interrogation, she said, "I don't remember nothing
that happened back then. Specifics, I don't remember who asked

me what or who said what or who did what. That was twelve years ago."

As far as the officer who had coached her at the police lineup was concerned, she said, "I didn't base nothing I said on anything anybody told me. It was what I seen. And I'm sorry I ever seen it."

"You're not the only one, I'm sure," Schaffer replied.

The subject of Errol Morris and his filmed interview with Emily Miller arose.

The witness turned to the judge and said, "May I get this clear on this videotape? This man [Morris] came to my house and told me that he was going to make a movie. . . . They were kicking it around in their heads about making a movie about the police shooting in Dallas. So I said O.K. He said, well, it would be interesting because, he said, 'In the first place, you're married to a black man.' This was his exact words. And I said, 'Well.' And he said, 'Do you mind? We're not sure we're going to film or anything. We're just going to kick it around.' And I said, 'Well, I don't exactly remember how everything went down back then.' And he said, 'Well, what the heck, it's just a movie, you know?' He said, 'Anything you don't remember . . . I'll remember for you.' Well, this went on . . . The movie wasn't accurate. It wasn't, you know . . . I went along because he said what the heck, it's a movie. . . . He . . . tried to make me look like trash."

During a recess, several reporters approached Morris—the courtroom was filled to capacity most of the three days of the hearing—and asked about Emily Miller's accusations. He pointed out that she had described the precise antithesis of his well-established interviewing style—his let-'em-talk-until-the-truth-flows technique —and he offered to roll the tape of the full interview for anyone who was interested. "She spoke extemporaneously, at length, without coaching, prodding, or interruption by me," he said. "It's quite clear that Emily Miller has no credibility."

Nevertheless, Emily Miller had accomplished something oddly significant: she had introduced the idea that *The Thin Blue Line* was a corrupt document. Months earlier, a reporter for *The Dallas Morning News* had said to Morris, "You know, Errol, there are two sides to every story," and he had replied, "Yeah, the truth and falsehood." Much as he still believed that about the Adams case, he also understood the mythology that attaches to movies, and he understood that in the iconography of this courtroom proceeding *The Thin Blue Line* had acquired a taint, as if it were some soiled version of the truth. Errol Morris, seated in the front row of the spectator section, wearing a blue plaid jacket, chinos, a white shirt, and a red paisley necktie, repeatedly heard himself referred to as "a filmmaker from New York"—a phrase chock-full of unflattering connotations. The word "movie" was chock-full of connotations. Robert Wood was dead, and Randall Adams had spent twelve years behind bars—those were virtually the only remaining unassailable truths. Almost every intervening fact had been tampered with by the police or lawyers or mysteriously motivated witnesses. In the immediate context, Randall Adams, in his jumpsuit, handcuffs, and leg irons, seated mutely with his back to the spectators, seemed more relevant to the proceeding than Robert Wood but less relevant than Errol Morris.

Other witnesses went out of their way to impugn Morris—most notably Gus Rose, a former homicide detective, whom Adams described in *The Thin Blue Line* as having pulled a gun on him during one interrogation session. Rose had come to court as the District Attorney's witness. During the direct examination by Leslie McFarlane, the appellate lawyer assigned to represent the Dallas County District Attorney, he made several statements that had Morris squirming in his seat and whispering to me things like "Don't these people get embarrassed lying? After all, this is only a man who was sentenced to death." Rose complained that Morris had misrepresented his intentions in soliciting an interview and then had been argumentative during the interview. "You should *hear* this interview," Morris said to me. "I'm barely present." When Rose testified that Adams had never denied murdering Robert Wood, Morris seethed, "That's a lie. He told me on film that Adams had denied it. This is all lies, lies, lies."

During cross-examination, Schaffer gave Rose reason to regret this particular portion of his testimony. Holding a transcript of *The Thin Blue Line*—proof of Rose's failure to keep his own story straight—Schaffer stood at the detective's side and read a passage in which Rose recalled that Adams, shortly after his arrest, "almost overacted his innocence." A hubbub arose in the spectator section, not unlike the inevitable moment when Perry Mason's assistant, Paul Drake, shows up with a previously elusive piece of physical evidence. A bearded man seated two rows behind Morris suddenly produced a videocassette of *The Thin Blue Line*, and Morris relayed it to George Preston, who passed it to Schaffer, who was able to taunt Rose with it, asking whether he wanted to see a moving picture of himself uttering words directly at odds with the testimony he had just given.

Trapped, Rose turned to Judge Baraka and said, "Your Honor, if the question is do I want to see the film the answer is no, I do not want to see the film or anything Errol Morris has anything to do with."

Baraka called a recess for lunch. In the hallway, I passed Mildred Adams, Randall's mother. A tall, broad-shouldered woman with light-blue eyes, blue-gray hair, and a beauty-shop permanent, Mrs. Adams was standing in a bath of bright light, being interviewed by a television reporter, saying not for the first or the last time, "If Dallas County will just admit that they made a mistake and let that boy come home . . ."

One evening, I went to the Dallas County jail to have a conversation with Randall Adams. I rode an elevator to the eighth floor of the courthouse building, signed in, presented a guard with a letter from Randy Schaffer authorizing my visit, and was directed to a pinkish-beige room about twice the size of a prison cell, along one wall of which was a row of telephone receivers and thick six-by-twelve-inch windows. Adams, standing on the opposite side of the wall and holding two adjacent receivers—one to each ear—was concluding a conversation with Nancy Bapst and Mary Baugess, his sisters. A black woman who had three children with her was talking on one of the other phones. When Nancy Bapst handed me her receiver, a wall clock said 8:45—which meant that we didn't have long before the visiting hour would expire.

Adams and I discussed Randy Schaffer's aggressive style ("I need somebody who can intimidate. That's what you need") and Doug Mulder, who was scheduled to testify the next morning ("I know what those people did to me, but I have no personal animosity toward them"), and then I turned the subject to Errol Morris.

"If it wasn't for him . . . I sat down there in Huntsville and this man listened to me—I was pleading for somebody and this man listened," Adams began, in a flat voice, which, although it originated only a couple of feet away, sounded distant and disembodied, as if it had traveled through water. "Errol Morris, when I talked to him, I talked to him for one purpose and one purpose only: for the investigation of my case, whether good or bad. I told him, 'Whatever you want to do—you can dig into my closet if you will allow me to look at whatever you turn up.' I knew what these people had done to me, but I couldn't prove it. Randy Schaffer and Mel Bruder [another appellate lawyer], they didn't know. The only one who knew was Dennis White, but he was shook up entirely and he was devastated. I agreed to talk to Errol Morris on the condition that he would share with me what he found out. I like to call Errol the Easter Bunny. I needed somebody to gather up all these facts and put them in one basket. He went and did his investigative work, and everything we're doing now is because of what he did with his investigation of the facts. That is what *The Thin Blue Line* did for me."

The next morning, Doug Mulder gave a poised and self-assured courtroom performance. As Leslie McFarlane lobbed him across-the-letters questions, Mulder, a handsome man in his late forties with a squarish face, not much of a neck, and a stocky, athletic build, effortlessly swatted them out of the ballpark.

McFarlane: "Everything that you discovered and everything that you reviewed in preparation for this case indicates Adams' guilt, is that correct? . . . Did you find anything inconsistent with that?"

Mulder: "Nothing that comes to mind, no."

Schaffer, when his turn arrived, proved somewhat less ingratiating. His gambit, for instance, went "Well, I guess today you've returned to the scene of one of your greatest crimes." Leslie Mc-Farlane objected to the argumentative tone, and the judge agreed with her, telling Schaffer, "That's not the way to start." From there on, Schaffer and Mulder duelled for more than an hour—until it was apparent that the judge had had enough and that Mulder was not going to throw up his hands and declare, "O.K., ya got me, my legal career's a shambles, I'm finished in this town." The judge's impatience with Schaffer belied the fact that he had already made up his mind on the basic question. After a masterly summation by Schaffer—sufficient in its eloquence for McFarlane, when her turn came, to apologize, accurately, that her closing argument would be notably devoid of eloquence—Baraka said he was ready with his decision.

Of the thirteen grounds for relief cited in Adams' writ, Baraka agreed on six: that Metcalfe, the original trial judge, had erroneously denied the admissibility of David Harris's prior criminal record; that Teresa Turko's initial statement describing the killer had been illegally suppressed; that, similarly, Emily Miller's initial statement describing the killer had been illegally suppressed; that evidence of Emily Miller's failure to identify Adams in the police lineup and subsequent coaching by a police officer had been suppressed; that Emily Miller had later committed perjury regarding her performance at the lineup; and that Adams had been denied effective assistance of counsel.

It seemed that, because Baraka had rejected seven of the contentions cited in the writ, a final observation he made was designed to eliminate any remaining ambiguity: "I think over all, when we look at this trial, all the nuances that are involved, I think there's no question that the defendant did not get a fair opportunity to a trial. I would not go so far as to say that the defendant is innocent of this. I would go so far as to say that if the defendant were to be retried, considering all the testimony elicited and what would be presented to the jury or a court, that more likely than not the defendant would be found not guilty."

The ruling did not mean that Adams was now at liberty to walk out of the courtroom; it meant that one judge officially believed that Adams had yet to receive a fair trial. As a practical matter, Baraka's recommendation could languish with the Texas Court of Criminal Appeals for months before a final ruling came down. And the court could, of course, reject Baraka's recommendation. Imminent freedom for Adams, in other words, was by no means a foregone conclusion. Knowing that Baraka lacked the authority to grant Adams bail in the meantime, Schaffer asked for it anyway, and the motion was denied. On that note, the hearing ended. There was applause, and a call for order from the court officers, and then the television and newspaper people were ready with their questions.

Adams, seated in a wooden armchair and still wearing handcuffs and leg irons, said he felt "numb"—the same word he had used in *The Thin Blue Line* to describe his frame of mind when, twelve years earlier, he heard himself sentenced to death.

A woman with a microphone asked Adams if he had anything to say to David Harris. No, he did not.

A reporter from *New York Newsday* asked, "Do you think you'd be here today if it hadn't been for Errol Morris?"

"Without the facts that came from the movie, no, I wouldn't be here in this courtroom today. We needed the facts, and the film helped. It helped immensely."

Roughly the same question was directed to Schaffer, who was standing nearby: "Do you consider that if the file that Errol Morris got out of Mr. Wade's office had not been found, we'd be here?"

In his summation, Schaffer had belittled the Dallas District Attorney, saying, "They'll give their file to a moviemaker, because he'll go out and make a movie and they'll be famous, but they won't give it to a defense attorney." Elaborating, he now said, "No, if Errol had not decided on his own that this was a story worth telling, Randall Adams would have been buried forever. Yes, that was the linchpin."

Mildred Adams, between bouts of crying for joy and kissing Morris and Schaffer and any willing members of the press, said she hoped people would remember Robert Wood and his family in their prayers. When the excitement had lasted close to half an hour, Morris suggested to Mrs. Adams that she and her daughters and sisters and brothers-in-law should join him for champagne at the Adolphus Hotel.

"Did I tell you what Randall Adams said to me about my movie?"

Morris asked me as we headed for the hotel, a few blocks east of the courthouse. "He told me another inmate asked him, 'How come your case is being argued in the entertainment section of the newspaper?' And you know what Randall's response was? He said, 'I'll argue my case anywhere I can, any way I can.' "

The Thin Blue Line made dozens of critics' lists of the ten best films of 1988; according to a survey by *The Washington Post*, in fact, it turned up on more ten-best lists than any other film. Both the New York Film Critics Circle and the National Society of Film Critics chose it as best documentary of 1988. Although its box-office receipts have not extended into the *Roger Rabbit* or *Crocodile Dundee II* vicinity—at the end of the year, it was playing in fifteen theaters around the country—Morris no longer faces the prospect that he will soon again be working as a private detective or dodging collection agencies. Immediately before the writ hearing in Dallas, he was in Italy, where *The Thin Blue Line* was shown at a festival in Florence. On the same trip, he made stops in London—where he screened it for some people from the London Film Festival— and in Munich, where he met with Reinhold Messner, the legendary Alpine climber and the first man to have scaled all fourteen eight-thousand-meter peaks on earth (including Mt. Everest without oxygen). Messner was planning an ascent of Cerro del Toro, in Chile, and he wanted Morris—who happens to be an experienced rock climber—to accompany him and make a film. "I'm thinking of doing it," Morris said, in Dallas. "Messner's a terrifically interesting person. He told me he's been doing a lot of walking recently. You or I might assume he meant he was taking long strolls in his neighborhood. What he actually meant was that he had just walked across Tibet. And he's planning to walk across Antarctica. He told me some interesting stuff about meeting the yeti—you know, the abominable snowman. He's seen two—the red yeti and the black yeti. Messner was very reassuring. He said, 'The only thing you really have to be scared of is when you hear the black yeti whistling—whistling through his nose.' "

Heading off to South America with Messner would mean delaying a couple of other projects that Morris was eager to carry forward. He still had plans to complete *Dr. Death*—the movie he had intended to make before the Randall Adams case sidetracked him. He also hoped to direct *The Trial of King Boots*, a feature-length examination of how an Old English sheepdog named King Boots —the most highly decorated performer in the annals of show-dog competition—became the only canine in Michigan history to be prosecuted, in effect, for homicide. Morris already had a vision of what the film's publicity posters would say: "Only Two People Know What Happened. One Is Dead. The Other Is a Dog."

If Morris could find the time to finish *Dr. Death*, he might at last tie together an odd mélange of material: interviews with Dr. Grigson himself; action shots of a lion tamer; scenes from lab research on a mammal called the African naked mole rat; archival footage from an Edison silent film called *Electrocuting an Elephant*; and a meditation on Zoar, an extinct utopian community in Ohio. After a previous trip to Europe, Morris had told me with satisfaction about finding the right music to accompany the Zoar material. "It's called 'Yodeler Messen,' " he said. "I'd been hearing this stuff on the radio in Zurich, and then I went into a record store and asked whether they had any liturgical yodelling. They came up with 'Yodeler Messen.' It's, like, based on the idea that God might be hard of hearing."

One afternoon, in his office near Times Square, Morris patiently tried to walk me through the connections between the elements that would compose *Dr. Death*, an exercise that struck me as analogous to a journey along the scenic route from the right side of his brain to the left. He told me that his fascination with Dr. Grigson's disturbing theories of sociopathy and recidivism had aroused an interest in lion taming, and that in 1985 this led him to the eponymous ringleader of a circus act called Dave Hoover's Wild Animals. Of the three basic schools of lion taming—what Morris delineated as "the persuasive, mutual-respect school, the behaviorist school, and the chairs-whips-guns school"—Hoover subscribed to the third. Having filmed Hoover at work for several hours—the soundtrack consists mainly of scary roaring noises and the determined voice of Hoover saying, again and again, "Bongo!

Come! Come to Daddy! Bad girl! Caesar! Get home, *Caesar!* Good
boy!"—Morris was uncertain what to do with the footage.

"After I'd looked at this stuff awhile, I decided, Oh, no, I can't
use this. It's too goofy," Morris said. "Then I got interested in the
mole rats. What's the connection between the lion tamer and the
mole rats? I don't know if there even is one. Mole rats spend their
entire lives digging tunnels. They have a rigid social system. They're
like wasps or bees—there's a queen and workers. Mole rats dig
at random, looking for tubers. Maybe they find a tuber, or maybe
they don't. They just dig away. At one point, I had thought the
mole rats addressed the utopian ideal of what it would be like if
there were no crime or criminals, if you could say hello to your
neighbor and your neighbor would say hello in return and we'd all
be assured that no one would attack us with an axe. Is aggression
innate in mammals? Well, supposedly not in mole rats. The mole
rat was thought to be the only mammal that lives in harmony with
its fellow-mammals, its fellow mole rats. *The* only. But it turns out
that mole rats are nonviolent only under certain circumstances—
that, in fact, they can be really nasty critters after all, who at times
really do seem to hate one another. When one colony of mole rats
meets another, they can be extremely vicious. Anyway, that was
my original idea—Dr. Grigson, lion tamers, mole rats. I then
decided to add to this compote *Electrocuting an Elephant*—which
was, if anything, a miscarriage-of-justice story."

When it became clear that I was unfamiliar with the once popular
habit—practiced during the first half of this century—of system-
atically executing "bad" elephants, Morris eagerly took a book
from a shelf next to his desk and handed it to me. It was a prolifically
illustrated memoir titled *I Loved Rogues*, by George (Slim) Lewis
and Byron Fish. Lewis was a passionate lover of elephants who
spent most of his working life in the employ of zoos and circuses,
and Fish was a newspaperman whose interest in elephants was that
of an involved amateur. The book had chapter titles like "They
Are Not House Pets" and "Ziggy Tries to Kill Me" and "How to
Feed and Water Your Elephant." The foreword included a reproduction of a painting labelled "George Lewis and Tusko"—Tusko
being a vast bull elephant who came close to being executed for

doing something deemed bad. A photograph on the facing page, captioned "Byron Fish painting Wide Awake," showed Fish perched on an elephant's shoulder, giving the animal a cosmetic treatment with a bucket of oil made from horse fat. The phone rang. While Morris took the call, I wrote down some more interesting captions and passages:

"Occasionally the victim of an elephant's attack is a man who was hated for reasons of the elephant's own" (p. 29).

"Black Diamond seemed to know that he was taking his last walk" (p. 47).

"After 170 shots by the firing squad, Diamond finally goes down" (p. 48).

"Joe Metcalf was another man Slim often met in his travels. The man with his head in the elephant's mouth was Alonzo Dever" (p. 62).

"Isn't that a wonderful book?" Morris said after he hung up. "I'd very much like to show you *Electrocuting an Elephant*. This elephant, Topsy, was, if anything, a *good* elephant rather than a bad elephant. Topsy was being electrocuted because, as I understand it, some guy was smoking a cigarette and gave the cigarette to Topsy, burning the tip of her trunk. Now, the tip of an elephant's trunk is the most sensitive part of an elephant. Topsy picked this guy up, tossed him in the air a couple of times, and hurled him onto concrete. I ask you: Does Topsy deserve the juice for this? The film of Topsy's electrocution is a 1903 Edison short—one of the first times electricity was used in capital punishment. And, coincidentally, the equipment malfunctioned and the person who pulled the switch almost electrocuted himself while he was electrocuting Topsy."

Morris paused. We could hear the traffic on Broadway, two floors below, and from the editing room, ten feet away, we could hear a litany of "Come, Bongo!"s and "Home, Caesar!"s.

"My favorite line in *Dr. Death*, I think, will be when the last living Zoarite is quoted as saying, 'Think of it—all those religions. They can't *all* be right. But they could all be wrong,' " Morris said. He looked down at his hands, massaged the tips of his little fingers—a characteristic tic—and then looked up, smiling his asymmetrical smile. "My two remaining ambitions are to have my picture hung up in my local Chinese restaurant and to have a sandwich named after me at the Stage Deli. And I guess I'll still keep making films. I always felt film was a good medium for me to work in, because if you don't finish, the level of embarrassment is so high."

CODA

At the time this Profile was published in *The New Yorker*, in February 1989, a decision about Randall Adams' legal fate, although imminent, remained unresolved. A further, unanticipated, development—an ironic postscript entirely worthy of an Errol Morris enterprise—was yet to come.

On March 1, three months after the habeas-corpus hearing in Judge Larry Baraka's courtroom, the Texas Court of Criminal Appeals unamimously overturned Adams' murder conviction. Three weeks later, Adams again appeared before Judge Baraka—this time for a bail hearing. John Vance, the Dallas County District Attorney, had at that point still not announced whether he intended to retry Adams. Confident that a new trial would result not only in acquittal and vindication but in humiliation for the District Attorney's office, Adams and his appellate lawyer, Randy Schaffer, made it clear that they hoped Vance would indeed pursue the case. Anything still seemed possible; from the time of Adams' arrest, in 1976, the conduct of the D.A.'s office is this matter had been characterized by a disdain for logic and due process. On the morning of the bail hearing, an assistant D.A. named Winfield Scott appeared before Judge Baraka. Scott, who had aided Douglas Mulder in the original prosecution of Adams, and had been incensed by Judge Baraka's ruling at the writ hearing, now sought to disqualify the judge, claiming that he had shown bias toward Adams. Although Scott ultimately did not prevail, he did perform a public service by rendering what many observers felt was an entertaining impersonation of a loose cannon.

Ignoring the fact that *The Thin Blue Line*, together with Schaffer's legal skill, had effectively impeached virtually all the state's witnesses, Scott told Baraka, "We have witnesses on standby and we are ready to try this case immediately," and then refused to participate in the proceeding. Scott's bombast brought to mind a declaration by John Vance to the *Dallas Times Herald* some months earlier that "as much as I'm convinced that Lee Harvey Oswald killed John Kennedy, I'm convinced that Randall Dale Adams is the man that shot Officer Wood." Since then, however, *The Thin Blue Line* had turned up in movie theaters, and Vance's assurance had been replaced by vacillation.

Judge Baraka released Adams on a $50,000 personal-recognizance bond. Within an hour, before Schaffer could physically escort Adams from the courthouse, Winfield Scott arranged a hearing before a more friendly judge who—evidently persuaded by rhetorical questions from Scott such as "What if Randall Adams isn't really going home to his mommy in Ohio? What if he tries to flee to Mexico or Canada?"—compliantly raised Adams' bail to $100,000, payable in cash or surety, pending a ruling on Judge Baraka's impartiality. Unable to make bail, Adams was forced to spend one more night in the custody of Dallas County.

The next day, a third judge reinstated the $50,000 personal-recognizance bond and Adams was released. Speaking to a reporter in Houston the day after that, Adams said, "No offense, but I hate Texas." The day after *that*, he flew to Columbus, Ohio, where his mother and two sisters lived. As he walked off the plane, the reporters who had gathered at the airport told him that John Vance, in Dallas, had just held a press conference. Despite having said earlier in the week, "I don't think Randall Dale Adams ought to be out on the street," Vance now acknowledged that his office lacked "sufficient credible evidence" and would therefore not retry the case.

Leslie McFarlane, the assistant D.A. who had been assigned to represent the Dallas County District Attorney in the habeas-corpus proceeding, apparently decided that the maladroitness of her colleagues was more than she could bear, and she soon resigned from that office. Around that time, the excitable and diverting Winfield Scott was fired. Dallas County has never formally stated whether David Harris, who since 1986 has been on death row in Texas for

the unrelated murder of Mark Walter Mays, will be tried for the
murder of Robert Wood.

Errol Morris was in the crowd at the airport in Columbus when
Randall Adams returned home, and Adams made a point of pushing
his way through the throng to warmly greet and embrace the person
he had come to refer to as "the Easter Bunny." At that moment,
it probably did not occur to either man that, within three months,
Adams would be filing a lawsuit against Morris—although Morris,
who all along had described the *Thin Blue Line* murder as a "tale
of error and confusion," perhaps should have seen it coming. The
personal affection that Morris felt for Adams did not extend to
Randy Schaffer. Morris had often differed with Schaffer's tactics
in the handling of Adams' appeal, and Schaffer, in turn, did not
really welcome Morris's freely offered advice on legal strategy. The
undercurrent of friction in the relationship blossomed into vindic-
tiveness when, in the late spring, Schaffer sent Morris a letter
threatening to sue him on Adams' behalf.

At issue was an agreement reached in December 1986, a year
and a half after Morris had filmed an interview with Adams at the
Eastham Unit. The agreement, which granted Morris a two-year
option to purchase the rights to Adams' life story, set forth a
schedule of potential payments—depending on the form in which
his story was, as they say in show business, exploited. If, for
instance, Adams' experiences became the basis for a "dramatic
motion picture intended for initial theatrical release," he would
receive $60,000 plus a share of net profits. If the medium of
exploitation was a made-for-television movie, Adams would receive
$40,000—and so forth. In the event a documentary film was made,
Adams would receive ten dollars—the same amount he was paid
by Morris for the option. The object of these token ten-dollar
payments was a mutual desire to eliminate any appearance of
impropriety or conflict of interest. At the time of the agreement,
neither Adams nor Morris was guided by mercenary motives. Rather,
Adams was trying to win his freedom and Morris was making a
documentary film that might be used in a courtroom to further that

endeavor. Paying Adams to appear in the movie might create an
unseemly taint. Indeed, no one who agreed to appear in the movie
was paid.

Beyond the pivotal role that *The Thin Blue Line* played in proving
Adams' innocence, it also elevated him to celebrity status, an
inevitability in the late eighties. Various book and movie offers
immediately materialized—blunt attempts by the usual opportun-
ists to further exploit what had happened to Adams. Morris, of
course, was also approached with similar offers to tell, for a price,
the story of how he got the story. By Texas statute, Adams could
not sue Doug Mulder or any of the other parties who had helped
bring about his twelve and a half years of unjust imprisonment.
Recognizing that fact, and taking into account the 1986 agreement
between Adams and Morris—and, above all, proceeding with the
mistaken assumption that *The Thin Blue Line* had produced a profit
and had earned Morris a lot of money—Schaffer sent his demand
letter in May 1989. On the one hand, Schaffer insisted that Morris
owed Adams $60,000, the amount that would have been due if
Adams' life story had become the basis for a "dramatic motion
picture intended for initial theatrical release." According to this
logic, *The Thin Blue Line* was not a documentary film. Demonstrating that logical consistency was not his first concern, however,
Schaffer also argued that Morris, having failed to exercise his option
by paying the $60,000, no longer owned the rights to Adams' story.
If within thirty days, Schaffer assured Morris, he did not agree to
pay the money *and* release Adams from the agreement, he would
be sued. As it happened, Morris was quite willing to return to
Adams the rights to his story. But he deeply resented what he
regarded as an extortion attempt by Schaffer, who, displaying an
extraordinary imagination, alleged that the filmmaker had manipulated his client through "fraud and duress." In particular, Morris
did not enjoy the passage in the lawyer's letter that went: "It seems
to me that your public image is presently at its peak. You are
perceived as a person who made a movie not for the money but to
help another human being. . . . If you cause this matter to go into
litigation your public image can only suffer as you will be perceived
as a New York filmmaker who came to Texas and took advantage

of a prison inmate to line your own pocket. If we go to court, for once I believe that Randall will be able to receive a fair trial from a Dallas jury."

Before the thirty days were up—during which time Morris and his lawyers thought they were fruitfully negotiating a settlement—Schaffer and a co-counsel went ahead and filed their lawsuit against Morris and Miramax Production Company, the film's distributor. The defendants' lawyers successfully removed the case from Texas state court to federal court, and before long the whole thing hit the newspapers. Unlike Schaffer's demand letter, the lawsuit did not ask for $60,000 or any other payment for alleged damages. Not insensitive to public relations considerations, Schaffer now made a point of telling anyone who asked that his client sought no money from Morris, but just wanted to control the rights to his own story. "They think they bought [Adams] lock, stock, and barrel for ten dollars, and that's unconscionable," he got in the habit of telling reporters. Nevertheless, the lawsuit attracted considerable publicity and much of it did not flatter Adams. "Now the envelope, please, for Ingrate of the Year," was the lead of an item in the New York *Daily News*.

As settlement discussions proceeded, Morris was good for a few colorful quotations of his own.

"Someone remarked that this started out as Kafka, then became Frank Capra, then Preston Sturges, then back to Kafka," he said to me at one point. "By the way, did I tell you the idea for my next film? I'm going to find an innocent man, frame him for murder, and then follow the case right up to and including the moment of his execution. What do you think of that idea? Do you like it?"

In a conversation a few days later, he said, "I've had a dream in which I'm on the witness stand in a courtroom and Randall Adams is sitting next to my mother in the spectator gallery, and as they're leading me away in chains to a period of indefinite incarceration, I see Randall lean over to my mother and say, 'Don't worry, Mrs. Morris, we're gonna get him out. I don't know how long it will take, but rest assured: I will spare no effort to win Errol's freedom.' "

I mentioned to Morris that I had been dining out on his fanciful description of the plan to frame and make a film about an innocent man. "And now I see you've modified that idea so that it stars yourself," I said.

"Yes, that's it," Morris replied. "I was determined to make a story about the framing of an innocent man, but because of my reluctance to do harm to an innocent person I'm being forced to make the movie about myself."

One could argue that, by making such a peculiar, hybrid documentary film as *The Thin Blue Line*, Morris brought Schaffer's lawsuit upon himself. Even Morris, however, with his gift for wry self-flagellation, was not pushing that line of reasoning. In any event, the issue became moot when, two months after the lawsuit was filed, a settlement was reached. Randall Adams got back the rights to his life story, Errol Morris got to keep the rights to his own life story, and no money changed hands. In the wake of the settlement, a Houston newspaper reported that Adams, twelve and a half years after being convicted of a murder that he didn't commit and five months after being certified, at last, a free man, had become a client of the William Morris Agency. Meanwhile, Errol Morris was not doing too badly himself: he had been named a recipient of a five-year "genius grant" from the MacArthur Foundation; he had won a Guggenheim Fellowship to support completion of *Dr. Death*; and the Stage Deli had decided to name a sandwich after him.

                                                            1 9 8 9